In Search of Boundaries

In Search of Boundaries

Communication, Nation-States and Cultural Identities

Edited by JOSEPH M. CHAN
and BRYCE T. McINTYRE

Advances in Communication and Culture
D. RAY HEISEY, *Series Editor*

ABLEX PUBLISHING
Westport, Connecticut • London

Library of Congress Cataloging-in-Publication Data

In search of boundaries : communication, nation-states and cultural identities / edited by
   Joseph M. Chan and Bryce T. McIntyre.
      p.   cm.—(Advances in communication and culture)
      Includes bibliographical references and index.
      ISBN 1–56750–570–8 (alk. paper)—ISBN 1–56750–571–6 (pbk. : alk. paper)
      1. Mass media.   2. Group identity.   3. Boundaries.   4. Globalization.   I. Chan,
   Joseph Man.   II. McIntyre, Bryce Telfer.   III. Series.
   HM1206.I5   2002
   302.23—dc21   2001022920

British Library Cataloguing in Publication Data is available.

Library of Congress Catalog Card Number: 2001022920
ISBN: 1–56750–570–8 (hc)
      1–56750–571–6 (pb)

First published in 2002

Ablex Publishing, 88 Post Road West, Westport, CT 06881
An imprint of Greenwood Publishing Group, Inc.
www.ablexbooks.com

Printed in the United States of America

The paper used in this book complies with the
Permanent Paper Standard issued by the National
Information Standards Organization (Z39.48–1984).

10 9 8 7 6 5 4 3 2 1

Contents

Preface

Recently an acquaintance of the authors, an American university professor, was visiting Japan. He had a conversation with a little Japanese girl who was excitedly discussing a visit to Tokyo Disneyland. When he mentioned that he had visited Disneyland in the United States, the girl exclaimed, "Is there really a Disneyland in America?" Her genuine but naive question speaks to our long-standing concern over communication across state borders and the impact it may have on cultural identities. One of the key questions that we ask is: How are the cultural boundaries defined and redefined in this age of globalized communication?

The book you are holding in your hands is a natural consequence of our interests and concerns regarding the search for boundaries and the globalization problem. In pursuit of these interests and concerns, we called a congregation of internationally known scholars in Hong Kong for a few days in June 1999. Events included scholarly presentations, city tours and other social activities. The scholars came from the United States, the United Kingdom, Israel, Singapore, Taiwan and, of course, Hong Kong. All of them were known for their scholarly publications on the search for boundaries and the globalization problem. The number of participants was limited to 20 in order to better facilitate the exchange of ideas in a focussed discussion. Invitations to the meeting were carefully weighed by a panel of scholars over a period of several months from 1998 to 1999, and of all the presentations, only those that were directly related to the theme of this book are included here. The Introduction and Chapter 1 were added later to provide perspective.

In planning the meeting, our objective was to bring together scholars from East and West to have a dialogue on the patterns, processes and theories of how boundaries are drawn and redrawn. It was our considered opinion that scholars of diverse backgrounds would heighten our comparative perspective, essential for understanding a subject of this nature.

The scope of this book is international in scale, but we thought it fitting and proper that Hong Kong should be the venue for such an exchange of ideas. In a sense, Hong Kong may be viewed as a metaphor for the search of boundaries and the globalization problem. Hong Kong has a vibrant, free-market economy that is often rated the "freest in the world" by organizations such as the Fraser Institute and The Heritage Foundation. Hong Kong also is situated on the doorstep of China, the world's last remaining large socialist state.

It is a veritable cliché that Hong Kong is the place where East meets West. Even today, more than 150 years after Great Britain added Hong Kong to its colonial empire, Hong Kong is still a place where great civilizations of the Orient and the Occident coexist and cross-fertilize. Hong Kong is thus a locale where boundaries continually are being drawn, dissolved and redrawn.

If this were not justification enough to hold such a congregation in Hong Kong, then the reader should be reminded that Hong Kong today is a Special Administrative Region of the People's Republic of China. Since the transition of Hong Kong from British to Chinese rule on midnight of June 30, 1997, Hong Kong has been governed under a "one country, two systems" policy that guarantees Hong Kong its way of life for 50 years.

In short, Hong Kong is not only a place where East meets West, but also a place where capitalism meets socialism, and where pro-democracy leaders often find themselves in stark confrontation with autocratic authorities from mainland China. Hong Kong is thus a metaphor for boundary dissolution, reconstruction and crossing.

This is to say nothing of the "silent revolution" that is taking place in China itself. From its birth in 1949 until 1978, the People's Republic of China had a Soviet-style, centrally planned economy that was sluggish and inefficient. In late 1978, under the stewardship of the late Paramount Leader Deng Xiaoping, China, at first slowly and then with increasing speed, opened up the economy. Limited experiments in capitalism have resulted today in a "socialist market economy" where one finds quasi-capitalistic enterprises operating under the close scrutiny of party-state officials.

Thus, China itself is witnessing the dissolution and reassertion of boundaries—boundaries between not only capitalism and socialism, but also between traditional and modern ways of life, and between Chinese and Western cultural values.

It was partly this fascinating and complex cultural milieu that inspired us to organize a meeting in Hong Kong on globalization and the search for boundaries. Hopefully, this book will add to our understanding of the social processes behind the question the little Japanese girl asks at the beginning of this preface.

Acknowledgments

This volume is the result of about two years of work and planning by dozens of people. We are heavily indebted to the individual contributors, most of whom not only traveled all the way to Hong Kong to share their ideas with us, but also assented willingly to our request to publish their presentations in book form. We are grateful to Professor Ambrose King for his support and benediction for the "In Search of Boundaries" meeting, and to Professor Ping Chung Leung, head of New Asia College at The Chinese University of Hong Kong, for his participation and for the college's financial contribution. We are grateful as well to The Cultural Foundation of the United Daily News Group and Ming Pao newspaper for their financial contributions. We are thankful also to Frank Biocca, Kinman Chan, Chin-chuan Lee, Deborah Davis, Louis Leung and Wei Ran for their presentations and comments, and to Leonard Chu, James Kenny, Kenneth Leung, Xu Yu and Jonathan Zhu for chairing discussions. Thanks also to those scholars who reviewed individual chapters—Anthony Fung, Todd Gitlin, Zhou He, Yu Huang, Linda Ku, Linda Lai, Tai Lok Lui, Toby Miller, Monroe Price, Clement So, Gerald Sussman, Joseph Straubhaar and Georgette Wang. And special thanks are owed to Professor Ray Heisey, editor of the Ablex series on Advances in Communication and Culture, for his enthusiasm and many encouragements. We are grateful as well to Paul Lee, Eric Ma, Zhongdang Pan and other members of the organizing committee. They aided immeasurably in refining the focus of the main events and in deciding on the list of invitees, as well as by sharing their ideas after the presentations had been made. And thanks also to Betty Co and Monique Leung, who comprised the secretariat. We owe thanks as well to Michelle Mui, Vien Lau and Mark Wong, who produced the program and publicity materials, and to Vincent Chau, K. K. Chan, Lam Kong and Sunny Tong for their technical support. We also thank Zhang Weiyu for her assistance in compiling the index. Finally, we are indebted to the School of Journalism and Communication of The Chinese University of Hong Kong for the many ways it supported this project.

Introduction

Joseph M. Chan and Bryce T. McIntyre

The rise and fall, construction and deconstruction of different types of boundaries—biological, psychological, geographical, cultural, social, political, economic—make up the very story of human civilization and of contemporary social transformation.

—T. K. Oommen, 1995, p. 251

[I]t is now not so much physical boundaries . . . that define a community or nation's "natural limits". Increasingly we must think in terms of communications and transport networks and of the symbolic boundaries of language and culture . . . as providing the crucial and permeable boundaries of our age.

—D. Morley and K. Robins, 1995, p. 1

No government happily accepts a loss of control over what happens within the boundaries. The normal response to foreign influence is to build walls.

—I. S. Pool, 1990, p. 66

While a country could avoid Cold War alignment, it cannot lack an identity. The question, "Which side are you on?" has been replaced by the much more fundamental one, "Who are you?" Every state has to have an answer. That answer, its cultural identity, defines the state's place in world politics, its friends, and its enemies.

—S. Huntington, 1996, p. 125

In his presidential address on "contested boundaries" to the International Sociological Association, T. K. Oommen (1995, p. 251) began by characterizing this world as one filled with contradictory "isms" or trends. It is a world of "endisms" (end of history, ideology, nature, geography), "postisms" (postindustrial, postcapitalist, postmodern) and "beyondisms" (beyond the nation-state, beyond the Cold War). Endisms represent the disappearance of boundaries, postisms signify the emergence of new boundaries and beyondisms allude to the elongation of boundaries. This keen observation speaks to the growing importance of the concept of boundary in social science and to the fact that boundaries are constantly contested and recreated. Indeed, there has been a renewed interest in boundary studies in the 1990s in various academic disciplines, including sociology (Silber, 1995), anthropology (Donnan & Wilson, 1999), political science (Anderson & Bort, 1998), geography (Newman & Paasi, 1998), media and cultural studies (Morley & Robins, 1995), history (Baud & van Schendel, 1997) and gender studies (Weedon, 1997). In academia, boundary studies is a growth industry.

The renewed interest in boundary studies is partly a result of the reterritorialization in Eastern Europe and elsewhere since the late 1980s (Newman & Paasi, 1998). This reterritorialization has raised questions over corresponding formation of national identity which, in the words of Schlesinger (1991) is the cultural constitution of the nation-state. Boundary studies owe their new life to the high frequency at which boundaries are defined and redefined in the midst of globalization, which leads to economic integration, cultural clashes, migrant dislocation, ethnic conflicts and blurring of social categories.

Another factor that fuels the interest in boundary studies is the general significance and relevance of the concept in various fields. To some social theorists, what constitutes "the very story of human civilization and contemporary social transformation" is the "construction and deconstruction of various kinds of boundaries" (Oommen, 1995, p. 251). A boundary is a theoretically telling metaphor that can capture emergent realities and provide an answer to the search for a new language in place of the obsolete (Silber, 1995). In sociology, for instance, spatial metaphors such as boundaries, fields and spaces are found to be compatible with a wide range of theoretical approaches and provide common conceptual links among competing schools and theories.

The study of communication has benefited from and contributed to the cross-fertilization of various fields. We trust that it will continue to do so by engaging in boundary studies. This very collection of articles forms part of what might be described as the "postmodern" discourse on boundaries, a discourse in which many disciplinary boundaries are being eroded. In the next two sections we shall explicate the concept of boundary and briefly review how it is related to communication, nation-state and cultural identities. Finally, we shall map out the major themes of the book.

BOUNDARY AS CONSTRUCTED REALITY

Although boundary can be defined differently as the research context varies, what appeals to us is its general meaning. A boundary is the interface between two entities; it marks the end of one and the beginning of another. Boundaries can be tangible, visible, spatial and physical, as in the case of territorial border, or intangible, invisible, temporal and virtual, as in the case of social categorization and symbolic representation. Boundaries exist at many different levels, and they may be cultural, social, spatial, territorial, political, sexual, racial or psychological. In other words, boundaries are "the bounds of limits of anything whether material or immaterial" (Pellow, 1996, p. 1). Boundaries constitute "the lines of separation or contact" in "real or virtual space" or "between groups and/or individuals" (Newman & Paasi, 1998, p. 191). Borrowing from Giddens (1984), boundaries are a metaphor, something we construct, and even reify, to create order out of chaos and to make sense of our world. Boundaries do not refer only to the interface between social systems and others contiguous upon it. They also refer to how boundaries mark members off from non-members, "us" vs. "them" (Wallman, 1978). Boundaries and identity are thus different sides of the same coin, with the former creating and being created through the latter (Newman & Paasi, 1998).

Boundaries are socially constructed, subject to the influence of various social forces. It follows that boundaries are always contested and recreated. There are a growing number of researchers who view boundaries as more permeable (Morley & Robins, 1995) and even disappearing (Shapiro & Alker, 1996), ending in a "borderless world" (Allen & Hamnett, 1995). However, there is no need for one to assume the arrival of a borderless world before one can agree that boundaries are negotiable. Boundaries are in a constant state of flux, being created, maintained, elaborated, contested, eroded and deconstructed. They are locked in dialectical relationships—simultaneously separating and unifying, including and excluding, transforming and being transformed.

It is increasingly recognized that the construction of boundaries is achieved through narrativity which informs how we make sense of the social world and constitute our social identities (Somers, 1994). Discourse analysis is an important approach to the study of boundaries as sociospatial identities or sociocultural differences. The rise of discourse analysis in the last two decades coincided with the general shift in epistemology in social studies towards constructionism (Jaworski & Coupland, 2000, p. 4), implying that the building of knowledge is largely "a process of defining boundaries between conceptual classes, and of labeling those classes and the relationships between them."

Discourse is inherently contestable and tied to the prevailing power structure. Discourse on boundaries is thus a sociopolitical act, representing the contestation over classification, communication, social control, resource allocation and order (Sack, 1986). As expressions of power relations, boundaries are the results of an individual's or group's success in limiting the actions and behaviors of others. From this vantage point, state boundaries are no longer taken for granted, nor are they treated as natural divisions between states (Newman & Paasi, 1998). They are recognized as discursive constructs whose meanings are thus alterable and historically contingent.

COMMUNICATION, NATION-STATE AND CULTURAL IDENTITIES

Out of the boundaries in different spatial contexts—local, national and international—the national is the most important for the identification with a national community. The state remains a basic parameter in the discourse on boundaries and national identities (Newman & Paasi, 1998). While the disappearance of national boundaries may apply to a small part of the world, such as Europe, territorial partitioning remains a global norm. Even if the meanings of sovereignty may be changing, states remain the sole representatives of the population living within the borders in the international arena (Murphy, 1996). Boundaries, especially when they take the form of national borders, are the sites and symbols of power (Wilson & Donnan, 1998). They also are political constructs, "imagined projections of territorial power" (Baud & van Schendel, 1997, p. 211). National boundaries both secure protection from violence and constitute a form of violence: While providing preconditions of identity, national boundaries also close off possibilities (Connolly, 1996). Boundaries can be institutions as well as processes. As institutions, they mark the limits of state sovereignty and individual citizenship (Anderson, 1996). As processes, they are instruments of the power of the state. State boundaries do not reflect only the institutions and policies of their states, but also mirror the changes in the "definitions of citizenship, sovereignty and national identity," thus becoming "meaning-making" and "meaning-carrying" entities (Wilson & Donnan, 1998, p. 4). Even though state boundaries may be arbitrary lines, they have deep symbolic, cultural, historical and religious, often contested, meanings for social communities.

Debates over the fate of the nation-state arose in response to the threats posed by multinational corporations, supranational trading blocs and political entities, globalization of culture and society and the perceived demise of imperialism and other forms of nationalistic enterprise (Wilson & Donna, 1998). Much of the debate centers on Europe, birthplace of the nation and the state. But the evidence is split between the view that the nation-state is diminishing and the view that the nation-state is as strong as ever. What both sides of the debate appear to agree on is that the nation-state, as an imagined community (Anderson, 1991), is being reimagined.

In this age of globalization, what defines a community or a nation is not so much the physical boundaries, but "communication networks and symbolic boundaries such as the 'spaces of transmission' defined by satellite footprints or radio signals" (Morley & Robins, 1995, p. 1). Nation-states are becoming less autonomous after the onset of globalization. States do not make decisions just for themselves; their decisions have repercussions that are felt in other countries (Held, 1997). Transnational actors and transnational forces cut across the state boundaries in trade, finance, production, security and defense, carrying implications for other national communities. Antithetical to national boundaries are the flows of capital, cultures, identities and human bodies (Ferguson, 1996). Through the migrations of people and mediated communications, cultures flow across established boundaries; cultures are no longer bounded by nation-states. Indeed, no culture is an island in this age of globalization.

Does globalization spell the end of national boundaries? While globalization is an elusive concept, it has been defined as the erosion of the borders of nation-states through expansion of international companies, international communications, international financial networks and homogenization of consumer culture. Globalization is a social process in which the constraints of geography on social and cultural arrangements recede and in which people become increasingly aware that they are receding (Waters, 1995). Critics argue that globalization is a "propagandistic ploy to mask the politico-economic objectives of neoliberal capitalism" by diverting public attention from the fact that it creates "new monopolists and oligopolists rather than free competitive markets" (Hamelink, 1999, p. 6). While it is doubtful that globalization is the conscious effort of any group, it is an impersonal force beyond the control of global corporations, transnational, nongovernment organizations and even supranational political organizations (Waters, 1995). A key feature of globalization concerns interconnectedness (Robertson, 1992): Globalization is "complex connectivity" (Tomlinson, 1999). While it is generally observed that the West dominates the cultural flow across borders, globalization does not represent a rigid, one-way process from the "West to the rest"; it is a disjointed and multi-directional flow characterized by its compression of time and space (Barker, 1999). There are "reverse flows," notably of musical cultures from Brazil, the Caribbean and sub-Saharan Africa, that result in a hybridization (Pieterse, 1995) of cultural products and, consequently, cultures themselves. Globalization is thus a complex interaction of globalizing and localizing tendencies—glocalization—a synthesis of local and universal values (Robertson, 1995; Scott, 1997).

The above brief review of the concept of globalization has led us to believe that globalization has indeed resulted in the increased and accelerating "interpenetration and interdependency of relations on a world scale," including industrial, financial and intellectual relationships (see Chapter 7 in this volume). While the nation-state may have been reimagined, it remains an important force that we have to reckon with in the discussion of cultural identities, communication and boundaries. This is illustrated in a comparative study of the world's coverage of the Hong Kong handover in 1997 (Lee, Chan, Pan & So, 2000) that found that, in the shadow of globalization, international newsmaking remains inherently ethnocentric, nationalistic and even state-centered. The media from various countries tend to domesticate and hype the news in accordance with the foreign policy, values and cultural orientations of their home countries. The study is an echo of the chapter by Akiba A. Cohen in this volume.

Another significant factor that helps reset boundaries is the onslaught of information technology, which is also viewed as a driving force of globalization. Such an impact can be dated back to the ancient days, when paper and the printing press were invented. National boundaries are especially vulnerable to the erosion of new information technologies such as satellite television and the Internet (Morley & Robins, 1995). Our senses of space and place are all being significantly reconfigured as a consequence of new technological forms of information delivery. The rise of virtual space is in some ways indicative of the disappearance of national boundaries; the Internet's ability to cross borders with impunity challenges traditional, state-based identity structures (Everard, 2000). While the erosion of national boundaries may be true in regard to the diffusion of information, the impact on cultural identities, which are anchored in blood, religion and ethnicity, is less clear. With the Internet, one can communicate with many people around the world. While the technology poses almost no barriers, the community the individual will communicate with is largely defined by social customs and structures (Pool, 1990). While some traditional boundaries may blur or disappear as a result of globalization, new boundaries are created as it promotes uneven development and structural inequality. Eighty percent of the world's population have never made a telephone call, and more than half of the world's population live more than 100 miles from the nearest telephone line (Everard, 2000). The emerging picture is clear: The world is not yet living with a global information superhighway that wires all the nations equally; some are more equal than others. Boundaries, both old and new, abound.

In this age of globalization, the nation-state still exerts important influence over the education system as well as the communication system, both of them key socializing agents in the formation of national identity. State borders are far from withering away. Indeed, the rise of ethnoterritorial entities and states, and the consequent replacement of existing boundaries with new ones, continue to render the nation-state an important player (Waterman, 1994, as cited in Newman and Passi, 1998). While the state's role in the economic sphere may be diminishing, this is not so in the politics of identity (Everard, 2000). In a time of change and uncertainty, people are turning to nationalism and engaging in regional conflicts over identity. This concurs with the view that nationalism is a process of border creation and maintenance (Conversi, 1995). Boundaries are needed to ensure a distinction between two or more groups, or the spaces they inhabit. Hence, in the process of nationality formation, the boundaries defining the national community are given prominent attention.

FOCUS OF THIS VOLUME

The above reviews are not intended to draw conclusions, but to set a theoretical stage for asking the questions we have asked in this book. We hope that readers will have a better understanding of the problematics involved after going through various chapters. It should be noted that the contributors are from diverse intellectual and ethnic backgrounds. This cosmopolitan mix should be conducive to the generation of comparative insights and perspectives.

The focus here is on how communication, nation-states and cultural identities interact in the search for boundaries in this age of globalization. Put in boundary terms, the central themes of this volume center on the dissolution and reconstruction of boundaries.

Boundary Dissolution

The avalanche of breakthroughs in information technologies has rendered communication insensitive to distance and national boundaries. To some, the Internet implies the end of national communication franchises. Concerns about communication across national boundaries and information sovereignty date back some three decades, and these concerns are magnified as communication is globalized. The globalization of television is a major force in the deconstruction and reconstruction of cultural identities. It is not just technological advancements that are at work, however: The downfall of communism and the global triumph of capitalist markets have hastened the blurring and reconstruction of national boundaries. Cultural boundaries seem to be receding in favor of stronger forces from outside. However, one cannot take this process for granted by assuming the inevitability of the homogenization of world culture (Smith, 1991). Thus, one must ask: Are the boundaries really dissolving? If they are, in what ways, how and why?

Boundary Reassertion and Reconstruction

If boundary dissolution characterizes major changes in the world, the other half of the equation is boundary reassertion and reconstruction. The processes of cultural disintegration and cultural integration take place at all levels—within states and across states. As the following pages testify, rather than succumbing to despair over the disappearance of local cultures, some scholars are surprisingly optimistic. Although boundaries appear to be shifting, the tug-of-war among various social forces in redrawing the lines is far from over. As alluded to above, in the process of boundary reconstruction, the nation-state remains a critical framework by holding onto traditions and by controlling the power to regulate inflows of cultural products. A few scholars, including some of those featured here, believe that national or local cultures will not lose their identities. Local cultures resist by virtue of tradition, or, alternatively, sometimes take on a new life by reinvention or hybridization. A twist on this view is that "introverted cultures" are receding into the background, while "translocal cultures" made up of diverse elements are coming into the foreground (Pieterse, 1995). Therefore, we must ask: How does national or local culture accommodate the challenge of foreign cultural influence? To what extent can national or local culture reassert its boundaries and identities? How do nation-states respond to cultural globalization? Is the nation-state losing its relevancy? How do people make sense of the world and their own identities as boundaries are crossed?

CHAPTER ORGANIZATION

This book is divided into five principal sections based on themes in the chapters. Part I, "Becoming Postmodern," contains only one chapter, "Transculturating Modernity." This chapter helps to set the stage for much of the rest of the book by arguing that, while modernity is historically grounded in the West, in fact many developing nations are creating their own modernities in the name of national sovereignty and out of sociopolitical necessity. Unlike the cultural imperialism thesis, in which Western cultures are alleged to dominate and overwhelm the cultures of developing nations, the thesis of this chapter is that there is a give-and-take among cultures wherever they encounter one another.

Part II, "Dissolution of Boundaries," focuses specifically on contemporary institutions and processes that tend to defy the international boundaries of sovereign nation-states. Chapter 2, "The Unification of the World under the Signs of Mickey Mouse and Bruce Willis," suggests that the alleged one-way flow of American popular culture is overly simplistic without an accounting of both supply-side and demand-side factors. In this chapter Todd Gitlin argues that, although indigenous populations prefer local cultural products when given a choice, American culture has an incontrovertible allure that limits the space for autonomous culture in other nations.

Chapter 3, "Consuming the Citizen," is a creative application of the theme of the New International Division of Labor to culture industries.

Just as manufacturing has fled from the First World, so has cultural production, though largely within the industrialized market economies. The chapter urges critical scholars to expose the contradictions of theories of the consumer and to strive for democratically accountable forms of intervention in the culture industries.

Chapter 4, "Three Processes of Dissolving Boundaries," is an analysis of major forces that lead to the dissolution of boundaries—internationalization, marketization and acculturation. Internationalization is the integration of nation-states into supranational organizations such as the United Nations and the European Union. Marketization is the integration of national economies into the capitalist world order through entities such as the World Trade Organization (WTO) and the Asia Pacific Economic Cooperation forum, while acculturation is the process of exchange of values across cultures. The chapter provides specific examples of each process at work.

Chapter 5, "Dissolving Boundaries," illustrates how new technologies can result in changes in social relations. Specifically, it is an abstract analysis of how on-line newspapers change spatial, temporal, social, conceptual and symbolic boundaries of traditional newspapers. Traditional newspapers are a form of *closed media code*, characterized by rigid classifications of information and its control over contents. On-line newspapers, on the other hand, represent a form of *open media code*, characterized by weak classifications of news texts and interactive contents.

While Chapter 5 was an abstract analysis of the phenomenon of on-line newspapers, Chapter 6 is a concrete analysis of 44 on-line English-language newspapers in 14 Asian nations. By content-analyzing the Web sites of these newspapers, the authors investigate how on-line journalism is affecting the traditional relationships between journalists and audiences. They found little evidence that long-standing power relationships—and the associated boundaries of information control between on-line journalists and their audiences—are eroding or being renegotiated because of the Internet and on-line newspapers. Despite the potential for change, journalists are reluctant to permit nonjournalists to have a say in the selection and presentation of news.

Part III of the book, "Reassertion of Boundaries," is an examination of processes that result in a redefinition of boundaries. These range from the domestication of foreign television news, in order to make it more relevant to local audiences, to the consequences of orbital slot assignments of communications satellites. Chapter 7, "Global Challenges and National Answers in the Information Age," is an overview of the major issues raised by globalization. Example: Many multinational corporations have a diverse ownership structure, so they are difficult to identify as belonging to a particular nation; thus, doubts must be raised about the ability of national governments to control their own economies because of pressures to conform to global market practices.

Chapter 8, "Urban Congregations of Capital and Communications," argues that the New International Division of Labor, particularly by means of the infrastructure of information and communications technology (ICT), is redefining social boundaries, intensifying and extending Fordism beyond traditional communities, regions and nation-states. The consequences are contradictory. Capital is becoming increasingly concentrated in the "first tier information" cities of Tokyo, New York and London, while at the same time smaller, more localized concentrations of capital have appeared in locales that have solved the "bandwidth" problem. Transnational corporations, of which there are some 40,000, situate branch offices in stable communities with low wages, weak labor laws, few tax liabilities and weak environmental regulations—but most of all the ICT necessary to maintain information flows from the headquarters.

Chapter 9, "Satellite Broadcasting as Trade Routes in the Sky," likens the trade routes of seventeenth-century sailing vessels to the transmission of electronic signals in the Information Age. In the Information Age, data is a principal commodity of trade, so the channels over which data flows—from server, to satellite uplink, to transponder and back down to earth again—are not randomly assigned, but are selected for speed and efficiency. The number of orbital slots is finite and, thus, they are contested, bargained for and "colonized."

With vast quantities of information flowing like great rivers over national borders, there is a need for contextualization and interpretation, especially when it comes to broadcast media. Chapter 10, "Globalization Ltd.," argues that television news in general, but especially foreign news, should be exempt from characterization in terms of globalization. The key variable is language: Foreign, imported television news requires translation, at the very least, not to mention editing by local producers. This is part of the broader process of domestication of the news, which is done in various ways—by drawing comparisons between the foreign event and local events, by suggesting the possible impact of foreign events on the local situation, by providing historical context from the perspective of the local viewing audience, and so on. Obviously such tasks have a significant effect on the meaning.

This theme is picked up and developed further in Chapter 11, "(Re)asserting National Television and National Identity Against the Global, Regional and Local Levels of World Television." Media imperialism and dependency theory are too simplistic to explain the phenomenon of television at the local and regional levels. This chapter calls for a multilevel analysis, one that takes into account local television production and local cultural consumption, as well as new regional flows from places such as Brazil and Hong Kong that export to surrounding nations.

The need to protect national sovereignty by controlling cross-national information flows is the theme of Chapter 12, "Restrictions on Foreign Ownership and National Sovereignty." Traditionally, the main concerns have been the need to keep telecommunications services under local control for security reasons and to regulate services and the flow of information within national boundaries. Since 1998, however, when 72 member nations of the WTO signed an agreement to open basic telecommunication services to competition, the situation has changed somewhat. This chapter reviews the current policies of the signatory nations and concludes that many nations have maintained restrictions on foreign ownership.

Part IV of the book, "Crossing Boundaries," represents a departure from the reassertion of boundaries to transformation of culture and tensions in cultural identities. Chapter 13, "Disneyfying and Globalizing the Chinese Legend Mulan," is a study of transculturation, the process by which a culture is transformed by another for assimilation. Using the Disney animated feature *Mulan* as a case study, this chapter demonstrates that transculturation is an evolving process involving both organizational routines and experimentation. The imported culture is first decontextualized, essentialized and universalized before reconfiguration and recontextualization for local purposes. Transculturation lies always in the hybridization of two or more cultures.

Political subjectivities such as nationalities are tied to historical narratives (Shapiro, 1996), and this is the theme of the next two chapters. Chapter 14, "Mapping Transborder Imaginations," recapitulates boundary-crossing experiences of immigrants to Hong Kong from mainland China. Through an analysis of consumption histories, the chapter suggests that aspirations to modernity are embodied in material culture. The first taste of ice-cold Coca-Cola or a mouthful of a fresh California orange, the colors of trendy clothing or the soothing comfort of a pair of jogging shoes—these are the lasting impressions of new immigrants from mainland China to Hong Kong. Such impressions also are the embodiment of modernity among the new immigrants. Chapter 15, "Sweet Comrades," follows a similar theme. Though an analysis of director Peter Chan's 1996 award-winning film *Sweet Comrades: Almost a Love Story*, the author not only explores the boundaries of identity between Hong Kong and mainland Chinese, but in the process also identifies the symbols of modernity in the minds of recent immigrants to Hong Kong. One of the film's characters, Li Chiao, played by Maggie Cheung, is a recent Hong Kong immigrant who regularly visits her local ATM for the sheer pleasure of checking the balance in her savings account. She also has entrepreneurial aspirations that lead her to financial ruin. Meanwhile, Li Xiao-jun, played by Leon Lai, is another recent immigrant who, delivering chickens from a butcher shop for HK$2,000 per month by bicycle, reflects on the fact that he earns more money than the mayor of his hometown in China, Tiensin. Such are the embodiments of modernity.

Like Part I of the book, Part V, "Getting Personal," contains a single chapter. Chapter 16, "Globalization and Me," is both a discussion of the disaggregation of the "hyphenated nation-state" as well as a personal reminiscence in which the author explores the relationships between global processes and the individual. The author's "radical subjectivity" is used to forge a "certain humility" in the study of others.

CONCLUDING REMARKS

When established boundaries dissolve, we face new challenges as social scientists. The challenges are not only to record, but also to understand and explain why—and how—such changes take place, and where such changes are leading us. The study of boundaries is essential for the understanding of human interactions. Recognizing and acting out boundaries have always been important parts of the human experience. The rigid definitions of boundaries are known to have led to extremist behavior such as ethnic cleansing and national isolationism. Our responsibility as social scientists is to find out how boundaries are dissolving and being reconstructed, which is an important step toward the understanding of our own limitations and opportunities. This understanding will enable us to interact with one another more empathetically and to share the globe in a more humane manner. It may also serve to generate mechanisms that would allow different peoples to live in peace, to share resources and to appreciate commonalities among differences.

REFERENCES

Allen, J., & Hamnett, C. (Eds.) (1995). *A shrinking world? Global unevenness and inequality*. Oxford: Oxford University Press and Open University Press.

Anderson, B. (1991). *Imagined communities: Reflections on the origin and spread of nationalism*. London: Verso.

Anderson, M. (1996). *Frontiers: Territory and state formation in the modern world*. Cambridge, MA: Polity Press.

Anderson, M., & Bort, E. (Eds.) (1998). *The frontiers of Europe*. London: Pinter.

Barker, C. (1999). *Television, globalization and cultural identities*. Buckingham: Open University Press.

Baud, M., & van Schendel, W. (1997). Toward a comparative history of borderlands. *Journal of World History*, 8(2), 211–242.

Connolly, W. E. (1996). Tocqueville, territory, and violence. In M. J. Shapiro & H. R. Alker (Eds.), *Challenging boundaries* (pp. 141–164). Minneapolis: University of Minnesota Press.

Conversi, D. (1995). Reassessing current theories of nationalism: Nationalism as boundary maintenance and creation. *Nationalism and Ethnic Politics*, 1(1), 73–85.

Everard, J. (2000). *Virtual states: The Internet and the boundaries of the nation-state*. London: Routledge.

Featherstone, M. (1995). *Undoing culture: Globalization, postmodernity and identity.* London: Sage Publications.

Ferguson, K. (1996). Unmapping and remapping the world: Foreign policy as aesthetic practice. In M. J. Shapiro & H. R. Alker (Eds.), *Challenging boundaries* (pp. 165–192). Minneapolis: University of Minnesota Press.

Giddens, A. (1984). *The constitution of society.* Cambridge: Polity Press.

Hamelink, D. J. (1999). The elusive concept of globalisation. *Global Dialogue,* 1(1), 1–9.

Held, D. (1997). Democracy, transnational problems and the boundary. *Social Alternatives,* 16(4), 33–37.

Huntington, S. (1996). *The clash of civilizations and the remaking of world order.* New York: Simon & Schuster.

Jaworski, A., & Coupland, N. (2000). Perspectives on discourse analysis. In A. Jaworski & N. Coupland (Eds.), *The discourse reader* (pp. 1–44). London: Routledge.

Lee, C. C., Chan, J. M., Pan, Z. & So, C. (2000). National prisms of a global "media event." In J. Curran & M. Gurevitch (Eds.), *Mass media and society* (3rd ed., pp. 295–309). London: Arnold.

Morley, D., & Robins, K. (1995). *Spaces of identity: Global media, electronic landscapes and cultural boundaries.* London: Routledge.

Murphy, A. B. (1996). The sovereign state system as political-territorial ideal: Historical and contemporary considerations. In T. J. Biersteker & C. Weber (Eds.), *State sovereignty as social construct* (pp. 81–120). Cambridge: Cambridge University Press.

Newman, D., & Paasi, A. (1998). Fences and neighbors in the postmodern world: Boundary narratives in political geography. *Progress in Human Geography,* 22, 186–207.

Oommen, T. K. (1995). Contested boundaries and emerging pluralism. *International Sociology,* 10, 251–268.

Pellow, D. (1996). Concluding thoughts. In D. Pellow (Ed.), *Setting boundaries: The anthropology of spatial and social organization* (pp. 215–226). Westport, CT: Bergin & Garvey.

Pieterse, J. (1995). Globalisation as hybridisation. In M. Featherstone, S. Lash & R. Robertson (Eds.), *Global modernities* (pp. 46–68). Thousand Oaks, CA: Sage Publications.

Pool, I. S. (1990). *Technologies without boundaries: On telecommunications in a global age.* Cambridge, MA: Harvard University Press.

Robertson, R. (1992). *Globalization: Social theory and global culture.* London: Sage Publications.

Robertson, R. (1995). Globalization: Time-sapce and homgeneity-heterogeneity. In M. Featherstone, S. Lash & R. Robertson (Eds.), *Global modernities* (pp. 25–44). London: Sage Publications.

Sack, R. D. (1986). *Human territoriality: Its theory and history.* Cambridge: Cambridge University Press.

Schlesinger, P. (1991). *Media, state and nation: Political violence and collective identities.* London: Sage Publications.

Scott, A. (Ed.) (1997). *The limits of globalization.* London: Routledge.

Shapiro, M., & Alker, H. (Eds.) (1996). *Challenging boundaries: Global flows, territorial identities*. Minneapolis: University of Minnesota Press.

Shapiro, M. J. (1996). Introduction to Part IV. In M. J. Shapiro & H. R. Alker (Eds.), *Challenging boundaries* (pp. 141–164). Minneapolis: University of Minnesota Press.

Silber, I. F. (1995). Space, fields, boundaries: The rise of spatial metaphors in contemporary sociological theory. *Social Research*, 62, 323–355.

Smith, A. (1991). *National identity*. London: Penguin.

Somers, M. R. (1994). The narrative construction of identity: a relational and network approach. *Theory and Society*, 23, 605–649.

Tomlinson, J. (1999). *Globalization and culture*. Chicago: University of Chicago Press.

Wallman, S. (1978). The boundaries of "race": Processes of ethnicity in England. *Man*, 13(2), 200–217.

Waters, M. (1995). *Globalization*. London: Routledge.

Weedon, C. (1997). *Feminist practice and poststructuralist theory*. Oxford: Blackwell.

Wilson, T. M., & Donnan, H. (Eds.) (1998). *Border identities: Nation and state at the international frontiers*. Cambridge: Cambridge University Press.

Part I

Becoming Postmodern

Chapter 1

Transculturating Modernity:
A Reinterpretation of Cultural Globalization

Joseph M. Chan and Eric Ma

Modernity is inherently globalizing.
—A. Giddens, 1990, p. 177

Essential to the idea of modernity is the belief that everything is destined to be speeded up, dissolved, displaced, transformed, reshaped.
—S. Hall, 1992, p. 15

Modernity is a global condition that now affects all our actions, interpretations, and habits, across nations and irrespective of which civilizational roots we may have or lay claim to. In this sense, it is a common condition on a global scale that we live in and with, engage in dialogue about, and that we have to reach out to grasp.
—J. Arnason, 2000, p. 59

INTRODUCTION

There are two general tendencies in the analysis of cultural globalization. The first is the liberal perspective, which views cultural globalization as a result of the triumph of the market economy and democracy around the world, especially in the wake of the collapse of communism in Eastern Europe. The global spread of modernity is conceptualized as a consequence of its diffusion or transplantation. The asymmetrical relationships among different cultures tend to be taken for granted. To be part of the globalized world is not only feasible, but also desirable. The second is the critical perspective, which builds on the notion of cultural imperialism and treats cultural globalization as a euphemism for the domination by Western or

American culture. The homogenizing effect of Western culture is emphasized. The preferred policy option is to distance oneself from the global
trend and to reassert one's cultural autonomy.

This chapter proposes a transcultural perspective that, as a synthesis of
the liberal and critical perspectives, views cultural globalization more as an
extension and adaptation of modernity on a world scale. Transculturation
is the process by which one culture is transformed by another for self-
aggrandizement when they come into contact with one another. From a
transcultural perspective, cultural boundaries are always in a state of flux,
subject to forces from within and without. Cultural sovereignty is rendered
less relevant as the world becomes more integrated technologically, economically and politically. But as a result of mediation by the nation-state,
local interests and the needs for local identity, foreign culture is not imposed but indigenized. What is absorbed and retained is what matches the
needs of the receiving culture at a given time. Our proposition of "transculturating modernity" represents an attempt to capture the push and pull,
the mix and break, of global cultural encounters, while at the same time
highlighting the forceful and directional nature of cultural formation. It is
not the simple, linear "diffusionist thesis" of early modernization theories,
since we propose that instead of diffusion from the West to the rest, what
we are now experiencing is a give-and-take among encountering cultures.
This is not a general, catch all "globalization thesis," since we are tracking
the power vector of modernization in uneven hybridization. This is not
another form of the "imperialism thesis" because we are analyzing the
multifaceted and dialectic consequences of modernity.

GLOBALIZATION AND MULTIPLE MODERNITIES

Globalization is sometimes conceived as a break that signifies the arrival
of a new epoch—postmodernity. While there is no denial that significant
changes such as the rearrangement of spatial relations of production, as
well as the extension and intensification of market relations, are having
powerful impacts on the contemporary world, they stop short of reversing
the organizing principles of modernity (Callhoun, 1999). This observation
agrees with Anthony Giddens's (1990) argument that globalization is an
extension and consequence of modernity. We are living in what he calls
"high modernity" (p. 163), the current phase of development of modern
institutions marked by the radicalizing and globalizing of the basic traits
of modernity. What has often been labeled as postmodern is merely "the
experience of living in a world in which presence and absence mingle in
historically novel ways" (p. 177). This close connection between modernity
and globalization prevents us from framing the transculturation of modernity in the postmodern discourses of simulacre, fragmentation and flu-

idity. Instead, we think that it is important to bring back the power vector of modernity.

Modernity can be viewed as "the rapidly developing and ever-densening network of interconnections and interdependencies that characterize modern life" (Tomlinson, 1999, p. 2). The notion of connectivity is found in one form or another in most contemporary accounts of globalization, implying an increase of global-spatial proximity, a compression of time and space and a stretching of social relations across distance. Institutionally, the nation-state and systematic capitalist production are of particular significance to the development of modernity. Modernity is as an aggressive and expansive project that has historical origins and a power center in Europe and other Western developed countries. After a century of rapid transculturation, the world is teeming with modernities. While the West is now experiencing high modernity, most other countries are immersed in the dream of modernization as a preferred form of social organization. Some countries are engaged in political and economic mobilization to catch up with the West; others are still struggling with the spell of postcoloniality in realizing the dream of modernity; still others are reinventing historical legacies to construct their own style of modernity in the name of national sovereignty. To the eyes of people in less affluent societies, modernity comes as a simplified and generalized imagination, which equates modernization with Westernization. Modernity comes from the West as commodities, management models, advertising, mediated images and all sorts of cultural products. Although the West is a mixture of wildly different cultures of very different historical formations, modernity is seen as an essential feature of an undifferentiated Western culture at the receiving end of the developing world. The sheer materiality of modern culture is often mapped into the hierarchy of a global cultural imagination in which the West is far more superior to the rest. The West becomes a simplified discursive category that embodies the utopian dream of modernity. Western material culture fuels the social desire of less developed communities to consume modernity of faraway places. These meaning transfers reconfigure cultural boundaries, install new aspirations and trigger complex ideological negotiations.

Contrary to what some contemporary rulers think, modernity is much more than the introduction of a liberal economy (Wittrock, 2000). It is a complex project also linked to democratic revolution, a package of social, organizational, technological and academic arrangements. Lash (1999) differentiates between first and second modernity. First modernity concerns rationality, mass production, global processes of development and mechanical reproduction. However, first modernity has been unfolding as a self-transforming project that increasingly absorbs reflexivity, historicity and uncertainty, thus becoming what is called second modernity. In connection with the process of transculturation, more historically specific cultures, ideas and practices are uprooted and translocated to alien cultures. They implode the trajectories of individual projects of modernization in different parts of the world. Thus, modernity is no longer a large scale, uniform process initiated in the West and transposed to the rest of the world. Second modernity is not a radical postmodern break; it retains many aspirations of first modernity—for instance, control, automation, bureaucracy, and so on. But it acknowledges the fact that modernity projects have different trajectories in different nations and that cultures can be translocated and thus influence the orbit of far away formations of modernities.

The expansion of modernity to engulf the world marked the most significant phase of globalization. It expanded from Europe and the West through various stages, including the period of geographical exploration, conquest, settlement, colonization, imperialism and neo-colonialism (Bocock, 1992). Modernity was at first viewed as an end state toward which all societies are inevitably moving. This teleological view of history assumes that the path of development taken by Western societies provides the universal model that all societies must follow sooner or later (Hall, 1992). However, comparative development has demonstrated that such unconditional universalism is fallacious: History simply does not unfold according to one logic; both paths and consequences may vary with contingencies. The successes of Japan, Taiwan, Singapore, Korea and Hong Kong in achieving modernities that are distinct from the West have formed what Berger (1988, p. 6) calls a "second case" of capitalist modernity, lending strong support to an alternate conception of historical formation that stresses more the varied paths to development—unevenness, contradictions, contingencies, contextual differences and diverse outcomes.[1] Modernity is thus not merely a diffusion of Western institutions around the world. It involves very diverse and complex historical processes that may give rise to multiple institutional and ideological patterns. Distinctly modern, these patterns all bear the imprints of the cultural premises, traditions and historical experiences of the reception cultures. After more than a century of modernization in some of the developing countries, modernization and Westernization are found *not* to be identical. Multiple modernities exist *not* only in the East, but also in the West, where modernity first took place. Indeed, the center of modernity gradually moved from Europe to the United States, whose institutional configurations markedly differ from those of Europe. One prominent example is that the state is assigned a much greater role in the operation of the market in Europe than in North America (Wittrock, 2000). The existence of multiple modernities in the West and East represents a refutation of the modernization theories that prevailed in the 1950s and 1960s, which assumed that all industrial societies would one day converge. The modernization experiences of various countries that span the world from Southeast Asia to the Islamic world and to Latin America have demonstrated that the homogenizing and hegemonic assumptions of this Western program of modernity were not realized.[2] Having said this, it would be wrong to push the argument so far as to deny modernity of its core axis of social organization that originated in Europe. Modernity implies various forms of universalism, representing a global condition that "affects all our actions, interpretations, and habits, across nations and irrespective of which civilizational roots we may have or lay claim to" (Wittrock, 2000, p. 59). The existence of this global condition is not necessarily bad because many countries have risen to its challenge by improving their welfare and power. To say the least, it has been a source of inspiration and aspiration for the developing world.

The idea of multiple modernities presumes that significant differences still exist between societies that are being transformed by globalization. The best way to understand the contemporary world and modernity, according to Eisenstadt (2000, p. 2), is to see it "as a story of continual constitution and reconstitution of a multiplicity of cultural programs." As modernity and Westernization cannot be equated, it makes less sense to speak of the Western patterns of modernity as being authentic. Of course, this does not dispute the fact that they enjoy historical precedence and continue to be a basic reference point for others. The idea of multiple modernities thus leads one to conclude that the package of modernity originated from the West can be disaggregated and reassembled in different ways. This makes it possible for transculturation to play an important role as cultures encounter, clash and compete.

THE TRANSCULTURATION OF MODERNITY

The process by which modernity spreads around the world is not linear. At every step of the way, it is adapted to suit local situations. Whatever works in one culture may not apply in a different context (Hannerz, 1996). Cultural mingling and recombinations are thus the norms. Imported culture will have to weave its way between context and organizational frameworks during transculturation. Based on a study of how a Chinese legend was transformed and incorporated by Disney (see Chapter 13), we have proposed the notion of transculturation to refer to the process by which a culture is transformed by another for self-aggrandizement. It is an evolving process involving both organizational routines and experimentation through which the foreign culture is decontextualized, essentialized, indigenized and recontextualized. Transculturation also involves the transfiguration of cultural forms, which affects the extent to which the original culture is changed. Transculturation always results in the hybridization of two or more cultures. While the relative weights of the component cultures may vary in various hybrids, cultural transculturators tend to strike a balance between the foreign and the indigenous in order to maintain a relatively stable self-identity. Through transculturation and globalization, what was once local is rendered global, and what was foreign is made indigenous. Although the concept of transculturation is initially applied to a cultural artifact such as legend, we think that it is also applicable to the analysis of macroscopic cultural encounters, including the indigenization and appropriation of modernity.

Cultural Appropriation and Cultural Recreation

The transcultural perspective distinguishes itself from cultural imperialism because the latter ignores the process of appropriation, which is an essential part of the circulation of symbolic forms. Cultural transfer does not take place in a linear way; it always involves "interpretation, translation, mutation, adaptation, and 'indigenization' as the receiving culture brings its own cultural resources to bear, in dialectical fashion, upon 'cultural imports' " (Tomlinson, 1999, p. 84). While the idea of active cultural appropriation is part of the perspective that views an audience as "active" consumers of media texts, there is no reason why it cannot be applied to the analysis of the adoption of foreign commodities or institutional arrangements.

When the East meets the West, especially at the stage of initial contact, both sides tend to think in dichotomous terms—East vs. West, traditional vs. modern, foreign vs. indigenous, global vs. local. It is not uncommon for the reception countries to move from one extreme position to another, rejecting or embracing modernity in total. The historical development in the last century shows that modernity cannot be wholly transplanted or imported. All social actions and thoughts have to be contextualized. Once contextualized, they are bounded by historicity and influenced by the cultural premises, traditions and social forces of the reception countries. Both the forces that promote and retard modernization will be brought to life, acting upon the direction and form of social change. Through transculturation, the foreign version of modernity will be imagined, interpreted, compromised and reinvented. What decides whether a new cultural element is assimilated depends on whether it can meet or create certain local needs. Transculturation allows many in non-European countries—especially elites and intellectuals—to appropriate foreign themes and institutions and to selectively reject many of their undesirable aspects in building up their new modern tradition. It entails "the continuous selection, reinterpretation, and reformulation" of the imported ideas, bringing about "continual innovation, with new cultural and political programs emerging, exhibiting novel ideologies and institutional patterns" (Eisenstadt, 2000, p. 15). The resulting cultural and institutional arrangements mark a balance between the aspirations of these countries to be modern and their ambivalent attitudes toward modernity in general and toward the West in particular. Transculturation thus facilitates the incorporation of some Western universal elements of modernity in the construction of their own new, yet traditional, collective identities.

Transculturation takes place when people are given a cultural choice. On the one hand, people not only possess a culture, but also are possessed by it (Hannerz, 1996). In other words, there is a strong tendency for people to reproduce what seem to be their own cultures. On the other hand, people tend to make use of new cultural resources that are made available to them for renewing their cultural heritage. These tendencies can be illustrated by the domestication and acculturation of foreign cultural products and values (see Chapters 4 and 10 in this volume). Sometimes, the decision to engage in the modernity project is not a free choice. Like China, some countries turn to modernity only when "national survival" is at stake. National survival is perceived to be a real problem in East Asian countries when they are challenged by modern Western society. It is a mix of cultural superiority and political inferiority (Hsiao, 1988). While this sentiment has never been part of Western modernity, it should have some direct or indirect influence on how East Asian countries respond to the challenge of modernity from the West. The encounter with modernity may result in far-reaching cultural transformations in traditional societies. As the implications of modernity for the traditional societies are not always known, modernization is to many a cultural adventure. With transculturation, people are more assured of the continuity of their own culture while new elements are adopted.

Deterritorialization and Transborder Imaginations

In this age of global communication, transculturation is less confined by space and time. In the initial stage of expansive modernity, military, missionary and commercial activities were largely territorialized. Encounters were spatially and temporally defined. Now expansive modernity and its consequences can be dislocated from the spatial and temporal boundaries of the West and the non-West, developed and developing countries. The key concept to this understanding of globalization is deterritorialization, which Tomlinson (1999, p. 107) defines as "the loss of the natural relation of culture to geographical and social territories." This is similar to Giddens's (1990) idea of "time-space distanciation," which allows for the stretching of relations across time and space. This disembedding does not mean that people cease to live their lives in "real" localities. What becomes important is the way in which this stretching of social relations affects the character of the localities that we inhabit. Deterritorialization is not a linear, one-way process. Deterritorialization is often accompanied by reterritorialization. Deterritorialization does not the spell the end of locality; it is only that the locality is rendered a more complex cultural space.

These deterritorializations and reterritorializations are both imaginative and materialistic. When cultures are transposed from one community to another, they are captured by the imaginations of very localized audiences. To put it in another way, foreign cultures have to be imagined through the mediation of transborder cultural products and socioeconomic encounters. Western nations are the historically precedent centers of modernity. However, the cultural imaginations of high modernity can be uprooted from these geographical centers, transposed to other parts of the world and developed as virtual discursive centers away from Western sites. Because of new media technologies, aspirations of Western high modernity such as nomadity, upward mobility and rationality can be domesticated in non-Western satellite cities. These imaginations of modernity as Westernization are expressing themselves as virtual sites in newly modernized societies. Transborder imagination of alien cultures can be deterrestrialized, stereotypically inflated, temporally compressed and reterritorialized into the local social network and circuits of meaning construction (see Chapter 14). These are especially true in times when information technologies are speeding up the circulation of cultural imaginations.

Transculturation is fuelled by transborder imaginations. However, it is also a form of cultural materialism in the sense that transculturation is embodied within materialistic exchanges and sustained by a transborder division of cultural labor (see Chapter 3). Contemporary culture flows within a few organizational frames: interpersonal relations, firms, markets and states.[3] It is through these frames that transculturation takes place. The interpersonal relations belong to what Hannerz (1996) refers to as the form-of-life. As people live out their daily lives, meanings of different origins are exchanged and appropriated. The cultural flow is mostly local in form as people are primarily sedentary and anchored in the same territories. In the contemporary world, where commodities form an important part of our environment, the interpersonal frame is closely linked to the firm and the market. As modernity is often embodied in the presence and consumption of commodities imported from the West or from modernized local companies, both the firms and the markets are heavily involved in the transculturation of modernity. The Hollywood studios that have strong followings around the world (see Chapter 2) are the cases in point. Global sales have become an important factor in their calculations of the potential appeal of their productions. Meanwhile, local firms in the developing world have to respond to the challenges from Hollywood through emulation and recreation.

Modernity is about mechanical production and standardizations. When cultural products and transnational commodities are massively produced and widely distributed on a global scale, the charms of innovative images and products will diminish in subsequent consumption. As Ritzer (1999) argues, globalization is "disenchanting" the world with standardized goods. Thus, there is a structural inclination for the local to enchant the disenchantment of transnational cultural flows. In short, the firm enchants, promotes and dramatizes modernity in order to build and exploit new markets, both globally and locally. In the end the audience will use both Western and local yet Westernized products in order to fulfill their own objectives. The state is more concerned with the translation of the modernity package into institutional arrangements. It regulates and nationalizes the process of transculturating modernity. The forms of the market and democracy, for instance, are as a rule installed by the state. These institutional arrangements are important in that they define people's way of life and the space in which individuals consume and make sense of what is produced by the firms. There are intense, multi-level negotiations between the national and the international (see Chapters 7 and 11).

The traditional emphasis is placed on the importance of the state in setting the parameters for the development of modernity in the less developed world. While we think that the state's role cannot be ignored, we should not slight the importance of the modernity project that is mediated through daily exchanges, firms and markets. The experience of Shanghai is a case in point. As modernity burgeoned in Shanghai before the Communist Party came to power in 1949, it was embedded in an urban-based print culture responsive to the logic of the marketplace (Lee, 2000). Modernity was found to be very much the product of a commodified culture of consumption. It was about the material transformation of everyday life for the general public, rather than the organizational mobilization of an elitist few for a well-articulated cause, implying that modernity is sometimes "about business rather than politics, the quest for a good life rather than a just society, the transformative capacity of private enterprises rather than collective action" (Yeh, 2000, p. 6). For about three decades after 1949, the state intervened in the development of Shanghai, putting a virtual stop to the modernity project as it was known in the West. Modernization embodied in the form-of-life began to rise in importance again as the state and the ruling elite began to take the path of modernization and marketization by the late 1970s. The consumption and business associated with the transculturation of modernity is destined to receive increasing attention as the world's economy becomes more integrated.

Although binary opposites—Eastern vs. Western, traditional vs. modern, global vs. local—are useful analytical categories in the discourse of globalization, the distinctions between them should not be stressed so much as to neglect the fact that they are dialectically linked. From the transculturalist perspective, modernity does not represent a total break from the traditional and the local; it is more like a combination of opposites. In both Orientalism and Occidentalism, there is a tendency to stress the cultural differences between East and West. The portrayal of other cultures as opposites serves to achieve a cultural binding within one's domestic community. At the same time, framing such differences as diametrically opposite tends to make each culture less tolerant of the other and more resistant to cross-fertilization. This undermines one's potential in transculturating other cultures to one's own advantage. While the Eastern and Western cultures differ from one another, they share some important universals. In addition, the transculturation of modernity can be a two-way process, with the early modernizing countries incorporating traditions and features from the later ones. Cultural borrowing in the reverse direction ranges from learning from the Japanese style of management to the co-optation of movie directors and kung fu techniques from Hong Kong. Indeed, what is Western and foreign is constantly changing. A rigid distinction between the East and the West is becoming inapplicable in this age of rapid transculturation.

The traditional and the modern are also dialectically linked. As evidenced by the history of the pro-modernization May Fourth Movement in China from 1917 to 1921, many anti-traditionalists were in fact scholars who were familiar with ancient philosophies (Yu, 1982). They made use of traditional teachings to promote modernization and even Westernization. Tradition is not a monolithic whole. It is filled with contradictions. People with different causes can exploit these internal differences for their own purposes. Given the compatibility between certain aspects of traditional and imported culture, it may not be appropriate to separate the traditional completely from the modern. Tradition is constantly evolving; it dies when it is found to be irrelevant to the contemporary. To the developing world, the modern originated from the West. The contemporary is a hybrid of the traditional and the foreign. What is foreign is constantly changing, too. Buddhism was imported from India and became an integral part of Chinese tradition which later, ironically, became a force resisting the importation of Christianity—a Western religion. All this shows that it is a futile exercise in the long run for one culture to try to maintain its purity and authenticity.

Self-Identity and Global Power

Transculturation is also about meaning transfer. Transculturating modernity is about the transfer of the meaning systems embedded in different modernities. In the above, it has been examined by looking into the imaginative and material aspects of transborder exchanges. However, transculturation can also be examined, on a sociopsychological level, by the ritual, which "inscribes" transculturated modernity. This is a process in which the meaning systems of high modernity are incorporated into self-identity. It is also a process by which we can cut across the macro-analytic and the micro-experiential (see Chapter 16). In transculturation, there is an interface between the macro and the micro, the transnational and the personal. The notion of "habitus" (Bauman, 1992; Bourdieu, 1984; Hannerz, 1996) can help to bridge transculturation at various levels, notably the macro process of global networking and the micro sociocultural process of identity formation. The habitus is defined in reference to particular agents or groups, so that the habits of different agents may overlap to various degrees. Thus, the concept can simply refer to a dwelling site where there are overlapping networks of social, cultural and economic resources available to an individual or a group of people. In sociological terms, the habitus of an agent could be said to consist of a network of direct and indirect relationships, stretching out wherever they may, within or across national boundaries. In cultural terms, habitats can become "webs of meaning" that offer agents symbolic resources to make sense of the world and restrictive categories to limit his or her cultural imagination. In short, it offers resources and constraints. Thus, habitus is a fuzzy concept that can explain stability and change, security and anxiety, and agency and structure.

Within emergent and transitory habitats, cultural identities are maintained in what Giddens (1991) called a protective cocoon balancing ontological security and existential anxiety. Ontological security is a sense of continuity offered to an individual from mythical ideologies and commonsensical order of events. In daily existence, this ontological security is constantly put to the test. The existential anxiety triggered from these daily encounters can be stabilized by social skills and practical know-how, which form what are called ethnomethodologies of day-to-day interpersonal interaction. Global expansive modernity can impinge on the micro configuration of habitats in sociological and cultural terms. The materiality and ideology of far away modernity in the West can be transferred to and recontextualized in local habitats. They install new aspirations in these habitats, destabilize and rearrange cultural categories and motivate transculturation on an intimate and personal level (Bauman, 1997; Firat & Dholakia, 1998; Friedman, 1994; Mathews, 2000). It is the macro transculturation of modernity expressed in the micro ritual of daily existence. The concept of ritual is used here liberally to refer to daily routines of habitual activities. To be modern involves the psychological process of changing one's "local skills." Deskilling and reskilling break the ontological security of the individual and unleash a series of floating and nonspecific anxiety. These anxieties of not knowing how to do things right (modern) are directly related to micro day-to-day encounters. A casual glance of disapproval or a gaze of contempt challenges and disturbs the daily survival skills of the individuals. The reskilling is motivated negatively by the feeling of shame and positively by the comfort and freedom offered by modern living. Transculturating modernity, as an interactive and capillary dynamic of cultural globalization, is both transnational and personal.

Finally, these macro and micro processes of transculturation may reconfigure the hierarchy of global power. Those countries that are more successful in transculturation rise in influence, causing the declining grip of the West over the rest of the world. This decline is not a result of the diminishing impact of the institutions that first arose there, but, on the contrary, a result of their global spread, which can be interpreted as globalization (Giddens, 1990). Modernity is a competitive project. Nations try to race to be the most efficient in their production of quality goods, services and culture. When Japan was found to be threatening to a few strategic industries in the United States, such as car manufacturing and electronics, in the 1980s, it was hailed as the world's "No. 1" producer, so its way of social organization was studied and transculturated in other parts of the world. In many ways, international trade in brand-name consumer products has become a binding force for nations engaging in the modernity project. Through political maneuvering and regulations of the international marketplace, the periphery can transform itself into a center if it has the will and the power. Needless to say, this should by no means be interpreted as to indicate the end of the general subordinating status of most developing countries. The globalized world has multiple modernities; it nevertheless retains a power vector which is centripetal to the developed centers. There are also satellite sites between centers of high modernity and developing modernities in the rest of the world. In developing countries, newly modernized cities, as satellite modernities, are reproducing, hybridizing and domesticating a simplified Western modernity for the consumption of less developed sister cites and territories within the same regions (Ma, 2001). Multiple modernities are still organized in a global network of powers.

HYBRIDIZED MODERNITY

Encounters of distinct cultures can result in creative confrontations that may lead to cultural blending and recreation. Associated with the transcultural perspective is a concern with the ideas of cultural mixing and hybridization, rather than with direct cultural imposition from the West. During transculturation, modernity or other values are essentialized, appropriated, transfigured, decontextualized and recontextualzed. As modernity spreads, cultural hybridization has become an inevitable consequence and cultural authenticity a growing impossibility. Hybridity is a global condition for all human cultures. It contains no zones of purity because they are subject to a continuous process of transculturation.

Cultural hybridization can be physical or chemical in nature. Physical hybridization is represented by the co-presence of two different cultural traits, which can take the form of commodities or behavioral choices. The traits are distinct, subject to the final choice of consumers or individuals. As the mixing is physical, the traits can be separated and withheld. This kind of physical cultural mixing is more prevalent at the initial stage of cultural encounters. Of more importance to the discourse of globalization is chemical hybridization. It carries what Tomlinson (1999, p. 143) refers to as the ideas of "intermingling, combination, fusion, and mélange." Hybridization assumes the emergence of a new synthetic culture that results from the combination of the formerly "pure" cultures. The transformation involved is chemical in nature, meaning that it is impossible to separate the component elements and to reverse the change. The synthesis has made the whole greater than the sum of its parts. The notion of cultural hybridity tends to neglect the role of power relations in structuring the hybrid mix and to suggest "equal measures" and a certain serendipity in the combination.[4] However, recognizing hegemonic structures does not necessarily lead to an offhand rejection of the idea of hybridity. While a hybridity has its independent cultural power, we should recognize the power of hegemonic force within it. The questions that follow are: How does this complexity of hegemony-hybridity operate? What are the conditions for mixing and melange? How is hegemony not merely reproduced, but refigured in the process of hybridization (Nederveen, 1995)? Given the inequity of the contemporary world system, there is no question that modernity anywhere is subject to the heavy pull of the centers based in the developed West. What is generally feared in the periphery is that this asymmetrical cultural relationship will result in political and economic subordination.

World history shows that the hybridization of foreign and domestic cultures is an important way by which cultural development is achieved. The transculturation of modernity represents a form of boundary crossing between the global and the local, and between the foreign and the indigenous. Transculturation and hybridization have rendered cultural boundaries blurry. What is considered to be foreign at a time will become indigenous if it has been successfully synthesized; the resultant hybrid, undeniably national, will then serve as a new basis for further hybridization. While the relative weights of the composing cultures may vary in different cultural hybrids, there is a tendency for the transculturator to strike a balance between the foreign and the indigenous, the global and the local. This is necessary because human beings have an enduring need to maintain some stability in their cultural identity, which is often tied to the soil, blood and religion.

TOWARD A TRANSCULTURAL PERSPECTIVE

Globalization was initially theorized as a homogenizing dynamic that would engulf the world. But history has shown that globalization and cultural homogenization, as theoretical imaginations, have not been fully actualized, and perhaps they might never be. Indeed, the world is far from being one, and boundaries, old and new, are still around us. More recent developments have seen a multiplicity of cultural and social formations going far beyond the very homogenizing aspects of the original version. The proposition of "the transculturation of modernity" is a reinterpretation of cultural globalization in light of these developments, which attest to the continual development of multiple modernities on a global scale. The trans-cultural perspective, we believe, can better explain the globalized dynamic of modernity. It refrains from a simple cultural homogenization argument and enriches the political economy perspective by highlighting the full complexity and dialectic nature of cultural globalization. It also differentiates from the random hybridization arguments of popular postmodernism and attempts to depict the uneven configurations of transcultuation in different modernities. As elaborated above, the thesis of transculturation captures the historicity, multiplicity, power asymmetry, reciprocal dialectic, uneven hybridization, creative synthesis, transborder imagination, material embod-iment and sociopsychological inscription in the global expansion of mo-dernity. We will briefly summarize these characteristics.

Transculturation stresses the creative mixing and blending of exotic and domestic cultures under historical conditions. The transculturation of mo-dernity is history specific, resulting in the formation of multiple modernities in different nations and at different periods of time. The transcultural per-spective also highlights the power hierarchy in these historical and cultural formations. In the expansive project of modernity, many of the phenomena labeled as postmodern are the compressed coexistence of different modes of modernities in which presence and absence mingle in dizzyingly novel ways. Nevertheless, the globalized world retains a power imbalance tilting in favor of the developed centers. The transculturation of modernity is the transborder and global circulation of different cultural systems. Although its centers are residing in the established modern societies, every encounter and exchange, we believe, is reciprocal and dialectic, combining creatively dominant global motifs and local preferences. Even the centers of high modernities are now absorbing and transforming the cultural heritages of less developed countries to reenergize their own cultural formations. Thus, cultural globalization is producing uneven hybridizations worldwide.

The transcultural perspective treats globalization as a dialectically syn-thetic process that embraces the contradictory dynamics captured by du-alities such as universalization vs. particularization, homogenization vs. differentiation, integration vs. fragmentation, centralization vs. decentrali-zation and juxtaposition vs. syncretization.[5] Transculturation of modernity is imaginative and materialistic. It is fueled by transborder imaginations, which are hybridized and heterogeneous, deterritorialized and reterritorial-ized, continuous and discontinuous. Cultural imaginations are often ster-eotypically inflated, temporally compressed, historically flattened and contextually reworked when they travel across national boundaries. How-ever, these transborder imaginations are also embodied within material ex-changes, which are managed by nation-states, transnational agents, local firms and the market. And finally, transculturation of modernity also in-volves sociopsychological processes at the personal and interpersonal levels, in which macro cultural transfers and hybridizations are inscribed in micro social habitats. The real lasting power of globalization lies in the transculturation of daily routines and habitual activities which de-skill and re-skill individuals into "modern" subjects. Transculturing modernity is global, transnational, reciprocal, social and personal.

NOTES

1. One case in point is the existence of subdued individualism in East Asia which, based on the Western experience, is thought to be inevitably linked to modernity. Japan, for one, demonstrates that a strikingly traditional culture is compatible with a fiercely modern, high-tech economy (Hall, 1992). As evidenced by the experiences of Germany, Japan and the Soviet Union, a dictatorship could be as effective an engine of industrialization as democracy in some other countries. Force, violence and coercion have played as decisive a historical role in the evolution of capitalism as peaceful economic competition.

2. For an extensive review of the modernizations that occur in various places, consult the special issue of *Daedalus* on Multiple Modernities (Winter 2000 edition).

3. The organizational frames identified by Hannerz (1996) include form-of-life, market and state. What we propose here is a modification and extension of his formulation.

4. Tomlinson (1999) calls for a better term than hybridization because it connotes equal contribution from two combining cultures. In this sense, transculturation is a preferred concept.

5. For a more detailed analysis of these dualities, see McGrew (1992).

REFERENCES

Arnason, J. (2000). Modernity: One, none, or many? European origins and modernity as a global condition. *Daedalus: Journal of the American Academy of Arts and Sciences*, 129(1), 31–60.

Bauman, Z. (1992). *Intimations of postmodernity*. London: Routledge.

Bauman, Z. (1997). *Postmodernity and its discontents*. New York: New York University Press.

Berger, P. (1988). An East Asian development model? In P. Berger & H.-H.M. Hsiao (Eds.), *In search of an East Asian development model* (pp. 3–11). New Brunswick, NJ: Transaction Books.

Bocock, R. (1992). The cultural formations of modern society. In S. Hall & B. Gieben (Eds.), *Formations of modernity* (pp. 229–274). Cambridge: Polity Press and Open University Press.

Bourdieu, P. (1984). *Distinction: A social critique of the judgement of taste*. London: Routledge & Kegan Paul.

Callhoun, C. (1999). Postmodernity as pseudohistory. In M. Waters (Ed.), *Modernity: Critical concepts: Vol. IV. After modernity* (pp. 188–208). London: Routledge.

Eisenstadt, S. N. (2000). Multiple modernities. *Daedalus: Journal of the American Academy of Arts and Sciences*, 129(1), 1–30.

Firat, A. F., & Dholakia, N. (1998). *Consuming people: From political economy to theaters of consumption*. London: Routledge.

Friedman, J. (1994). *Cultural identity and global process*. London: Sage Publications.

Giddens, A. (1990). *The consequence of modernity*. Cambridge: Polity Press.

Giddens, A. (1991). *Modernity and self-identity: Self and society in the late modern age*. Cambridge: Polity Press.

Hall, S. (1992). Introduction. In S. Hall & B. Gieben (Eds.), *Formations of modernity* (pp. 1–16). Cambridge: Polity Press and Open University Press.

Hannerz, U. (1996). *Transnational connections: Culture, people, places*. London: Routledge.

Hsiao, H.-H.M. (1988). An East Asian development model: Empirical explorations. In P. Berger & H.-H.M. Hsiao (Eds.), *In search of an East Asian development model* (pp. 12–26). New Brunswick, NJ: Transaction Books.

Lash, S. (1999). *Another modernity: A different rationality*. Oxford: Blackwell.

Lee, O.-F. Leo. (2000). The cultural construction of modernity in urban Shanghai: Some preliminary explorations. In W.-H. Yeh (Ed.), *Becoming Chinese: Passages to modernity and beyond* (pp. 31–61). Berkeley: University of California Press.

Ma, E. (2001). Consuming satellite modernities. *Cultural Studies*, 15(3/4), 444–463.

Mathews, G. (2000). *Global culture/individual identity: Searching for home in the cultural supermarket*. London: Routledge.

McGrew, A. (1992). A global society? In S. Hall, D. Held & T. McGrew (Eds.), *Modernity and its futures* (pp. 61–116). Cambridge: Polity Press.

Nederveen, P. (1995). Globalization as hybridization. In M. Featherstone, S. Lash & R. Robertson (Eds.), *Global modernities* (pp. 45–68). London: Sage.

Ritzer, G. (1999). *Enchanting a disenchanted world: Revolutionizing the means of consumption*. Thousand Oaks, CA: Pine Forge Press.

Tomlinson, J. (1999). *Globalization and culture*. Chicago: University of Chicago Press.

Wittrock, B. (2000). Modernity: One, none, or many? European origins and modernity as a global condition. *Daedalus: Journal of the American Academy of Arts and Sciences*, 129(1), 31–60.

Yeh, W.-H. (2000). Introduction: Interpreting Chinese modernity, 1900–1950. In W.-H. Yeh (Ed.), *Becoming Chinese: Passages to modernity and beyond* (pp. 1–30). Berkeley: University of California Press.

Yu, Y. (1982). *Historiography and tradition*. Taipei: China Times Press (in Chinese).

Part II

Dissolution of Boundaries

Chapter 2

The Unification of the World under the Signs of Mickey Mouse and Bruce Willis: The Supply and Demand Sides of American Popular Culture

Todd Gitlin

The dominance of American popular culture as a global *lingua franca* can only be understood by taking into account both supply-side and demand-side factors. Supply-side factors include economies of scale, the organization of distribution networks, the absorptiveness of American culture, its eclipse of less popular forms in American history and the sway of the English language. Demand-side factors include American culture's modernist themes and styles, especially in film and music, and its ambiguities. Although audiences around the world often prefer indigenous material when given the choice, they attach themselves to populist aspects of American products. Four genres in which this taste is manifest are action movies, road movies, cartoons and physical comedies. These provide, in however reduced a form, accessible versions of freedom, mobility, materialism and the return of the repressed, themes and topics that they can adapt to their own purposes. Still, the coarsening effects of American popular cultural styles cannot be neglected. The fact that American popular culture is distinctly susceptible to multiple interpretations is compatible with its allure, an allure that attracts cultural practitioners from many countries, turns Hollywood into a global export platform, and, over time, limits the spaces available for autonomous culture in the world.

This chapter concerns the interplay of supply and demand, the dialectic of cultural powers and pressures that results in the unification of the world under the signs of Mickey Mouse and Bruce Willis. If it seems perverse to speak of the unification of the world by Mickey Mouse and Bruce Willis, this is not, I hope, strictly because I am perverse, but because the world is peculiar.

A few years ago I visited the champagne cellar of Piper-Heidsieck in

Reims, France. At the entrance is a plaque recording that the cellar was dedicated by Marie Antoinette. At the end of the tour, offered in six languages, the visitor walks upstairs from the cellar into a small museum consisting entirely of photographs of famous people drinking champagne. And who are they? Are they perhaps members of today's royal houses? Are they Nobel Prize winners, economic titans, presidents or prime ministers of great nations? Of course not. They are movie stars, almost all of them American—Marilyn Monroe to Clint Eastwood. Perhaps by now Leonardo has been added—not da Vinci, but di Caprio. The symmetry of the exhibition is obvious, the premise unmistakable: Hollywood stars are the royalty of this century (more popular by far than the doomed Marie).

Hollywood is the global cultural capital—capital in both senses. Hardly anyone is exempt from its force. French resentment of Mouse, Willis and the rest of the force-fed products of American civilization is well known. A few years ago in France there took place a great struggle over import quotas, and of course the Americans, for whom entertainment is the nation's second largest export—just after aerospace—cried foul. A similar struggle erupted in the 1920s. What is less well known, and usually not acknowledged by the French, was that *Terminator 2* sold 5 million tickets in France during the month it opened—with no submachine guns held at the heads of the ticket buyers. The same Culture Minister Jack Lang who achieved a moment of predictable notoriety in the United States for declaring that *Dallas* amounted to cultural imperialism, conferred France's highest honor in the arts to Elizabeth Taylor and that paragon of cultural achievement, Sylvester Stallone. I am not pointing my finger at hypocrisy pure and simple, but at something deeper: dependency. American popular culture is that nemesis that hundreds of millions of people, perhaps billions, love, and love to hate. The antagonism and the dependency are inseparable.

How shall we understand the antagonism, the dependency and the consequences? How shall we understand the little Japanese girl a few years ago who asked an American visitor, "Is there really a Disneyland in America?" How shall we understand the Hong Kong T-shirt that says—as a student once told me—"I Feel Coke"?

I want to argue that the omnipresence of American popular culture has a complex meaning—overlapping with the complex meaning of American popular culture itself. On the one hand, American popular culture is the closest approximation there is today to a global *lingua franca*, drawing especially the young, urban and urbane classes of most nations into a federated cultural zone. Or to use another metaphor: American popular culture has become the central bank of international mythologies. Retailing these mythologies, American, Japanese and European multinational corporations—their ownership more dispersed than the styles they circulate— are the administrators of most of the stories that enable the world, at least the so-called developed world, to share some dreams in common. Two major dreams in particular: the dream of freedom and the dream of wealth. The clash can be interesting. The compatibility, too.

Cultural bilingualism is routine. One is local but cosmopolitan at the same time, in many possible hybrid forms. Omnipresent American popular culture is, for worse and sometimes for better, a global *lingua franca*, just as English is the most common second language, and partly, of course, *because* English occupies that position. America presides over a sort of World Bank of styles and symbols, an International Cultural Fund of images and celebrities. Whether circulated by American, European or Japanese multinationals, American popular culture is the latest in a long succession of bidders for global unification. It succeeds the Latin imposed by the Roman Empire and the Catholic Church, and the so-called Marxism-Leninism of the three-quarters of a century following 1917. Michael Jackson, Madonna, Charles Bronson, Clint Eastwood, Bruce Willis, the multicolor chorus of Coca-Cola and the next flavor of the month or the universe are, thanks to the multinational corporation, the icons of a curious sort of one-world ideology, or, better, a global semiculture, helping to integrate at least the urban classes of most nations, and especially the younger population, into a single cultural zone.

What people experience in the form of American television, American movies, American soft drinks, American-label running shoes and T-shirts is more than immediate sensory experience; it is the taste of a certain cultural citizenship. Consuming a commodity, even wearing a slogan, one signifies, to a certain degree, an identity. One joins with others, even vicariously, perhaps "virtually." By partaking of the signs and objects of popular culture, one enters into virtual membership in an abstracted assembly, so that to wear a Hong Kong T-shirt that reads, "I Feel Coke," is to borrow some of the effervescence that is supposed to emanate from this American staple. Such identifications are peculiarly strong for the young, who through the media in relation to real and virtual peers are encouraged to form a sort of horizontal society (Friedman, 1999). Increasingly, the young want to "feel Coke"—that is the main way they interpret what it means to be American, by which they mean not only prominent on a world scale, but also quintessentially modern, contemporary, happening, *now*. In a world of ubiquitous images, easy migration, feverish capital flows and casual tourism, the young often desire to identify not only locally and nationally, but globally. Even when they are nationalist, they also aspire to some sort of universal credentials.

The depth of such identifications should not be exaggerated. Indeed, in the United States, "identity" is a vastly overused term, the very overuse suggesting that the phenomenon casually called "identity" is something relatively shallow, evanescent, overlapping and coexisting with other "identities" in a mélange of memberships, none of which may by itself be compelling. Traditional social bonds do not evaporate altogether in the flux of

contemporary life, just as nation-states do not dissolve in the face of globalizing tendencies. Rather, traditional bonds bend to accommodate the expressions that circulate in popular culture, so that family ties are
consolidated with joint visits to Disney World, children affiliate with their
parents by playing the "oldie" music of the parental generation and ex-
changing team sport statistics with them. The values and practices that
result from this bending, from the juxtaposition and recombination that
characterize American popular culture, feature a diversity that cannot be
reduced to a simple set of variations on American themes. Still, the repertory of cultures in the world is today shaped by American or American-
based models and styles more than by any other single factor. In the course
of a century of success, the giant corporations that specialize in entertainment, starting with the Hollywood studios, have cultivated popular expectations for entertainment, expectations that have hardened into genres and
formulas that are ignored by competitors at their financial peril.

The economic dimension of the American predominance is itself immense, explaining why U.S.-based multinationals steadily aim to increase
their foreign markets. Some statistics will convey the scale of American
popular culture's dependency on global exports, notably in film. In 1991–
1993, according to Ilott (1996, p. 18), "Hollywood derive[d] 45% of its
theatrical revenues, 33% of pay-TV, 36% of video and 55% of free-TV
from non-US markets." Among the 10 most lucrative Hollywood films of
1997, total foreign box office receipts amounted to $1,713.5 million, ex-
ceeding total domestic box office of $1,672.2 million, according to the
January 30, 1998, edition of *Entertainment Weekly*. Little imagination is
required to understand why the global entertainment conglomerates feel an
incentive to imitate formulas they have seen work, even if they exaggerate
the degree to which they do work. As for television, I have shown, in a
study of the American networks (Gitlin, 1983/1994), that, even in the early
1980s, when the three major networks had little competition in prime time,
more than 60 percent of the new shows they launched each year failed to
draw a large enough audience to warrant being renewed for a second year;
by the strictly economic criteria that are virtually all that matter to the
networks, they failed. Still, what the culture industry knows best how to
do is to imitate, vary and recombine formulas it has once found successful;
thus the inertia of tested "product."

Note that American economic preeminence in the culture industry is
nothing new. Economies of scale have always sided with the United States
because of the size of the American market. The United States was already
a major force in European movie theaters by the second decade of the
twentieth century. Even against competition from the British, French and
German industries, this dominance began in the silent era, accelerated with
the devastation of Europe in World War I, accelerated further in the sound

era and benefited from the second destruction of 1939–1945. American companies proved especially adept at positioning themselves for sales, striking deals with foreign distributors, establishing high-powered marketing operations. In many countries the United States could monopolize theaters, which would sooner take a chance on American goods than the available alternatives. America was already a sales culture, a master of mass production and mass promotion. Thus, according to a recent study (Vasey, 1997, p. 7), "Between the world wars, the principal film companies derived an average of 35% of their gross revenue from the foreign field."

A host of industrial advantages in production and marketing continue to accrue to the United States in the case of television, where American assembly-line methods help Hollywood companies undersell other suppliers. In the early 1980s, a program procurer in Copenhagen could lease one hour of *Dallas* for less than $5,000—the cost of producing one original minute of Danish drama. Moreover, around the world, as in the United States itself, American formulas have, over time, helped establish the conventions which productions outside the United States aim to match, even though there is evidence that when faced with a choice, majorities in many countries prefer programs produced in their own countries to the American goods. All over the world, young filmmakers aspire to be the next Spielberg. For around the world, over time, as in the United States itself, American formulas have helped establish the conventions that subsequent production—like East Asian kung fu and splatter films, "Europop," French imitations of *Dallas*—aims to match.

But the supply-side argument won't suffice to explain global cultural dominance, because after all no one forced the Danes to watch *Dallas*. In fact, as the former chief of Danish TV entertainment recently told me, when he assumed that position and proceeded to cancel the show, thousands of protest letters poured into headquarters, and hundreds of Danes demonstrated against his decision. He bowed and reversed himself. In other words, the dominance of American popular culture is a soft dominance—in a certain sense, a collaboration with audiences.

The American advantage in this sort of collaboration is partly a function of the polyglot, multirooted nature of the society. By the time it leaves American shores, popular culture has already been "pre-tested" in a heterogeneous public—a huge internal market with hybrid tastes and a tradition of juxtaposition and recombining disparate elements, melting them down into a Hollywood mélange. But the roots are in American diversity. American popular culture is, after all, the rambunctious child of Europe and Africa. Our main contributions in popular music derive from the English and Irish, but increasingly from African slaves and their descendants. Our comic sense derives principally from English settlers, East European Jews and, again, African Americans (though Hispanic infusions are growing). Our stories come from everywhere—consider Ralph Ellison's *Invisible Man*, inspired jointly by Dostoyevsky, African-American folktales and jazz.

Most deeply, American popular culture never had to fight to establish its legitimacy against an established high culture. As the British researcher Jeremy Tunstall (1977) has argued, American popular culture has from its inception been driven by a single overriding purpose: to entertain. Tradition counts. For at least a century and a half, America's prime cultural tradition has been to cultivate popularity. Popular culture never had to fight to establish its legitimacy against an established high culture. Already a generation before the Civil War, it reigned supreme over its ecclesiastical rivals. Aristocratic claimants to cultural supremacy were weak. In the 1830s, when Alexis de Tocqueville visited the United States to see what a democratic culture looked like, long before Hollywood, before George Gershwin, Michael Jackson, or the Internet, American culture was already sensational, emotional, melodramatic and informal. Tocqueville (1835/1945, pp. 50, 52, 54, 62–63) wrote: "Democratic nations cultivate the arts that serve to render life easy in preference to those whose object is to adorn it." What results, he added, are "many imperfect commodities" that

substitute the representation of motion and sensation for that of sentiment and thought. . . . Style will frequently be fantastic, incorrect, overburdened, and loose, almost always vehement and bold. Authors will aim at rapidity of execution more than at perfection of detail. . . . There will be more wit than erudition, more imagination than profundity. . . . The object of authors will be to astonish rather than to please, and to stir the passions more than to charm the taste.

Because of these long-lived features of American culture, beyond the distribution advantages and economies of scale, it is easy to see why the American goods have outdone most of the competition—British goods, with their aristocratic lineage, developed in large part for high-culture elevation; Islamic goods, with their religious thrust; or previously, Soviet, Maoist and other Communist goods developed for didactic purposes. So it is not completely disingenuous that, as one Euro Disneyland official was quoted as saying in October 1991, denying that it would constitute American cultural imperialism: "It's not America, it's Disney. . . . We're not trying to sell anything but fun, entertainment."

Language is also certainly an advantage for the American cultural industry. By the time commercial work emerges from Hollywood, New York or Nashville, it is already "pre-marketed" in the principal world language— spoken as a second language more frequently than any other. Yet the English language by itself is not a sufficient explanation for global popularity. It should be borne in mind that Hollywood products depend little on the spoken word. The camera tracks and swoops, the edits crackle, while speech is auxiliary. Non-English-speakers everywhere can understand

Schwarzenegger without difficulty. No competitor from Europe and Asia can make this claim.

In a certain sense, "American" popular culture does not emanate from a specific physical place. "Hollywood" uses capital, hires personnel and depicts sites from many countries. To sustain its market advantages, the Americocentric multinationals, ever-thirsting for novelty, steadily import, process and export styles and practitioners from abroad. Consider, among many other examples, the Beatles, *All in the Family*, the Macarena, Ridley Scott, Paul Verhoeven. (The big movie of 1996, *Independence Day*, dotted with many a national feature, was directed by the German Roland Emmerich.) Hollywood, the global export platform, is where much talent wants to be and often enough the black hole into which it vanishes. It is not difficult to absorb foreign talent into American models of work. Even the locales come from everywhere, or nowhere—it is striking how many blockbusters take place in transnational space (*Star Wars*), in remote locations (*Jurassic Park*), in the future (the *Terminator* films), or at sea (*Titanic*).

The result of all these processes is a popular culture with all the appeals of fun. Our themes and styles converge in what psychologists Wolfenstein and Leites (1950) called fun culture. Ours is a popular culture of comfort and convenience. If it has any other mission than to amuse, that is to offer a populist morality—a celebration of common decencies against wicked authority. Masters of a universe of formula, American moguls offer accessible reassurances. This is an analgesic culture: take one formula and lie down. The all-too-bearable lightness of American product offers relief from complexities and psychic burdens. Not for American culture the televisual intricacies of Rainer Fassbinder's *Berlin Alexanderplatz*, or Dennis Potter's *Singing Detective*, or the inwardness of the great European filmmakers, or the social scale of Latin Americans and Japanese.

No one should underestimate the range of the formulas, ranging from sagas of unblemished good, as in Disney, to images of unbleached evil, as in "action movie" mayhem. Consider four major formulas: the "action movie," the road movie, the cartoon and the wacky comedy.

The so-called "action movie," an extension of video games with its relentless cuts, its gruesomeness and one-liners, reliably offers the experience of the kinetic sublime—a cutting loose from the terrestrial gravity of everyday life into a stratosphere of pure motion, suspense and release. After jeopardy comes relief—the spectator survives. The spectacle of redemptive savagery, from *Rambo* on up, belongs to a tradition that the literary historian Richard Slotkin (1973) called "regeneration through violence"—a staple of American popular writing since the frontier myths and captivity narratives of the seventeenth century. The *Rambo* grunt, the Schwarzenegger one-liner, the *Die Hard* machine-gun burst—for all that they degrade the human spirit, they evidently speak to some taste, some sensibility, some reorganization of the sensory apparatus, throughout the periphery as well as the center of modernity, for these films are box-office successes virtually everywhere they show. *Rambo* was a success in places where the American war in Vietnam was far from popular—Vietnam itself, for example. Four films produced by one man (*Die Hard 1* and *2, Lethal Weapon 1* and *2*) are said to have grossed $1 billion worldwide.

Like soft drinks, which marketers have learned to identify with youthful effervescence, road movies offer icons of freedom, risk and literal mobility. In 1989, an East German student told the historian Paul Buhle that the night the Berlin Wall came down she had dreamed of Route 66. The Route 66 she dreamed of, of course, is not the one that exists today, largely bypassed by a superhighway. It was the American TV series of the early 1960s that had entered into her imagination.

The Disney-based cartoon offers the pure joy of adorableness. The smooth faces of Disney characters are signs of perpetual innocence. Life has not yet produced scars. As Ariel Dorfman has written (1996), the appeal of childishness seems well-nigh universal. The various Disneylands specialize in a particularly highly produced, conflict-free, crewcut, streamlined, smoothed-down style of innocent fun. The Disney style of fun is arguably America's most potent export in popular culture.

Wackiness offers yet another appeal. Slapstick, rubbery faces and related shtick, from the Marx Brothers through Jerry Lewis to Jim Carrey, suggest the joys of transcending social convention. Insouciance and wildness, a sort of American savagery, kindle a happy release. Authority is ridiculed without cost.

Obvious American culture celebrates material pleasures, and these are of interest to modern people who don't want to accept their lot. Transgressions with happy endings—this is an American staple. Our pictures and music exalt icons of freedom, celebrating a society conducive to upward mobility, informality, egalitarian irreverence and vital life-force. This exaltation has its appeals in an age when people want to partake of the good life American style, even if as political citizens they are aware of the downside for ecology, community and equality. During the late days of communism, the most popular television shows in Hungary were two police dramas of the 1970s, *Kojak* and *The Streets of San Francisco*. I asked a Hungarian media researcher for an explanation. It was his considered opinion (in research that the regime would not permit to be published) that Hungarians appreciated the casual, informal, approachable American cops. They were, in a sense, utopian police—preferable to the local regime's.

Yet while people everywhere revel in America's spectacles, they would not necessarily admit to admiring the behavior that amuses them. Here again American culture is useful. It invites acceptable voyeurism—a projection of unacceptable feelings elsewhere. This is, after all, one thing people do with culture—they use it as a projective screen, to behold that which they long for and fear. A number of years ago, I asked a Chinese student visiting Wyoming what Chinese viewers think when they watch the Academy Award ceremonies. "We think Americans are wild and crazy people," she said. I think this sentiment is typical. Elisabeth Rosenthal of the *New York Times*, writing of the tremendous popularity of the NBA championship series televised in Beijing, quoted a Chinese junior wearing jeans and a T-shirt on the subject of Dennis Rodman. "I couldn't accept this from a Chinese player, but he's an American, so we expect it." If Americans look like "wild and crazy people," we are not only sources of value, we are the world's necessary other—the global outlaw and buffoon, wrapped up in one.

American goods succeed in this collaboration partly because, from their inception on the American screen, they specialize in equivocation. The sociologists Tamar Liebes and Elihu Katz (1990) have argued that Israeli families of Russian, North African, American and native provenance interpret the same *Dallas* episode in different ways and like it for different reasons. This can, of course, be true even within the confines of a single culture. The Brazilian anthropologist Ondina Fachel Leal asked professional-class and working-class groups of Brazilians to talk about the same Brazilian soap opera, and found that they told quite distinctly different stories of what they had seen. Indeed, I believe that the commercial strength of many American television programs has lain in their capacity to speak out of several sides of their mouths at once. In short, the American movies and TV shows are peculiarly plastic, inviting multiple pleasures for multiple audiences and demanding little of them.

In short, the demand side for American goods has to be taken into account to help explain the popularity of American popular culture. The relation between the culture of the United States and others is not one of simple imposition. As dominant as American styles are—especially the insistence on entertainment—it is important to note that arrows of influence point in both directions. The cultural import-export business may be intricate, especially in music, where the cost of entry is relatively low. In music, what exactly is an "American" style anyway, or a "foreign" style? Consider the career of reggae music. American rhythm-and-blues got to Jamaica in the 1950s, and was rhythmically refined through several stylistic generations, whose product was called reggae, which was exported to Britain, from which it was reimported to the United States, whose version was then reexported. The result is not an American equivalent of the *mission civilisatrice*—arguably it is even an inversion, in which American teenagers shimmy through the malls to the rhythms of the wretched of the earth.

So the reasons for the spread of American popular culture are various. But what are the consequences? The ubiquity of Coke, Mouse, Schwarzenegger & Co. give rise to the fear, expressed by M. Jack Lang, among others, that America's marketing practices will succeed in paving over the profusion of global cultures. Once overstated, the fear is easy—too easy—

to sweep aside. Obviously, American popular culture does not erase all the vernacular alternatives—all the local forms by which artists and writers give forth their styles and stories. The emergence of a global semi-culture coexists with local cultures and sensibilities more than it replaces them. As the Norwegian researcher Helge Rønning suggests, it's plausible to suppose that global, largely American popular culture has become, or is in the process of becoming, everyone's second culture. It doesn't necessarily supplant the indigenous culture, but it does activate a certain cultural bilingualism. People from Australia to Zimbabwe acquire a sort of second cultural membership, switching with ease from local news to the American Oscar ceremonies, and vice versa. American pop culture becomes everyone's second choice—degraded in some ways, liberating in others.

But clearly, over time, for all the hybridization and multiple interpretations among diverse audiences, American exports threaten to produce a narrowing down, an ecological simplification with bad effects on the world's cultures. Especially in the movies, where the cost of entry is high, Hollywood's premium style diminishes the cultural repertory of makers and audiences alike. America's so-called "high production values" are largely glib, slick, mechanistic and mindless. Inwardness is deplored, spirituality trivialized, reflectiveness overwhelmed. The mainstream Hollywood movie today specializes in drowning language beneath gaudy pictures and stripping down pictures to their most banal common denominators. Hollywood is driven by a hideous Bernoulli principle of the senses, as if in imitation of Marshall McLuhan's most simple-minded idea—the belief that when artistic work plays on one sensory capacity (sight) it is obliged to sacrifice a previously dominant sense (the capacity for language). That most relentless of free market principles, Gresham's Law, comes into play: bad culture drives out the taste for the good. Not only is American politics dragged to the level of Eastwoodian lines like "Make my day" and "Read my lips," and Schwarzeneggerian lines like "Hasta la vista, baby," but even literate young screenwriters in America and elsewhere aim to dumb themselves down to the writing level of Steven Spielberg and George Lucas. This is largely true even within America's so-called "independent film."

While the reach of American media has its limits, what remains true is that Gresham's Law of fun operates globally. Local industries can rarely compete with Hollywood. The Central and Eastern European industries have been freed of the heavy hand of state censorship only to be deprived of state subsidy, and as a result are in a state of collapse. Small countries that make a handful of films a year are drowning in American movies, and young filmmakers in Europe and the Third World find it hard to make careers against the pressure of American imports. Indeed, arguably the ascendancy of Hollywood exports, along with Americans' declining taste for foreign work (less than 1 percent of American prime time television on the networks and public channels combined comes from abroad, and most of this consists of English mysteries), helps explain the fact that the great European film-making generation of Bergman, Fellini, Antonioni, Godard, Truffaut, Rohmer and Resnais seems largely barren of successors. It is much harder to build a coherent career now confined to the markets of Europe. The American mode is—again, with rare exceptions—to process promising filmmakers from around the world into banality, Hollywood's premium style.

The fear of banalization reaches its peak with anxiety about the violence of popular media, many of them American. The sheer everyday shock and real-world violence that riddle our time cannot, all by themselves, account for the violence of popular culture today, for modernity is always with us but violent images are not—at least not in such vividness and profusion. Today's movies are far more violent than the streets. The industry is in the grip of inner forces that amount to a cynicism so deep as to defy parody. The movies are driven by economic and technological incentives to revel in the means to inflict pain, to maim, disfigure, shatter the human image. And they are also beset by a zeitgeist that slashes and burns, that wants to hurt—in every sense: to reach out to cut someone; to inflict pain, to maim, disfigure, shatter the human image. And they are also beset by a zeitgeist that slashes and burns, that wants to hurt—in every sense: to reach out to cut someone; to cause pain; to fight back; to suffer; and also to be anesthetized, to feel no pain. Wounded masculinity is screaming, and what it screams ends up in grotesque pictures and Dolby sound.

Over the years of chain saws, sharks, abdomen-ripping aliens and the like, movie violence has come to require, and train, numbness. Although no statistics can demonstrate this conclusively, I think it is clear that anesthesia becomes necessary equipment for steering through the thousands of limb tearings and arterial spurts which the movies have made more common than dependent clauses. To be hip is to be inured, and more—to require a steadily increasing boost in the size of the dose required. Writers learn to sprinkle "jeopardy" into the action to paper over vast holes in the narrative. Mangled flesh rescues a mangled plot.

The predilections of financiers, directors, writers, makeup artists and audiences come together to ratchet the frequency and magnitude of violence upward. Directors draw craft pride from their ability to surpass each previous round of abominations. Financiers see no reason to temper the cycle and every reason not to; studio bosses, bankers and distributors conclude that, but for a few romances and exercises in the supernatural, nothing is more riveting than the furies of jeopardy, frights, wounds, machine-gun bursts and fireballs, exploding helicopters, car chases and crashes—and no motivation more alluring than revenge, power-lust, or all-around viciousness. Encouraged by the industry, young screenwriters learn to "write" this way—using violence as an easy and formulaic expression of the unexpected, even as punctuation. The truncated sense of what constitutes a commercial movie is coarsened further by all the garish "advances" in make-up and stunts, the better to assault the imagination with picturesquely wounded or bared flesh which (at this writing) the television networks will still not permit on their airwaves—all the dirty words, shark gouges, ax gashes, dentists' drills and machine-gun spatters which end up dotted throughout even the most modest thriller.

If the rage and nihilism that well up on the screen record the rage and nihilism of their makers, they also collect, contain, focus, channel, reflect back the free-floating anxieties of their spectators. Uprooted people are often in a sour mood. They want to lash out. American movies give them the apparently harmless occasion. Recognizing the formula, the knowing spectator everywhere settles down in the dark holding his shield up. Cynicism becomes a normal response. The secret of the global box-office success of these films is that they evoke a forbidden pleasure in the victim's pain. There is a delirium of delight in the perpetrator's ability to get away with murder. The sheer volume and magnitude of mayhem is utterly severed from any conceivably rational objectives of criminals. The viewer who doesn't close his eyes is not drawn to identify with the victims, who are barely on the screen long enough to warrant second thoughts. The visitor from another planet, screening all the splatters and slashes, would have to conclude that in the United States of America today, life is cheap.

And yet, there is another America, the circulatory system for other American values, also playing a part in the export of American goods—and arguably it is here that American culture makes its contribution to the spread of democratic principle, egalitarian irreverence, personal freedom and vital life-force. Here modernity's passions find their often imperfect, often sentimental, often (in one way and another) shoddy replicas.

In the mid-1980s, with much fanfare, a galaxy of rock stars including Michael Jackson and Bruce Springsteen recorded a song called "We Are the World." Many critics called it sentimental. I was inclined to agree. And then, in South Africa, a multicolored group of protesters marched into an all-white neighborhood singing "We Are the World."

In 1991, according to John Sweeney of London's *Observer*, several Serbian students arrested by the Belgrade riot police after an opposition rally were

beaten . . . with truncheons, fists, and walkie-talkies . . . , then forced to stand with their hands up against a wall for the next four hours. When anyone dropped their hands, they were kicked in the knees. Come the shift change, the policemen forced them to stand on tiptoe. Students who disobeyed were beaten. Anyone who wanted to go to the lavatory had to face the gauntlet of police officers. The tiptoe torture was followed by a mockery of a trial. When one student asked for a defence lawyer, he was told: "You have been watching too many American films!"

It's all American pop culture: the coupling of irreverence and brutality; the exaltation of the common man alongside the degradation of women; the love of the road and its freedoms alongside the degradation of the word; a music of the spirit alongside "death metal." This amalgam fills the world cultural space for worse and for better. In unknowable proportions, it invites immigration, emulation and revulsion.

Not exclusively, of course. There are plenty of other currents in global circulation: Mexican and Brazilian telenovelas, Hong Kong action, the various domestications of American formula, along with the un-Americanized small-circulation productions: Kieslowski's Polish existentialism, Mike Leigh's and Ken Loach's English naturalism, the Kaurismaakis' Finnish comedy, even some American independents, and others of which I am ignorant, all scrambling for the niches left in the corners of the American-dominated mass market. Still, on balance, with mass distribution and oligopoly there comes a standardization of form and style—a shrinkage in the cultural gene pool. The box office in the modern world is driven by Hollywood's (and the theater-owners') only passion—the maximization of market share. It is a tribute to the variety of human culture that the great repertory of the world's social relations, sentiments and activities continues to be replenished anyway.

REFERENCES

Dorfman, A. (1996). *The empire's old clothes: What the Lone Ranger, Babar, and other innocent heroes do to our minds.* New York: Pantheon.

Friedman, L. M. (1999). *The horizontal society.* New Haven, CT: Yale University Press.

Gitlin, T. (1983/1994). *Inside prime time.* London: Routledge.

Ilott, T. (1996). *Budgets and markets: A study of the budgeting of European film.* London: Routledge.

Liebes, T., & Katz, E. (1990). *The export of meaning: Cross-cultural readings of Dallas.* New York: Oxford University Press.

Slotkin, R. (1973). *Regeneration through violence: The mythology of the American frontier, 1600–1860.* Middletown, CT: Wesleyan University Press.

Tocqueville, A. de. (1835/1945). *Democracy in America*, rev. F. Bowen, ed. P. Bradley. New York: Vintage.

Tunstall, J. (1977). *The media are American: Anglo-American media in the world.* New York: Columbia University Press.

Vasey, R. (1997). *The world according to Hollywood, 1918–1939.* Madison: University of Wisconsin Press.

Wolfenstein, M., & Leites, N. (1950). *Movies: A psychological study.* Glencoe, IL: The Free Press.

Chapter 3

Consuming the Citizen: The New International Division of Cultural Labor and the Trade in Screen Texts

Toby Miller

Think of the Mexican entertainment market, with its young population and fast-growing middle class, as a teenager out looking for a good time after being cooped up for too long. For economically emerging peoples all over the globe, Hollywood speaks a universal language.
—L. Gubernick and J. Millman, 1994, p. 95

Worried that free trade is making their indolent lifestyle less viable, the French are blaming sinister conspiracies and putting quotas on American movies.
—D. Brooks, 1994, p. 34

INTRODUCTION

Montreal hosted the fourteenth quadrennial World Congress of Sociology in the late summer of 1998. The conference marked the end of postmodernity—in a sense. A trope that had been ever-present four years earlier was gone, erased (or at least rendered palimpsestic) by globalization: "and the postmodern/the postmodern and" saw their status as suffix and prefix written all over. So polysemous was globalization that it included sameness, difference, unity and disunity—in short, globalization, like postmodernity before it, had come to stand for nothing less than *life itself*. What the *Financial Times* ("The G-Word," 1997) calls "the G-Word" is not the exclusive property of sociologists, of course. The concept has great currency with businesses, unions and governments—*Forbes Global* magazine was launched in 1998 via a full-page social realist-like advertisement, complete with red flags (which included currency motifs in their design), Castro- and

Mao-garbed workers and the slogan "Capitalists of the World Unite!" The avowed intent was to acknowledge and sell "the final victory of capitalism" as embodied in the new magazine. But in the cultural sphere, globalization is still associated by most of the United States with what the French call *le défi américain*.

What does this signify for ideas of sovereignty in relation to film and television? That is my core concern here. And it is an urgent one. The year 1998 saw the major U.S. film studios increase their foreign rentals by a fifth on 1997, to well in excess of $2.5 billion, with the overseas box office of $6.821 billion just below the domestic figure of $6.877 billion. That proportion of the world market is double what it was in 1990. Between 1988 and 1993, international box office receipts for Hollywood increased by 14 percent, domestic ones by just over half that figure. To give you an idea of how dramatic this is, in 1980, the American film industry relied on exports for a third of its annual revenue, the same as 50 years ago. So this decade has seen a truly foundational change. The most popular 39 films across the world in 1998 came from the United States, and the condition of other major filmmaking countries is declining. The year 1998 saw the percentage of the box office taken by indigenous films down to 10 percent in Germany, 12 percent in Britain, 26 percent in France, 12 percent in Spain, 2 percent in Canada, 4 percent in Australia and 5 percent in Brazil— all dramatic decreases, to record-low levels in some cases ("Foreign Bums," 1998; Groves, 1994, 1999; "H'wood Buries," 1999; Mayer, 1947; Woods, 1999a). Although its dominance is there for all to see, the United States is mounting major governmental and business assaults on the concept of national self-determination in the domain of culture in order to develop this share of the market. The United States has the rest of the world on notice that it will use the notorious provisions of the 1974 Trade Act. Hong Kong has been made a particular target for what the United States likes to call screen "piracy" (odd that this concept is never put dialectically into play with the development dictum of the free exchange of ideas and open communication, isn't it?). Meanwhile, my country's government eyes China's 140,000 film theaters (Barshefsky, 1998; USIA, 1997; World Trade Organization, 1998). This chapter looks for ways to explain and intervene in this environment.

The chapter picks up previously developed arguments about audiovisual textual trade (Miller, 1991, 1993a, 1993b, 1996, 1998a, 1998b). *The Well-Tempered Self* (Miller, 1993b) addressed theories of subjectivity underpinning cultural policy. It tracked the history to discourses of cultural protectionism in the domain of screen trade, especially film and television, from the 1920s to the final round of the General Agreement on Tariffs and Trade (GATT). I located these discourses inside a notion of ethical incompleteness, associated with post-Romantic notions of selfhood that encouraged characterological introjections from dramatic texts onto reading subjects via identification and a particular training in decoding texts. I suggested that this ethical incompleteness was then mapped onto citizenship, such that national screen drama was held to be a critical component of fealty to the state. *Technologies of Truth* (Miller, 1998a) addressed the New International Division of Cultural Labor (NICL) in the global screen economy. In an increasingly global division of cultural labor, how citizenship is theorized and actualized matters enormously for working people. Can their participatory rights be asserted in terms of: (1) where they live, were born, or work; (2) the temporary or permanent domicile of their employer; or (3) the cultural impact of a foreign multinational on daily life? Although those questions form the backdrop to this chapter, I hope readers will keep them in view. The chapter begins with a discussion of screen consumption and citizenship, goes on to explain the theory of the NICL (with specific application to Britain) and finally discusses events and trends in the World Trade Organization (WTO).

SCREEN CONSUMPTION, SCREEN CITIZENSHIP

> Entertainment is one of the purest marketplaces in the world. If people don't like a movie or record they won't see it or buy it. The fact that the American entertainment industry has been so successful on a worldwide basis speaks to the quality and attractiveness of what we're creating.
>
> —Robert Shaye, chair of New Line Pictures
> (quoted in Weinraub, 1993, p. L24)

> FBI + CIA = TWA + Pan Am.
> —graffito written by Eve Democracy in the film
> *One + One* by Jean-Luc Godard (1969)

There is a complicated relationship between the citizen and its logocentric double, the consumer. The citizen is a wizened figure from the ancient past. The consumer, by contrast, is naive, essentially a creature of the nineteenth century. Each shadows the other, the *national* subject versus (or is it *as?*) the *rational* subject. We all know the popularity of the consumer with neoclassical economists and policy wonks: the market is said to operate in response to this ratiocinative agent, who, endowed with perfect knowledge, negotiates between alternative suppliers and his or her own demands, such that an appropriate price is paid for desired commodities. The supposedly neutral mechanism of market competition sees materials exchanged at a cost that ensures the most efficient people are producing and their customers are content.

This model may occasionally describe life in some fruit and vegetable markets today. But as an historical account, it is of no value: the rhythms of supply and demand, operating unfettered by states, religions, unions, superstition and fashion, have never existed as such. Or rather, they exist today as enormously potent prescriptive signs in the rhetoric of international financial organizations, bureaucrats and journalists, at least since economists achieved their hegemony via the Keynesian end to the Great Depression, and then worked to maintain it, despite 1970s stagflation, via their mass conversion from demand- to supply-side doctrines. The consumer has become the sexless, ageless, unprincipled, magical agent of social value in a multitude of discourses and institutions since that time. Even consumer-*protection* legislation has fallen before the altar: consumers are *so* clever that they don't require paternalistic governments to outlaw dangerous goods.

The consumer looms large in global discussions of textual exchange. In the final GATT of 1993, the United States unsuccessfully took on the rest of the world in a debate over film and television. The United States argued from a *laissez-faire* position, claiming that the revelation of consumer preferences should be the deciding factor as to who has comparative advantage in screen production—whether Hollywood or Sydney is the logical place for audiovisual texts to be produced. The United States claims there is no room for the public sector in screen production, because it crowds out private investment, which is necessarily more in tune with popular taste. Both the active face of public subvention (national cinemas and broadcasters) and the negative face of public proscription (import barriers to encourage local production) are derided for obstructing market forces. The GATT's successor, the WTO, has focused initially on telecommunications and other industries, but is turning its oleaginous hand to culture, with just this agenda.

It seems sensible to evaluate *laissez-faire* as an account of U.S. screen production, to question: (1) whether Hollywood is truly a free market based purely on consumer demand; and (2) whether the industry realizes the stated aims of public policy based on the tenets of neo-classical economics. I have four tests of worth here, based on the promises and premises of neo-classical economics. They are important background to my later discussion of the New International Division of Cultural Labor.

Freedom of Entry to New Starters

It is certainly true that there have been new owners of major Hollywood studios, such as Australia's Channel Seven and News Corporation, Canada's Seagrams and Japan's Sony, plus a new venture in Dreamworks, but control of studio output remains with New York management and Los Angeles creativity.

No State Subsidies

The U.S. government endorses trust-like behavior overseas, while prohibiting it domestically. Its local film industry has been aided through decades of tax-credit schemes, State and Commerce Department representation, the Informational Media Guaranty Program's currency assistance and oligopolistic domestic buying and overseas selling practices that (without much good evidence for doing so) keep the primary market essentially closed to imports on grounds of popular taste (Guback, 1984 and 1987; Schatz, 1988; Thompson, 1985; Vasey, 1997). After World War II, Hollywood's Motion Picture Export Agency referred to itself as "the little State Department," so isomorphic were its methods and contents with Federal policy and ideology. The U.S. Department of Commerce continues to produce materials on media globalization for Congress that run lines about both economic development and ideological influence, problematizing claims that Hollywood is pure free enterprise and that its government is uninterested in blending trade with cultural change (Ferguson, 1992; Jarvie, 1998). Meanwhile, the Justice Department is authorized to classify all imported films, which it can prohibit as "political propaganda" (as it has done with Canadian documentaries on acid rain and nuclear war, for instance) (Parker, 1991; Sorlin, 1991). The United States has 205 state, regional and city film commissions, hidden subsidies to the film industry (via reduced local taxes, free provision of police services and the blocking of public wayfares), State and Commerce Department briefings and plenipotentiary representation (negotiations on so-called video piracy have resulted in People's Republic of China offenders being threatened with beheading, even as the United States claims to be watching Chinese human rights as part of most-favored-nation treatment) and copyright limitations that are all about preventing the free flow of information (which, as noted above, the United States is forever instructing less-developed countries to permit in order that they might prosper).

A Relationship between the Cost of Production and Consumption

Costs are not reflected in the price of tickets or cable fees. They are amortized through a huge array of venues, so reusable is each copy of each text, unlike a car or painting. The huge domestic market, plus years of selling into the English-language sector, is a powerful legacy.

Textual Diversity

In the 1960s, imports accounted for 10 percent of the U.S. film market. In 1986, that figure was 7 percent, and today it is 0.75 percent. Foreign films are essentially excluded from the United States as never before ("Shall We," 1997). This is due to the corporatization of cinema exhibition plus increases in promotional costs, to the point where subtitling and dubbing become insupportable for independent distributors. In television, the proliferation of channels in the United States over the past 10 years has required companies to change their drama offerings significantly. In 1990, action-adventure, the most expensive TV genre, occupied 20 percent of prime time on the networks; 4 years later, the figure was around 1 percent (Schwab, 1994). Now we are seeing the sudden decline of the soap opera. Reality television, fixed upon by cultural critics who either mourn it as representative of a decline in journalistic standards, or celebrate it as the sign of a newly feminized public sphere, should frankly be understood as a cost-cutting measure and an instance of niche marketing.

So much for the accuracy and utility of consumer-based rhetoric from Hollywood and its Washington lackeys. What of the other side to our couplet, the citizen? Against the 1993 U.S. demand for a free market stood a coalition that saw thousands of European artists, intellectuals and producers signing a petition in major newspapers calling for culture to be exempt from the GATT's no-holds-barred commodification (Van Elteren, 1996a). They did so in the name of a different figure from the consumer—the citizen. Western Europe's Community law enshrines freedom of expression through media access—the EU's alibi for putting quotas on U.S. screen texts, along with the claim that the screen is not a good but a service. The 1993 coalition opposed the idea that the GATT ensure open access to screen markets, on the grounds that culture must be deemed inalienable. To U.S. critics, this was a smokescreen, with cultural rights secreting the protection of inefficient culture industries and outmoded *dirigiste* statism (Kessler, 1995; Van Elteren, 1996b; Venturelli 1998).

The citizen has been with us for millennia, but has undergone a major revival in the last decade. Social theorists and policymakers have shifted their attention from class to citizenship as a magical agent of historical change. More easily identified than class, and more easily mobilized as a justification for state action, citizenship has become a site of hope for a left that has lost its actually existing alternative to international capital. I want to consider the utility of this move in the context of film and television.

There are two basic accounts of screen citizenship. In their different ways, each is an effects model, in that they both assume the screen *does* things *to* people, with the citizen understood as an audience member. The first model derives from the social sciences and is applied without consideration of place. I'll call this the *domestic* effects model, or DEM. It is universalist and psychological. The DEM offers analysis and critique of such crucial citizenship questions as education and civic order. It views the screen as a machine that can either pervert or direct the citizen, entering young minds osmotically, alternatively enabling or imperiling learning. And it also drives the citizen to violence through aggressive and misogynistic images and narratives. The DEM assumes three kinds of screen impact on citizenship. We can identify them as: (1) learning and self-control, (2) training and the superego, or (3) preparation and responsibility. Each has a grisly antonym, respectively (1) ignorance and self-indulgence, (2) guesswork and the id, or (3) lassitude and selfishness. The DEM is found in a variety of sites, including laboratories, clinics, prisons, schools, newspapers, psychology journals, TV network and film studio research and publicity departments, everyday talk, program classification regulations, conference papers, parliamentary debates and state-of-our-youth or state-of-our-civil-society moral panics (see Buckingham, 1997; Hartley, 1996).

The second way of thinking about screen citizenship is a *global* effects model, or GEM. The GEM is specific and political rather than universalist and psychological. Whereas the DEM focuses on the cognition and emotion of individual human subjects via replicable experimentation, the GEM looks to the knowledge of custom and patriotic feeling exhibited by collective human subjects, the grout of national culture. In place of psychology, it is concerned with politics. The screen does not make you a well- or ill-educated person, a wild or self-controlled one. Rather, it makes you a knowledgeable and loyal national subject, or a duped viewer who lacks an appreciation of local custom and history. Cultural belonging, not psychic wholeness, is the touchstone of the global effects model. Instead of measuring responses electronically or behaviorally, as its domestic counterpart does, the GEM looks to the national origin of screen texts and the themes and styles they embody, with particular attention to the genres of drama, news, sports and current affairs. GEM adherents hold that local citizens should control local broadcast networks because they alone can be relied upon to be loyal reporters in the event of war, while reflectionist claims for the role of fiction are thought to mean that only locally sensitized producers make narratives that are true to tradition and custom. This model is found in the discourse of cultural imperialism, everyday talk, broadcast and telecommunications policy, international organizations, newspapers, cultural diplomacy, postindustrial service sector planning and national-cinema discourse.

Let me run through the problems with these models. The DEM suffers from all the disadvantages of ideal-typical psychological reasoning. Each massively costly laboratory test of media effects, based on, as the refrain goes, "a large university in the mid-West," is countered by a similar experiment, with conflicting results. As politicians, grant givers and jeremiad-wielding pundits call for more and more research to prove that the screen makes you stupid, violent and apathetic—or the opposite—academics line up at the trough to indulge their hatred of popular culture and ordinary life and their rent-seeking urge for public money. As for the GEM, its concentration on national culture: (1) denies the potentially liberatory and pleasurable nature of different takes on the popular; (2) forgets the internal differentiation of viewing publics, (3) valorizes frequently oppressive and/ or unrepresentative local bourgeoisies in the name of national culture's maintenance and development, and (4) ignores the demographic realities of its "own" terrain.

Consider Europe. The abiding logic of the EU's audiovisual policy is really commercial; it clearly favors existing large concerns that can be built upon further. And the NICL has served to bring into doubt the opposition of U.S. entertainment versus European education, with art cinema effectively a "Euro-American" genre in terms of finance and management, and, as was noted earlier, much of Hollywood itself owned by foreigners (Lev, 1993). In this sense, the seeming discontinuity with earlier concerns, when the EU had a primarily economic personality, is misleading: a notion of cultural sovereignty underpins concerns *vis-à-vis* the United States, but so too does support for monopoly capital and the larger states inside its own walls (Burgelman & Pauwels, 1992). Meanwhile, the old notions of state cultural sovereignty that were so crucial to Europe's political traditions are being attenuated by the twin forces of "bruxellois centralization" from outside and separatist ethnicities from within (Berman, 1992).

Where should the left go with screen citizenship? In an era of globalized film and television, the idea that audiovisual spaces should be accountable to local viewers, as well as far-distant shareholders, is a powerful one. But how much can be expected from citizenship ideals when: (1) for the first time, trade between corporations exceeds that between states, (2) deregulation sees huge monopoly capitalists converging and collaborating, (3) screen texts are designed to transcend linguistic and other cultural boundaries, and (4) many of us live in societies that deny or limit our citizenship claims? In the United States, it is basically discriminatory to privilege citizenship, given recent moves toward the destruction of educational opportunity and economic security for resident workers. It is no accident that the majority of pro-citizen writers and advocates live in their countries of origin or in places that have a tradition of remarkably homogeneous migration. You won't find many folks on the left in countries with disenfranchised guest labor forces endorsing the idea. In fact, much of the push for a citizen address in screen culture is profoundly anti-democratic, in that it laments the passing of "happier" times, when all was stable and resolved and a patrimony was, well, a patrimony. And like its supposed other, the consumer, the citizen is an ideal type. Of course, countries like France and Australia are committed to retaining local audiovisual drama for some of these reasons, but they also have immensely powerful local media that benefit from protection of the culture industries. I am not convinced by either model of the screen citizen. So let's think about a labor-theory-of-value approach to media citizenship, for bringing together the economy and textuality of the screen necessitates looking at the terrain of trade and work.

In other words, I am arguing for an outlook on culture based on fundamental shifts in the division of labor, not psychological health or national consciousness.

THE NEW INTERNATIONAL DIVISION OF CULTURAL LABOR

> During the months leading up to the signing of the GATT protocols in 1993, production of the TV series *White Fang* in New Zealand was halted, and workers left unpaid, because French finance was in disarray awaiting the outcome.
>
> —GATT, 1993, p. 1

> We have created a product that by, say, putting the name of Warner Brothers on it is a stamp of credibility. But that could be an Arnon Milchan film, directed by Paul Verhoeven, starring Gerard Depardieu and Anthony Hopkins, and shot in France and Italy, and made with foreign money.
>
> —John Ptak, Creative Artists Agency of Hollywood
> (quoted in Weinraub, 1993, p. L24)

The expression "division of labor" refers to sectoral differences in an economy, the occupations and skills of a labor force and the organization of tasks within a firm. Life-cycle models of international products suggest they are first made and consumed in the center, in a major industrial economy, then exported to the periphery and finally produced "out there," once technology has become standardized and savings can be made on the labor front. Goods and services owned and vended by the periphery rarely make their way into the center as imports (Cohen, 1991; Evans, 1979; Keynes, 1957; Lang & Hines, 1993; Strange, 1995).

The idea of a New International Division of Labor (NIDL) derives from re-theorizations of economic dependency theory that followed the inflationary chaos of the 1970s. Developing markets for labor and sales, and the shift from the spatial *sen*sitivities of electrics to the spatial *in*sensitivities of electronics, pushed businesses beyond treating Third World countries as suppliers of raw materials, to look on them as shadow-setters of the price of work, competing amongst themselves and with the First and Second Worlds for employment. This broke up the prior division of the globe into a small number of industrialized nations and a majority of underdeveloped ones, as production was split across continents. Folker Fröbel and his collaborators (1980) christened this the NIDL.

I am suggesting that just as manufacturing fled the First World, cultural production has also relocated, though largely within the industrialized market economies (IMECS), as factors of production, including state assistance, lure filmmakers. This is happening at the level of popular textual production, marketing, information and high-culture, limited-edition work. Toronto, for instance, has doubled as New York City in over 100 films, thanks to the appeal of government subsidies. Labor market slackness, increased profits and developments in global transportation and communications technology have diminished the need for colocation of these factors, which depresses labor costs and deskills workers. Animation, for example, is frequently undertaken in Southeast Asia and Europe by employees at lower rates of pay than U.S. workers. The trend toward off-shore work is gathering pace: between 1990 and 1998, 31 national film commissions were set up across the globe. Many of them are solely concerned with attracting foreign capital ("Culture Wars," 1998; Lent, 1998; McCann, 1998).

Obviously, the U.S. film industry has always imported cultural producers, such as the German Expressionists. But this was one-way traffic during the classical Hollywood era. Post-War anti-trust decisions and the advent of television compelled changes to the vertically integrated studio system. The decade from 1946 saw production go overseas. Location shooting became a means of differentiating stories, and studios purchased facilities around the world to utilize cheap labor. Between 1950 and 1973, just 60 percent of Hollywood films in production began their lives in the United States. American financial institutions grew practiced at buying foreign theaters and distribution companies, thus sharing risk and profit with local businesses. This was in keeping with the close historic relationship between the film industry and finance capital: as American banks looked overseas for sources of profit through the 1960s, so they endorsed and assisted efforts by Hollywood to spread risk and investment as widely as possible. By the end of the 1980s, overseas firms were crucial suppliers of funds invested in American film or loans against distribution rights in their countries of origin. Joint production arrangements are now well established between U.S. firms and French, British, Swedish and Italian companies, with connections to theme parks, cabling and home video. Co-production sees host governments working together or with the United States, as when the film *JFK* was funded by a Hollywood studio, a French cable network, a German production house and a Dutch financier, while *The Full Monty* is of course owned by Fox. For some critics, this represents a restructuring from the vertically integrated production line and vertically integrated studios of the 1930s and 1940s to a flexible system where finance, management and production are physically and industrially splintered. To others, the fact that U.S. management prevails is the relevant fact (Briller, 1990; Buck, 1992; Christopherson & Storper, 1986; Kessler, 1995; Marvasti, 1994; Miège, 1989; "The PolyGram Test," 1998; Wasko, 1982, 1994, 1998; Wasser, 1995).

Any decision by a multinational firm to invest in a particular national formation carries the seeds of insecurity, because companies move on when tax incentives or other factors of production beckon (Allan, 1988; Browett & Leaver, 1989; Fröbel, Heinrichs & Kreye, 1980; Welch & Luostarinen, 1988). The hold on foreign capital is always tenuous and depends heavily on foreign exchange rates. This too relates to state activity—the UK government's decision to float the pound and free the Bank of England from democratic consultation contributed to a situation in 1998 where a strengthening currency raised costs for overseas investors and encouraged locals to spend elsewhere, with severe implications for offshore film funds. So the late 1990s offshore-production boom in Australia and Canada, driven in part by scenery, infrastructure, language and lower pay levels than the United States combined with equivalent skill levels, still depended on weak currencies (Pendakur, 1998; Woods, 1999b).

There are two difficulties with the NIDL and the NICL. First, they aggregate investment and trade data, assuming a correlation between the movement of capital and the division of labor that is not necessarily accurate, especially given the role of the state. And second, privileging production and distribution in the cultural arena may negate the importance of meaning in the circulation of texts. So the model is tentative (Beaverstock, 1996; Cohen, 1991; Miège, 1989). And like the scenery and convenience aspects of tourism, the international screen has some peculiarities that do not apply to manufacturing. It is risky on all but a huge scale, with most investments complete failures, and while new technology reduces the need for colocating shooting, editing and financing, it also problematizes "authenticity."

Back in the United States, the American Film Institute is anxious about any loss of cultural heritage to internationalism, critics question what is happening when U.S. drama is scripted with special attention to foreign audiences and political economists argue that a newly transnational Hollywood no longer addresses its nominal audience. George Quester laments that British costume history crowds out the space for indigenous "quality" television, claiming there is more Australian high-end drama on U.S. TV than locally produced material (Quester, 1990). But the trend remains for North America to attract talent developed by national cinemas to compete with it. Peter Weir's post-production for *The Truman Show* or *Witness* might take place in Australia, satisfying off-screen indices of localism in order to obtain state financing, but does that make for a real alternative to the United States? What does it mean that Michael Apted, James Bond and *7 Up* series director, can speak with optimism of a "European-izing of Hollywood" when Gaumont points out that "a co-production with the Americans . . . usually turns out to be just another U.S. film shot on location" (Apted quoted in Dawtrey, 1994, p. 75; Gaumont quoted in Kessler, 1995, n. 143; Top, 1994)? Attempts by the French film industry in the 1980s to attract U.S. filmmakers may have the ultimate effect of U.S. studio takeovers, while diplomatic efforts to maintain local screen subsidization continue even as Hollywood producers and networks purchase satellite and broadcast space across Europe (Hayward, 1993). AOL-Time Warner, Disney-ABC, Viacom, NBC and others are jostling their way into the center of the vast and growing Western European industry as sites of production as much as dumping grounds for old material. The new stations throughout the Continent invest in local programming with cost savings from scheduling American filler (Stevenson, 1994).

Localization also occurs at the level of the consumer, as international audience targetting becomes increasingly specific: Sean Connery is cast as a Hollywood lead because European audiences love him, while each U.S. film is allotted a hundred generic descriptions for use in specific markets (*Dances with Wolves* was sold in France as a documentary-style dramatization of Native American life, and *Malcolm X* was promoted there with posters of the Stars and Stripes aflame) (Danan, 1995; Wasser, 1995).

Britain has been a major player in the NICL recently, as both a foreign investor and a recipient of offshore production funds. The long-term strategy of successive governments in Britain since 1979 has been to break up unions within the media in order to become a Euro-Hollywood by default: the skills generated in a regulated domain of the screen would be retained without the "inefficiency" of the so-called "X-factor"—labor. In short, flexibility was to supplant wage stability and texts were to be oriented towards export. As a consequence, the United Kingdom now has a negative balance of screen trade for the first time in history. Associated deregulation produced a proliferation of networks and the inevitable search for cheap overseas content (Cornford & Robins, 1998). From the 1980s, it became impossible to recoup the cost of most British feature films domestically. The necessity of finding jobs for skilled workers and their employers made the industry a true welcome mat. In 1991 a British Film Commission (BFC) was formed to market UK production expertise and locations by providing overseas producers with a free service articulating talent, sites and subsidies and generating a national network of urban and regional film commissions. In 1997, seven Hollywood movies accounted for 54 percent of expenditure on feature film production in the United Kingdom, but Britain faces increasing competition to capture Hollywood production finance. The government opened the British Film Office in Los Angeles in an attempt to normalize traffic with Hollywood by offering liaison services to the industry and promoting British locations and crews, and the BFC announced the Blair Government's outlook on cinema: "set firmly at the top of the agenda is the desire to attract more overseas film-makers" (British Film Commission, n.d.; Guttridge, 1996; Hiscock, 1998).

One key agency, the London Film Commission, was formed in 1995 with a grant from the Department of National Heritage to attract offshore film production (you work out the connection to the portfolio). The Commission promotes the capital to overseas filmmakers, arranges police permits and negotiates with local residents and businesses. Its defining moment was *Mission: Impossible*, when the Commissioner proudly said of that film's Hollywood producers: "They came up with all these demands and I just went on insisting that, as long as they gave us notice, we could schedule it" (Jury, 1996).

In order to keep British studios going, regulations were promulgated under John Major that meant films entirely made in Britain counted as British, regardless of theme, setting, or stars. So *Judge Dredd* with Sylvester Stallone was "British," but *The English Patient* did too much of its postproduction work abroad to qualify. Until 1998, 92 percent of a film had to be created in the United Kingdom. At the end of that year, the government reduced this requirement to 75 percent to encourage American companies to make their films in Britain (Woolf, 1998).

Britain was a late starter as a co-production partner, although an intergovernmental treaty of 1965 spawned some Anglo-French productions. This agreement specified films of high quality, but assistance was routinely granted to money-spinners when the local industries were in trouble (financing was made available to the James Bond film *Moonraker*, for example). The stimulus of European co-operation in the early 1990s launched new projects, though few were commercially successful (Jäckel, 1996).

What do film industry mavens make of this? Michael Kuhn (1998), managing director of Polygram Filmed Entertainment (PFE), the company which dominated the British film industry in the 1990s, considers that "Europe (when you talk about mainstream movies) is almost a vassal state to that Hollywood business." Only "supra-national government institutions" can turn this around, because of the lack of a firm financial base to compete with Hollywood's mix of production and distribution and the United States' cartel-like discrimination against European producers. Ironically, PFE has now been taken over by Seagram, and its interests will merge in some form with another of Seagram's subsidiaries, the Hollywood major Universal.

In contrast to Kuhn, Rupert Murdoch (1998) welcomes "new joint ventures between the Hollywood majors and both public and private broadcasting" in Europe, citing the numbers of European workers invisibly employed in the making of *Titanic*: "this cross-border cultural co-operation is not the result of regulation, but market forces. It's the freedom to move capital, technology and talent around the world that adds value, invigorates ailing markets, creates new ones." This view finds support in the upper echelons of the European Union, which has offered U.S. film marketers unhindered access to the European marketplace.

There are other models of the NICL. Consider the Grundy Organization. It produced Australian TV drama and game shows from the 1950s that were bought on license from the United States. The company expanded to sell such texts across the world, operating with a strategy called "parochial internationalism" that meant leaving Australia rather than exporting in isolation from relevant industrial, taste and regulatory frameworks. Following patterns established in the advertising industry, it bought production houses around the world, making programs in local languages, based on formats imported from Australia that themselves drew on U.S. models. From a base in Bermuda, Grundy Organization produced about 50 hours of television a week in 70 countries across Europe, Oceania, Asia and North America until its sale in the mid-1990s to Pearson. This is the NICL offshore, utilizing experience in the Australian commercial reproduction industry to manufacture American palimpsests in countries relatively new to profit-centered television. The benefits to Australia, where a regulatory framework birthed this expertise by requiring the networks to support such productions as part of cultural protection, are unclear (Cunningham & Jacka, 1996; Moran, 1998; Stevenson, 1994). In each case, the GEM is underwriting local cultural bourgeoisies.

In an era when U.S. network television is desperately cutting costs, there are opportunities for outsiders, but only major players. The trend seems to be toward smaller investments in a larger number of programs for television, in the simultaneously splintered and concentrated media domain of North America. Put another way, a huge increase in the number of channels and systems of supply and payment is also producing unprecedented concentration of TV ownership. Some examples of the NICL represent a form of vertical investment, with production processes fragmented across the world. But what may be more significant for the future is horizontal licensing and joint ventures that mirror domestic retailing systems. For the culturalist remit of the GEM, the ability to make locally accented infotainment is one way of nations using the NICL (Roddick, 1994; Schwab, 1994).

To summarize, the screen is back where primary and secondary extractive and value-adding industries were in the 1960s, needing to make decisions not just about export, but about the site of production. Advances in communications technology permit electronic off-line editing across the world, but also enable special effects problematizing the very need for location shooting. The trend is clearly toward horizontal connections to other media, global economy and administration, and a break up of public-private distinctions in ownership, control and programming philosophy (Marvasti, 1994; Wedell, 1994). TV texts are fast developing as truly global trading forms. This is where the GEM is so influential: U.S. late-night talk-show host Jay Leno's promotional spot for the NBC's Pan-European Super Channel promised "to ruin your culture just like we ruined our own." The GATT and the WTO are the devices of that "ruination."

THE GATT AND THE WTO

Who can be blind today to the threat of a world gradually invaded by an identical culture, Anglo-Saxon culture, under the cover of economic liberalism?
—François Mitterrand (quoted in Brooks, 1994, p. 35)

If the European Commission governments truly care about their citizens' cultural preferences, they would permit them the freedom to see and hear works of their choosing; if they are really concerned about a nation's cultural heritage, they would encourage the distribution of programming reflecting that heritage.
—Jack Golodner, president of the Department for Professional Employees (Golodner, 1994, p. H6)

From its emergence in the late 1940s as part of a range of new international financial and trading protocols, the GATT embodied in contractual form central aspects of the First World's rules of economic prosperity: nondiscrimination, codified regulations policed outside the terrain of individual sovereign states and multilateralism. It was born under the sign of North American growth evangelism, whereby standardized methods, vast scales of production and an endless expansion of markets would engineer economic recovery and development for the West European detritus of World War II, although initial plans for an independent organization were shelved because the U.S. Congress resisted ceding individual sovereignty. This is part of a long wave of restructuring capitalism.

The GATT stood for the paradoxically bureaucratic voice of neo-classical economics, dedicated beyond the call of parochial national interests and state intervention to the higher service of promulgating free trade. Officials worked like puritans ordered by some intellectual manifest destiny to disrupt trading blocs and restrict distortions to the putative natural rhythms of supply and demand as determined by consumer sovereignty and comparative advantage. Such pristine forms of theorization routinely enunciate quite specific and partial material interests; in this instance, the agenda of the United States, which was suited by such arrangements until Japan and Western Europe became powerful economic agents that were able to make some rules of their own. In any case, by the 1980s, there were serious doubts inside the United States about the utility of free-trade absolutism. The seemingly transcendental nature of marginalist economics, which set up good/bad antinomies in the form of liberalism versus mercantilism, became a conditional argument, to be used as and when it suited the purposes of its self-interested enunciators (the United States was extremist in one direction over cinema and television, in another on agriculture). The highly moral mode of the GATT itself became its legalistic ruination, as new forms of protectionism appeared via nontariff implements and industry policy to match the varied positions of member-states.

From the early days in the 1940s, the United States sought coverage of cinema by the GATT, without success (Jarvie, 1998). The services sector of the developed world expanded massively over the last decade, to the point where it now comprises 70 percent of gross domestic product in the industralized nations and 50 percent in much of the Third World, accounting for U.S.$1 trillion a year in trade, perhaps a fifth of the global total ("Disquieting," 1994; Drake & Nicolaïdis, 1992). The GATT was slow to notice this growth, in part because the tenets of neo-classical dogma, and the technological limitations of the "human" side to the sector (restaurants, for example), were not especially amenable to conceptualizing and enumerating its frequently object-free exchange. But as the Western powers saw capital fly from their manufacturing zones, and sought to become net exporters of textuality, they discovered ways of opening up the area to bureaucratic invigilation. Trade in Services (TIS) was found to comprise, *inter alia*, film, television and broadcast advertising production and distribution (Grey, 1990; Sjolander, 1992–1993). The Punta del Este Declaration of September 1986 put TIS at the center of GATT debates, because of pressure from the United States (always the main player in negotiations) in the service of lobbyists for American Express, Citibank and IBM. A decade on, TIS accounted for 60 percent of Gross Domestic Product in the IMECS and more than a quarter of world trade. And the entertainment sector was a significant subcategory. After the United States failed to have cultural industries incorporated in the 1988 Free Trade Agreement with Canada, its foreign service and trade officials were concerned to thwart EU plans for import quotas on audiovisual texts. The Community's "Television Without [intra-European] Frontiers" directive drew particular ire for its 50 percent limit on imported texts. But attempts to have the Uruguay Round of the GATT derail such policies were almost universally opposed, with significant participation from India, Canada, Japan, Australia, all of Europe and the Third World, in the name of cultural sovereignty. This position equated cultural industries with environmental protection or the armed forces as beyond neo-classicism. Of course, American negotiators argued that the GATT must "agree to disagree on motives—cultural sovereignty or business opportunity—and then start negotiating" (quoted in Miller, 1993a, p. 97).

As Daniel Toscan du Plantier, then president of the French government's film marketing body, put it in 1994: "cinema used to be side salad in world commerce. Now, it's the beef." And the illegal copying of electronic texts was estimated at $70 billion in 1994, a further copyright incentive in the area of intellectual property (du Plantier, quoted in Cohen, 1994; Hills, 1994; Hoekman & Kostecki, 1995; Mayrhofer, 1994). The final agreement struck to end the seven-year Uruguay Round was negotiated by a small number of industrialized nations and then delivered to a hundred other countries with a weekend to ponder the final draft (Childers, 1994).

The screen was excluded—an agreement to disagree. So the Americans lost the last battle of the GATT. But they are winning the war. As noted earlier, half of Hollywood's revenue comes from overseas, with Western Europe providing 55 percent. The United States supplies three-quarters of the market there, up from half a decade ago. The consolidation of Europe into one market has been a huge boon to Hollywood, along with deregulation of television ("After GATT," 1994; "Culture Wars," 1998; Van Elteren, 1996b). The European screen trade deficit with Hollywood grew from $4.8 billion to $5.65 billion between 1995 and 1996 ("Culture Wars," 1998; "Déjà vu," 1994; Hill, 1994). Until recent downturns, the Hong Kong industry was the world's second biggest exporter of film, but some distance behind (Miller, 1993b; World Trade Organization, 1998).

U.S. firms are negotiating on a country-by-country basis over most communications issues, regardless of the European bloc's stance at the GATT ("Superhighway," 1994). Sony Entertainment published a report in mid-1994 that argued against quotas as inimical to the very producers they are designed to assist. The EU made both hostile and friendly sounds, with many commercial TV networks failing to observe national production quotas (Stern, 1994a, 1994b; Zecchinelli, 1994). Meanwhile, France and the United States held informal bilateral talks, and Steven Spielberg was reinvented by Paris. After *Jurassic Park*, he was derided in Europe for rampant commercialism, drawing particular opprobrium from French Culture Minister Jacques Toubon. And Spielberg was among the Hollywood directors who argued against the European position in the GATT. But less than a year later, *Schindler's List* was hailed as a triumph of serious filmmaking, and he was invited to meet Mitterand to discuss both the Holocaust and the film industry. Spielberg left the Élysée Palace full of support for local filmmaking and the maintenance of cultural heritage ("After GATT," 1994; Williams, 1994). But there was a more serious backdrop, in the form of the new WTO that was developing even as they met.

In January 1995, the WTO replaced the GATT agreements and bought the latter's *detritus* of GATTocrats. The last gasp of the GATT came with the 20,000-page protocols, weighing 850 kilograms, that were agreed upon in Geneva in December 1993, signed in Marrakesh in April 1994 and ratified domestically by 125 members and fellow travelers over the next eight months. But its effects will be felt—through the work of the WTO—beyond its life. The WTO has a legal personality, a secretariat and biennial ministerial conferences. This new machinery makes it easier for multinational corporations to dominate trade via the diplomatic services of their home governments' representatives, to the exclusion of environmental and other matters of public interest, which no longer have the *entrée* that GATT gave via recognition of non-government organizations. Multinationals will find it easier to be regarded as local firms in their host countries, and Third World agricultural production has been further opened up to foreign ownership (Dobson, 1993; Lang & Hines, 1993). But despite its high theory commitment to pure/perfect competition, political pressures mean the WTO does devote care to archaeological, artistic and historic exemptions to free-trade totalizations, as even the GATT routinely did (Chartrand, 1992).

The WTO's operating protocols stress transparency, most-favored-nation precepts and national treatment (identical policies on imported and local commodities), tariffs versus other protective measures and formal methods of settling disputes. The year 1997 was the WTO's first major movement into culture industries, a case concerning the Canadian version of *Sports Illustrated*. The WTO ruled that Canada could not impose tariffs on the magazine for enticing local advertisers. Such cultural issues were excluded from the first NAFTA, so WTO was the place to go. This case is regarded as beginning the Organization's cultural push (Magder, 1998; Valentine, 1997). And the new U.S. move is to cluster cultural issues under the catch-all rubric of intellectual property (Venturelli, 1998).

CONCLUSION

What should progressive politics do now? We need to utilize contradictions on each side of the discursive divide between the consumer and the citizen, criticizing both neo-classical accounts of consumers and DEM/GEM takes on citizenship. We must beware falling for the rhetoric of citizenship adopted in discriminatory and exclusionary ways (think always of the *non*-consumer, the *non*-citizen and their fate), and require each part of the consumer-citizen divide to illustrate: (1) the history to their account of either consumption or citizenship; (2) the relationship between multinational capital, democracy and diversity; and (3) the role of the state in consumption and of corporations in citizenship. Finally, we must look to minority, indigenous and migrant interests any time we are told consumers are unmarked, or that citizens are at the center of culture within borders.

If cultural imperialism has lost intellectual *cachet* (even as it has gained diplomatic and political adherents), perhaps the left should go back to where we began, to the person as laborer rather than viewer. The model of citizenship accompanying that, however, will have to deal with de-domiciled workers, with all the dispossession entailed in that status. Citizenship assumes governmental policing of rights and responsibilities. Does this apply when a NICL is in operation, and deregulation or the protection of retrograde media bourgeoisies seem the only alternatives? And to whom do you appeal as a person unhappy with the silencing of your local dramatic tradition through TV imports, but demoralized by the representation of ethnic and sexual minorities or women within so-called national screen drama or network news? We have seen first the slow and now the quick dissolution of cultural protectionism in television. That hardly seems an effective place to struggle. We know that globalization of the industry involves a reconfiguration of the labor force, so perhaps that might give a solid material backing to our discussions. DEM/GEM theorists have held the high ground for a long time. I suggest we look somewhere else and see what happens. In as labor-intensive an industry as the screen, we know that Leno's promised "ruination" will involve over a million working people in the United States alone, most of whom have low weekly earnings. These groups have important internal divisions between so-called "talent" and "craft" and between heavily unionized film and broadcast workers and non-union cable employees; but their numerical growth and willingness to strike during the dominance of Republican union-busting was a beacon through the 1980s. But anti-union legislation in so-called "right-to-work" states of the United States, the appeal to capital of the NICL and pressure for Hollywood workers to deunionize in order to retain employment has been successful. International solidarity has been minimal, with U.S. entertainment unions supporting *laissez-faire* screen trade (Christopherson, 1996; Gray & Seeber, 1996a, 1996b; Wasko, 1998).

If the day comes when the United States complains that Japan's ideological objections to organ transplants are non-tariff barriers to the export of the American heart, or takes issue with the French for prohibiting patents on DNA maps on the grounds that they represent an inalienable human heritage, we shall see this debate played out on less entertaining terrain. For this is the crowded hour of the *first* instance of economic versus cultural determinations; an hour we should all spend contemplating Daniel Singer's oxymoron: "GATT culture, that is to say, the resistible reign of merchandise" (1994, p. 56). The difficulty is that lurking behind the DNA and the heart are equally fetid forms of commodification that are just as alienated from citizen rights as any multinational. Our task must be to expose the contradictions at the center of consumer-citizen rhetorics and strive for democratically accountable forms of intervention. The backdrop must be an awareness of our New International Division of Cultural Labor.

REFERENCES

After GATT pique, pix pax promoted. (1994, June 8). *Daily Variety*, 1, 16.

Allan, B. (1988). The state of the state of the art on TV. *Queen's Quarterly*, 95(2), 318–329.

Barshefsky, C. (1998). Testimony of the United States Trade Representative before the House Appropriations Committee Subcommittee on Commerce, Justice, State, the Judiciary and Related Agencies, 31 March.

Beaverstock, J. V. (1996). Subcontracting the accountant! Professional labor markets, migration, and organizational networks in the global accountancy industry. *Environment and Planning A*, 28(2), 303–326.

Berman, N. (1992). Nationalism legal and linguistic: The teachings of European jurisprudence. *New York University Journal of International Law and Politics*, 24(1), 1515–1578.

Briller, B. R. (1990). The globalization of American TV. *Television Quarterly*, 24(3), 71–79.

British Film Commission. (n.d.). [On-line]. Available: http://www.britfilmcom. co.uk/content/filming/site.asp.

Brooks, D. (1994). Never for GATT. *American Spectator*, 27(1), 34–37.

Browett, J., & Leaver, R. (1989). Shifts in the global capitalist economy and the national economic domain. *Australian Geographical Studies*, 27(1), 31–46.

Buck, E. B. (1992). Asia and the global film industry. *East-West Film Journal*, 6(2), 116–133.

Buckingham, D. (1997). News media, political socialization and popular citizenship: Towards a new agenda. *Critical Studies in Mass Communication*, 14(4), 344–366.

Burgelman, J. C.; & Pauwels, C. (1992). Audiovisual policy and cultural identity in small European states: The challenge of a unified market. *Media, Culture & Society*, 14(2), 169–183.

Chartrand, H. H. (1992). International cultural affairs: A fourteen country survey. *Journal of Arts Management, Law and Society*, 22(2), 134–154.

Childers, E. (1994). Old-boying. *London Review of Books*, 16(16), 3, 5.

Christopherson, S. (1996). Flexibility and adaptation in industrial relations: The exceptional case of the U.S. media entertainment industries. In L. S. Gray & R. L. Seeber (Eds.), *Under the Stars: Essays on labor relations in arts and entertainment* (pp. 86–112). Ithaca, NY: Cornell University Press.

Christopherson, S., & Storper, M. (1986). The city as studio; the world as back lot: The impact of vertical disintegration on the location of the motion picture industry. *Environment and Planning D: Society and Space*, 4(3), 305–320.

Cohen, R. (1991). *Contested domains: Debates in international labor studies*. London: Zed Books.

Cohen, R. (1994, January 2). Aux armes! France rallies to battle Sly and T. rex. *New York Times*, pp. H1, 22–23.

Cornford, J., & Robins, K. (1998). Beyond the last bastion: Industrial restructuring and the labor force in the British television industry. In G. Sussman & J. A. Lent (Eds.), *Global productions: Labor in the making of the "Information Society"* (pp. 191–212). Cresskill, NJ: Hampton Press.

Culture wars. (1998, September 12). *Economist*, n.p.

Cunningham, S., & Jacka, E. (1996). *Australian television and international mediascapes*. Melbourne: Cambridge University Press.

Danan, M. (1995). Marketing the Hollywood blockbuster in France. *Journal of Popular Film and Television*, 23(3), 131–140.

Dawtrey, A. (1994, March 7–13). Playing Hollywood's game: Eurobucks back megabiz. *Variety*, 1, 75.

Deja vu. (1994). *Film Journal*, 97(6), 3.

A disquieting new agenda for trade. (1994). *Economist*, 332(7872), 55–56.

Dobson, J. (1993). TNCs and the corruption of GATT: Free trade versus fair trade. *Journal of Business Ethics*, 12(7), 573–578.

Drake, W. J., & Nicolaïdis, K. (1992). Ideas, interests, and institutionalization: Trade in services and the Uruguay Round. *International Organization*, 46(1), 37–100.

Evans, P. (1979). *Dependent development: The alliance of local capital in Brazil*. Princeton, NJ: Princeton University Press.

Ferguson, M. (1992). The mythology about globalization. *European Journal of Communication*, 7(1), 69–93.

Foreign bums on seats. (1998, August 15). *The Economist*, n.p.

Fröbel, F., Heinrichs, J. & Kreye, O. (1980). *The new international division of labor: Structural unemployment in industrialised countries and industrialisation in developing countries*, trans. P. Burgess. Cambridge: Cambridge University Press; Paris: Éditions de la Maison des Sciences de l'Homme.

GATT quota row puts muzzle on *White Fang*. (1993). *On Film*, 11, 1.

Golodner, J. (1994, February 27). The downside of protectionism. *New York Times*, H6.

Gray, L. S., & Seeber, R. L. (1996a). The industry and the unions: An overview. In L. S. Gray & R. L. Seeber (Eds.), *Under the stars: Essays on labor relations in arts and entertainment* (pp. 15–49). Ithaca, NY: Cornell University Press.

Gray, L. S., & Seeber, R. L. (1996b). Introduction. In L. S. Gray & R. L. Seeber (Eds.), *Under the stars: Essays on labor relations in arts and entertainment* (pp. 1–13). Ithaca, NY: Cornell University Press.

Grey, R. de C. (1990). *Concepts of trade diplomacy and trade in services*. Hemel Hempstead: Harvester Wheatsheaf.

Groves, D. (1994). O'seas B. O. power saluted at confab. *Variety*, 356(4), 18.

Groves, D. (1999, April 12–18). A major force o'seas. *Variety*, 9.

Guback, T. H. (1984). International circulation of U.S. theatrical films and television programming. In G. Gerbner & M. Siefert (Eds.), *World communications: A handbook* (pp. 153–163). New York: Longman.

Guback, T. H. (1987). Government support to the film industry in the United States. In B. A. Austin (Ed.), *Current research in film: Audiences, economics and law* (Vol. 3, pp. 88–104). Norwood, NJ: Ablex.

Gubernick, L., & Millman, J. (1994). El Sur is the promised land. *Forbes* 153(7), 94–95.

Guttridge, P. (1996, July 11). Our green and profitable land. *Independent*, 8–9.

The G-Word (1997, July 30). *Financial Times*, 15.

Hartley, J. (1996). *Popular reality: Journalism, modernity, popular culture*. London: Arnold.

Hayward, S. (1993). State, culture and the cinema: Jack Lang's strategies for the French film industry. *Screen* 34(4), 382–391.

Hill, J. (1994). Introduction. In J. Hill, M. McLoone & P. Hainsworth (Eds.), *Border crossing: Film in Ireland, Britain and Europe* (pp. 1–7). Belfast: Institute of Irish Studies.

Hills, J. (1994). Dependency theory and its relevance today: International institutions in telecommunications and structural power. *Review of International Studies*, 20(2), 169–186.

Hiscock, J. (1998, July 24). Hollywood backs British film drive. *Daily Telegraph*, 19.

Hoekman, B. M., & Kostecki, M. M. (1995). *The political economy of the world trading system: From GATT to WTO.* Oxford: Oxford University Press.

H'wood Buries Overseas Pix. (1999, January 25–31). *Variety,* 1, 90–91.

Jäckel, A. (1996). European co-production strategies: The case of France and Britain. In A. Moran (Ed.), *Film policy* (pp. 85–97). London: Routledge.

Jarvie, I. (1998). Free trade as cultural threat: American film and TV exports in the post-war period. In G. Nowell-Smith & S. Ricci (Eds.), *Hollywood and Europe: Economics, culture, national identity, 1945–95* (pp. 34–46). London: BFI.

Jury, L. (1996, July 4). Mission possible: Red tape cut to boost film industry. *Independent,* 3.

Kessler, K. L. (1995). Protecting free trade in audiovisual entertainment: A proposal for counteracting the European Union's trade barriers to the U.S. entertainment industry's exports. *Law and Policy in International Business,* 26(2), 563–611.

Keynes, J. M. (1957). *The general theory of employment interest and money.* London: Macmillan; New York: St. Martin's Press.

Kuhn, M. (1998). How can Europe benefit from the digital revolution? Presentation to the European Audiovisual Conference, Birmingham, April 6–8.

Lang, T. & Hines, C. (1993). *The New Protectionism: protecting the future against free trade.* New York: New Press.

Lent, J. A. (1998). The animation industry and its offshore factories. In G. Sussman & J. A. Lent (Eds), *Global productions: Labor in the making of the "Information Society"* (pp. 239–254). Cresskill, NJ: Hampton Press.

Lev, P. (1993). *The Euro-American cinema.* Austin: University of Texas Press.

Magder, T. (1998). Franchising the candy store: Split-run magazines and a new international regime for trade in culture. *Canadian-American Public Policy,* 34, 1–66.

Marvasti, A. (1994). International trade in cultural goods: A cross-sectional analysis. *Journal of Cultural Economics,* 18(2), 135–148.

Mayer, G. M. (1947). American motion pictures in world trade. *Annals of the American Academy of Political and Social Science,* 254, 31–36.

Mayrhofer, D. (1994). Media briefs. *Media Information Australia,* 74, 126–142.

McCann, P. (1998, August 14). Hollywood film-makers desert UK. *Independent,* 7.

Miège, B. (1989). *The capitalization of cultural production,* trans. J. Hay, N. Garnham & UNESCO. New York: International General.

Miller, T. (1991). Splitting the citizen. *Continuum,* 4(2), 193–205.

Miller, T. (1993a). National policy and the traded image. In P. Drummond, R. Paterson & J. Willis (Eds.), *National identity and Europe: The television revolution* (pp. 95–109). London: BFI.

Miller, T. (1993b). *The well-tempered self: Citizenship, culture, and the postmodern subject.* Baltimore and London: Johns Hopkins University Press.

Miller, T. (1996). The crime of Monsieur Lang: GATT, the screen and the new international division of cultural labour. In A. Moran (Ed.), *Film policy* (pp. 72–84). London: Routledge.

Miller, T. (1998a). *Technologies of truth: Cultural citizenship and the popular media.* Minneapolis: University of Minnesota Press.

Miller, T. (1998b). Hollywood and the world. In J. Hill & P. C. Gibson (Eds.), *The Oxford guide to film studies* (pp. 371–381). Oxford: Oxford University Press.

Moran, A. (1998). *Copycat TV: globalisation, program formats and cultural identity*. Luton: University of Luton Press.

Murdoch, R. (1998). Untitled presentation prepared for the European Audiovisual Conference, Birmingham, April 6–8.

Parker, R. A. (1991). The guise of the propagandist: Governmental classification of foreign political films. In B. A. Austin (Ed.), *Current research in film: Audiences, economics and law* (Vol. 5, pp. 135–146). Norwood, NJ: Ablex.

Pendakur, M. (1998). Hollywood north: Film and TV production in Canada. In G. Sussman & J. A. Lent (Eds.), *Global productions: Labor in the making of the "Information Society"* (pp. 213–238). Cresskill, NJ: Hampton Press.

The PolyGram test. (1998, August 15). *Economist*, n.p.

Quester, G. H. (1990). *The international politics of television*. Lexington, MA: Lexington Books.

Roddick, N. (1994). A hard sell: The state of documentary film marketing. *Dox*, 2, 30–32.

Schatz, T. (1988). *The genius of the system: Hollywood filmmaking in the studio era*. New York: Pantheon.

Schwab, S. (1994, March 1). Television in the '90s: Revolution or confusion? Tenth Joseph I. Lubin Memorial Lecture, New York University.

Shall we, yawn, go to a film? (1997, February 1). *The Economist*, n.p.

Singer, D. (1994). GATT and the shape of our dreams. *The Nation*, 258(2), 54–56.

Sjolander, C. T. (1992–1993). Unilateralism and multilateralism: The United States and the negotiation of the GATT. *International Journal*, 48(1), 52–79.

Sorlin, P. (1991). *European cinemas, European societies 1939–1990*. London: Routledge.

Stern, A. (1994a, June 27–July 3). Film/TV future tops confab agenda. *Variety*, 39.

Stern, A. (1994b, June 23). Valenti denies Euro TV crisis. *Daily Variety*, 1, 17.

Stevenson, R. W. (1994, February 6). Lights! Camera! Europe! *New York Times*, 1, 6.

Strange, S. (1995). The limits of politics. *Government and Opposition*, 30(3), 291–311.

Superhighway Summit (1994). *Emmy*, 16(2), A1–69.

Thompson, K. (1985). *Exporting entertainment: America in the world film market 1907–1934*. London: BFI.

Top 100 all-time domestic grossers. (1994, October 17–23). *Variety*, M60.

USIA. (1997). 1997 National trade estimate report—European Union. *M2 Press Wire*.

Valentine, J. (1997). Global sport and Canadian content: The *Sports Illustrated* controversy. *Journal of Sport & Social Issues*, 21(3), 239–259.

Van Elteren, M. (1996a). Conceptualizing the impact of U.S. popular culture globally. *Journal of Popular Culture*, 30(1), 47–89.

Van Elteren, M. (1996b). GATT and beyond: World trade, the arts and American popular Culture in Western Europe. *Journal of American Culture*, 19(3), 59–73.

Vasey, R. (1997). *The world according to Hollywood, 1918–1939.* Madison: University of Wisconsin Press.

Venturelli, S. (1998). Cultural rights and world trade agreements in the information society. *Gazette,* 60(1), 47–76.

Wasko, J. (1982). *Movies and money: Financing the American film industry.* Norwood, NJ: Ablex.

Wasko, J. (1994). *Hollywood in the information age: Beyond the silver screen.* Cambridge: Polity Press.

Wasko, J. (1998). Challenges to Hollywood's labor force in the 1990s. In G. Sussman & J. A. Lent (Eds.), *Global productions: Labor in the making of the "Information Society"* (pp. 173–189). Cresskill, NJ: Hampton Press.

Wasser, F. (1995). Is Hollywood America? The trans-nationalization of the American film industry. *Critical Studies in Mass Communication,* 12(4), 423–437.

Wedell, G. (1994). Prospects for television in Europe. *Government and Opposition,* 29(3), 315–331.

Weinraub, B. (1993, December 12). Directors battle over GATT's final cut and print. *New York Times,* L24.

Welch, L. S., & Luostarinen, R. (1988). Internationalization: Evolution of a concept. *Journal of General Management,* 14(2), 34–55.

Williams, M. (1994, March 7–13). Euros bury dinos, fete "List" auteur. *Variety,* 55–56.

Woods, M. (1999a, January 11–17). That championship season. *Variety,* 9, 16.

Woods, M. (1999b, May 3–9). Foreign pix bring life to biz. *Variety,* 37, 44, 46, 59.

Woolf, M. (1998, December 20). Why the next English patient will be British. *Independent on Sunday,* 9.

World Trade Organization. (1998). Audiovisual services: Background Note by the Secretariat. S/C/W/40 of June 15.

Zecchinelli, C. (1994, June 26). Gaps seen for EU TV meet. *Daily Variety,* 13.

Chapter 4

Three Processes of Dissolving Boundaries: Internationalization, Marketization and Acculturation

Paul S. N. Lee

By the end of the twentieth century, humankind witnessed a shrinkage of the globe as a result of advancements in communication and transport technologies, increase in world incomes, improvement in working conditions and increase in leisure. The idea of a global village aroused great interest in the 1990s. The interest in globalization was renewed by impressive achievements in telecommunications and computer technologies. The "plain old telephone" suddenly became the "information superhighway" as a result of digitization, compression technologies, satellite proliferation and invention of fiber optics. In the final few years of this century, it became clear to almost everyone that the changes brought about by the emergence of the Internet would be tremendous. It would change not only our conventional entertainment forms and cause genuine information explosion, but alter existing commercial practices, interpersonal interactions, legislation, taxation, education, etc.

In the process of globalization, three major areas are being affected, namely, national, economic and cultural. This chapter examines the three processes involved in the changes in these three areas and the implications of each to human societies. To be sure, there are other processes in globalizing human societies, such as technological changes, imperialism and movements of internationalism, etc. The three processes examined here are, however, the most obvious and immediate in the present era.

GLOBALIZATION AND BOUNDARY CROSSING

To Giddens (1990), modernity is inherently globalizing. Modernity changes so fast that it has extended its global reach and transformed profoundly traditional societies. Giddens conceptualizes a Western-based model being extended to the rest of the world. A few authors take issue with this Eurocentric conception of globalization. Featherstone (1995), for example, considers it insufficient to assume a neat sequence of social change based upon a western European experience, with other places condemned to follow the same route. Instead, he proposes to conceive global modernities in "plural forms." Robertson (1992) noted that globalization is a process involving the interpenetration of the universalization of particularism and the particularization of universalism. The process cannot be considered simply as an outcome of the Western project of modernity. Tomlinson has the following conception of globalization: It is a "rapidly developing process of complex interconnections between societies, cultures, institutions and individuals world-wide" (1997, p. 170).

No matter whether globalization is conceived of as an extension of a hegemonic culture to the rest of the world, or as a melding of diverse particularities (Woodiwiss, 1996), original boundaries in various societies are being pushed, crossed or changed. Various reactions to the "complex interconnections between societies" in different realms of societies are seen. Three most affected areas are the state, market and culture. In the "interconnections," three processes are taking place, namely, internationalization, marketization and acculturation. Each of the processes is discussed in order.

INTERNATIONALIZATION

Internationalization is defined as a process in which different national systems work together to form a larger supranational unit for mutual benefits. In the nineteenth and early twentieth centuries, the Western powers had successfully brought the social organization of nation-states to the world through imperialism. The nation-state has become the dominant and most powerful political unit in human societies. Nevertheless, when issues demanding concerted efforts of multiple states emerge, international organizations are needed. As early as 1865, the International Telegraph Union (ITU) was formed by 20 nations including Prussia, France, Italy and Russia to deal with the technical problems of telegraphy. In 1932, over 70 nations met at Madras to deal with issues of radio spectrum and change the ITU's name to International Telecommunication Union.

Another prominent international organization was the General Agreement on Tariffs and Trade (GATT), which was the predecessor of the World Trade Organization (WTO). The GATT was set up at Geneva in 1948 with 23 signatories. It aimed at encouraging free trade and full employment. Although it was not a formal international organization, it played the de facto function of one. In its 1986 Fourth Uruguay Round negotiation, the World Trade Organization was proposed to be established in January 1995.

From the experiences of these two international organizations, the nation-state's sovereignty in some areas like trade or technical standards are compromised. However, such compromises are usually voluntary and non-detrimental to state interests. The concessions made by the state are compensated for usually by benefits gained in other areas. For example, the ITU's radio spectrum allocation helps individual nations avoid interference from frequencies used by other parties. Similarly, the concession by Japan in opening up its food market was compensated for by its free access to the industrial markets in the West.

Internationalization is a voluntary process in which states could choose to join or not join, to agree or not to agree. Technical standards are a case in point. Take the standard of high-definition television (HDTV) for example. At present, there are three standards of HDTV, namely, Japanese, European and American. No side is willing to compromise its standard, or to accept another's. It has resulted in slow growth and acceptance of this technology among the general public. But no party can be coerced in the ITU to adopt another's standard. Another example of the voluntary nature of internationalization is China's entry into the WTO. Despite great benefits for China's trade, China was hesitant in joining the WTO for years because its local industries might be jeopardized if the local markets were liberalized too much.

FEATURES OF INTERNATIONALIZATION

There are several features of internationalization. First, it entails some recession of national sovereignty in some areas. To some people, this feature testifies to the erosion of nation-states' sovereignty. However, due to other features listed below, the nation-states' sovereignty remains largely intact. The second feature of internationalization is the formation of larger geo-political units that have specific goals to accomplish. These goals can be political and military, such as found in the North Atlantic Treaty Organization (NATO); economic, as in the WTO and Asia-Pacific Economic Cooperation (APEC); or social and educational, such as in the World Health Organization (WHO) and UNESCO.

Third, the state generally retains the right not to follow the majority decisions and withdraw its support from one particular action, or from the organization altogether. The consequences of withdrawing from international organizations vary with the power and the need of the state. For powerful nations like the United States or the United Kingdom, for instance, their withdrawal from the UNESCO in the mid-1980s did not do much harm to their national interests. As for North Korea, another example, it does not conceive of a need for joining the Asia-Pacific Economic Cooperation (APEC), which promotes open trade in the region.

Fourth, consensus is generally sought in international organizations. Although some nations have little bargaining power in international organizations, most of them are given equal status and their consent is needed for important decisions. With this feature, internationalization as a globalizing force does not alter fundamentally the nation-state system. National boundaries are not trespassed. The nation's authority is eroded by the forces other than internationalization, namely, marketization and acculturation.

THE EUROPEAN UNION IN INTERNATIONALIZATION

The European Union is a good example of voluntary association of different nation-states. It originated from the European Economic Community formed by the Treaty of Rome in 1957, signed by Belgium, West Germany, France, Italy, Luxembourg and the Netherlands. In 40 years of evolution, the European Union was formed after revising the founding treaties three times: in 1987 (the Single Act), in 1992 (the Treaty on European Union) and in 1997 (the draft Treaty of Amsterdam).

The goals of the European Union are "to promote economic and social progress which is balanced and sustainable, assert the European identity on the international scene and introduce a European citizenship for the nationals of the Member States" (European Union, 1999). It has two important structures, the Council of Ministers and the Parliament. The Council of Ministers consists of ministers of the 15 member states. Its presidency rotates every six months. There are three pillars of policies laid down by the Treaty on European Union.

Pillar one covers a wide range of Community concerns such as agriculture and environment. In a majority of cases, including fisheries, agriculture, environment and transport, the Council decides by qualified majority votes. Taxation, industry, culture, regional and social funds in Pillar One, however, remain subject to unanimity. For policies in Pillar Two (common foreign and security policy) and Pillar Three (cooperation in the fields of justice and home affairs), unanimity is the rule. This indicates that consensus is also sought in international organizations with regard to important decisions affecting member states.

The European Parliament has three functions: to legislate, to approve the budget and to supervise the executive. It shares the power of decision with the Council in a large number of cases. The co-decision procedure applies to a wide range of issues including free movement of workers, consumer protection, education, culture, health and trans-European networks. Every five years, the Parliament appoints the president and members of the Commission, which shares the executive power with the Council of Ministers and their representatives.

Since the European Union is formed on a voluntary basis, compromises and rules of unanimity are crucial to its survival. In important areas, no uniform action can be taken if no consensus is reached. The introduction of the Euro is an example. In January 1999, a unified currency—the Euro—came into existence in member states of the European Union except the United Kingdom, Sweden, Denmark and Greece, which did not sign the agreement with the EU in the first wave of introducing the currency; they have different financial and economic considerations at home. This demonstrates well the integrity of national sovereignty in the process of internationalization. If a nation does not see the benefits, it can refuse to participate in some joint actions.

So far as the internationalization process is conducted on a voluntary basis with nation-states as the basic operational units, state autonomy and sovereignty remain largely intact. Indeed, the process of internationalization may strengthen the system of nation-states by binding nations together to form into a more powerful bloc so as to protect common national interests. National sovereignty would be eroded by internationalization only if the basic unit of interactions in the world change from nation-states to individual members of each nation. Should this scenario appear, the nation as a social form would wither away.

MARKETIZATION

Much has been said about the role of capitalism in transforming the world into a single market. Classical Marxist theory conceives a progressive role of capitalism in transforming all primordial forms of production. Accordingly, capitalism has a mission to fulfill—turn the globe into a single market mediated through monetary exchange and contractual social relations. Warren (1980) argued in his work *Imperialism: Pioneer of Capitalism* that the underdeveloped world was changing into capitalistic societies, a prerequisite for their eventual transformation into socialism. By the end of the twentieth century, we can see that the mission is nearly completed with the exception of North Korea and, to some extent, Cuba. Neither state is expected to hold out long against the temptations of capitalism.

In 1820, the ratio of merchandise exports to gross domestic product of the world was only 1 percent, while the figure reached a record high of 13.5 percent in 1992. World trade is getting more integrated than ever and countries are trading each other's manufactured goods (Baker, Epstein & Pollin, 1998). A study showed that a weakening of the Japanese yen against the U.S. dollar tends to reduce the economic growth rates of South Korea, Taiwan, Hong Kong and Thailand, while raising those of Singapore, Malaysia and the Philippines. The winner/loser profile would be reversed in the case of a strengthening of the yen against the U.S. dollar. The reason seems to be that countries competing with Japan suffer from a weaker yen because it will make Japanese exports cheaper to third markets (Davis, 1996).

In 1950, the total amount of funds raised on international financial markets relative to world exports was 0.5 percent. By 1985, the ratio was increased to 13.5 percent and by 1996, the ratio increased further to 20 percent, showing a dramatic rise of capital flows. Measuring by interest parity relations, international financial markets are more integrated now than in the 1950s and 1960s (Baker, Epstein & Pollin, 1998). As regards foreign direct investment, it has been growing four times faster than international trade since the early 1980s, with a large increase of flows to developing countries (Baker, Epstein & Pollin, 1998). World capital is flowing around the globe to seek profits.

The products from the most advanced capitalist state, the United States, are seen everywhere in the world. Coca-Cola, McDonald's and Disney go hand in hand in the world market. Today Disney has more than 350 stores worldwide, deriving 23 percent of its income from overseas. Chairman and CEO Michael Eisner aimed at a split of 50–50 in its international and domestic incomes by 2000 (Gershon, 1997; Herman & McChesney, 1997). McDonald's feeds 35 million people a day with more than 24,500 restaurants in 115 countries (Sutcliff, 1999).

Transnational commercial activities increased greatly in the last few years due to spiral effects of competition by business giants across borders. According to *The Economist* ("The Science," 1998), some 32,000 commercial alliances have been formed around the world in the past few years, and three quarters of them were across borders. Among the nine firms that dominate the world's mass media, all but two are based in the United States. The two largest, Disney and Time Warner, have almost tripled in size this decade (McChesney, 1997).

The global concentration of economic power by transnational corporations (TNCs) is remote and difficult to be controlled by the state. The international market force is conceived to be disruptive. The TNCs are found to be adept at circumventing national borders and state control. They not only seek cheap labor and consumption markets, but also alter people's preferences for goods, jeopardizing local economies and subverting local cultures through control of media channels and contents.

FEATURES OF MARKETIZATION

The process of marketization has several features. First, it brings about standardization of products through mass production. Second, mass advertising is needed to promote the sales of huge quantities of goods. Third, it encourages mass consumption to sustain production growth. Fourth, it

seeks international division of labor in lowering costs and increasing profits.

The marketization process is undertaken by agents including the TNCs,
foreign capital, transnational advertising agencies and, sometimes, the
home government of the TNCs, as well as international financial organizations such as the International Monetary Fund (IMF) and the World
Bank.

The TNCs have interests in getting low wages, low taxes and minimum
regulations from host countries. Through their investments and creations
of employment, TNCs can often extract concessions from host governments
in taxes, land purchases and regulations. They circumvent the state's power
in deciding domestic politico-economic affairs. Rapid inflows and outflows
of international capital have created economic instability and financial crises in host countries. Coca-Cola, Nestlé, Exxon and Procter & Gamble
advertise through international advertising agencies not only their products
but the associated values too.

There have been cases of interference by TNCs' home governments into
other countries' economic decisions. France once warned an African government that it would withdraw government guarantees on outstanding
loans if Alcatel did not win a $20 million telecom switching contract. And,
in order to win a $30 million supercomputer order from Brazil, the Bank
of Japan said it would credit the purchase against Brazil's existing debt to
Japan (Gershon, 1997). The IMF has often been criticized for peddling the
"neo-liberal" agenda to developing countries, opening their markets for
unbridled international capital. The most recent example was the austerity
program imposed on Indonesia after its financial meltdown.

The process of marketization is eroding the state authority, breaking
down national boundaries and stripping away traditional identity fostered
under nationhood. Strange (1996) describes it as a shift of political authority from states to markets. Kaplan (1994) views political postmodernism as an epoch in which the classificatory grid of nation-states is to be
replaced by a jagged glass pattern of city-states, shanty-states, nebulous and
anarchic regionalisms.

However, the destructive force of marketization on nationhood is dis-
puted. Chang (1998) argues that while TNCs are increasing in importance,
the phenomenon is by no means a truly "global" and even process. Most
TNCs are still "national" firms with peripheral operations abroad rather
than truly "stateless" bodies globally rearranging their activities in search
of higher profits. The alleged importance of TNCs in the developmental
process of East Asia also turns out to be highly exaggerated.

While the flows of foreign direct investment to low-wage developing
countries have been increasing, the bulk of it is still concentrated in the
industrialized economies. Furthermore, over 70 percent of the foreign investment that is going to developing countries is targeted at only 10 coun-

tries, and China alone received over 25 percent of the developing economies' foreign direct investment (FDI) between 1990 and 1994. Most of their governments have taken "strategic," rather than *laissez-faire*, attitudes toward TNCs to one degree or another and tried to influence the direction and the terms of engagement of incoming FDI. For example, the two "star performers" of East Asia, namely, Korea and Taiwan, employed two important policies in regulating TNCs—restricted entry and ownership. Joint ventures were encouraged once entry was granted and foreign ownership was rarely allowed to exceed 50 percent except in some "strategic" industries.

In addition, data show that in both the advanced and developing countries, the government has played an increasingly important role, especially after the post–World War II period, in seeking to increase economic welfare within domestic economies. For example, the total government expenditure as a share of GDP for six OECD countries rose from 10 percent in 1880 to 45 percent in 1999 (Baker, Epstein & Pollin, 1998). The nation-states' role has been expanding rather than shrinking since World War II.

MCDONALD'S IN MARKETIZATION

Since McDonald's is one of the most familiar TNCs worldwide—its outlets are spread as far afield as the Arctic Circle—I use it as a case to examine more closely the process of marketization in globalization.

McDonald's does not only produce uniform products throughout the world, such as french fries, Big Macs and Egg McMuffins, but also its pricing in various countries has been used by *The Economist* magazine as a measure for the calculation of currency valuations. The Big Mac index establishes the relative over- and undervaluing of world currencies by converting them into the price of a Big Mac in each country and then comparing parities. McDonald's also set the model for fast food chains in many countries. It spends heavily on advertising, urging people to consume or discard its burgers. Amidst the craze of redeeming Snoopy toys through eating McDonald's in 1998, thousands of hamburgers were dumped into litter bins every day in Hong Kong. People simply could not consume that many burgers, purchasing them merely for the sake of the Snoopy collections. McDonald's is also noted for hiring minimum-wage laborers to maintain low costs of production.

With all these features, McDonald's is playing an active role in globalizing the world into a single market. However, McDonald's is seldom reported to have troubles with the host countries. On the contrary, it is reported to have conceded to government demands, such as the removal of its Beijing restaurant to a new place in Beijing after the city government refused to honor a long lease signed by both parties.

It should also be pointed out that TNCs are not necessarily successful in their globalizing mission. For example, McDonald's has been in Hong Kong for more than two decades. In its early days in Hong Kong, it was given a cold shoulder. Its stores grew very slowly before the 1980s. Hong Kong people prefer rice to hamburgers in their daily diet. It was only after the 1980s that Hong Kong people, especially the younger generation, started to accept burgers—mainly a fast means to fill the stomach and a treat for children on holidays. In Hong Kong, 53 percent of the population eat there at least once in any given week. Of the 25 busiest stores world-wide, 16 are in Hong Kong (Sutcliff, 1999).

Nevertheless, McDonald's does not dominate the fast food industry in Hong Kong. The total number of Chinese-style fast food stores is much bigger than McDonald's. The two largest competing chains are Cafe de Coral and Maxim. All provide Chinese dishes as well as Western drinks and snacks. The number of corner stores providing fast food in all housing estates in Hong Kong is beyond estimation. Despite its well-known brand name all over the world, McDonald's does not dominate the fast food industry in Hong Kong, not to say the food supply industries. After all, McDonald's serves less than 1 percent of the world's population (Sutcliff, 1999).

Marketization is taking place and turning world economies alike in many respects, including modes of production, product features, brand names, shopping malls, commercial practices, mass advertising and consumerism. However, below the surface of sameness and similarities, there are great variations and diversities in both material and spiritual cultures of different societies. We see commonness across many societies, but we see even more differences if we shift our attention to the variations.

States seem to be losing control of their boundaries, but a closer look shows that the states are regulating cross-border capitalism actively. The state may lose some economic sovereignty in the process of marketization; however, it gains more political power by utilizing the economic benefits generated by the market. The Chinese Communists' position in China to-day, for example, is bolstered by economic growth after the Tiananmen Massacre in 1989.

The state is pretty alive although the market gives it more work to do. The relationship between state and market should not be viewed as a per-manent contest (Scott, 1997). Instead, they are collaborators for mutual benefits. The state collaborates with the market to aggrandize itself through economic growth, while the market helps the state in order to grab more profits.

ACCULTURATION

In the discussion on globalization, culture is often treated as a victim to be protected by the state, defending against the intrusion of the market.

The state is the protector of culture while the market is a destroyer. Capitalism is viewed as evil in its displacement of traditional values of indigenous cultures. It is, however, debatable whether the consumption of Disney videos entails the consumption of American values. Even granted that consumerism is embedded in capitalistic culture, it is doubtful whether it will replace important local values, especially the deeply entrenched ones.

Cultural sovereignty is the least affected in the process of globalization because adoption and absorption of cultural values are not subject simply to state policies or market forces. Culture belongs to people and is practiced by people in everyday life. Even if the state loses some of its sovereignty (and dignity) in failing to regulate satellite television, for example, this does not mean that people subsequently lose their cultural sovereignty in determining what to watch and what values to adopt. There are cases in which global television needs to localize before being accepted by people with different cultures. Zee TV in India is one of the examples. Star TV needs to use Indian content and actors in this channel to hold the Indian audience. Anglo-American programs fail most of the time to reach the prime time slots in non-English-speaking channels in Latin America or Asia.

Cultural development, if not distorted by coercive force, has its own logic. It is resilient in resisting unpopular values from the outside, yet open to values compatible with existing practices. The values associated with capitalism are mainly materialism and consumerism. The change of culture cannot be affected just by these two values. The most dominant force for globalization will come from acculturation rather than internationalization or marketization.

Acculturation is a process whereby different cultures come in close contact and interact on a day-to-day basis, with mutual influences, adaptation and absorption. Under this process, people in different territories share similar cultural, rather than national identities, just as the nobility did in Medieval Europe (Kobrin, 1998). This process is voluntary and the ongoing interactions are spontaneous although initial contacts can be made intentionally.

The values adopted by people through the process of acculturation will be universal. Although in the foreseeable future, a "global" culture with universal values shared by humankind is not likely, "intermediate-level" culture(s) shared by people within certain class, ethnic, or geographical boundaries can be dated back to the time when human beings appeared on this planet. Through conquests or contacts, tribal cultures were destroyed or transformed into cultures of city states or modern states with larger populations. What differentiates the final decade of this century from the previous era is a general sentiment against "conquests" in international society. The use of state violence is not viewed as heroic and glorifying, as it was in the past century.

FEATURES OF ACCULTURATION

Acculturation has several features. First, it is a voluntary process of interactions among different cultures. Second, the state and people do not feel threatened by such contacts. Third, cultures will influence one another, with spontaneous rejection, adaptation and absorption. Fourth, it takes time for the change of culture to occur. Fifth, it is a never-ending process since people are confronted with changing physical and social environments.

The process of acculturation is occurring more rapidly and frequently among different cultures due to increased contacts, thanks to technological advancements. One of the most active areas in acculturation is the audiovisual materials which are in great demand as a result of channel proliferation in media. Contents are badly needed to fill multiple channels of cable television, satellite television, video-on-demand and Internet pages. Television and films have undergone the process of acculturation most remarkably. The international exchange of television programs and films is conducted on a voluntary basis. Producers may withhold the sales of their products, while buyers can choose one product or producer over another. And the audience may switch off their television sets or stop going to the cinema.

Some argue that American films and television programs dominate the international market; people in other countries have little choice because U.S. products are cheap due to economies of scale and have higher viewership than local programs. This argument's second point is most crucial. Appeal of media products is essential to their success at home or overseas. One should not be blind to the fact that many U.S. films or television programs do not reach foreign countries. Local programmers will not buy programs from overseas that do not appeal to the home audience. On the other hand, if people have access to local programs of similar quality, their preference is always local rather than foreign (Lee, 1998; Straubhaar, 1991).

Herman and McChesney (1997) argue that the crucial incursion of global media in host countries is the implantation of the model, which defines the path that will be taken and brings the country in question into the orbit of interest of the dominant powers. In other words, they conceive that people in other countries who choose U.S. products are doing so "unconsciously" or "involuntarily." This assumption of "unconscious" choice (or false consciousness) on the part of the audience, however, has not been substantiated by empirical evidence.

On the other hand, we can see some blending of different cultural elements in some American media products. The release of *Mulan* by Disney in the summer of 1998 is one example. It was a Chinese classic story. It adapted not only the story line, but also conveyed some traditional Chinese cultural values like filial piety and loyalty to friends. *Aladdin, Snow White* and *Little Mermaid* are also examples of acculturation. The original story lines of these three Disney classics did not originate in the United States. In the following, I would like to use recent developments of Hollywood action movies to illustrate the process of acculturation.

HOLLYWOOD ACTION MOVIES IN ACCULTURATION

In recent years, Hong Kong movies have experienced decline in audience. The typical Hong Kong movie genre of kung fu comedy is not frequently seen in Cantonese cinema any more. But a few famous stars and directors have gone to Hollywood and participated in a few action movies. Jackie Chan's *Rumble in the Bronx* in 1995 drew a huge audience in Hong Kong. Most people then considered it simply another Jackie Chan movie shot in America with an American cast. Hong Kong director John Woo's *Hard Target* (1993) and *Broken Arrow* (1996) were some disappointments for Woo fans in Hong Kong. His *Face/Off* in 1997, however, was quite a success—Woo had regained his style and blended it successfully with American cinema: less outraged violence with mainstream conventions. Woo was then invited to direct *Mission: Impossible 2* (2000) for Paramount Pictures.

Apart from John Woo, Chow Yun-Fat and Jackie Chan, both superstars in Hong Kong movies, should also be mentioned. In 1998, Chow Yun-Fat made his debut in *The Replacement Killers*, co-starring with Oscar winner Mira Sorvino. He performed in similar styles as he did in *A Better Tomorrow* (1987) directed by John Woo in Hong Kong. But *The Replacement Killers* is definitely mixed with a typically American sense of humor, represented well by Sorvino, and high-energy action sequences of American cinema.

Jackie Chan's *Rush Hour* in 1999 was an even greater success. It blended Jackie's usual style of slapstick in the midst of a fistfight with an American black cop performed by Chris Tucker. They are a perfect match. This movie topped the box office when it was screened in Hong Kong and America. In fact, American movies have been imitating the genre of action-comedy for years. In *Tango & Cash* (1989), for example, Sylvester Stallone pulled a stunt right out of Jackie Chan's *Police Story* (1988).

The action genre of the Hong Kong movie is absorbed not only in the examples cited. A recent Warner Bros. Production, *The Matrix* (1999), combined hi-tech, fantasy and kung fu together. The producers specifically hired Hong Kong fight choreographer Yuen Woo-ping and his team of wire specialists to plan the action. Yuen directed the *Drunken Master* in 1978 in Hong Kong, which made Jackie Chan a star. The actors in *The Matrix* all went through several months of kung fu training prior to shooting. The movie mixed the Hong Kong genre well with American cinema.

Although Hong Kong movie genres or elements will not dominate Hol-

lywood movies, the cited examples demonstrate a voluntary process of acculturation. Two cultures, after coming into contact with one another, will
mutually influence each other. As a matter of fact, the kung fu genre was
started by Bruce Lee cast as Kato in the American television series of *Green
Hornet*.

CONCLUSION

From a historical point of view, globalization has been going on for a
long time. People have always been inclined to overcome distance and time
and to get closer. It is only due to recent technological developments that
people really have the possibilities of contacting one another. The globe
seemed to shrink rapidly in the final years of the last century. Nevertheless,
getting communicatively or physically closer does not mean socially or culturally closer. Acculturation will be the only peaceful means of achieving
a genuine global community in which people share a common culture and
identity.

Marketization cannot achieve a global community although it helps in
familiarizing people with some common material goods. Neither is internationalization able to form a global community since nation is an antith-
esis to global community. With rapid development in transportation and
communication technologies, people will interact more frequently than
ever. Acculturation is a slow process, but the formation of a global community should not be a utopia.

REFERENCES

Baker, D., Epstein, F. & Pollin, R. (Eds.). (1998). *Globalization and progressive
economic policy*. Cambridge: Cambridge University Press.
Chang, H. (1998). Globalization, transnational corporations, and economic devel-
opment: Can the developing countries pursue strategic industrial policy in a
globalizing world economy? In D. Baker, F. Epstein & R. Pollin (Eds.),
Globalization and progressive economic policy (pp. 97–113). Cambridge:
Cambridge University Press.
Davis, B. (1996, January 3). Asia Pacific outlook. *Australian*, 28.
European Union. (1999, June 20). [On-line]. Available: http://europa.eu.int/abc-
en.htm.
Feathersone, M. (1995). *Undoing culture: Globalization, postmodernism and iden-
tity*. London: Sage Publications.
Gershon, R. (1997). *The transnational media corporation: Global messages and
free market competition*. Mahwah, NJ: Lawrence Erlbaum Associates.
Giddens, A. (1990). *The consequences of modernity*. Cambridge: Polity Press.
Herman, E., & McChesney, R. (1997). *The global media: The new missionaries of
corporate capitalism*. London: Cassell.
Kaplan, R. (1994, February). The coming anarchy. *The Atlantic Monthly*, 44.

Kobrin, S. (1998). Back to the future: Neomedievalism and the postmodern digital world economy. *Journal of International Affairs*, 51(2), 361–381.

Lee, P. (1998). Toward a theory of transborder television. In A. Goonasekera & P. Lee (Eds.), *Television without borders: Asia speaks out* (pp. 274–286). Singapore: AMIC.

McChesney, R. (1997). The global media giants: The nine firms that dominate the world. *FAIR—Fairness and Accuracy in Reporting*, 10(6), 11–18.

Robertson, R. (1992). *Globalization: Social theory and global culture*. London: Sage Publications.

The Science of Alliance (1998, April 4). *The Economist*, 69–70.

Scott, A. (1997). *The limits of globalization: Cases and arguments*. London: Routledge.

Strange, S. (1996). *The retreat of the state: The diffusion of power in the world economy*. Cambridge: Cambridge University Press.

Straubhaar, J. (1991). Beyond media imperialism: Assymetrical interdependence and cultural proximity. *Critical Studies in Mass Communication*, 8(1), 39–59.

Sutcliff, T. (1999, June 11). Big Mac just keeps on getting bigger. *South China Morning Post*, 17.

Tomlinson, J. (1997). Cultural globalization and cultural imperialism. In A. Mohammadi (Ed.), *International communication and globalization: A critical introduction* (pp. 170–190). London: Sage.

Warren, B. (1980). *Imperialism: Pioneer of capitalism*. London: NLB.

Woodiwiss, A. (1996). Searching for signs of globalization. *Sociology*, 30(4), 799–810.

Chapter 5

Dissolving Boundaries: The Electronic Newspaper as an Agent of Redefining Social Practices

Alice Y. L. Lee and Clement Y. K. So

Boundaries of various kinds exist in human society, and they are affected by different forces. Among them, technology is one major force that can bring changes to existing boundaries. This chapter examines how the electronic newspaper as a new medium is dissolving old boundaries and creating new ones, and then explores the social implications of these boundary changes.

Throughout history, people live and act according to the rules of their social territories such as ethnicity, nationality, profession and family, as well as private and public domains. Social territories can be understood as spatial strategies to influence and control people, phenomena and social relationships. However, the boundaries that divide social territories are continually changing and these changes lead to successive redefinitions of social relationships. Toward the twenty-first century, anthropologists, political scientists and geographers are enthusiastically examining the boundary shift of human territoriality and its social implications (Gradus & Lithwick, 1996; Pellow, 1996; Prescott, 1987; Sack, 1986).

For most of them, boundaries are socially constructed and limits are altered by human determination. However, this chapter does not follow the humanistic approach but tries to examine boundary change from a technological perspective. As Hut (1996, p. 178) puts it, "Every technological revolution has changed society as well as individual lives in ways that were never anticipated." While the invention of the airplane has turned every city into a port city, the invention of the telephone, radio and television has further brought access to remote countries. With the advent of the Internet, now most places on Earth have been turned into an information port, putting our life "on edge" in various ways. Regarding communication technology as an important force in breaking boundaries and resetting limits, we select the electronic newspaper as a case to look at the process and consequences of the change.

Based on boundary theory and medium analysis, this chapter scrutinizes the format of the electronic newspaper to see how it changes the spatial, temporal, social, conceptual and symbolic boundaries of the traditional newspaper. We put forward the notions of open and closed media codes to facilitate boundary interpretation. The format of the traditional newspaper is considered a kind of "closed media code" while the media format of the electronic newspaper is an "open media code." We argue that the conversion from closed to open media codes may bring along a series of boundary changes and social consequences in the new millennium.

BOUNDARY, SOCIAL TERRITORY AND SOCIAL CHANGE

Boundary study has long been the interest of scholars in many fields, as all people have to live under the constraints of different kinds of boundaries, no matter if they are formal or informal, salient or hidden. Hall (1996, p. viii) points out that in order to survive in a society, "one must be in command of the system of boundaries as defined by one's own group, as well as others that impinge on that group." Therefore, boundary analysis is essential to understand human activities and relationships. Holdich (1916, p. 2) says that "Nature knows no boundary line. Nature has her frontiers truly, but lines . . . are abhorrent to her." Boundaries, therefore, are human creations. Social scientists are eager to know how and why boundaries are set and in what ways they regulate the thinking and behavior of individuals and social groups.

Scholars from different disciplines have various ideas about the concept of "boundary." Since our concern is how a new medium like the electronic newspaper interacts with its social and cultural environment, we choose to adopt an anthropological notion of boundary to examine the interface of technology and human relationships. Here, boundary is defined as a demarcation, which "serves to indicate the bounds of limits of anything whether material or immaterial" (Pellow, 1996, p. 1). There are many forms of boundary, including physical, social, temporal, conceptual and symbolic ones. A boundary can be permeable and negotiable; it can be created, maintained, elaborated and dismantled. Most importantly, it is transformative, and in fact many boundaries are constantly being blurred and changed. The transformative feature of a boundary and its relation to social change are what we are most concerned about.

Boundaries set perimeters, delineating what is in and what is out, who is a member and who is not, what has status and what does not (Pellow, 1996). The area within a boundary is usually referred to as a territory, which Sack (1986) specifically calls "human territoriality." A territory is an expression of social power. Territoriality in human society implies a control over an area that is conceived of and communicated. Sack defines the use of territoriality as an attempt by an individual or group "to affect, influence, or control people, phenomena, and relationships, by delimiting and asserting control over a geographic area" (Sack, 1986, p. 19). Boundaries of a territory mold behavior and affect power structure. A boundary serves the functions of classifying, communicating and enforcing control. First, through classifying membership, group identity can be built and insiders protected. It also sets a spatial context through which members of the group experience the world and give it meaning. Second, through communicating, it can help coordinate efforts, specify responsibilities and allocate resources. Third, through enforcing control, it is able to create and maintain order and prevent people from getting in each other's way.

For Sack (1986), boundaries of territory are alterable and the change reflects or leads to social transformation. As mankind moves from a primitive to a modern society, there are fewer autonomous territorial units and the world is subdivided into varied territorial sub-units. The new delimitation subsequently leads to change in human relationships. Modern human territoriality defines realms of control and hierarchies of responsibility and creates impersonal relations in complex bureaucratic structures. Other studies also show that spatial boundary change will be followed by political transformation (e.g., the collapse of the Berlin Wall) (Pellow, 1996), a national identity shift (Rotenberg, 1996), changing class relations (Carlisle, 1996) and reconceptualizations of self/society (Lawrence, 1996). Boundary breaking in the physical, socio-cultural or conceptual sense has important social implications.

Anthropologists, geographers and political scientists tend to single out certain social groups as the driving forces for creating and breaking boundaries. While they conclude that boundaries are human constructions (Pellow, 1996), some communication scholars do see that, apart from human agency, technology also plays a significant role in establishing and dissolving a boundary and thus leads to social change. For example, Meyrowitz (1985) claims that television makes people have "no sense of place." The impact of television on social behavior is through altering the boundary between private and public spaces and breaking the myth between children and adults, men and women, and politicians and common citizens. As a result, television brings blurring of age, gender and authority distinctions. Morley and Robins (1995) also point out that the emergence of global media, such as satellite television, introduces a breakdown of national boundaries. New communication media provide the permeable boundaries of our age. Modern people's senses of space and place are all being significantly altered, resulting in the reconfiguration of contemporary cultural identities. With increasing popularity and importance of the Internet and new media, it is worth examining how new communication technology such as the electronic newspaper generates boundary changes and socio-cultural transformation.

In the field of business, Hammer and Champy (1993) advocate that technology can be disruptive in the sense that it is able to break the rules that limit how we conduct our work and thus it is critical to look for competitive advantages. Rigid boundaries are crumbling as "modern structures . . . must be open and flexible if they are to keep up with the pace of change" (Hammer, 1996, p. 168). The notion of "boundarylessness" is proposed by Jack Welch of General Electric to describe the dissolution of all walls within and around a business.

Although boundaries are usually understood together with the spatial metaphors of territory and domain, it can also be examined in terms of the concepts "limit," "cutting edge" and "frontier." Limits can be defined as "enclosing something, setting part of the world apart from the rest, by making it off-limits" (Hut, 1996, p. 174). The cutting edge is where important new things can be expected. People proceed toward the edge of what is known and usually discover that an edge is not a place to fall off. The status of "on edge," for Hut, is to expect nothing in particular, to be fully open to whatever new situation presents itself and to greet the unknown with open arms. So, life at the frontier means one is present at the edge between the known and the unknown and pushing the limit toward a new horizon. The frontier can be a battlefield, a newly explored territory or newly conceived activities. The electronic newspaper, as we shall see in the following section, is making mankind stretch the limits of the existing information system and explore the frontiers of cyberspace in a new communication landscape. This new landscape inevitably signifies a completely new socio-cultural pattern.

MEDIUM ANALYSIS AS SOCIAL INQUIRY

While traditional analyses of the media usually focus on media content and its effects, a small but significant group of scholars choose to look at the media format, and they even proclaim that the format is much more important than the content. Canadian economist and historian Harold Innis is perhaps the first to recognize the unique role of the media format. In his study of how technological innovations affect social and cultural institutions, Innis (1951) differentiates time-biased media such as stone and clay and space-biased media such as paper and papyrus. He argues that time-biased media are favorable to the past, religious authority and tradition, while space-biased media are conducive to the rise of modern empires, decentralization and secular political authority. Marshall McLuhan (1964) has popularized Innis's ideas and proclaimed that communication technologies affect human beings' five senses and change their order of importance. He maintains that new technologies alter the way people react to things and thus affect their entire lives and society. The format of a medium is much more important than the sum of all the messages of that medium, and so it goes his famous phrase "the medium is the message." Other medium theorists have also picked up on the cues from Innis and McLuhan and discussed the impact of media format on society. For example, some of them focus on the effects of the shift from orality to literacy (Havelock, 1963; Ong, 1967, 1971), while others study the impact of the change from script to print (Chaytor, 1966; Eisenstein, 1979). Still others look at the effects of electronic media on individuals and social organizations (Boorstin, 1978; Ong, 1982; Schwarz, 1974).

From a sociological perspective, Altheide and Snow (1979, 1991) explicate the "media logic" as constituted by different elements of media format, including the grammar of the medium and the norms that are used to define content. The grammar is viewed as an important variable in the process of developing meaning and it ultimately affects how phenomena are perceived. For example, the grammatical features of the electronic media include how time is used, how the content is organized and scheduled, and other special features of verbal and nonverbal communication. As a consequence, radio as a medium is used by listeners to create a temporal framework and stay in touch with realities. In contrast, television viewers often equate what they see as representative of the real world and thus they come to develop a false sense of participation. Furthermore, as television is basically an entertainment medium, it tends to "entertainmentize" everything on it, including news, politics and religion. Meyrowitz (1985) focuses on how media format affects social behavior. For example, the physical characteristics of a book make it a private possession and reflect one's cultural tastes. They are discriminatory and selective in terms of readership. On the other hand, television is "public" in nature as its programs are shared by many viewers regardless of sex, age and social class. Television as a medium is inclusive and boundary-blurring as exemplified by its "lowest common denominator" or "least objectionable program" strategy.

Postman (1985, 1992) also criticizes television. Regardless of the content, its entertainment format makes it a culturally debasing instrument. He further questions whether we should embrace a new technology without first knowing what it brings. In explicating McLuhan's relevancy in the digital age, Levinson (1999, p. 7) reiterates McLuhan's idea that "centers are everywhere and margins are nowhere" to show that the power structure in the new information millennium is changed. The digital age is decentralized more than ever. As individuals become their own information gatekeepers, the traditional gatekeepers such as news organizations have to switch their roles to become matchmakers.

Canadian scholar Richard Ericson and his colleagues have studied the relationship between the mass media and other social phenomena such as the law and criminal justice (Ericson, Baranek & Chan, 1991). In delineating the influence of the media on the social justice system, they made a systematic comparison among major forms of media in terms of their various characteristics and argued that the format of the media plays a central role in affecting their presentations and contents. While their analysis only includes print newspapers, television and radio, we adopt their classification scheme and expand it to include the electronic newspaper as well. The differences in format among the four types of mass media are listed in Table 5.1.

Scholars in the McLuhanesque tradition postulate that the change in media format would inevitably lead to a boundary change, and then new social patterns would emerge. Format analysis has thus become a form of social inquiry with high level of relevancy in the information age. The rapid development of new communication technologies gives birth to the electronic newspaper which represents a whole new media format. Before we discuss what social impacts this new format brings, let us first look at the defining characteristics of the electronic newspaper as a new format.

THE NEW FORMAT OF ELECTRONIC NEWSPAPERS

Inspired by Basil Bernstein's (1971) analysis on educational code, here we put forward "closed media code" and "open media code" as a pair of concepts to contrast the format of the traditional newspaper from that of the electronic newspaper. "Code" means systemic set of laws (Swannel, 1989) and it refers to a "regulative principle which underlies various message systems" (Atkinson, 1985, p. 136). The media code, therefore, could be understood as a systemic set of laws that regulate the format of a medium. It can be examined from two aspects. The first is about the classification of content and the other is the mode of transmission. Classification refers to "the nature of the differentiation between contents" (Bernstein, 1971, p. 88). If classification is strong, contents are insulated from each other by strong boundaries, and the reverse is also true. In terms of mode of transmission, it refers to the degree of control possessed by the transmitter and receiver over the selection, organization, pacing and timing of the information transferred. Strong mode of transmission means that the transmitter is in full control of the transmission process, while weak mode of transmission refers to the receiver's increase of power in the communication process. Here closed media code refers to the media organization's strong classification between information contents and its rigid control of information transmission. Open media code is characterized by weak classification between information contents and interactive information transmission. Table 5.2 summarizes the format of the traditional and the electronic newspaper from the perspectives of organization of content and mode of transmission.

In Table 5.2, we can see that the traditional newspaper organizes its

Table 5.1
Comparison of Characteristics among Various Media*

Characteristics	Print Newspaper	Electronic Newspaper	Television	Radio
Mode of message	Visual	Primarily visual but also audio	Visual and audio	Audio
Validation of context	Weak	Medium	Strong	Medium
Level of redundancy	Lowest	Low	Medium	Highest
Demand on imagination	Medium	Medium	Lowest	Highest
Characteristics of message	Narrative/ Symbolic/ Abstraction	Narrative/ Somewhat abstract	Dramatic/ Entertaining/ Concrete	Somewhat abstract/ Entertaining/ Concrete
Level of personalization	Lowest	Low	Highest	Medium
Structure with time/space	Space	Space	Time	Time
Immediacy	Lowest	Medium	Medium	Highest
Amount of message	Highest	Highest	Medium	Lowest
Permanence of message	Permanent record	Can be permanent	Ephemeral/ Evanescent	Ephemeral/ Evanescent
Structure of message	Linear/ Sequential	Linear/ Mosaic	Mosaic/ Episodic	Mosaic/ Episodic
Message flow	Static	Basically static but also dynamic	Dynamic/ Continuous	Dynamic/ Continuous
Mode of information processing	Self-pacing	Self-pacing	Imposes own pace	Imposes own pace
Nature of activity	Individual/ Primary	Individual/ Primary	More social/ Secondary	Most social/ Secondary

*Expanded on the basis of Ericson, Baranek and Chan (1991), p. 22.

Table 5.2
Comparison of the Traditional Newspaper and the Electronic Newspaper

Traditional Newspaper	Electronic Newspaper
A. Organization of Content:	
1. Hierarchical distinction among sections	1. Weak hierarchical distinction among sections
2. Hierarchical distinction among pages	2. No page distinction
3. Hierarchical distinction among stories	3. Weak hierarchical distinction among stories
4. News items stand alone	4. News items linked to background materials and databases
B. Mode of Transmission:	
1. One-way communication Top-down-to-readers mode Full copy delivery No customized versions	1. Interactive communication Readers control selection Customized version delivery possible
2. Linear story-telling (independent treatment of news items) Simple, holistic retrieval steps	2. Non-linear story-telling (with media Links) Multiple retrieval steps
3. Retail distribution in paper form	3. Web distribution in electronic form
4. With limit in space	4. Exterior browsing, no space limit
5. Mass distribution	5. Point-to-point in a mass scale
6. Print presentation (photo + word)	6. Multimedia presentation (sound + image + word)
7. No back-issue link	7. With back-issue link
8. News update on daily basis	8. Constant news update

content into distinct categories such as news, entertainment, business, sports, horse racing, feature columns and classified advertisements. Each page has a strong territorial boundary and each story has a particular physical location. For example, sports news will not be placed in the entertainment page and a travel feature will not appear in the news page. Moreover, the traditional newspaper has its content organized in a hierarchical way. There are strong hierarchical distinctions among sections, pages and stories. Placement, layout and use of signposts manifest the hierarchical order. Thus, information placed in "section A" is usually regarded as more important than the other sections like news, sports, entertainment, finance and education, which are also organized in certain order. There is also segregation within the news section. It is divided into "major news," local news and international news as they are clearly numbered in terms of order as well as importance. Stories within a page are also hierarchical presented through placement and headline size. Some are leading stories and others play subordinate roles. This arrangement implies some pages have higher status and some stories are more important.

In contrast, the electronic newspaper does not organize its content in a strictly hierarchical way. The electronic newspaper is not a pile of paper and therefore has no natural sections. In the home page of an electronic newspaper, there are only icons classifying the content into different page categories. These icons facilitate readers to look for content they like to read. However, the hierarchical distinction among these icons/categories is weak. Although icons are ranked in certain order, compared with the traditional newspaper, their priority is not very salient. As readers click an icon and pull down the screen of an individual page category's "menu," they can see stories and features listed in brief headings with similar font sizes. Except for the headline story of the day, again there is little indication to show which item is more important than the others. Furthermore, the classification of content is not strong. Although information in the electronic newspaper is classified into different categories, there may be "hyperlinks" connecting information across page categories. The story link is a unique characteristic of the electronic newspaper and it breaks down the strong boundaries among content. While individual news stories in the traditional newspaper stand on their own and have strong territorial identities, through the links news stories in the electronic newspaper are embedded in an information network. They are not only connected with stories in another page in another day, but are also linked to information or raw materials in databanks somewhere else. It is becoming increasingly difficult to distinguish news from data. In brief, information in the electronic newspaper is presented in a flat or network pattern.

In Table 5.2 we see that the transmission mode of the electronic newspaper also contrasts greatly with that of the traditional newspaper. First, the traditional newspaper involves a one-way communication process that allows no instant feedback from the readers. It is a "top-down" mode in terms of control of the transmission. Editors of the traditional newspaper select what information to transmit and decide on the format and pace of the transmission. Readers' needs and opinions are only conveyed to the reporters and editors through channels like market surveys and letters to the editor. Moreover, the traditional newspaper delivers its product in full. No filtering is done during the delivery process and customized versions are not the norm. As a result, editors are active gatekeepers and agenda-setters while readers are passive receivers. Second, in terms of presentation format, it is "linear story-telling" in the sense that readers' information retrieval is simple in procedure and uninterrupted. Information retrieval is usually limited to one step as readers flip to a particular page to locate a story. Each story is accompanied by a headline and possibly sidebars, graphics and photos. Together they stand as an independent information unit. Readers understand the story at one time without delay or interruption. Each story is understood as an isolated item and not as a part of an information chain.

Third, as the traditional newspaper is distributed in paper form as a retail product, its circulation is under great spatial constraint. Although transportation technology has rapidly advanced in recent years, a newspaper (with the exception of a few national newspapers) is still mainly produced for local consumption. Both its content and style have to meet local tastes. Fourth, since the traditional newspaper is printed on paper, it has a space limitation. Newspapers nowadays are much thicker, but there is still a limit in physical size and information volume. News has to be brief and not much space can be devoted to background information. Comprehensive journalism remains an ideal yet to be achieved. Fifth, the traditional newspaper as a mass medium transmits its information from a center to numerous receiving points. So its content has to remain appealing to the mass in order to sustain a healthy circulation. Its nature and method of distribution do not allow it to provide specialized information to segregated readers as narrowcasting (like cable television) does.

Sixth, information in the traditional newspaper is transmitted through words accompanied by some graphic designs and photos in a static way. Without sound and moving images, the traditional newspaper is monotonous and less attractive. Seventh, old newspaper copies are usually stored only in libraries and readers find it inconvenient to get back issues. Traditional newspaper output, therefore, can be regarded as perishable. Finally, the traditional newspaper is published on a daily basis. Any news happening after the daily deadline will be discarded or printed in the next day's issue. Therefore, this medium is temporally constrained.

On the contrary, the electronic newspaper is free from many spatial and temporal constraints the traditional newspaper faces. First, the electronic newspaper is unique in its interactive ability. Through on-line newspaper chat rooms, interactive news forums and e-mail communication, readers can instantly air their views and establish conversation with reporters/editors and even fellow readers. The reporters and editors are no longer in full control of the information transmission process, as readers can be more selective in choosing what they want to read. For some advanced electronic newspapers, their readers can also order customized versions of news and information. Second, the electronic newspaper provides media hyperlinks to audio soundbites, video clips, archived stories, stories in other page sections, relevant Web sites and databanks. With various media links, the electronic newspaper presents information in a "non-linear story-telling" format (Tremayne, 1999). Through multiple retrieval steps, readers can comprehend an issue from different perspectives and with different contexts. They can also decide how deep they would like to go into an issue.

So to a certain extent readers, rather than the editors, control the pace, amount and content of the information transmission.

Third, the electronic newspaper delivers its product through the World Wide Web in electronic form. The transmission cuts across national borders and geographical boundaries and reaches global readers in high speed and inexpensive way. Since it is globally distributed, its content and style are subsequently adjusted to fit the global context. Free from spatial constraint, the electronic newspaper can be run with a broader vision and in greater variety. Fourth, the electronic newspaper is distributed in the cyberspace and virtually has no limit in terms of information quantity. With extensive browsing and rich media links, readers can have access to full texts of speeches, lengthy interviews, court documents, legislative records, survey results, maps, statistics, commentaries and all kinds of other background materials that do not fit the format of the traditional newspaper. Readers can also print articles, retrieve photos, download statistical tables and search back-issues. News, for the first time in history, is possible to be reported in a comprehensive and in-depth way without worrying about space limitation. Fifth, the electronic newspaper, unlike other mass media, delivers its message point-to-point on a mass scale. Its characteristic of personal access, together with its customizability, enable it to deliver specialized information and customized news to fit individual needs.

Sixth, the electronic newspaper allows multi-media presentation of its information. The combination of words, sounds and images makes its transmission more lively and attractive. Seventh, with back-issues stored on-line, readers can have easy access to archived stories and information. News is not just a piece of perishable information as before but is accessible as easy reference material. Finally, for the electronic newspaper, reporters and editors can update news and information at any time they want without being confined by the once-a-day format. Therefore, readers can get the latest news as soon as possible. Live reporting on-line is also technologically possible.

FROM FORMAT CHANGE TO BOUNDARY CHANGE

From the above analysis, we find that newspaper format has undergone revolutionary changes as it moves from print to an electronic version. The format difference is manifested in the ways they organize their content and transmit information. The traditional newspaper rigidly classifies its content, organizes it in a hierarchical way and delivers it in a top-down and one-way communication mode. We use the term "closed media mode" to describe this rigid and asymmetrical communication format. In contrast, the electronic newspaper uses media links to cut across topic categories and is interactive and flexible in information delivery. We call this kind of media format "open media code." The result of the change from closed media

Table 5.3
Implications of Boundary Blurring Brought by the Electronic Newspaper

Boundary Blurring	Implications
A. Organization of Content:	
1. Front page/Inside pages	• Decline of agenda-setting • Decline of common body of knowledge
2. Important page/Ordinary page	• Decline of agenda-setting • Change of journalistic practice
3. Leading stories/Non-leading stories	• Decline of agenda-setting • Change of journalistic practice
4. News/Data	• Higher degree of information freedom for readers
B. Mode of Transmission:	
1. Sender/Receiver	• Decline of agenda-setting • Changing pattern of information seeking • Changing mode of knowing (Understand an issue from multiple dimensions, not just fact-finding)
2. Event/Context	• Change of journalistic practice • Change of mode of knowing
3. Local/Global	• Reconfiguration of cultural identity • Decline of political control • Development of global journalism • Development of global information seeking
4. Physical space/Virtual space	• Change of journalistic practice
5. Mass communication/Personal Communication	• Network communication
6. Print/Broadcast	• Media convergence
7. Present/Past	• Changing mode of knowing
8. Time/Space	• Decline of gatekeeping

code to open media code is a series of boundary dissolution that can have significant social implications (see Table 5.3). With regard to content, the electronic newspaper blurs the boundaries between front page and inside page, important page and unimportant page, leading stories and non-leading stories (Ma, 1998). It also blurs the distinction between news and data. The traditional newspaper divides its content into well-defined territorial units (sections and pages). Each territory has its distinct identity. For example, the writing style of news stories differs from that of features. The design of the entertainment page is also in great contrast with that of the forum page. Some territories enjoy higher status (e.g., news page) and get better placement, while some have lower status (e.g., feature page) and are placed in less visible sections. Accordingly, the news desk becomes more important and resourceful than the feature desk. Territorial boundaries thus signify power relationship. Besides, since pages and stories are arranged in hierarchical order, the media organization indirectly tells its readers which pages are worth reading first and which stories are more important. The agenda-setting function is clear and sharp.

For the electronic newspaper, media links dissolve page boundaries and weaken territorial identities. For example, when a story about a knee injury by U.S. President Bill Clinton first appeared in the general news page, it was then linked to a relevant story in the medical page and another story in the political page. Therefore, the territorial boundary among pages is weakened. Without placement and page design, the electronic newspaper has to organize its content in a flat pattern and so the hierarchical relationships among pages and among stories are less salient. There is little indication that some pages are more important than others. For some electronic newspapers, within news pages there are still some distinctions between leading and non-leading stories, but they are far less obvious when compared with those of traditional newspapers. That means the electronic newspaper does not tell its readers which page is more important, as it does not present the stories in a strictly hierarchical order. The readers can make their own choices, as the agenda-setting function of the press is reduced.

These boundary changes have two implications. The first is the weakening of the agenda-setting function, as journalists do not instruct readers what to read and how to read. Second, the weakened distinction between pages will affect the division of labor in news organizations. For example, reporters in an electronic newspaper are not only responsible for reporting, as they may also have to conduct research and assemble information from various databanks. The changing journalistic practices will lead to changes in the role of journalism. We shall elaborate this point in a later section.

In the electronic newspaper, news stories are sometimes linked to relevant background information or data banks. The distinction between news and data is blurred as some scholars even suggest that the new definition of news in the electronic newspaper is "data." In the past, news was a piece of information well processed by journalists who articulate stories with special angles, while readers had no access to original statistics and data. In some sense, journalists played a role of tight information control. But in the electronic newspaper, journalists may provide links that connect a story to some relevant raw data or reference materials. Readers can have access to information that is less processed and thus they enjoy higher degree of information freedom. Since readers may study an issue through self-exploration, they can free themselves from the constraint of understanding the issue from a particular angle set by journalists.

With regard to mode of transmission, the interactivity of the electronic newspaper blurs the boundary between sender and receiver. News organizations which provide customized news to their on-line readers are no longer powerful gatekeepers, as they are less capable of setting the news agenda anymore. Electronic newspaper readers select what they like to read and they are in control of the sequence, pace and amount of information transmission. They are crossing the "border" into the territory of the communicator. Making use of the search, browse and hyperlink functions, readers are engaging in a new information-seeking pattern that privileges their critical autonomy. The power shift in the communication process from editors to readers redefines the social relationship between news organizations and their readers. As readers are surfing in cyberspace, they have the tendency to scan through a number of electronic newspapers rather than being logged into a particular one. Since they surf and shop around for information, their loyalty toward certain newspapers naturally decreases. Reader identity is no longer as distinct as in the past.

Borrowing from Bernstein's (1990) pedagogic analysis, interactivity brings along three aspects of change. The first is from explicit hierarchical rules in which the relations of authority are clear and the power relationship between transmitter and receiver is explicitly defined (Sadovnik, 1995), to implicit hierarchical rules in which the power relationship is "masked or hidden by devices of communication" (Bernstein, 1990, p. 67). This also applies in the case of the electronic newspaper, as the top-down power relationship between journalists and readers has been changed. Journalists' authority will continue to decline as they will neither be able to monopolize the information channels nor to directly instruct readers what and how to consume the news. The second aspect of change is from (journalists') strong to weak manipulation of the transmission sequencing and pacing since the two-way communication function enables readers to decide what to read first and at what pace. The third aspect of change is from a single and explicit criterion to multiple and implicit criteria. With a single explicit criterion, the rules of legitimate expectations are made clearly available to the receiver by the transmitter. But when criteria are implicit, the receiver has more freedom to create his/her individualized criteria for evaluation, and the rules are then more numerous and diffuse (Sadovnik, 1995). For the traditional newspaper, front-page news and headline news is explicitly presented so that what readers are expected to know is clear. For the electronic newspaper, news is presented in a diffused and less hierarchical way. As a result, editors take the role of a facilitator rather than a transmitter.

The non-linear story-telling format of electronic news breaks the norm of reporting an issue as merely a current event. With media links, a news issue can be comprehended through a sequence of news stories. The issue at hand may be reported together with ample background materials and is embedded in a contextual information cluster. Traditional news stories are usually seen as too simple and out of context. The electronic newspaper's non-linear story-telling format can contribute to more comprehensive reporting. Besides, electronic newspaper readers with their computer mouses in hand can decide how many archived stories they will retrieve, how many links they will visit and how much they want to know about the issue. Their goal of information seeking is no longer restricted to fact-finding but understanding an issue from multiple dimensions.

Electronic newspapers are distributed on the Internet and their distribution format breaks the boundary between the local and the global. Electronic newspapers reach their global readers by crossing national, ethnic and cultural boundaries. The electronic newspaper is not confined to local readership, as in many cases over half of the readers come from overseas. So the content of this new medium is gradually moving from a local to a more global perspective. For on-line readers, their scope of information seeking is also extended from local to global. They are no long satisfied with localized information as they can gather information worldwide.

The electronic newspaper has no space limit and thus can break the physical boundary of the printed paper. The volume of an electronic newspaper can be virtually unlimited. The breaking of the physical space limit enables electronic newspapers to provide information in larger quantity and wider variety. News can be reported in a more comprehensive way and new sections can be introduced to meet the needs of specialized on-line readers.

Point-to-point distribution on a mass scale is one of the unique characteristics of the electronic newspaper that blurs the boundary between mass communication and personal communication. More than an efficient mass communication tool, electronic newspaper's advantages lie in its personal links with individual readers and the possibility of customized information service and network communication. According to Castells (1996, p. 471), our society is evolving to become a "network society" in which "the work process in increasingly individualized, labor is disaggregated in its performance, and reintegrated in its outcome through a multiplicity of interconnected tasks in different sites." Society as a whole is moving toward network forms of management and production while organizations need to be "reengineered" to cope with the new technological and competitive environment (Hammer & Champy, 1993). The network information service provided by electronic newspapers is expected to play an important role in people's work as well as their personal relationships.

Electronic newspapers can carry soundbites and video clips. This feature breaks the boundary between print and broadcast journalism, signifying the convergence of communication technology. The multimedia electronic newspaper is not replacing the traditional newspaper format but supplementing it with the function "which has the immediacy and liveness of broadcasting, while retaining the depth and space provided by print" (McNair, 1998, p. 138). In the past, print and broadcast journalism have been two distinct fields that employed different news packaging principles and produced very different outputs. Print journalists and broadcast journalists differed a great deal in mentalities as well as in skills. As the electronic newspaper dissolves the territorial boundary between print and broadcast journalism, it blurs the difference between print journalists and broadcast journalists as well. Journalists in the future may have to be able to handle information in many forms, including text, graphics, sounds and images. This new form of journalism will surely lead to changes in the workforce, job routines and relationships among news people.

With the storage and search functions of the electronic newspaper, readers can easily gain access to information from past issues. Breaking the boundary between the present and the past makes news no longer perishable on a daily basis. The updating ability of the electronic newspaper also overcomes the time-space barrier. The gap between the actual news event and the information delivered to the audience has become almost nonexistent. The disappearance of the time-space "lag" and the ascendancy of real-time news are exciting developments, but they also threaten the depth and quality of news (McNair, 1998). Real-time news privileges style over substance. Besides, reporters and editors actually have very little editorial control on what is delivered. This decline in the gatekeeping function leads to concern about the accuracy of news and related ethical issues.

FROM BOUNDARY CHANGE TO SOCIOCULTURAL CHANGE

The format of the electronic newspaper leads to various types of changes in physical boundaries (front page/inside page, important page/unimportant page, leading story/non-leading story and print/broadcast), spatial boundaries (physical space/virtual space and local/global), temporal boundaries (present/past and time/space), social boundaries (sender/receiver) and conceptual boundaries (event/context, mass communication/personal communication and news/data). These boundary changes also may trigger changes in human relationships and social practices at the individual, organizational, social and cultural levels. Due to space limitations, here we concentrate on the change in information seeking behavior and the change in the role of journalism.

As postindustrial information society is "increasingly structured around a bipolar opposition between the Net and the Self" (Castells, 1996, p. 3), many people will turn to the Net for information. Electronic newspapers and other on-line news services will become major information sources in the new millennium. The new medium format of the electronic newspaper, identified here as the "open media code," fosters a completely new pattern of information seeking. As Jon Katz (McNair, 1998, p. 142) put its, "No other medium has ever given individual people such an engaged role in the movement of information and opinion or such a proprietary interest in the medium itself."

This new pattern of information seeking has several characteristics. First, it is active in the sense that readers search for information instead of being fed. Second, readers have greater power in selection as they are in control of "what" to read. Third, in a two-way communication mode, the new medium's characteristics of interactivity, connectivity and search functions enable readers to decide "how" to read. They are in command of the sequence and pace of the information flow. Fourth, information seeking can become multidimensional since electronic newspaper readers are able to understand an issue from more perspectives instead of just knowing specific facts. Fifth, it is global-oriented. Readers can have easier access to things happening both locally and globally. The new medium of the electronic newspaper cuts across national boundaries and further fosters this kind of global mind-set. Sixth, the new pattern emphasizes on seeking information that is relevant to everyday life. "Worthwhile knowledge" certified by authorities is becoming an outdated concept originating in the industrial era. The usefulness of news and information very much depends on the acquirer's own needs and wants.

In the "network society" characterized by increasing individualization, diversification of working relationships, social fragmentation and globalization (Castells, 1996), new economic development puts emphasis on personalized devices, interactivity and networking. Stehr (1994) coins the postindustrial information society as "knowledge society" to highlight the importance of the role knowledge plays in the new social structure. In this knowledge society, everyone becomes an individual "expert" and knowledgeable citizen to survive in the highly competitive environment that treasures ideas and innovations. In order to succeed in the new society, Mak (1998) advocates the enhancement of "infoledge" (the combination of information and knowledge) while Hasegawa (1997) calls for the build-up of one's "information power." That means in the new society, people are self-motivated to actively acquire information and knowledge. The individualized pattern of labor force requirement apparently privileges relevant knowledge instead of authorized knowledge. The new information seeking behavior and the social requirement of the postindustrial society are somehow interlocked.

On-line readers are surfing the Net. With media hyperlinks, they are trekking from screen page to screen page and from the present to the past. As news stories are contextualized in an information network, readers are travelling across the borders between newspapers, between sections and between current/back issues to locate what they need and what they like. This kind of self-regulated information seeking behavior clearly represents a new pattern of knowledge inquiry in the information age. As readers move from reading one or two traditional newspapers to surfing among a number of electronic newspapers, the knowledge they get proceeds from "deep knowledge" to "surface knowledge" and from local information to global information. As industrial society requires a submissive and inflexible person, the twenty-first century demands a conforming but flexible person (Bernstein, 1971). People's knowledge base in postindustrial society needs to be multi-dimensional and rich in variety, stressing analogy and synthesis. The electronic newspaper, in fact, fits in well with this postindustrial landscape.

While readers are in a better position to make their own judgment and are less manipulated by a news organization's ideological perspective, individually they may risk losing touch with one another. Since individual readers only look for news that is relevant and interesting to themselves, collectively they may lose sight of something which is important to the whole community. No common news agenda may lead to fragmented concerns and lack of consensus among members of the society. This could undermine the basis for a civil society and an informed democratic system. Besides, the format of the electronic newspaper demands its readers to be computer literate, to have a strong desire for information and convenient access to the Net. This inevitably raises the concern about the widening gap between the information rich and the information poor (Donohue, Tichenor & Olien, 1975).

The boundary changes brought by the electronic newspaper could foster a new pattern of information seeking and may also alter the top-down relationship between journalists and their readers. Newhagen and Levy (1998, p. 9) propose that the innate structure of communication technologies "reflect the societal power relationships they embody" and the change in format architecture naturally upsets the existing power equilibrium. Old social systems always need to struggle to maintain their integrity within the structural context defined by new technology. We come to the same conclusion that journalism is at this juncture when it moves to the computer-based technological environment. Newhagen and Levy (1998) describe the architecture of traditional journalism as "an hour-glass shape," which means "large amounts of information flow in linear fashion from among sources through a narrow, journalistic 'neck' and on to a mass of readers or viewers" and "the ability to control this linear flow rests almost exclusively with the journalist" (Newhagen & Levy, 1998, p. 9). As we have pointed out, editors in the traditional newspaper set the news agenda by hierarchically organizing their news content with the assistance of placement and page design. Through the distinction between different pages and stories, they have been successful in telling the readers what to think *about*

(McCombs & Shaw, 1972). However, the computer-mediated technology greatly challenges their established authority. With the interactivity and media link devices, the electronic newspaper has conceded large parts of their news selection and "meaning creation" power to the readers. As a result, we predict that with the increasing popularity of digital news, journalists' existing high status may gradually be eroding.

Print newspaper sets news agendas not only through placement of stories but also through the amount of coverage and emphasis on some stories as illustrated by headline, photo, background and analysis. Thus, the electronic newspaper is still able to set the agenda through the non-linear structure, such as links, background information and databases. However, there is a difference between "manifest" and "latent" agenda-setting. For the traditional newspaper, the strong manifest agenda-setting function is achieved through eye-catching placement and one-step retrieval page design delivered to the readers directly. For the electronic newspaper, the more latent type of agenda-setting is operated through less eye-catching placement and multi-step links. The readers are less directly affected by the format and so the agenda-setting effect is weaker.

Traditional journalism is basically a product of industrial society and it is operated within the mass media system. In the coming postindustrial society, future journalism (which may be called "i-journalism," signifying a totally new mode of on-line journalism with interactivity as its major characteristic) will be operated in a more individualized media system and advanced technological environment. The role of the news industry shall undergo revolutionary changes as the society evolves. First, in the past the print newspaper was a strong agenda-setter and it was presented like an "information supermarket" to be consumed by individual readers in a "buffet style." In contrast, the role of the electronic newspaper is moving to become more of an information broker. The supermarket display of information and buffet style of consumption will likely stay, but the electronic newspaper is more capable of providing customized individual services which are automatic and pre-ordered. Second, with the features of interactivity and immediacy, the on-line newspaper is able to operate multiple opinion forums to be participated spontaneously by readers from all over the world. Its role of acting as opinion facilitator is larger while its role of a traditional opinion leader may shrink. Third, the format of the Web also facilitates the growth of electronic commerce conducted through the electronic newspapers' Web sites. So and Lee's (1999) study indicates that many electronic newspapers have already set up their own marketplace sections. They are evolving from mere advertising carriers to cyber traders.

While journalism is searching for a new role to play, the news industry also needs to go through changes to accommodate the new environment which will affect the authority of editors, the power of reporters, the status of technicians and the role of advertising staff. Their changing job relationships and professional roles will be another worthwhile topic of study in the digital age.

With the advances of communication technology and shifts in various boundaries, how do we cope with the resulting sociocultural changes? We suggest that in the information age individuals should be well-equipped with media literacy and computer literacy skills. With the diminishing role of journalists as gatekeepers, part of the burden of information verification is shifted to the readers, who are accustomed to the interactive format of the electronic newspaper. As Newhagen and Levy (1998, p. 17) worry, "the interactive information searches will call on the users to employ a set of highly effortful cognitive skills they may not now possess." The electronic newspaper benefits its readers by providing abundant information, but readers in the digital age are in danger of being overwhelmed by too much information. Information overload makes them lose their ability to sort, make sense of and evaluate information (McNair, 1998). Therefore, as digital news will certainly become more prevalent in the new millennium, media literacy training should be imperative. Media users have to master efficient, logical and purposeful searching skills as well as to be able to understand, analyze, use and influence the new media (Lee, 1999). Only can a media literate population be truly benefited from the new medium of interactivity.

Lessons from history indicate that technology is an intruding social force that is responsible for many major changes in social structure. The info-media revolution (Koelsch, 1995) in the 1990s gave birth to interactive new media and again they are dissolving social boundaries and bringing significant social changes. Different media embody different formats that are regulated by particular code systems. Studying the electronic newspaper from a structuralist approach, we attempt to link micro analysis of media format (open media code) to macro analysis of the transformation of social practices (boundary changes). The purpose is to examine how a new form of medium (the electronic newspaper) classifies, organizes, transmits and reproduces public knowledge (news and information) and to inquire about its social consequences. The content of the new medium does matter but the influence of the new media format may even be more profound.

This chapter theorizes that the change in format will lead to the blurring of many boundaries and thus it has important social implications. However, studies (e.g., Levy & Massey, 1999) done recently discover that electronic newspapers only have very limited impact on professional journalists and readers. The discrepancy may partly be explained by the time frame involved. This chapter discusses the format effect in a longer term, but empirical studies usually focus on the present. Another reason is related to the evolutionary stages of the electronic newspaper. So and Lee's (1999) study of English and Chinese on-line newspapers indicates that some major newspapers in the United States have already developed highly sophisticated on-line editions that clearly show changes in journalistic practices and reader relationships. However, most Chinese electronic newspapers in Asia are still in the early stage of development, as their electronic editions are only copies of their print counterparts. Future studies may benefit from identifying and comparing the electronic newspaper's various stages of development, and see how different social, political, economic and cultural factors affect its locus of development.

REFERENCES

Altheide, D. L., & Snow, R. P. (1979). *Media logic.* Beverly Hills, CA: Sage Publications.

Altheide, D. L., & Snow, R. P. (1991). *Media worlds in the postjournalism era.* New York: Aldine de Gruyter.

Atkinson, P. (1985). *Language, structure and reproduction: An introduction to the sociology of Basil Bernstein.* London: Methuen.

Bernstein, B. (1971). *Class, codes and control: Vol. 1. Theoretical studies towards a sociology of language.* London: Routledge & Kegan Paul.

Bernstein, B. (1990). *Class, codes and control: Vol. 4. The structuring of pedagogic discourse.* London: Routledge.

Boorstin, D. J. (1978). *The republic of technology: Reflections on our future community.* New York: Harper & Row.

Carlisle, S. (1996). Boundaries in France. In D. Pellow (Ed.), *Setting boundaries* (pp. 37–54). Westport, CT: Bergin & Garvey.

Castells, M. (1996). *The rise of the network society.* Oxford: Blackwell.

Chaytor, H. J. (1966). *From script to print: An introduction to medieval vernacular literature.* London: Sidgwick & Jackson.

Donohue, G. A., Tichenor, P. E. & Olien, C. N. (1975). Mass media and the knowledge gap: A hypothesis reconsidered. *Communication Research, 2,* 3–23.

Eisenstein, E. L. (1979). *The printing press as an agent of change: Communications and cultural transformations in early modern Europe.* New York: Cambridge University Press.

Ericson, R. V., Baranek, P. M. & Chan, J. B. L. (1991). *Representing order: Crime, law, and justice in the news media.* Milton Keynes: Open University Press.

Gradus, Y., & Lithwick, H. (Eds.) (1996). *Frontiers in regional development.* Lanham, MD: Rowman & Littlefield.

Hall, E. T. (1996). Foreword. In D. Pellow (Ed.), *Setting boundaries* (pp. vii–viii). Westport, CT: Bergin & Garvey.

Hammer, M. (1996). *Beyond reengineering: How the process-centered organization is changing our work and our lives.* New York: HarperBusiness.

Hammer, M., & Champy, J. (1993). *Reengineering the corporation: A manifesto for business revolution.* New York: HarperBusiness.

Hasegawa, K. (1997). *Information power.* Tokyo: Sunmark Publishing.

Havelock, E. A. (1963). *Preface to Plato.* Cambridge, MA: Harvard University Press.

Holdich, T. H. (1916). *Political frontiers and boundary making*. London: Macmillan.

Hut, P. (1996). Structuring reality: The role of limits. In J. L. Casti & A. Karlqvist (Eds.), *Boundaries and barriers: On the limits to scientific knowledge* (pp. 148–187). Reading, MA: Addison-Wesley.

Innis, H. A. (1951). *The bias of communication*. Toronto: University of Toronto Press.

Koelsch, F. (1995). *The infomedia revolution: How it is changing our world and our life*. Toronto: McGraw-Hill Ryerson.

Lawrence, D. (1996). Tourism and the emergence of design self-consciousness in a rural Portuguese town. In D. Pellow (Ed.), *Setting boundaries* (pp. 71–90). Westport, CT: Bergin & Garvey.

Lee, A.Y.L. (1999). Infomedia literacy: An educational basic for the young people in the new information age. *Information, Communication & Society, 2,* 134–155.

Levinson, P. (1999). *Digital McLuhan: A guide to the information millennium*. London: Routledge.

Levy, M., & Massey, B. (1999, June). Asian online newspapers and the challenge to professional, personal and political boundaries. Paper presented at the conference "In Search of Boundaries: Communication, Nation-States and Cultural Identities," Department of Journalism and Communication, The Chinese University of Hong Kong, Hong Kong.

Ma, K. F. (1998, December 2). Go digital: Ideals journalism rookies should have. *Hong Kong Economic Journal, 25* (in Chinese).

Mak, S. (1998). *Infoledge: A reader's guide to reading*. Dou Liou, Taiwan: Ban Tau Cultural Publishing Company (in Chinese).

McCombs, M. E., & Shaw, D. L. (1972). The agenda-setting function of mass media. *Public Opinion Quarterly, 36,* 177–187.

McLuhan, M. (1964). *Understanding media: The extensions of man* (2nd ed.). New York: New American Library.

McNair, B. (1998). *The sociology of journalism*. London: Arnold.

Meyrowitz, J. (1985). *No sense of place: The impact of electronic media on social behavior*. New York: Oxford University Press.

Morley, D., & Robins, K. (1995). *Spaces of identity: Global media, electronic landscapes and cultural boundaries*. London: Routledge.

Newhagen, J. E., & Levy, M. R. (1998). The future of journalism in a distributed communication architecture. In D. L. Bordon & K. Harvey (Eds.), *The electronic grapevine: Rumor, reputation, and reporting in the new on-line environment* (pp. 9–21). Mahwah, NJ: Lawrence Erlbaum Associates.

Ong, W. J. (1967). *The presence of the word: Some prolegomena for cultural and religious history*. New Haven, CT: Yale University Press.

Ong, W. J. (1971). *Rhetoric, romance, and technology: Studies in the interaction of expression and culture*. Ithaca, NY: Cornell University Press.

Ong, W. J. (1982). *Orality and literacy: The technologizing of the word*. New York: Methuen.

Pellow, D. (1996). Introduction. In D. Pellow (Ed.), *Setting boundaries* (pp. 1–8). Westport, CT: Bergin & Garvey.

Postman, N. (1985). *Amusing ourselves to death*. New York: Viking.

Postman, N. (1992). *Technopoly: The surrender of our culture to technology*. New York: Knopf.

Prescott, J.R.V. (1987). *Political frontiers and boundaries*. London: Allen & Unwin.

Rotenberg, R. (1996). Tearing down the fences: Public gardens and municipal power in nineteenth-century Vienna. In D. Pellow (Ed.), *Setting boundaries* (pp. 55–70). Westport, CT: Bergin & Garvey.

Sack, R. D. (1986). *Human territoriality: Its theory and history*. Cambridge: Cambridge University Press.

Sadovnik, A. R. (1995). *Knowledge and pedagogy: The sociology of Basil Bernstein*. Norwood, NJ: Ablex.

Schwarz, T. (1974). *The responsive chord*. Garden City, NY: Anchor.

So, C.Y.K., & Lee, A.Y.L. (1999, August). Using "open media code" to evaluate online newspapers: A study of English and Chinese e-papers. Paper presented at the 52nd Annual Convention of the Association for Education in Journalism and Mass Communication, New Orleans, LA.

Stehr, N. (1994). *Knowledge societies*. London: Sage Publications.

Swannel, J. (1989). *The little Oxford dictionary*. Oxford: Clarendon Press.

Tremayne, M. (1999, May). Use of nonlinear storytelling on news web sites. Paper presented at the 49th annual Conference of the International Communication Association, San Francisco, CA.

Chapter 6

Asian On-line Newspapers and the Challenge to Professional, Personal and Political Boundaries

Mark R. Levy and Brian L. Massey

> In the last quarter of this fading century, a technological revolution, centered around information, has transformed the way we think, we produce, we consume, we trade, we manage, we communicate, we live, we die, we make war, and we make love.
>
> —M. Castells, 1998, p. 1

There is no doubt, as Castells so aptly observes, that we are living in an era of potentially radical change. Ironically, no aspect of this revolutionary potential has received greater public attention and less scholarly investigation than the information environment itself. This chapter attempts to redress that scholarly neglect by suggesting a set of benchmarks against which current and future developments in one highly visible media form— the on-line newspaper—can be charted.

Web newspapers, we believe, are a particularly fruitful research site because they exemplify the convergence of a well-established mass medium, the newspaper, with computer-based information networks.[1] At moments of convergence, old social systems and the information technologies that sustain power relationships within them often struggle against the emerging technologies to maintain the status quo (McLuhan, 1994).

Journalism, for instance, now finds itself at such an historic juncture as it attempts to understand the new challenges to its now-mature norms and canons that were established during the reign of mass circulation newspapers. The distributed architecture of the Internet is rapidly replacing the journalistic "gate" (Newhagen & Levy, 1998) that has kept content producers at the top of the information-flow hierarchy, separated from content

consumers at the bottom. How this change in the "shape" of communication challenges traditional boundaries of power and information control
between journalists and their audiences is one focus of this chapter. What
we will examine is, to put it simply, who controls what gets onto the newspaper's World Wide Web site.

The institution of journalism is, however, not the only societal actor with
an interest in a fuller understanding of convergent on-line communication.
Some writers (Massey & Levy, 1999; Morris & Ogan, 1996; Tucher, 1997)
contend that the chief benefit of on-line journalism lies in its capability for
interactivity, thus making individuals and social groups additional stakeholders in the new communication environment. More specifically, Web
newspapers can be characterized by the level of interpersonal interaction
they afford their audiences and by how interactively users of news Web
sites can engage content producers or other reader/users. Each of these
questions *au fond* is a matter of whether Web newspapers facilitate the
reformulation of boundaries between mass communicators and audiences
and/or the social connections within the mass media audience itself.

Finally, at least for purposes of this chapter, we wish to examine the
degree to which on-line newspapers provide news and information that
transcends national boundaries. Obviously, whenever a newspaper—be it
transmitted via electrons or on dead trees—publishes foreign news, it is
offering its reader/users information that, by definition, transcends national
boundaries. But how, if at all, is that act different when it is carried out
through an on-line newspaper? Indeed, what heuristic value might we find
in conceptualizing an individual on-line newspaper as the local edition of
the global village's daily press (Cohen, Levy, Roeh & Gurevitch, 1995).

Our exploration of Web newspapers will be guided by the following
three research questions:

RQ1: How, if at all, is on-line journalism affecting the traditional relationships of power and information control between journalists and their
audiences?

RQ2: To what extent is this new form of *mass* communication also facilitating increased *interpersonal* communication on-line and the creation
of new social boundaries, also in cyberspace?

RQ3: Are Web-based newspapers providing news and information that
reaches across national borders; are they bringing the world to their audiences or do they concentrate primarily on providing local news?

RESEARCHING THE WEB-BASED PRESS

As of June 1999, an estimated 27 million people in the Asia/Pacific region
had access to the Internet, accounting for approximately 15 percent of the
global total (NUA Internet Surveys, 1999). Asia watchers (Jansen, 1998)

Table 6.1
Asian English-Language On-line Newspapers

Bangladesh	*Daily Star; Independent*
Brunei	*Borneo Bulletin*
China and Hong Kong SAR	*China Daily; Hong Kong Standard; South China Morning Post*
India	*Deccan Chronicle; Deccan Herald; Hindu; Indian Express; Pioneer; Times of India*
Indonesia	*Indonesian Observer*
Japan	*Asahi Shimbun; Japan Times; Yomiuri Shimbun*
Malaysia	*Borneo Mail; New Straits Times; Sabah Daily Express; Sarawak Tribune; Star; Sun*
Nepal	*Kathmandu Post*
Pakistan	*Dawn; Frontier Post; Hindustan Times; Nation; News International*
Philippines	*Freeman; Independent Post; Manila Bulletin; Manila Times; Philippines Daily Inquirer; Philippines Star; Visayan Daily Star*
Singapore	*New Paper; Straits Times*
South Korea	*Chosun Ilbo; Joong Ang Daily News; Korean Herald; Korea Times*
Sri Lanka	*Daily News*
Thailand	*Bangkok Post; Nation*

have noted that the region's newspapers have experienced a dramatic growth in demand for their Web-based versions.

For our study, daily, general circulation English-language newspapers in Asia that publish companion Web editions were identified from the major Net search engines, as well as database compilations of on-line newspapers.[2] This effort yielded 50 Net "addresses," although 6 were later found to reach either non-working sites or ones that publish only news summaries in English. The final data set included 44 Web newspapers from 14 Asian countries (see Table 6.1).

English-language newspapers were selected first, because English is often used in Asia as a *lingua franca* among local elites and the expatriate community; and second, because newspapers that publish in this shared language thus often are among a nation's most influential (Merrill, 1991). Ideally, a more complete census of Asian Web newspapers would include those published in each of the languages indigenous to countries in the region; pragmatically, however, hiring and training all of local-language coders required by this strategy would be prohibitive in terms of cost.[3]

The unit of analysis was the entire newspaper Web site, beginning at the "front page." At about half of the 44 sites, the "front page" was accessible only through a "home page." Following Li's (1998) operationalizations, we defined "home page" as a newspaper's initial, or opening, screen on the Web. Home pages typically provide information about other stories in the same publication or about stories or files on computers located on remote networks. By contrast, the "front page" of an on-line newspaper can be accessed either through the home page or itself serve as the newspaper's initial Web screen, and is recognizable by its similarity in appearance to an ink-and-newsprint newspaper's front page. Each on-line newspaper site we identified was coded for the presence or absence of various types of content and features that tap into the technology of the Net and that are relevant to our research concerns.

The Power of Journalists and Audiences

The first research question—the potential of on-line newspapers for changing the relationship between journalists and their audiences—was examined through the following four indicators:

- Whether the Web site permitted its users to create a package of "customized" news, based on their own news and information preferences.
- Whether hypertext links were provided to allow readers to "jump" from one on-line story to either some form of on-site background content or to an external Web site.[4]
- A three-item index[5] that measured the ease by which readers could contribute, or upload, information and opinions to the on-line newspaper; specifically, letters to the editor,[6] postings to electronic bulletin boards and "votes" in reader polls on news topics of the day.
- A two-part indicator of journalistic responsiveness to audience members, which was split into an index of "potential for responsiveness," by which we meant the provision of one or more of six different possible e-mail links to journalists at the Web newspaper;[7] and a second measure of "actual responsiveness." To gauge the latter, the study's coders sent a standardized e-mail message to the newspapers, requesting minimal data about how the newspapers' sites functioned.[8] We then recorded whether a response was received and, if so, the elapsed time to its receipt.

Interpersonal Communication and Social Bonds

Research question no. 2, which asked whether on-line newspapers facilitate interpersonal communication and the formation of social bonds between users, was measured by coding for the presence on the newspaper's Web site of moderated or unmoderated chat rooms or bulletin boards/

newsgroups.[9] Chat rooms are generally understood to be "places" in cyberspace where people "converse" by entering text messages and where all users see those messages as a scrolling list. As Damer (1998, p. 485) put it, "Chat rooms don't look like rooms at all, but like a teletype machine running in a window in your computer."

In contrast, to the synchronicity of communication that is a characteristic of chat rooms, bulletin boards (BBS) are asynchronous discussion forums, more like the printed page (read anytime, respond anytime) than are chat rooms. Still, even in the short history of the Web, BBS have played and continue to play a significant role in the development of on-line communities (Baym, 1998; Rheingold, 1993).

Content That Transcends National Boundaries

To the third research question, the degree to which Web-based newspapers provide news and information that transcends national boundaries and enlarges the amount of "foreign" news available to reader/users was studied by coding on-line news content. News items were classified as international, regional, national, local, business, sports, or weather (either headlines or in a Web-page box). "International" stories were distinguished by the inclusion of a dateline and were defined as foreign news that did not occur in the same geopolitical region as the nation from which the Web newspaper being coded is published. Stories were coded "international" even if nationals of the newspaper's home country were involved in the news. "Regional" news was defined as news from and about neighboring (i.e., Asian) nations, and "local" news was defined as articles reporting on a given Web newspaper's home-base city.

Admittedly, some "sports" and "business" news could be considered "international" news as well, thus posing the potential for non-exclusive coding categories. Yet we defined "international" news to be that of the "hard" or "straight" news variety—reporting of political, social or military events, for example—and we considered sports and business reports to be specialized, or special-interest, topics. Furthermore, although there is no universally agreed upon categorizations scheme for news-story content, we nevertheless attempted to follow what appears to be a common practice (Cohen, Levy, Roeh & Gurevitch, 1995; Sreberny-Mohammadi, Nordenstreng, Stevenson & Ugboajah, 1982).

Data Quality

The first author of this chapter and 11 master's degree students in the School of Communication Studies, Nanyang Technological University, Singapore, coded the Web sites. Each site was accessed twice between March 23 and April 10, 1998, once on the initial visit and then a second time

24 hours later. This double-accessing method demonstrated the relative stability of Web-site appearance over time and helped to insure that our data were reliable (Li, 1998).

Some 11 percent of the Asian newspaper Web sites were visited independently by two coders during one coding session to gauge intercoder reliability. For each of the 37 variables requiring coder judgment, intercoder agreement ranged from 80 percent agreement, a widely accepted threshold (Lacy & Riffe, 1996), to perfect agreement, using Holsti's (1969) formula.

ASIAN ON-LINE NEWSPAPERS: A BENCHMARK

This section presents the empirical evidence that will inform our discussion of the current and future impact of on-line newspapers on professional, personal and political boundaries.

Journalistic Norms and Audience Control

Only three of the 44 English-language, Asian Web newspapers—Japan's *Asahi Shimbun*, the *Indonesian Observer* and Malaysia's *New Straits Times*—offered their users the necessary on-line software to create a "basket" of customized (i.e., user-selected) news. Similarly, only the *Asahi Shimbun* and the *South China Morning Post* of Hong Kong SAR allowed readers to "jump" by hypertext link from an on-line story to a relevant, external Web site. Seven of the Web newspapers—the *South China Morning Post*, India's *Deccan Chronicle*, the *Sun* of Malaysia, Pakistan's *Dawn*, the Philippines' *Freeman* and *Philippines Daily Inquirer* and Singapore's *Straits Times*—provided links to other, related news items in their on-line editions.

Sixteen of the newspapers (36.4 percent) did not allow consumers to create and add content to their Web sites. More than half provided one of the three features comprising the adding-information dimension, while five—India's *Indian Express*, Malaysia's *New Straits Times*, the *Korean Herald*, Pakistan's *Frontier Post* and the *New Paper* of Singapore—offered two of these features. The average score on this dimension was .25 (*s.d.* = .22), with the letter to the editor being the most frequently observed method of allowing consumers to upload content. It was present at 56.8 percent of sites.

The newspapers generally scored low on "Potential for Responsiveness" (mean = .33, *s.d.* = .20). All of the newspapers, except for the *Japan Times*, *Korea Times*, Malaysia's *Sarawak Tribune* and the *Nation* of Thailand, averaged no more than two of the six types of e-mail links coded for. Specifically, they provided a "feedback" link for the general delivery of reader e-mail to the newsroom, and almost half offered a link to "webmaster." The *South China Morning Post* and *Freeman* of the Philippines stood out, providing all of the six types of the e-mail links measured.

For "actual responsiveness," the coders' e-mail messages generated responses from only 18 percent of the on-line newspaper sites. Replies were received from the *China Daily* of the People's Republic of China, the *South China Morning Post*, India's *Deccan Herald*, Korea's *Chosun Ilbo* and *Korean Herald*, Pakistan's *Dawn* and the Philippines' *Manila Times* and *Philippines Star*. Of these eight replies, the average time-to-respond was more than two days (mean = 51.6 hours, *s.d.* = 47.1 hours), with *Manila Times* being the fastest at nine hours and *Chosun Ilbo* the slowest at seven days.

Creating an On-line Community

Net-based venues for synchronous, interpersonal communication were found in less than one-fifth of the Asian newspaper Web sites studied. The *South China Morning Post* was alone in offering its site as a conduit for both moderated and unmoderated real-time conversations between readers. Moderated chat rooms were provided by *Manila Times*, Pakistan's *Dawn* and the *Nation* of Thailand, while unmoderated chat rooms were present at the Philippines' *Freeman*, India's *Hindu* and the *News International* (Pakistan). Only five on-line newspapers—*Korean Herald*, *New Straits Times* of Malaysia, the Philippines' *Manila Bulletin* and *Independent Post* and Singapore's *New Paper*—had e-bulletin boards.

Transcending Geographic Boundaries

The 44 English-language Asian Web newspapers generally scored very high on the index of "news by substantive category" (mean = .81, *s.d.* = .12). Indeed, it is not surprising that all of the Web newspapers published some articles about local, regional, national and international events. Three-fourths of them offered coverage of business and three-fourths reported on sports. A meager 11 percent (namely, the *South China Morning Post*; Malaysia's *Borneo Mail*, *Star* and *Sun*; and Thailand's *Nation*) carried weather news. The *South China Morning Post* and Malaysia's *Sun* were alone in providing on-line all of the seven types of news content measured.

No precise accounting was undertaken of the amount and placement of these various types of news. However, it is our observation that, in keeping with widespread journalistic routines and norms of newsworthiness (Shoemaker & Reese, 1996), the "play" of on-line news items tended to mirror patterns of coverage typically found in the newsprint editions. Thus, local and regional news tended to receive the highest priority; international news generally was not given prominent display.

CHALLENGING COMMUNICATION BOUNDARIES

There is, we believe, little doubt that Castells (1998) is fundamentally correct. We are in the midst of a profound change in the communication environment and that change is certain to affect the underlying power relations of society that are embodied in those very communication technologies that are experiencing change. What is far less clear, as this study demonstrates, is just how fast this social transformation is occurring in the arena of Web newspapers. Indeed, it is worth remembering just how difficult it is to change social structures, norms and behaviors (Smelser, 1988). Social, political and economic change rarely comes easily, whether at the individual, institutional or societal level; and genuine revolution itself is a blessedly rare social phenomenon.

More specifically, in the case of Asian cyber-journalists and their audiences, we found little evidence that long-standing power relationships and the associated boundaries of information control between on-line journalists and their audiences are eroding or being renegotiated because of the Internet and on-line newspapers. Despite the enormous potential for such change, Asian on-line journalists, like their counterparts in the traditional media of Asia and the West, are generally behaving in a way that can only be interpreted as a reluctance to allow non-journalists to have a say in the provision or selection of news. Throughout modern media history, of course, journalists world-wide have claimed the "right" to determine what appears in the press, often justifying that claim by asserting that a poorly informed and essentially disinterested public needs and wants journalistic professionals to make difficult editorial judgments and then package the results for them (Bardoel, 1996; Fidler, 1997). However, this power- and boundary-maintaining behavior is antithetical to the "spirit" of the Internet (every person his or her own reporter and editor) and thus (temporarily) thwarts the Web's "prosumerist" potential (Khoo & Gopal, 1996) to empower the audience.

Further, our findings demonstrate another carryover from traditional Western journalistic norms: the reluctance of on-line journalists to interact with the mass audience directly and in timely ways. Journalists often show little interest in knowing their audiences, either as individuals or collectively (Gans, 1979). This attitude of disinterest and the accompanying distancing behavior is exemplified in the structure of most English-language, Asian newspaper Web sites, since few scored in potential or actual responsiveness to user/readers.[10]

Perhaps Asian Web journalists wish in part to avoid interacting with their audience because they share a misperception common to cyber-journalists in the United States (Newhagen, Cordes & Levy, 1995; Ross & Middleberg, 1999), namely, that providing on-line links and e-mail addresses will produce a deluge of undesired criticism from site-users. In sum, then, it seems reasonable to conclude that so far, the impact of Asian on-line news-papers on journalistic practice and professional power has been limited. Why this may be so is an area that deserves further study, and the quali-tative methodologies of ethnographic interviews and field observations would seem appropriate to that task.

Both of these conclusions raise interesting questions about the existence and success of a so-called Asian model of journalistic practice. For instance, Asian journalists, especially those in comparatively new nation-states, often espouse a professional rhetoric that stresses the obligation of the media to further national development (MacBride, 1980). Part of nation-building journalism involves, as Datta-Ray (1998, p. 29) notes, a "heightened awareness of the community" with which the newsworkers interact. One could therefore expect Asian Web newspapers to make greater use of the Net's technology to better interact with their communities, in part at least, in the name of nation-building. Generally speaking, they are not.

Moreover, as the MacBride Commission observed, a new world infor-mation order cannot come about until the news media redefine what they consider to be news, and to do so would require greater citizen involvement in the process of news creation. Here, too, our study suggests that while most journalists from the developing nations of Asia subscribe to a profes-sional norm of increased community involvement, few have reached out to the public via their on-line newspapers.

We do not, of course, mean to suggest that these two dimensions rep-resent the entire set of professional norms and behaviors of the Asian jour-nalist. We do wish to point out, however, that since the Asian Web newspapers by and large are not tapping into the Net's potential for reader/user involvement, this poses a challenge to those who seek to differentiate between a hypothetical model of "involved, community-aware" Asian jour-nalism and an equally hypothetical model of "detached, uninvolved" West-ern newswork.

Turning from content creators to their audiences, we found little support for the case that this new form of *mass* communication (Web newspapers) may be facilitating increased *interpersonal* communication on-line. Only a handful of the Web newspapers studied sought to facilitate discussion be-tween users by providing real-time chat rooms or electronic bulletin boards. We believe this is unfortunate. Although discussion of public issues and interests already takes place in many locations in cyberspace (Poster, 1997), the paucity of on-line interactions at newspaper Web sites seems to us to be a wasted opportunity, a historical moment in which it might just be possible to reinvigorate and reinvent the newspaper-reading, coffee-drinking public sphere.

Finally, with regard to whether Asia's on-line newspapers are presenting information that somehow reduces or even negates the geographic bound-aries of the nation-state, our data clearly show that, as a group, the English-language Web newspapers do publish some foreign news—and occasionally a great deal. Of course, foreign news is foreign news, whether it appears on newsprint or on a computer monitor. Thus, local user/readers are probably getting as much or as little foreign news as audience members who rely on the printed newspaper. Indeed, for most domestic users, foreign news is nothing more than repurposed copy, often shoveled on to the Web without any additional journalistic manipulation, except to cut the story down to fit the on-line template (layout). As such, most on-line news stories probably are of little consequence vis-à-vis national political boundaries.

There is, however, one potentially significant possibility that arises when news goes on-line. The news/information becomes accessible to virtually anyone, anywhere in the world, who has a computer and an Internet service provider. Based largely on anecdotal evidence, we believe that many readers of Asia's on-line press are persons living outside the nation in which the newspaper is printed, but who have family, ethnic or historical ties to that country. Thus, users outside of the home country may read "local" news in order to maintain social bonds and psychological ties. In short, by establishing a presence on the Internet, Asia's English-language newspapers are also reaching out, beyond the political and physical boundaries of the nation-state, to inform Diaspora communities.[11] And to the extent that on-line newspapers can be thought of as facilitators of social bonds across national boundaries, then Web-based newspapers must have some, as yet relatively unexplored, implications for the social, political and economic centrality of the nation-state.

NOTES

1. We acknowledge that Internet portal sites like Yahoo.com offer their users news content on-line too, and as such they perhaps could be defined as the truest form of Web newspaper. But they are not the focus of the present study. Instead, our interest lies in how traditional newsprint-and-ink newspapers are making the transition to the new communication medium represented by the Net.

2. The databases included *American Journalism Review*'s listing of Asia/Mideast newspapers (http://www.newslink.org/nonusa.html). Keywords used in search-engines included "Asia and news," "Asian and newspaper" and country names taken from profiles in the *Asian Communication Handbook* (Goonasekera & Holaday, 1998). The Southeast Asian nation of Brunei is not included in the *Handbook*'s profiles, yet it was included in the analysis because its English-language, general circulation daily, the *Borneo Bulletin*, is also published on-line.

3. A middle-ground strategy could be to tackle Asia by sub-region. That would require fewer local-language coders at any one time and thus likely would not represent an overly costly exercise. Future research on Asian Web newspapers should consider this strategy.

4. Embedding hypertext links into a Web-published story has been criticized (Noth, 1996) for giving readers a false sense of interactive control over content and

simultaneously defended as an undervalued technique for empowering users (Lasica, 1997).

5. In creating the indices "Ease of Adding Information" and "Potential for Responsiveness," scores on the dichotomous variables comprising them were summed and then reported as ratios, where the total site score was the numerator and the total number dichotomous variables in the index was used as the denominator. For example, if two of the three variables in the "Ease of Adding Information" dimension were observed at a newspaper's Web site, that newspaper received an index score of .67.

6. On-line letters to the editor were included in the ease-of-adding-information index, rather than in the "responsiveness to user" measure, because we believed that users generally do not consider on-line letters to be an e-mail link to the journalists. Letter writers do not expect a personal response from cyber-journalists, believing instead that their letter will be published (added to the on-line file) for all to read. For a cross-media and cross-cultural comparison, see Newhagen, Cordes & Levy, 1995.

7. The e-mail addresses were coded for: (1) "feedback" link, or the on-line newsroom's general-delivery e-mail address; (2) "chief newspaper editor," or the executive responsible for the on-line and traditional newsrooms; (3) "chief on-line editor," defined as the Web edition's journalist-manager; (4) editors of specific on-line sections; (5) on-line reporters; and (6) the site's "webmaster."

8. The same message was sent to each of the 44 Asian Web newspapers. Coders e-mailed it through a "feedback" link, or, if listed, to the site's chief on-line editor or webmaster. The message asked about criteria for selecting news for the on-line newspaper, the job title of the person(s) doing the choosing, and the total number of journalists and IT specialists assigned to the Web site.

9. We have used the presence of chat rooms and bulletin boards (BBS) on Web newspaper sites as indicators of site potential to stimulate interpersonal communication and social bonding, largely because that is what is currently there. We also realize that other features of the Internet (for example, e-mail, listservs and avatar-based virtual worlds) may play an equal or even greater role in the generation of cyber-communities.

10. It is also possible that these under-developed aspects of interactivity are caused in part by lack of money and personnel to create, manage and maintain more elaborately interactive on-line newspaper sites. Re-purposing news for on-line consumption can be "tedious and time consuming, taking up many hours of employees' days" (Martin, 1998).

11. In the course of our research, we found a handful of on-line newspapers that were published in the United States, but which carried mastheads suggesting that they came from Web sites in Asia. Some of these U.S.-based sites reprinted stories from Asian newspapers, while others were largely compilations of wire-service reports and commentary.

REFERENCES

Bardoel, J. (1996). Beyond journalism: a profession between information society and civil society. *European Journal of Communication*, 11(3), 283–302.

Baym, N. (1998). The emergence of on-line community. In S. Jones (Ed.), *Cybersociety 2.0: Revisiting computer-mediated communication and community* (pp. 35–68). Thousand Oaks, CA: Sage Publications.

Castells, M. (1998). *The information age: Economy, society, and culture: Vol. 3. End of millennium*. Oxford: Blackwell.

Cohen, A., Levy, M., Roeh, I. & Gurevitch, M. (1995). *Global newsrooms: Local audiences*. London: John Libbey & Co.

Damer, B. (1998). *Avatars! Exploring and building virtual worlds on the Internet*. Berkeley, CA: Peachpit Press.

Datta-Ray, S. (1998). Press freedom and professional standards in Asia. In A. Latif (Ed.), *Walking the tightrope: Press freedom and professional standards in Asia* (pp. 25–39). Singapore: Asian Media Information and Communication Centre.

Fidler, R. (1997). *Mediamorphosis: Understanding new media*. Thousand Oaks, CA: Pine Forge Press.

Gans, H. (1979). *Deciding what's news*. New York: Vintage Books.

Goonasekera, A., & Holaday, D. (Eds.). (1998). *Asian communication handbook*. Singapore: Asian Media, Information and Communication Centre.

Holsti, O. (1969). *Content analysis for the social sciences and humanities*. Reading, MA: Addison-Wesley.

Jansen, P. (1998, May). *New look for* Straits Times Interactive [On-line; no longer available].

Khoo, D., & Gopal, R. (1996, June). Implications of the Internet on print and electronic media. *Journal of Development Communication*, 7, 21–33.

Lacy, S., & Riffe, D. (1996). Sampling error and selecting intercoder reliability samples for nominal categories. *Journalism & Mass Communication Quarterly*, 73(4), 963–973.

Lasica, J. D. (1997, November). So you want to be an on-line journalist? *American Journalism Review* [On-line]. Available: http://www.newslink.org/ajrjd23.html.

Li, X. (1998). Web page design and graphic use of three U.S. newspapers. *Journalism & Mass Communication Quarterly*, 75(2), 353–365.

MacBride, S. (1980). *Many voices, one world*. Paris: UNESCO.

Martin, S. (1998, Spring). How news gets from paper to its on-line counterpart. *Newspaper Research Journal*, 19, 64–73.

Massey, B. L., & Levy, M. R. (1999, Spring). Interactivity, on-line journalism and English-language web newspapers in Asia. *Journalism & Mass Communication Quarterly*, 76, 138–151.

McLuhan, M. (1994). *Understanding media: The extensions of man*. Cambridge, MA: The MIT Press. (Original work published 1964).

Merrill, J. (1991). *Global journalism: Survey of international communication* (2nd ed.). New York: Longman.

Morris, M., & Ogan, C. (1996). The Internet as mass medium. *Journal of Communication*, 46(1), 39–50.

Newhagen, J., Cordes, J. & Levy, M. (1995). Nightly@nbc.com: Audience scope and the perception of interactivity in viewer mail on the Internet. *Journal of Communication*, 45(3), 164–175.

Newhagen, J., & Levy, M. (1998). The future of journalism in a distributed communication architecture. In D. L. Borden & K. Harvey (Eds.), *The electronic grapevine: Rumor, reputation and reporting in the new on-line environment* (pp. 9–21). Mahwah, NJ: Lawrence Erlbaum Associates.

Noth, D. P. (1996, February). Interactive or hyperactive? Newspapers and other sites abuse the term [On-line]. Available: http://206.216.217.100:80/dom/colinter.html.

NUA Internet Surveys. (1999, June). How many on-line? [On-line]. Available: http://www.nua.ie/surveys/how_many_on-line/index.html.

Poster, M. (1997). Cyberdemocracy: The internet and the public sphere. In D. Holmes (Ed.), *Virtual politics: Identity and community in cyberspace* (pp. 184–211). London: Sage Publications.

Rheingold, H. (1993). *Virtual communities*. Reading, MA: Addison-Wesley.

Ross, S., & Middleberg, D. (1999). Media in cyberspace study [On-line]. Available: http://www.mediasource.com/cyber-study/intro.htm.

Shoemaker, P., & Reese, S. (1996). *Mediating the message: Theories of influences on mass media content* (2nd ed.). White Plains, NY: Longman.

Smelser, N. (1988). Social structure. In N. Smelser (Ed.), *Handbook of sociology* (pp. 103–130). Newbury Park, CA: Sage Publications.

Sreberny-Mohammadi, A., Nordenstreng, K., Stevenson, R. & Ugboajah, F. (1982). *Foreign news in the media: International reporting in twenty-nine countries*. Paris: UNESCO.

Tucher, A. (1997, July/August). Why web warriors might worry. *Columbia Journalism Review* [On-line]. Available: http://www.cjr.org/html/97-07-08-warriors.html.

Part III

Reasserting of Boundaries

Chapter 7

Global Challenges and National Answers in the Information Age

Frank Webster

INTRODUCTION

It is now commonplace for commentators to state—as a matter of plain fact—that today we inhabit an "information society." Grander still, Manuel Castells (1996–1998) has titled his massive and influential trilogy the "Information Age." While it is easy to appreciate that, at least in very general terms, these concepts capture something of the reality of the contemporary situation, it also must be admitted that it is extremely difficult to say, with any precision of definition, just what is meant by an "information society." For instance, is it an economic phenomenon (where the monetary worth of information is telling)? Or is it a matter of changed occupations (where increased numbers of people are employed in informational jobs such as teaching and research)? Or is it, more straightforwardly, distinguished by the prevalence of information and communications technologies (and thus a matter of technology)? Is it more to do with spatial relations (such that the "flows" of information between "networks" of people and places are the critical variable)? Or is it a cultural issue (where what matters is the explosion of symbols and signs in television, fashion, design and so on)? Or is the "information society" something which is characterized by a shift away from "practical" toward "theory" (hence a society in which abstract models shape social destiny)?

Each of these conceptions has been forwarded by serious and thoughtful scholars—and each has, in turn, been contested by equally serious thinkers.

Of course, the pragmatist will insist that the "information society" is a composite of all of these elements. Perhaps it is hoped thereby to advance analysis rather than getting stuck in debates about definitions. Unfortunately, however, pragmatism does not help very much, since the question must then be put: If it is a composite, just how is the "information society" composed? Is it primarily economic, cultural or occupational? Or does technology stand as the most significant factor in its constitution? With such questions, we come face-to-face with the paradox: however confidently people may assert that we inhabit an "information society," we are in considerable confusion when it comes to defining the concept with any exactitude.

I have written extensively about this imprecision of definition elsewhere (Webster, 1995). I have done this not to score points in an academic game, but to challenge the ready presumption that this "information society" is something distinctively and self-evidently new in human history. If something cannot be accurately distinguished, then it is accordingly rather difficult to assert that it is novel. Asking skeptical questions about how commentators characterize the "information society" is also to stop in their tracks those who are overly enthusiastic in announcing the arrival of a new and radically different type of society.

Actually, it is my belief that the continuities in society today are at least as significant as are the novelties. There is a great deal more information in circulation nowadays, and this plays an unprecedented part in everyday affairs, but very familiar forces continue to tell even in the vastly expanded informational domain. The presence of these established phenomenon must raise doubts about the credibility of the argument that the "information age" is something markedly new. There is more information around, yet this information remains under the control of long-established forces. Here then are good reasons to doubt claims that we are entering a new era. More information in itself surely does not make for an "information society." Accordingly, such skeptical reasoning may well lead people to resist endorsing the argument that we live now in an "information age," and—more serious still—to doubt its corollary, that adaption to this novel situation is a necessity.

In this chapter I want to put issues of definition to the side, so that I may focus on more compelling matters. I say "to the side" only because discerning readers will be able to see that, even in the more substantive discussion that follows, definitional issues are, in fact, constantly in play. My major concern in the next few pages is to ask: What is happening in the world today, particularly with regard to the more advanced and affluent societies of Europe, North America and the Far East? What are the major contours of development and what options and constraints do these trends present? As I address these questions, it will be seen that information is indeed central to what is taking place, though it is my argument that talk of an "information society" does little if anything to illuminate what is actually going on.

GLOBALIZATION

High on any list of pertinent developments must be the phenomenon of globalization and its associated traits. Globalization refers to the increased—and accelerating—processes of interpenetration and interdependency of relations on a world scale, relationships in which time and space are "compressed." Relationships—industrial, financial, intellectual—are conducted across and draw on a global stage, and every one of us is influenced by these trends, whether it is in terms of the foods we eat in our homes, the ways in which we work, or the media we see and hear. Of course, this is a tendential and complex process, and there is plenty of life which remains intensely local, but there can be little argument about the realities of globalization. Its roots lie in the distant past, traceable at least to the sixteenth century and the beginnings of colonial exploration, when the spatial divisions of the world began to be overcome. The temporal barriers were later in being lowered, but today we do indeed have "real-time" activities operating around the world, making it possible to conduct affairs across distance more or less immediately.

Globalization ought not to be seen as a straightforwardly homogenizing force. One argument has it that American corporations especially have foisted upon the world their ways of conduct and their ways of seeing, leading to an "Americanization" of life across the globe. This is the familiar theme of Coca-Colonization. Against this, other commentators observe that globalization is much more complicated than a one-way flow. They suggest that it brings hybridization of cultures, a result of mixtures of cultures and massive movements of peoples, something evident in the wide range of cuisines available in any sizable city around the world, in ethnic fashions combined with indigenous styles found just about everywhere, in the remarkable popularity, say, of reggae music across the globe.

It would be shortsighted to ignore this pluralism that has accompanied globalization. But it is equally naive to suggest that globalization does not reflect power differentials which do, in large part, impel considerable homogenization. Think, for example, of the financial networks that now traverse the globe, and one must concede that these fit in with, and express, the domination of Western organizations. Again, the globalization of manufacture has not led to significant hybridity—the lion's share goes to large-scale corporations that have their bases in Europe, North America and Japan. And, while it is true that music draws on many influences from many places, no one can deny that it is British and American practices which account for the most part of popular music at least.

What I am insisting on here is that globalization, while it is an extraordinarily complex phenomenon (Scott, 1997) does, for the most part, shape the world in ways that bring it into conformity with Western ways. In saying this, let me stress that I do not wish to suggest that bringing the world into line with Western ways has brought stability. On the contrary, another major feature of globalization is an intensification of competition, as once separate realms are brought into relation with others, and this impels deep uncertainty (Greider, 1997; Soros, 1998) and an acceleration of change itself as well as allowing many expressions of hybrid cultural forms (Lash & Urry, 1987). What I do want to emphasize here is that globalization expresses, above all else, the triumph of what one might call "business civilization." By this I want to underline that the world, however much variety we may witness in it, has been brought together under a common set of principles which have been historically most closely associated with the West (Robinson, 1996). These principles include:

1. Ability to pay is the major criterion determining provision of goods and services.
2. Provision is made on the basis of private rather than public supply.
3. Market criteria—that is, whether something makes a profit or loss—is the primary factor in deciding what, if anything, is made available.
4. Competition—as opposed to regulation—is regarded as the most appropriate mechanism for organizing economic affairs.
5. Commodification of activities—that is, relationships are regarded as being amenable to price valuations—is the norm.
6. Private ownership of property is favored over state holdings.
7. Wage labor is the chief mechanism for organizing work activities.

To be sure, these are idealizations of what happens in practice, but what seems to be unarguable is that these principles have spread around the globe at an accelerated pace in recent decades (de Benoist, 1996).

There are complex reasons why this should be so, and there remain to this day important pockets of resistance to their spread, but it appears to me that we have witnessed the massive intrusion of "business civilization" in recent years. This has been, it may be emphasized, both an intensive as well as an extensive affair. Intensive in so far as market practices have enormously intruded into areas of intimate life hitherto relatively immune even in the West. One thinks here, for instance, of child rearing (the plethora of diversionary toys and television for the young), of the provision of everyday foodstuffs (just about everyone nowadays is reliant on the supermarket for food, while not so long ago many families self-provided, at least in large part, through gardens and allotments which allowed vegetables to be grown and useful animals to be reared), and of the decline of self-providing activities such as dressmaking and knitting (cf. Seabrook, 1982).

Extensively, of course, we may instance the spread of globalization, a process which has colonized many areas that previously were self-supporting. The obvious, if underestimated, instance of this is the elimination of the peasantry from most quarters of the earth. This, by far the majority of the world's population throughout recorded time, is now on the eve of destruction (Worsley, 1984). And the reason is clear: The peasantry is antipathetic to market civilization. Peasants are largely self-supporting; they are skeptical of technological innovation, resistant to wage labor, and distanced from market organization. As such, their ways of life have been diminished by what Kevin Robins and Webster (1999) refer to as the "enclosure" of the earth by business practices, by which we mean the incorporation of activities once outside into the routines of the business realm.

Should there be some readers who perceive, on reading this, a nostalgia for times before the triumph of capitalism, let me stress a number of things. First of all, the penetration of market mechanisms does not, by any means, mean that there is hardship among consumers. On the contrary, for those with the wherewithal, reliance on the store for one's foods is preferable to the dreary round of home baking, and having to endure ill-fitting and unfashionable clothing. Moreover, compared with the lives of most peasants, even an impoverished existence inside capitalism offers an enviable standard of life (Figes, 1996). Second, the peasantry has been destroyed by various methods. Repression and dispossession certainly, but probably of more consequence has been the pull of the market society, offering change and opportunities that the peasant way of life could never match. Finally, no one should refer to the success of capitalism without acknowledging the failure of its major rival, communism. Politically discredited, communism also failed in economic matters, being incapable of matching the dynamism of the West. Together these are important qualifications to any account which might imply regret about the triumph of business civilization. Nonetheless, what must be accepted is that capitalism has won out, and its success has meant that the world has been enclosed within its orbit, within its ways of organization.

I would also emphasize that this success—of what has been called, appropriately, the "neo-liberal consensus," to underscore the ways in which this is the foundational principle of all governments around the world nowadays—represents no return to a former capitalist age. Not least, globalization has ensured that there is no going back to the days of *laissez-faire*. Much of business civilization is familiar, and would be recognized by nineteenth-century free traders, but it is undeniably now in new circumstances. Prominent among these is the presence of corporations with global reach which, if they are engaged in intense and rivalrous competition among themselves, exclude from the fringes of activity the small-scale entrepreneurs. Today's capitalism is one dominated by huge corporations—the likes of General Motors, Shell, Matsushita and Siemens—with breathtaking research and development budgets (often in excess of a billion dollars per annum), international leverage and worldwide marketing campaigns (Dicken, 1992). In addition, global capitalism today is linked in real-time by world financial markets—markets that trade in excess of a trillion dollars every day—the size and speed of which is unprecedented, and the consequences of which have been evident in massive upheavals of national economies such as Russia, Malaysia, Mexico and Spain in the 1990s. Again, today's capitalism is one that exercises global reach in many aspects of its operation, as witness the tendencies toward and practices of the world marketing of products, international divisions of labor and creation of global brands (Harvey, 1989).

Nevertheless, while I am at pains here to emphasize the novel features of the current era, it seems to me essential that we appreciate that these are consolidations and extensions of long-established principles. That is, today's global economy represents the spread and growth of capitalist ways of behavior—witness the increased use of market mechanisms, of private rather than public provision, of profitability as the *raison dêtre* of organizations, of wage labor and of the ability to pay principle as the determinant of goods and services supply. In short, the "global network society" in which we find ourselves today expresses the continuation—transmutation if one prefers—of long-held capitalist principles.

DECLINE OF NATIONAL SOVEREIGNTY

Of the many consequences of these trends, one I think stands out above all others. This is the fact of the relative decline of the economic sovereignty of nations. Bluntly, governments have relatively less capacity to control the national economy than they formerly did. This is not to say that governments are helpless when it comes to exercising influence over economic behavior within their own territories (cf. Held, McGrew, Goldblatt & Perraton, 1999). Governments still maintain considerable power over those economic activities which are restricted to their territories. However, in this age of 24-hour per day electronic financial flows, when world stock markets are constantly trading in foreign currencies to the tune of billions upon billions of dollars, then the nation-state must feel increased pressure to maintain the "confidence" of these markets. The evidence is plain for all to see: Where a country loses the confidence of the world financial markets, then its economic strength rapidly collapses, as witness the disinvestments from the Far East in 1998 and several nations before that. Further, the global capitalist economy, one in which global corporations are the major players, is astonishingly difficult to trace to any clearly identifiable national economy. What, for instance, constitutes the British economy? Do companies such as Nissan or Rover—significant employers within the country—represent the British economy because they have plants here, though they are owned by non-British parents and their stockholders come from around the world (and trading in these stocks is a ceaseless activity)? Much the same might be asked of Nokia: It seems quintessentially Finnish, and is certainly important in the employment of many Finns, yet its ownership comes predominantly from outside their home nation. Furthermore, many corporations that straddle the globe not only have a diverse ownership structure, they also are hard to identify straightforwardly as belonging to a particular nation because so much of their activity is undertaken outside the "home" nation. Indeed, corporations such as Sony, Hitachi and Mitsubishi proclaim that they belong to no nation, having—as global businesses—loyalty to whichever place or places in which they happen to be conducting their affairs.

Put simply, there are nowadays serious questions to be asked about the capacity of national governments to control their nation's economy because of the pressures to conform to global market practices, and these are compounded by problems of identifying who owns a company and to what extent it might be identified as belonging to a particular country. One result of this has been a general acquiescence from governments to the fact that they cannot do much to plan their economy. Of course, conservative governments have long had faith that their nations would thrive so long as they left the economy alone, so this has not presented them with particular challenges. It has been social democratic regimes that have most had to change their ways. Their former inclination toward collectivist policies— for example nationalization of key sectors of industry—has been stifled in the 1990s, and they have had to accept the "neo-liberal consensus" if they intend to avoid rapid fiscal crisis.

EDUCATION, EDUCATION, EDUCATION

But if the economy cannot be touched by government, then just what are politicians to do? One key policy has led to a prioritization of education, and the reasoning behind this is easy to understand. The argument goes that most people attend the education systems of the nations in which they are born. Therefore, government has leverage in this realm, if not in the economy. Now, in this freewheeling global market economy in which we find ourselves, it is estimated (Reich, 1992) that about 20 percent of all the available jobs will go to those who occupy the upper levels of this system. These are what the most significant proponent of this account, Robert Reich, calls "symbolic analysts" (i.e., those whose work involves deal-making, communication, management and such like) in the world economy. Manuel Castells (1998), adopting the same reasoning, identifies this as "informational labor," which he estimates at 30 percent of jobs in OECD countries, those which oil the wheels of this "network economy" by organizing, designing, trading and innovating.

Let me emphasize that "informational labor" is a widely differentiated group, ranging from highly creative filmmakers to professional accountants, but it does share two characteristics. The first is a capacity to change itself, and to adapt to change, as a matter of routine. Informational labor is always on the alert for novelty and new learning, constantly updating its skills—traits essential for prosperity in today's highly competitive global economy. A constant refrain here is the need for "flexibility," and symbolic analysts have this quality in abundance. The second characteristic informational labor shares is a crucial contributor to this adaptability—high level education, not in a specific skill, but in a capacity to "self-program" (or, in language popular in British policy circles, in having "learned how to learn" and thereby become equipped for "lifelong learning"). Attendance at higher education institutions cultivates the "transferable skills" so essential to symbolic analysts because these are what is required by the global market economy that is intensively dynamic. Indeed, no learning, at however high a level, is nowadays likely to last more than a decade or so— except for the capacity to re-educate oneself in readiness for meeting the challenges of constant change.

So what does this mean for national governments? The answer is that a government that can command a disproportionate share of this 20 to 30 percent of top jobs worldwide may deem itself successful because large numbers of its citizens will be in well paid and rewarding occupations. And what the government can do toward meeting the challenge of the "information age" is encourage first rate educational services so that large numbers of its young people emerge with qualities required by the global economy. Such is precisely the reasoning articulated by Robert Reich before and during his service as Secretary of Labor in the Clinton administration (1992–1996). And because the same refrain is echoed by Prime Minister Tony Blair in his ambition to make "London the knowledge capital of Europe" by prioritizing "education, education, education," the British New Labour government has been described as "Reichian" in its outlook. The policy means that one can resign oneself to the play of market forces at the global and national level by placing the onus of policy on producing the "human capital" that most appeals to this world system.

Incidentally, those nations that lack the necessary educational infrastructure will be doomed to supplying the workers who are to be acted upon by the symbolic analysts. In addition, there is likely to be serious internal stratification even within prosperous nations, since those people who fail to take advantage of the fine education available in nations such as the United States and Britain, are likely to suffer badly in this era of informational capitalism. For a start, the old options—semi- and unskilled labor in factories and coal mines—are increasingly not available, not least because information labor has arranged for much of these to be automated and/or to be undertaken abroad. After all, while the undereducated in metropolitan states may be poor as compared to their countrymen, in comparison to the labor forces in China and the Philippines, they are expensive to hire, and these days informational labor is quite adept at organizing things so that necessary non-skilled work is conducted at far distances.

Thus, a distinct prospect is for further polarization of classes within relatively advantaged nations: While government does its best to encourage informational labor that appeals to the global economic system, should it try to implement measures that militate against polarization by redistributing resources to the under-achieving, then it risks losing the confidence of the world's markets which frown on policies which introduce "distortions," just as it is likely to estrange the successful symbolic analysts who resent high taxation (and who are often capable of migrating with their high-level skills). Indeed, politicians will need to negotiate a fine balance between satiating global capital and meeting the reluctance of the better off to pay taxes, while also ensuring that the social fabric of the nation remains sturdy enough to appeal to investors and the symbolic analysts who need to be persuaded to stay inside the nation. After all, if an "underclass" develops to an extent that the quality of life of the affluent is threatened (unsafe areas of the city, high levels of street crime and the like), then no matter how sophisticated electronic defense systems are (commentators make much of the spread of CCTV systems in the inner city, of the "gated communities" which insulate the well-off [Blakely & Snyder 1997]), significant numbers of advantaged people will leave (European readers who are skeptical might reflect here on their reaction to the fact that, in the United States, around 10,000 people die annually from handguns; in European nations the equivalent figures rarely rise above two dozen). For the most able symbolic analysts, Geneva or Copenhagen might appeal more than Los Angeles or Baltimore if violent crime especially continues to grow. It is precisely this fear which drove Robert Reich to advocate what might be called post-Reagan policies for the United States in the 1990s. The poor cannot be thrown to the vagaries of the market if the social fabric is to be maintained, so socially ameliorative policies are recommended, but these must be mild enough not to incur the displeasure of the better off or global capital.

CULTURE

It is very easy to give all of one's attention to the economic forces in play, and to the policies adopted by governments which try to gain relative advantage in this new situation. However, the cultural dimensions of the current epoch ought not to be ignored because they too are of enormous consequence. When I refer to culture I wish to point especially to the symbolic realm of life, that arena which feeds into one's identity and consciousness. I should like here to identify four issues that pose enormous challenges to nations—and indeed the entire world—today.

Globalized Media

Globalization profoundly challenges the well established practice of national broadcast media. In evidence one might point to the technological innovations which bring us satellite television services as well as the Internet while bypassing national frontiers. But one needs to add that, since national broadcast systems, at least those outside the United States, have been brought to us largely by state-funded organizations, these have felt the destructive impact of a changed climate of opinion. State-sponsored systems are out of step with today's stress on private rather than public provision of services, and accordingly where they survive they have to face continued diminution of their revenue as well as competitive pressures from commercial suppliers. Digitalization of television, as well as additional terrestrial channels and cable services, for instance, will mean that it will become increasingly difficult for state-funded television to justify its funding.

In addition, the ethos which came to justify such services, at least in social democratic societies, was the doctrine of public service broadcasting, one which was conceived as a national service to be delivered by public servants who were imbued with a vocation to promote in broadcasting "information, education and entertainment" (as went the famous formulation of the founding Director General of the BBC, Lord Reith). Today, this is regarded on many fronts as unacceptably élitist as well as antipathetic to commercial services where entertainment prevails. The old-fashioned services produced programs about which audiences had little or no choice, audiences getting what they were given in return for an obligatory tax on TV ownership. Nowadays such form of supply is seen as unaccountable to those who pay for the service. Again, the program makers tended to be highly educated and from privileged backgrounds, ones which predisposed them toward programming which stressed "worthy" and "educational" output—this today is regarded with suspicion, as being out of touch with the consumer's right to have the programming which he or she desires. Moreover, public service broadcasting rather presumed that it could engage the entire nation in a "conversation with itself." The BBC (British Broadcasting Corporation), in this regard, might be seen to have contributed to a "public sphere," broadcasting to the whole country, where, through diverse programming, the nation could come to see itself in its variety as well as its distinctiveness (Scannell & Cardiff, 1991). This "public sphere" devoted a large amount of air time to the coverage of news and current affairs (at least double that provided by commercial channels in the United Kingdom), since, ran the argument, a genuine public service ought to privilege information about political (public) affairs. Moreover, the BBC also endeavored to expand on this commitment to promote high-quality dramas, documentaries and even music.

Today, one may readily understand that these days of public service broadcasting as well as a single public sphere are numbered (Tracey, 1998). For a start, there are many legitimate critiques which highlight the failures of the former system: This public sphere as often excluded as it included, as often projected a narrow view of the nation as it did a plural one. Anyway, "narrowcasting" is ensuring that the notion of a national audience is collapsing—instead there are many segmented audiences, occupied with specialist interests, often receiving their programming from abroad.

The question then is, does one relinquish television to the world market? This may turn out to be the future reality whatever governments may desire and, while the short-term will surely see the ascendancy of transnational organizations such as Rupert Murdoch's satellite channels, Star TV and MTV, the spread of Internet-type services may offer a good deal of diverse programming even where it is organized on commercial terms.

A second question raises the matter of the public sphere, and with that matters of identity. In the old days of public service broadcasting, it was presumed that the nation could be addressed more or less collectively and, at least to a degree, citizens of a given country could see a reflection of themselves in those sorts of programming. Today, one might more accurately talk of the development of multiple public spheres, of many means by which people may be informed and entertained, either through television or computerized networks. Some thinkers contend that this can be a positive force for extending pluralism, with more opportunities for the participation of citizens and for their reception of a more diverse sort of programming.

But there must also be anxieties expressed about the potential for fragmentation of identities and outlooks this may bring. For if the prospect is of multiple sites of information, and of people receiving highly diverse programming in the privacy of their own homes, then how might a national consciousness be addressed? How might citizens speak to fellow citizens? To be sure, one might reply that in the past such a practice has been deeply divisive, homogenizing very different peoples and proving incapable of catering for the diversity of a nation's population. Yet the ambition to talk as a nation disappears with "narrowcasting" and, while there may be gains in terms of the individual or at the small scale level (the football fan in London can readily access his team in Barcelona, the Turk in Berlin keeps in touch with his ethnic community in Istanbul), there may too be put at risk the ability to conceive of a nation as a phenomenon with a collective consciousness.

But perhaps things will not turn out so negatively. John Keane (1998) suggests that what might develop is a multiple level of "public spheres": an extension at the supranational level (e.g., trans-European television services, even global programming), the continuation of national broadcasting systems (even in commercial form, but also in terms of services which remain reliant on public funding), as well as a proliferation of localized (if global in reach) and specialized services that might link specialist communities. In such ways, the optimist suggests, the complexities of identity in today's world might be attended to, with citizens capable of reaching out beyond their own country for some matters (perhaps to think of themselves as European in particular ways), turning to their own nation for others, while always able to fulfil particular informational requirements by the proliferating specialist services—for instance, "I am a European, but am also Hungarian, while simultaneously an ethnic Jew who has a particular interest in the fortunes of Inter-Milan football club." Perhaps it is such "multivocalism" that is most consonant with the postmodern culture characteristic of the globalized capitalism within which we live. For sure, national governments will be called upon to negotiate the difficult terrain of this new media map.

Place Image

Historically, places have always been important, but the reason for their importance seems to be changing. In the past, places were important largely because of their physical location—for instance, Gibraltar commanding the entry to the Mediterranean, Cairo the mouth of the Nile and Istanbul the Bosporus Straits. In recent times, this physical reason for the importance of place is in decline, to be replaced by the primacy of "image." This stems, of course, from the fact that space has been, in large part, diminishing in significance. When, for example, one may organize affairs through telecommunications connections, then the former reasons for location are of less precedence.

However, this is not to say that places are no longer important. Not at all. For a start, this global network economy requires that there are central switching points, what might be conceived of as "nodes" amid the world's information circuits. Several scholars have, in this regard, pointed to the emergence of "global cities"—preeminently London, New York, Los Angeles and Tokyo—as locations where congregated key world players such as corporate headquarters, key government departments, financial services, media and marketing centers are (Sassen, 2000). With these come the essential occupational groups, composed heavily of symbolic analysts, whose work calls for their location close to "where the action is." However, what is interesting is that these places attain, and aspire toward, particular imagery—as action-packed, as galvanizing, as powerful, as centers of cultural innovation and availability. A crucial point is that these places do not automatically attain a particular image, but this imagery requires active involvement to be developed—and the wrong image may have negative effects on the prosperity of a place. For these reasons, what we are witnessing is a great investment being made in the imagery of places—because it can have very real consequences for jobs and positioning in the global economy.

The point can be made negatively easily enough. Consider, for instance, Johannesburg, South Africa, a city located in a potentially strategic nation for African development, blessed with rich natural resources and situated in a region with good quality educational institutions. It also happens, however, to be projecting an image of being crime-infested and dangerous, scarcely the place to draw the symbolic analysts and investors of global capital. One might also instance the case of Birmingham in this regard, Britain's second largest city, and one developed through industrialism (more precisely, engineering) and its location at the center of canals, railways and roads in the eighteenth and nineteenth centuries. De-industrialization has led to a massive collapse in traditional employment in manual occupation, while much of the place-image was dull and boring, a city ill-suited to change and weighed down with outdated industry. But over the past two decades or so huge investments have been made in reinventing Birmingham—to which end the city center has been radically overhauled (to stress its civic grandeur as well as fine cultural facilities—its theatres, its orchestras, its conference and performance venues). Its multiculturalism has been heavily publicized to stress Birmingham's capacity to adapt to and precipitate change as well as to offer huge varieties of experience, its canals have been rescued from industrial decay and abandonment to become walkways into the heart of a city of around 1.5 million citizens, its airport developed to become an international service, media organizations encouraged, universities expanded and so forth. The upshot has been a massive expansion of service employment, the increased attraction of Birmingham to entrepreneurial informational labor and a heightened role as a hub in the British, European and world networks along which affairs are conducted. In this regard, consider also the situation of Budapest, a large central European city of unsurpassed architectural beauty and with a rich history of music and the arts. However, it is a city that is, relatively, little known on a world stage, since it has been distanced from the world's media and incapable, in the Communist era, of projecting itself in desirable ways. This is likely to change, though it will take enormous amounts of energy to "reinvent" Budapest—to establish the communications infrastructure necessary for success, from roads and air transport to media systems, to an open, innovative and stable commercial sector.

The general point that place image is of heightened importance may be better appreciated beyond consideration of metropolitan centers. Tourism, one of the world's biggest industries, puts an enormous premium on imagery. The likes of Greece and Spain are heavily dependent on carefully crafted and assiduously maintained images for around 30 percent of total employment. Few believe the myths of "authenticity" that are projected ("unspoiled" places, "genuine" people and the like), but still these places draw tourists in significant part because they project a particular sort of imagery—of their folk cultures, their cuisines, their hospitality and their safety (Urry, 1990). This imagery does not appear by happen chance; it must be worked upon if it is to continue and be capable of adopting to ever-changing requirements. Governments—national, regional, supranational and local—will undoubtedly be called upon to play a central role in this recreation.

Heightened Cosmopolitanism

The accelerated globalization that has taken place over recent years brings with it a generalized heightening of cosmopolitanism. This is evident, for example, in the increased awareness of different cultures and histories that comes from world-wide media (which is not to say that this coverage is in any way representative). But cosmopolitanism stems from many other factors too—from awareness of the increasingly international origins of products, from knowledge that one's work activities draw in many other countries, from the massive growth in foreign travel (of both work and tourism), from interaction with migrants from many different cultures, from the rapid development of English as the de facto *lingua franca* around the world (which eases communication between members of minority linguistic groups), and from daily consumption of foods bought in the local supermarket that come from all corners of the earth.

This heightened cosmopolitanism must be one of the most important characteristics of living at the dawn of the second millennium. However, the experiences of cosmopolitanism are not equally distributed. The relatively privileged symbolic analysts are among the most cosmopolitan of all groups. After all, they are routinely in touch with people from around the world (via the Internet, business travel, because they work in metropolitan—and thereby variegated—centers, by their capacity to enjoy the fruits of multicultural life [the restaurants, the cinema and theater, etc.]) and thereby comfortable with variety and differences among peoples.

This might be contrasted with the experiences of those, disproportionately concentrated in the least advantaged sectors of society, who feel most threatened by globalization. These are the groups whose employment prospects are uncertain and whose options are limited, whose ways of life are challenged by the extension of the global market, who find globalization not an opportunity but an anathema which promises to uproot everything once thought secure. Not surprisingly perhaps, these who are threatened are readily drawn to fundamentalisms of one sort or another (militant Islam, born-again Christianity, neo-Fascism, deep environmentalism) because fundamentalism gives certainty in an uncertain world. Fundamentalism provides a faith in established creeds, offering a "return" to a secure and certain order that has appeal especially to those who are unsettled by the global market's dynamic (Barber, 1996).

At least two things are striking about this situation. The first is that those attracted to fundamentalism are found in every nation of the world, but especially among the most marginal. The second is that fundamentalisms articulate a creed that is the very opposite of the cosmopolitanism of the wider society (though fundamentalists are not averse to using the latest technologies to advance their views). By, for instance, evoking a mythical past (of national history, race or religion), fundamentalism sets itself against the internationalism of the more fortunate members of society. Moreover, a good deal of fundamentalism is extremely dangerous, expressing itself in racist attacks, or in terrorism and civil conflict, aimed as a rule at minority ethnic groups or an imagined enemy (the "great Satan" of the West). The most disturbing expression of it in Europe in recent years has been the waves of "ethnic cleansing" in the former Yugoslavia, directed at minority populations in the name of a mythically pure nation and national identity. This accounted, during the 1990s, for at least a quarter of a million deaths in the Balkans (Rieff, 1995).

What one might project from this potential polarization between those who are more cosmopolitan and those who are unsettled by globalization is that conflicts between nations will decline. Anthony Giddens (1994) goes so far in this respect to write of "states without enemies" in the post–Cold War situation. This is a remarkable phenomenon, since wars for most of the past several centuries have been between nations over territory. This form of warfare seems to be receding, to be replaced by conflicts between groups within nations (when one, for instance, proclaims that it epitomizes the "true" national creed, something which requires the expulsion of foreign, contaminated and contaminating, "outsiders"—who may well have lived inside the nation for centuries) and across national boundaries (where a bond is forged between fundamentalisms against a common enemy). As we are witnessing in Kosovo, and before this in Bosnia and Croatia, these challenges are formidable to nations as well as to the wider international community.

Migration

Globalization presupposes the movement of peoples as well as information. And how pleasant travel is for those of us blessed with credit cards, prepaid flights and the promise of well paid employment. Still more enjoyable is it to be a tourist, to visit other parts of the world at one's leisure, where one will be chaperoned, attended to and pampered. We are familiar with this sort of migration: the visiting scholar, the international businessman or the annual vacation in Antibe or Marbella.

But of course this is but one part of migration. The other, a part which has grown to unprecedented levels since 1945 and especially since the 1980s, involves the poor who travel to find a better way of life. Such migration is by no means new—think of the Irish who sailed to the United States, forced out of their nation by famine in the mid-nineteenth century, or consider the Italian exodus from the South of that country where the land could not offer sufficiency. Nonetheless, in recent decades migration has grown enormously, and most of it is for reasons of economics. The world's poor, wherever they are and whenever they can, migrate to where they might find better opportunities. For the most part, this means that peoples move from the South toward the North (the majority, of course, do not move since migration is a last-ditch option, and the majority who do move only make it to the urban centers of their own nations, but still the impulse is evident everywhere, and chiefly it is to try to make a better livelihood).

There are a great many consequences of this migration, but Zygmunt Bauman (1998) puts his finger on perhaps the most telling. In a world of high-level migration, the privileged are "tourists" who are, as such, encouraged to travel freely and with pleasure, while those at the bottom of the social heap are the "vagabonds," are those who are regarded as tramps and discontents who ought really to "remain where they come from." In Bauman's terms, the migrants from the South are those who most disturb those in the (relatively) privileged North—their skin color is different, they dress differently, their cultures do not conform to our own, their languages are incomprehensible. As such, Bauman continues, they are the nightmarish *alter egos* of those free-travelers who are the beneficiaries of globalized capitalism. Accordingly, they are a source of conflict and tension that must be addressed.

I do not believe that we can wish away this conflict by saying that people should simply be tolerant of one another. Of course, I earnestly advocate this, but it is not enough. Migration is but one important dimension of a global market society which is subject to constant change. Indeed, migration at the levels we experience today is a concomitant of this fluidity of advanced capitalism. However, this upheaval necessarily weakens the bonds that develop among stable peoples, not least (if not only), by bringing into play others ways of life, other backgrounds, other—strange—ways of behaving. Encountering others is surely an important stimulant for innovation, and one might welcome many aspects of other cultures' experiences, yet still a key issue then remains: How might people retain a sense of commonality, of togetherness, while living with differences? What are the bounds of tolerance? Where might the line be drawn between sufficient difference to stimulate change while at the same time maintaining constancy? This is indeed an extraordinarily problematical issue, and it is one which surely must be tackled by many agencies, at many levels from the local to the global, now and increasingly in the future. If ever there was a global challenge which requires national (and other) answers it is this: How might we live together amidst differences?

REFERENCES

Barber, B. R. (1996). *Jihad vs. McWorld*. New York: Ballantine.

Bauman, Z. (1998). *Globalization: The human consequences*. Cambridge: Polity Press.

Blakely, E., & Snyder, M. G. (1997). *Fortress America: Gated communities in the United States*. Washington, DC: Brookings Institution.

Castells, M. (1996–1998). *The Information Age: Economy, society and culture* (Vols. 1–3). Oxford: Blackwell.

Castells, M. (1998). *The Information Age: Economy, society and culture*. Vol. 3. *End of Millennium*. Oxford: Blackwell.

de Benoist, A. (1996, Summer). Confronting globalization. *Telos*, 108, 117–137.

Dicken, P. (1992). *Global shift: The internationalization of economic activity* (2nd ed.). London: Paul Chapman.

Figes, O. (1996). *A people's tragedy: The Russian Revolution, 1891–1924*. London: Pimlico.

Giddens, A. (1994). *Beyond Left and Right: The future of radical politics*. Cambridge: Polity Press.

Greider, W. (1997). *One world, ready or not: The manic logic of global capitalism*. Harmondsworth: Penguin.

Harvey, D. (1989). *The condition of postmodernity*. Oxford: Blackwell.

Held, D., McGrew, A., Goldblatt, D. & Perraton, J. (1999). *Global transformations: Politics, economics and culture*. Cambridge: Polity Press.

Keane, J. (1998). *Civil society*. Cambridge: Polity Press.

Lash, S., & Urry, J. (1987). *The end of organized capitalism*. Cambridge: Polity Press.

Reich, R. (1992). *The work of nations*. New York: Vintage.

Rieff, D. (1995). *Slaughterhouse: Bosnia and the failure of the West*. London: Vintage.

Robins, K., & Webster, F. (1999). *Times of the technoculture: From the information society to the virtual life*. London: Routledge.

Robinson, W. I. (1996). Globalization: Nine theses on our epoch. *Race and Class*, 38(2), 13–31.

Sassen, S. (2000). Global cities. In G. Browning, A. Halcli and F. Webster (Eds.), *Understanding contemporary society: Theories of the present*. London: Sage Publications.

Scannell, P., & Cardiff, D. (1991). *A social history of British broadcasting: Vol. 1*. Oxford: Blackwell.

Scott, A. (Ed.). (1997). *The limits of globalization: Cases and arguments*. London: Routledge.

Seabrook, J. (1982). *Working class childhood*. London: Victor Gollancz.

Soros, G. (1998). *The crisis of global capitalism: Open society endangered*. London: Little, Brown.

Tracey, M. (1998). *The decline and fall of public service broadcasting*. New York: Oxford University Press.

Urry, J. (1990). *The tourist gaze*. London: Sage Publications.
Webster, F. (1995). *Theories of the information society*. London: Routledge.
Worsley, P. (1984). *The three worlds of development*. London: Weidenfeld and Nicholson.

Chapter 8

Urban Congregations of Capital and Communications: Redesigning Social and Spatial Boundaries

Gerald Sussman

Seek ye first the political kingdom, and all things will be added to you.
—Kwame Nkrumah

THE PROBLEMATIQUE OF TECHNOLOGICAL CHANGE

The infrastructure of information and communications technology (ICT) has coevolved with industry and transportation as central properties of the metropolis, bringing new symbolic landscapes and cultural meanings to urban life. Local, regional, national and increasingly globalized information and communication networks have broadly inflated a range of social and spatial boundaries—that is, the reach of active social connectivity—yet remain unmistakably centered in the metropolitan core.[1] Although the Internet appears in its charming illusion to have no "place," its principal segments in fact are designed and situated in well defined spaces, where large research, development, software production, mass media, commodity manufacturing, sales and advertising, finance, commerce, state intelligence and other commanding interests usually congregate—and where most strategic decision making and revenue streams ultimately reside. On the strength of the concentrated presence of these forces, the first-tier information (and world) cities are New York, Tokyo and London (Sassen, 1991).[2]

Modern discourses on cyberspace, deregulation and neoliberalism tend to dissociate social interaction from regimes of political economic power, depicting imagined online communities and their boundaries as emancipated from temporal and spatial constraints. Such impressions are premised on the "revolutionary" and liberatory character of technological change.

Those who view technology as an inherently autonomous and largely be-
nevolent force also tend to reject public intervention in regulating its development and uses. Murray Edelman (1988), taking the more critical
stance, sees the "communications revolution" as little more than a grand
"political spectacle," a bedazzling language construct of interest groups
that commission its meaning, symbolism and social status.

Though some may celebrate the radically transformative power of mi-
croelectronics over everyday life, the microcomputer, the Internet and the
domain of digital multimedia technologies actually have demonstrated little
positive impact on the social structure of class-divided societies since the
arrival of the personal computer in the early 1980s. Jeremy Rifkin, deriding
current representations of advanced technology as the *deus ex machina* of
the late twentieth century, notes that when electricity was introduced as a
commercial medium in American cities a century earlier, "scientists and
engineers of the day predicted that its widespread use would make the cities
green, heal the breach between the classes, create a wealth of new goods,
extend day into night, cure age-old diseases, and bring peace and harmony
to the world" (Rifkin, 1995, p. 43). Thomas Edison added a measure of
hyperbole in 1922, familiar in many contemporary refrains about the Internet, that "the motion picture is destined to revolutionize our educational
system and . . . in a few years it will supplant largely, if not entirely, the
use of textbooks" (cited in Oppenheimer, 1997, p. 45). Similar exalted
claims were made about early radio and television. There is also a wide
misinterpretation that the automobile and the motorway rewrote all previous definitions of time and place and of social and spatial boundaries.
This often repeated maxim is among the many that mystify industrial and
technological history and the social forces that propel its motion and designs.

The concept of the "social production of distance" describes how organized institutional power imposes dissimilar boundaries on people within its
jurisdiction. Distance is measured not strictly in linear space but more essentially in terms of social, political and functional reach, and increasingly
it is swept aside via electronic modes of communication. It does indeed
appear that social interchange is now less constricted by occupation or
residential location, as communicative networks allow many "ordinary
people," at least in the more affluent strata, to take advantage of opportunities for distant associations that were unknown to their forebears. At
the same time, the development and diffusion of electronic communications
and the modern means of transportation have helped to *normalize* a degree
of industrial, commercial, social and familial separation that was also unknown to earlier generations.

The availability of a worldwide labor pool enlisted to the tasks of agriculture, mining, manufacturing and service industries, along with the existence of utilities for global management, enable organized capital to set

the conditions of social diaspora. Networked information circuits free business clusters to choose the location of their operational headquarters for command and control. Information cities as the pillars of the global economy are established through the convergence of business management; by the propinquity of finance capital, communications and other vital producer services; and with flexible options for production and profiteering on a vast spatial and material scale. The current political environment is one in which the power of the state to intervene in major markets is constrained in part by private global ICT networks endowed with a "velocity of information flow . . . [that] permits the firm to circumvent government disincentives whether embodied as taxes, rules, interest payments or capital restrictions" (Graham, 1994, p. 418).

Focusing on the postwar restructured world economy, this chapter discusses the urban social and spatial boundary changes, primarily in the United States, that have occurred under a system of "flexible accumulation," so-called post-fordism,[3] particularly as these changes relate to uses of information and communications technology. The argument challenges the notion that a post-historical and post–urban epoch has arrived that renders as immaterial past organizational and locational forms of economic exchange and power relationships. It offers in its place a critical political economic reading of social change in a heavily information-lubricated, urban-based world economy. The New International Division of Labor (NIDL) provides a holistic framework for explaining the reconstitution of politics at the local and global levels. It also explains how political economic opportunities and outcomes are engendered in technological infrastructure, and how expanded social and spatial boundaries, seen here as capacities for education, job satisfaction and upward mobility, are largely regulated on behalf of a small stratum with high regime status.

A confident technological rationality that underlies the dominant discourse about the "information society" and about material and cultural development in general is not particularly revealing of historical processes of interest formation, articulation, mobilization and circulation. The dominant discourse conceals embedded political economic power and controversy in an effort to convert public consciousness to an almost mystical faith in scientific expertise and unfettered technological enterprise. As Michael Borrus remarks:

Specific choices within the frontier of technological possibilities are not the product of technological change; they are, rather, the product of those who make the choices within the frontier of possibilities. Technology does not drive choice, choice drives technology. Grasping this point is critical, for there is nothing determinative, nothing inevitable about the ways in which the new technological possibilities of telecommunications will be implemented. (cited in Cohen & Zysman, 1987, p. 183)

THE RISE OF URBAN COMMUNICATIONS STRUCTURES

Choices driving technological change are framed within historical, social, cultural and political economic contexts. Information cities that emerged in the late twentieth century are direct extensions of the late eighteenth and early nineteenth century phases of industrialism and urbanism. Then as now, the compelling necessity and force behind the development of tele-communications drew more on the power ambitions and demands of cap-ital and state than on enlightened populist ideals of a broader democratic franchise. Throughout the era of early industrialization, organized interests, not households, steered the development and location of wires, investments and cities. (A social history of technology is presented in Sussman, 1997, chs. 3, 4.) State-subsidized telegraphy, and later submarine cable and te-lephony, conferred generous rewards to large-scale commercial and indus-trial markets, growing international trade and imperialist projects when "for the first time, information could reliably travel faster than people" (Herman & McChesney, 1997, p. 12). Long-distance messaging (i.e., tele-communications) served the practical needs of banking, manufacturing, commerce, brokerage, transportation, mass media, advertising, fire and po-lice work and military actions, along with the commodities markets and other modes of organized gambling.

Telegraphy and telephony encouraged companies to wire and locate in urban central business districts, which in turn created local concentrations that allowed for convenient meetings with producers and specialized service providers (finance, accounting, law, advertising, software design and so on). Wired communication was deployed in connecting the downtown office with the distant factory, field management, warehouses, railroad compa-nies, middlemen, wholesalers, retail shops, Pinkertons and union busters. Factories could be removed to fringe areas outside the city centers, where owners could take advantage of lower land values, while enjoying the amenities of urban bourgeois life. Private-line telegraphy, in particular, had the effect of demonstrating "the feasibility of office/plant separation given an appropriate communications technology, thus preparing the way for the more flexible telephone." This more fully enabled physical as well as con-ception/execution divisions in the industrial process, preparing the way for a fordist and taylorist manufacturing economy (Tarr, Finholt & Goodman, 1987, p. 48). Communications thus aided scale commodity producers in creating national markets, perfecting the system of pricing and, together with railroad, rationalizing the system of distribution (Du Boff, 1984). In the United States, this eventually led to monopoly control in several key information industries, including telegraph (Western Union), telephone (AT&T) and news distribution (Associated Press).

Between 1845 and 1871, eleven commodity exchanges were set up in the major U.S. cities, aided by the telegraph and one of its adaptations, the stock ticker, a device for which one of its innovators, Thomas Edison, was richly compensated. Communications was instrumental in consolidating New York City's preeminent position in the securities markets and bringing bankers more actively into agribusiness and the internal colonization of urban spaces. On the eve of the Civil War, Wall Street was setting commodity prices for every big city in the country and establishing the pace and standard of capital transactions. "Attracted by the demand, inventors and entrepreneurs such as Thomas A. Edison and Moses G. Farmer gravitated to the big cities to set up workshops and to market their devices" (Tarr, Finholt & Goodman, 1987, pp. 41–42). By the end of the nineteenth century, electric communications, together with the railroad and horse-drawn railed streetcars, were closely associated with corporate concentration and higher urban densities, even as they also facilitated the rise of suburbs and class and ethnic segregation.[4]

Although urban agglomeration persisted throughout the twentieth century, the obituary of the city continued to be written and rewritten. Spurred by post–World War II rapid industrial expansion and liberal G.I. Bill housing benefits, white middle and upper classes began a flight to American suburbs, driven both by anticipation of a greener, less congested life and the demons of their racialist anxieties. By the 1980s, a new wave of privately developed investment in finance, real estate and other service sectors dedicated to the affluent became the new urban development paradigm. Businesses won major concessions from urban politicians, including zoning permits and renewal projects for upscaling formerly working class residential areas of the cities, which nurtured locational preferences for high rise business centers. Teleports linking financial and industrial firms on a distance-annihilating, worldwide 24-hour clock were set up as public-private ventures to attract corporate headquarters to the city. Rooftop dishes and "smart" wiring were included in building designs, accommodating the need for remote management of decentralized transnational operations, while a precipitous decline in union membership and an influx of low-wage immigrant labor reduced business concerns about worker resistance to restructuring, downsizing and wage deflation.

A globalization and opening of previously defined boundaries undeniably has been occurring, but in limited and selective domains, primarily in spaces dedicated to market exchange and flexible capital restructuring and circulation. In these areas, the appropriation of telecommunications has fostered a new economic and cultural reconceptualization of space. Mark Wilson notes that

Metaphorically, continents and countries are moving closer together in telecommunications cost space, with Britain moving from being over $1 per minute away from the United States to being only 20 cents per minute away. . . . Many developing countries unable to afford electronic technology remain in place or lose ground, or they have major cities centrally placed in information space and hinter-lands far distant because of outmoded domestic telecommunications systems. Sim-ilarly, parts of Manhattan may well be integral to the information world, whereas blocks away such connectivity may be irrelevant or impossible. (Wilson, 1998, p. 43)

Does the development and diffusion of information and communications technology constitute a "revolutionary" phase of social history, what Bell (1973) and others have called "post-industrialism"? Or is this condition better construed as an intensified form of industrialism, a hyperindustrial-ism, extended beyond manufacturing to the production of consumption and culture? Acknowledging the fluidity and flexibility of contemporary civil society that post-modernists observe, David Harvey sees the core of the post-modernist view as the expression of an accelerated commodifica-tion of culture and time-space compression in late capitalism: "Precisely because capitalism is expansionary and imperialistic, cultural life in more and more areas gets brought within the grasp of the cash nexus and the logic of capital circulation" (Harvey, 1990, p. 344). It is the capitalist re-gime of production—more and more enveloping cultural practices, changes in conceptual knowledge and the designs of social architects—rather than specific technological forms (e.g., information technology) that properly should be identified as the propelling force of social change. "Each distinc-tive mode of production or social formation," he writes, "will, in short, embody a distinctive bundle of time and space practices and concepts" with "material consequences for the ordering of daily life" (p. 204).

Political economy, although certainly incomplete in its various depictions of social-institutional dialectics and in its attention to the cultural domain, seems to offer the most sober and compelling interpretation of contempo-rary social and political transformations and changes in urban communi-cations and industrial complexes. It is particularly pertinent within the U.S. historical experience that custody of print media, terrestrial and submarine cable, electronic voice and message transmission, and broadcasting was established in legally sanctioned property and First Amendment rights, a juridical definition of business corporations as "persons" under the Con-stitution, and large state subsidies and economic protections accorded to private capital. One academic who attaches much importance to telematics in the rise of the urban political economy laments that the two rarely have been conjoined. He writes: "Cities, and the corridors between them, are the prime sites for the development of corporate telematics networks. Ur-ban restructuring increasingly relates to the hidden and silent applications that are being constructed on these networks" (Graham, 1994, p. 429).

Political economy is also contending with technological determinist dis-courses that often present the social and productive relations of the modern world and its future as little more than the progressive results of laboratory science. An MIT architecture and planning professor, for example, sees the potential social boundaries of the "information highway" as essentially a "bandwidth" problem:

If you cannot get bits on and off in sufficient quantity, you cannot directly benefit from the Net. . . . Accessibility is redefined; tapping directly into a broadband data highway is like being on Main Street, but a low baud-rate connection puts you out in the boonies, where the flow of information reduces to a trickle, where you cannot make so many connections, and where interactions are less intense. The bondage of bandwidth is displacing the tyranny of distance, and a new economy of land use and transportation is emerging—an economy in which high-bandwidth connectivity is an increasingly crucial variable. (Mitchell, 1995, p. 17)

For critical observers, the imagined bandwidth constraint is restated as political and class struggle: telematics as a battleground, a highly uneven one, between competing needs and interests. How cities and communities become wired internally and externally, and the political, economic, social and cultural outcomes, is not simply about technical parameters but more centrally about how various stakeholders are identified or not identified in corporate-regulated public space and in policy decisions about technology. As Andrew Gillespie notes, "Telecommunications are not neutral technologies. They are not equally amenable to all users which can be envisaged; an inherent bias is already 'locked in' to them, through the network design process" (cited in Graham, 1994, p. 417). The largest cluster of telecommunications users since the government deregulation wave in the 1980s has been "[b]anks, securities brokers, and insurance companies [that] have invested the most heavily in new telecommunications technologies and have reaped the greatest returns" (Warf, 1989, pp. 260–261). The biggest of these operate globally, employing rapid transport of information and goods to facilitate the circulation of money into commodity forms (or other scrip) and back again to money, reducing frictions of exchange in the world economy.[5]

THE POLITICAL ECONOMY OF BOUNDARIES

There is also a power geography of space and information. Income redistribution has been associated in recent years with an expanding spatial division of labor that employs new communications systems for greater decentralization of branch plant production and related services ("flexible fordism") and that more easily accommodates customized products as well as market volatilities.[6] Decentralization enables transnational corporations (TNCs), some 40,000 worldwide, to seek stable locations for branch operations, often those with the smallest tax liabilities, least stringent environmental regulations, lowest wages and weakest labor laws.[7] Flexible

corporate networks are central in "facilitating significant horizontal reorganizations in firms in a wide range of sectors," which help "resolve the
tension between spatial separation and functional integration of business
activities." This allows large firms to rationalize their operations by relying
more on information flows than on physical movement of facilities and
people and, at the same time, shifting activities and taylorizing production
by "exploit[ing] geographical differentiation while maintaining their functional integrity" (Li, 1995, p. 1640). In this way, large firms can retain
headquarters status and critical producer services in major nodal cities
while shifting labor-intensive and other subsidiary operations to more remote locales, thereby becoming decentralized without being decentered
(Amin & Thrift, 1992).

ICT provides significant benefits to networked firms, particularly those
that operate beyond local and regional levels, promoting increased concentration of large scale users and licensing a "new logic of agglomeration"
(Sassen, 1998, p. xxiii). TNCs with branch plants or service facilities in
two or more countries could not operate without the strategic advantage
of global communications that ties together vast networks of information
and encourages greater intrafirm commodity and service flows, increased
temporal and spatial mobility and new options for value-added investment.
Services now comprise at least a quarter of all international trade and probably a third of U.S. exports (Warf, 1995), and this is both a causal factor
and effect of the rapid pace of innovation in ICT. The high cost requirements of ICT also force out all but the largest firms that seek to compete
internationally, a barrier that has reduced the range of trade and investment
in most global industries to oligopolies.[8]

Communications has had powerful effects on the style and functions of
cities. Perhaps not since the rise of dominant world cities such as London,
Antwerp, Venice and Amsterdam have cities had such a prominent role in
the world economy. Saskia Sassen notes that as the power of nation states
has declined in recent decades, the control of modern world cities, particularly New York, Tokyo and London,[9] has increased (Sassen, 1994). Castells and Hall (1994) have written about the rise of technological R&D
centers, what they call technopoles, in such areas as Silicon Valley (south
of San Francisco), Route 128 (near Boston), Paris Sud, Cambridge (United
Kingdom), Kanagawa (south of Tokyo), Daegu (South Korea), Los Angeles
and Munich, which have transformed both the economic structure of their
respective regions, countries and the world economy. Another indication
of the influence of ICT in the reshaping of the metropolis is the fact that
by 1991 a quarter of the Fortune 500 wealthiest individuals and families
made all or a large portion of their income from mainly urban-based media
and communications industries (Bettig, 1997).

Given such a degree of economic and informational concentration and
integration, does place still matter? The dominant "information society"

narrative suggests that it does not and that workers had better prepare for a highly adaptable life of frequent job changes, retraining and relocation in order to survive. Such a narrative has an elitist bias, Sassen argues (1994), that fails to take into account the place-bound and labor-intensive requirements of a viable globalized information economy. Telecommunications is not an independent variable; it can "neither obliterate the importance of space nor iron out uneven development, but serve to replicate both phenomena" (Thomas, 1995, p. 95). Paul Knox finds that the universalizing impacts of transnationalism only strengthen the need for locational identity: "The faster the information highway takes people into cyberspace, the more they feel the need for a subjective setting—a specific place or community—that they can call their own" (Knox, 1997, p. 21).

Moreover, it is demographically evident, even with reclassifications over time, that agglomerations of people choosing to live in close proximity to one another are increasing and will remain the pattern of metropolitan society well into the twenty-first century. Cities, comprising 3 percent of the world's population in 1800 and 10 percent in 1900, will be the residence of almost 50 percent of humanity by the year 2000, much of this reflecting the overwhelming urbanization in the Third World. In 1950, 285 million people in the Third World, 16 percent of its total population, lived in cities; by 1990, it was 1.5 billion and 37 percent. By the early twenty-first century, it is projected that 2 billion people, 40 percent of the world's population, will reside in cities, areas designed for much lower densities; this number is expected to expand to 4.4 billion (80 percent) by 2025. At the end of the twentieth century, one-third of city dwellers were projected to be living in the more than 300 cities with greater than 1 million population (Kasarda & Parnell, 1993). The prospects for sustainability in most of them, unfortunately, are very grim.

Information cities in the First World also are rent with contradictions. In 1994, the poorest quintile in the United States' premier information center, New York City, with more than 1 million people living on welfare supplements, averaged $5,237 in income, while the wealthiest fifth averaged $110,199. In another information city, Los Angeles, the respective income gaps were $6,821 and $123,098 (Schiller, 1996). The *Los Angeles Times* determined in 1996 that of all households in the southern California region below the $25,000 income range, only 22 percent had computers at home, whereas among those with $50,000 or above, the figure was 69 percent. Another study, done in 1998, found that the figure rose to 80 percent for families with over $100,000 income. Among Los Angeles' central city households below $15,000 income, 9 percent had computers (Goslee, 1998). Nationally, 6.6 percent of blue-collar workers used networked information services in 1993, compared to 11.4 percent for the whole population, while 4 percent of service users account for 50 percent of all telecommunication revenues. In 1996, there were 6.5 million Americans without telephone service (Chapman, 1996; Hepworth, 1989). In 1989, nearly a third of all families dependent on food stamps and half of women-headed households with children living at or below the poverty line were without telephone service (Schement, 1995).

Compared to the West, the structure of ICT access in the Third World has become considerably more polarized. With the exception of a few newly industrializing countries (NICs),[10] namely Singapore, Hong Kong, South Korea and Taiwan, and elite centers in the rest of the periphery, the vast majority of Third World citizens are not wired to information networks. The 29 OECD countries have less than 20 percent of the world's population but transmit more than 80 percent of the world's telephone traffic (nine of them with three-quarters of all telephones), and have 90 percent of the world's mobile telephone users and 95 percent of all computers. Almost 85 percent of the world's people have no telephones, and well over half have never made a telephone call. New York City, with about 7.3 million people, has more telephones than all of sub-Saharan Africa, with over 650 million people—12 percent of the world's total but less than 2 percent of the world's telephones. Britain has more television sets than all of Africa, and Japan has more than all of South America. The United States and the former Soviet Union (now Commonwealth of Independent States), with about 10 percent of the world's population, control more than half of the world's geostationary orbits, while the South uses less than 10 percent. U.S. annual advertising expenditure is greater than all but 17 countries' gross domestic products (Clark, 1996; Hamelink, 1994; Sussman, 1997).

BOUNDARIES, LOST AND FOUND

To this point, the discussion of boundaries has focused mainly on spatial divisions and connectivity. There is little question of the capacity of communications to make heretofore remote places seem closer at hand, such as through long-distance telephone, the Internet or live satellite television transmission. But are we to conclude that electronic communications necessarily opens social bridges to community, other cultures, the political process, better work and income prospects, improved health and education, and other opportunities on both the personal and collective levels? Such a presumption has not been well demonstrated. Several studies, in fact, have argued that ICT access patterns reinforce if not intensify national, class, gender and racial divisions within and across nation states (Civille, 1995; Floyd, 1996; Harmon, 1998; Henderson & King, 1995).

Electronic communications also does not substitute the need for direct personal communication within institutions and clusters, even in the major urban nodes of the global economy. The key transnational executives of the world, such as those in New York's financial district, Wall Street, require direct and regular interaction with one another and with other corporate players to survive in the high stakes game of casino capitalism. "Telecommunications cannot replace these networks beyond the possibility of acting on new information obtained in a face-to-face encounter. The complexity, imperfect knowledge, high risk, and speculative character of many endeavors . . . heighten the importance both of personal contact and of spatial concentration" (Sassen, 1994, p. 85). Businessmen of means prefer to conduct dealings where there is fresh air, green surroundings, space for exercise, and opportunities for long walks and conversation—the fairway. (Denied this costly option, labor organizers are more likely to prefer picnic grounds, the pub, or the union hall.)

With flexible accumulation, the corporate chain of command is organized with increased hierarchies in the internal flow of information as well as greater geographical separations of front office from back office, both tendencies facilitated by electronic communications. As one study of corporate networks has noted,

people working within the new informational boundaries may access what they are entitled to and such entitlement is primarily decided by the rank and responsibility of the person in the overall organizational hierarchy. Generally speaking, from the top-down in the corporate hierarchy, information accessibility decreases both in scale and in scope. The immediate result is that people at higher levels can organize the exclusive information to their advantage. (Li, 1995)

Although the technology policy process in the United States may sometimes bring to the table conflicting parties, including grassroots interests, it typically is not contested on a level playing field. Were society as a whole to experience the so-called communications revolution as truly *revolutionary*, there would need to be a corresponding revolutionary transformation of the political and economic class/participatory structure. With little evidence of such a requisite social change, it is perhaps better to construe the present ICT structure, if anything, as a force of *counter-revolution*. Social indicators in the United States since the introduction of the personal computer in the early 1980s do not at all support the premise of Daniel Bell (1960; 1973) and others that the essential "neutrality" of technology disposes of the need for oppositional political intervention in the policy process.

In the era of government deregulation, the ground rules for information access and political participation are increasingly being put on an ability to pay basis. A study by Mitchell Moss and Steve Mitra found that "the data show that the subscriber density is negatively correlated with the density of blue collar workers in an area. This result is important because the Internet is widely regarded as the great job-creation engine of the future." They also found that the cost of using the Internet "may exclude certain segments of our society. Furthermore, if this price goes up when broadband access to the home becomes a reality, the increase may exacerbate and clearly carve out class divisions on the Internet" (Moss & Mitra, 1998). According to a 1999 study of the Consumers Union and the Consumer Federation of America, since the 1996 Telecommunications Act, 75 percent of American households have been spending significantly more for basic telecommunications services (Wolf, 1999).

CAPITALS OF CAPITAL

Although there has been a relative suburbanization of capital investment, the target areas are largely within the commuting spaces of major urban centers, intensifying transportation and environmental problems. Urban sprawl associated with cities such as Los Angeles and Dallas has been extended to newly rising metropoles such as Phoenix, Orlando and Las Vegas, to edge cities, and to the suburbs. For many years, downtown commercial business districts in many cities have lost their customer bases to the outlying malls. As one example, the Sears Tower built in downtown Chicago in 1974 was almost completely abandoned by its owners by the early 1990s, as Sears moved 5,000 jobs from that building to the suburbs (Mitchell, 1995). In recent years, rising untaxed Internet sales have eroded downtown business, municipal and state revenues.

One of the expected outcomes of ICT was a significant rise in telecommuting. Between 1980 and 1990, a decade of extensive growth in the use of personal computers, there was in fact a national, though unremarkable, 31 percent increase (from 2.26 percent to 2.96 percent) of people paid to work out of their homes. However, in 1990 the ratio of home workers in the world's premier information city, New York City, was only 2.32 percent, well below the national average, suggesting that propinquity and regular in-person contacts with producer service providers are critical to the operation of global enterprises. The next four largest U.S. cities, Los Angeles, Chicago, Houston and Philadelphia, had ratios of 2.73 percent, 2.10 percent, 2.07 percent and 2.26 percent, respectively, also below the national average (U.S. Department of Transportation, 1993). Another reality is that in the age of digital communications, American workers on average have not decreased but significantly increased time spent in the office and shop-floor and, as companies relocate from urban areas to suburbs or edge cities, on the road as well. Moreover, as one study found,

proponents of telecommuting may well have overemphasized the positive elements of working at home (flexibility, lifestyle decisions, avoidance of the physical stresses of commuting) relative to the negative aspects of homeworking (isolation, poorer terms of employment) and the *positive* aspects of actually working in an office (everyday face-to-face contacts, social relationships and a feeling of being in touch with what is "going on"). (Gold, 1991, p. 336)

Expectations that ICT will bring about the demise of urban investment are misplaced. It is reductionist to assume that only direct production costs

matter in capital location decisions. Many industries will cluster in particular cities and districts because of the positive externalities they offer, such
as access to good roads, services, research centers and universities; the quality of housing, schooling and the environment; the big city atmosphere; and
so on. At the same time, the workforces of large corporations are far more
geographically dispersed than they were 50 years ago, a decentralization
process that *has* been aided by the development of ICT. Expert systems
have been used to move much of the information-intensive labor in many
industries, especially airlines, finance, telephony and insurance, to smaller
labor markets—cities like Salt Lake City, Omaha and Tallahassee—or "offshore" to Jamaica, East Asia and Ireland.

The notion that there is a general transcendence of social and spatial
boundaries as a result of ICT arises from a technocentric viewpoint and
otherwise pertains mainly to those within the hierarchies of the political
economic decision-making chain. Examining the technological determinist
reading of social history, there is little reason to think (anthropomorphi-
cally) that ICT significantly broadens the horizons of most people. The era
of liberalization and flexible accumulation has in many respects actually
narrowed the range of occupational and social mobility and the possibilities
of relative national political, economic and cultural autonomy. Relatively
few people in the First World, fewer in the Third World, have the time,
the financial means, or the supporting technical environment to take advantage of the possibilities that ICT might otherwise offer in a society
where the time and space dimensions were appropriated less by matters of
private accumulation and more by concerns of social distribution.

In the core TNC headquarters and information cities, New York, Tokyo
and London, it is reasonable to expect that these preeminent business, finance and information centers will assume more control over local, regional, national and world economic behavior (King, 1990a). The
boundaries of economic and informational power, however, are largely
contiguous with social and spatial location within the new international
division of labor. Jacques Ellul notes that "there is an aristocracy of transmitters and a plebeian mass of receivers, audiences and spectators. Great
specialists have huge power and cannot be controlled. The division between
the information-rich and the information-poor more profoundly divides
society than the former social classes" (Ellul, 1993, p. 339). Leading the
way to hyperindustrialization, information cities are the new congregations
of capital and communications.

NOTES

This chapter originally appeared as Gerald Sussman, "Urban Congregations of
Capital and Communications: Redesigning Social and Spatial Boundaries," *Social
Text* 60 (Fall 1999), 35–52. Copyright 1999, Duke University Press. Reprinted with
permission.

1. Active connectivity here refers to communicative transmission rather than mere reception. A television viewer is regarded as passively connected communicatively; the one who transmits is the active agent. Metropolitan refers to the regional, national, and global concentrations of business, cultural, entertainment, intellectual, mass media and informational exchange.

2. Information cities refer to the major urban centers of mass media, multimedia, advertising, public relations, universities, publishing, transnational headquarters, international finance, Internet domains, teleports, producer services, software design and other information-intensive strategic industries. Sassen's dominant world cities are also the leading information cities.

3. Vincent Mosco nicely summed up fordism as a "system of mass production for mass consumption led by large, integrated companies whose market dominance is secured with support from the state in return for maintaining economic and, by extension, political stability" (Mosco, 1996, p. 109). Danielle Leborgne and Alain Lipietz elaborate on fordism as a governing set of organizational principles within an industry. It coordinates levels of production with consumption in the accumulation process and regulates individual and societal adjustment so that the "regime of accumulation" can be sustained (summarized in Capello & Gillespie, 1993; pp. 35–36).

4. Chicago's population grew from less than 30,000 in 1850 to 1.7 million in 1900. More than half of the American population lived in cities by 1910 (Britain and Belgium by the 1850s, Australia by 1870, Germany in 1895, Sweden around 1920, France in 1931, and the USSR around 1950) (Jones, 1990). Britain, which could still claim the leadership of the capitalist world economy in 1914, was the most heavily urbanized with 80 percent of its people living in cities and towns (King, 1990b).

5. Even the conservative seat of the Catholic church, the Vatican, employs modern telecommunications to maintain its influence and interests and hired a private corporation, GE, to operate its global data network for communications with dioceses all over the world (Barnet & Cavanagh, 1994).

6. Robert Cohen, one of the early theorists on global cities described them as "centres for business decision making and corporate strategy formulation . . . for the co-ordination and control of the new international division of labour" (Cohen, 1981, p. 300).

7. The largest 300 TNCs have a quarter of the world's productive assets and effectively control the system of global trade and investment. About 90 percent are headquartered in the United States, Japan, or western Europe, with some 180,000 subsidiaries and over $6 trillion in worldwide sales. By the 1980s, TNCs represented 54 percent of both U.S. exports and imports, and of the latter about 80 percent were intrafirm transfers (Barnet & Cavanagh, 1994; Knox, 1997; Schwartz, 1994).

8. The demands by TNCs for state-of-the-art telecommunications has been the most important pressure point for privatization and deregulation of the section in Third World countries. In the sell-off of the Bahamas Telecommunications Company, the prime minister conceded that the state was "unable to maintain the telecommunications infrastructure demanded by the business community" (Herman, 1997, p. 13).

9. New York City and Tokyo are the dominant TNC headquarters cities in

their countries. Central London is the home of 80 percent of Britain's largest 51 TNCs.

10. Of these four "newly industrializing countries," two, Hong Kong and Taiwan, are not in fact countries but regions of China. Another, Singapore, is essentially an island city state of 3 million people.

REFERENCES

Amin, A., & Thrift, N. (1992). Neo-Marshallian nodes in global networks. *International Journal of Urban and Regional Research*, 16(4), 571–587.

Barnet, R. J., & Cavanagh, J. (1994). *Global dreams: Imperial corporations and the new world order*. New York: Simon and Schuster.

Bell, D. (1960). *The end of ideology*. Glencoe, IL: The Free Press.

Bell, D. (1973). *The coming of post-industrial society: Venture in social forecasting*. New York: Penguin.

Bettig, R. V. (1997, June). The enclosure of cyberspace. *Critical Studies in Mass Communication*, 14, 138–157.

Capello, R., & Gillespie, A. (1993). Transport, communications and spatial organisation: Future trends and conceptual frameworks. In G. Giannopoulos & A. Gillespie (Eds.), *Transport and communications innovation in Europe* (pp. 24–56). New York: Belhaven Press.

Castells, M., & Hall, P. (1994). *Technopoles of the world: The making of the 21st century industrial complexes*. New York: Routledge.

Chapman, G. (1996, June 10). Internet adds a new dimension to universal telecom service. *San Jose Mercury News*, 3E.

Civille, R. (1995). The Internet and the poor. In B. Kahin & J. Keller (Eds.), *Public access to the Internet* (pp. 175–207). Cambridge, MA: MIT Press.

Clark, D. (1996). *Urban world/global city*. New York: Routledge.

Cohen, R. B. (1981). The new international division of labour, multi-national corporations and urban hierarchy. In M. Dear & A. J. Scott (Eds.), *Urbanization and urban planning in capitalist society* (pp. 287–315). New York: Methuen.

Cohen, S. S., & Zysman, J. (1987). *Manufacturing matters: The myth of the post-industrial economy*. New York: Basic Books.

Du Boff, R. B. (1984, October). The telegraph in nineteeth-century America: Technology and monopoly. *Comparative Studies in Society and History*, 26, 571–586.

Edelman, M. (1988). *Constructing the political spectacle*. Chicago: University of Chicago Press.

Ellul, J. (1993). Preconceived ideas about mediated information. In A. Alexander & J. Hanson (Eds.), *Taking sides: Clashing views on controversial issues in mass media and society* (2nd ed., pp. 330–340). Guilford, CT: Dushkin.

Floyd, B. B. (1996, December 20). Program in Afro-American studies explores the racial gap in access to technology. *Chronicle of Higher Education*, A19–A20.

Gold, J. R. (1991). Fishing in muddy waters: Communications media, homeworking and the electronic cottage. In S. D. Brunn & T. Leinbach (Eds.), *Col-*

lapsing time and space: Geographic aspects of communications and information (pp. 327–341). London: HarperCollins.

Goslee, S. (1998). *Losing ground bit by bit: Low-income communities in the information age.* Online report produced by the Benton Foundation and the National Urban League [Online]. Available: http://www.benton.org/Library/Low-Income/one.html.

Graham, S. (1994). Networking cities: Telematics in urban policy—A critical review. *International Journal of Urban and Regional Research*, 18(3), 416–431.

Hamelink, C. J. (1994). *The politics of world communication: A human rights perspective.* Thousand Oaks, CA: Sage Publications.

Harmon, A. (1998, April 17). Racial divide found on information highway. *New York Times*, A1, A18.

Harvey, D. (1990). *The condition of postmodernity: An enquiry into the origins of cultural change.* Oxford: Basil Blackwell.

Henderson, C. C., & King, F. D. (1995). The role of public libraries in providing public access to the Internet. In B. Kahin and J. Keller (Eds.), *Public access to the Internet* (pp. 154–171). Cambridge, MA: MIT Press.

Hepworth, M. E. (1989). *The geography of the information economy.* London: Belhaven Press.

Herman, E. S. (1997, September/October). The global attack on democracy, labor, & public values. *Dollars and Sense*, 10–15.

Herman, E. S., & McChesney, R. W. (1997). *The global media: The new missionaries of global capitalism.* London: Cassell.

Jones, B. (1990). *Sleepers wake! Technology & the future of work.* New York: Oxford University Press.

Kasarda, J. D., & Parnell, A. M. (1993). Introduction. In J. D. Kasarda & A. M. Parnell (Eds.), *Third World cities: Problems, policies, and prospects* (pp. ix–xvii). Thousand Oaks, CA: Sage Publications.

King, A. D. (1990a). *Global cities: Post-imperialism and the internationalization of London.* London: Routledge.

King, A. D. (1990b). *Urbanism, colonialism, and the world-economy: Cultural and spatial foundations of the world urban system.* London: Routledge.

Knox, P. L. (1997, May). Globalization and urban economic change. In D. Wilson (Ed.), Globalization and the changing U.S. city. Special Issue of the *Annals of the American Academy of Political and Social Science* (pp. 7–27). Thousand Oaks, CA: Sage Publications.

Li, F. (1995). Corporate networks and the spatial and functional reorganizations of large firms. *Environment and Planning A*, 27, 1627–1645.

Mitchell, W. J. (1995). *City of bits: Space, place, and the infobahn.* Cambridge, MA: MIT Press.

Mosco, V. (1996). *The political economy of communication: Rethinking and renewal.* Thousand Oaks, CA: Sage Publications.

Moss, M., & Mitra, S. (1998). *Net equity* [Online]. Available: http://urban.nyu.edu/research/net-equity/.

Oppenheimer, T. (1997, July). The computer delusion. *Atlantic Monthly*, 45–62.

Rifkin, J. (1995). *The end of work: The decline of the global labor force and the dawn of the post-market era.* New York: G. P. Putnam's Sons.

Sassen, S. (1991). *The global city: New York, London, Tokyo.* Princeton, NJ: Princeton University Press.

Sassen, S. (1994). *Cities in a world economy.* Thousand Oaks, CA: Pine Forge Press/ Sage Publications.

Sassen, S. (1998). *Globalization and its discontents: Essays on the new mobility of people and money.* New York: The Free Press.

Schement, J. R. (1995). Beyond universal service: Characteristics of Americans without telephone: 1980–93. *Telecommunications Policy,* 19(6), 477–485.

Schiller, H. I. (1996). *Information inequality: The deepening social crisis in America.* New York: Routledge.

Schwartz, H. M. (1994). *State versus markets: History, geography, and the development of the international political economy.* New York: St. Martin's Press.

Sussman, G. (1997). *Communication, technology and politics in the Information Age.* Thousand Oaks, CA: Sage Publications.

Tarr, J. A., Finholt, T. & Goodman, D. (1987, November). The city and the telegraph: Urban telecommunications in the pre-telephone era. *Journal of Urban History,* 38–80.

Thomas, R. (1995). Access and inequality. In N. Heap, R. Thomas, G. Einon, R. Mason & H. Mackay (Eds.), *Information technology and society: A reader* (pp. 90–99). London: Sage Publications.

United States Department of Transportation. (1993, November). *Journey-to-work trends in the United States and its major metropolitian areas, 1960–1990.* Final report. Washington, DC: U.S. Department of Transportation.

Warf, B. (1989). Telecommunications and the globalization of financial services. *Professional Geographer,* 41(3), 257–271.

Warf, B. (1995). Telecommunications and the changing geographies of knowledge transmission in the late 20th century. *Urban Studies,* 32(2), 361–378.

Wilson, M. I. (1998). Information networks: The global offshore labor force. In G. Sussman & J. A. Lent (Eds.), *Global productions: Labor in the making of the "information society"* (pp. 39–56). Cresskill, NJ: Hampton Press.

Wolf, A. M. (1999, February 4). Telecommunications rates increase despite phone, TV laws, report says. *The Oregonian* (Bloomberg News Agency), B2.

Chapter 9

Satellite Broadcasting as Trade Routes in the Sky

Monroe E. Price

The metaphor of trade routes—used from time to time to think about the distribution of ideas and imagery—ought to nourish our conception of transnational paths of delivery of electronic communications. Our minds are full of Rupert Murdoch and Disney, CNN and the BBC as traders in information, great shippers of data, distributors of sitcoms and news and advertisements. In the common reading of the world of electronic signals, the media is considered "global," and the general impression is of a constant and ever-present net that can deposit information everywhere, disregarding boundaries. Our common and most recent experiences with the Internet seem, at first blush, to confirm and underscore a belief that data careers around the world from server to server, in patterns that seem virtually impervious to purposive planning or political and legal intervention (Volokh, 1995). Sender and receiver are linked in ways that appear indifferent to the route or mode by which they are connected. The obsolescence of boundaries is reinforced. So, too, has been the effect of the seamlessness of telephony in the developed world, obliterating distance and time. In telephony, transmission pathways seem invisible, or at least irrelevant, to the substantive decisions of most users. Although users are almost never conscious of it, all these modes of communication (postal service, telegrams and telephones) required the construction of international systems of regulation. Assurance of adherence to worldwide standards was a condition for their instantaneous nature and compatibility. The predominance of the West in terms of development and control of access to technology dictated the change in structure of international communication, putting pressure on non-Western members to Westernize, in order to comply with the prevailing system's bureaucratic rules.[1]

Central to this vision is the idea that the world's electronic umbrella is such that information and data are ubiquitous, capable of distribution everywhere, even if there are inequities in the manner and pattern of uploading and gaps in the earthbound infrastructure to receive them. But satellite routes for the distribution of images—even though digitally communicated—are neither entirely random nor random in the sense of indifference to historic and arbitrary boundaries of nation-states. Rather, as with their nautical counterparts for ports of call, certain orbital slots for communications satellites have advantages over other information routes. It is no longer fear of pirates or factors equally cinematographic that help determine a choice of passage. Nevertheless, issues of security in carrying goods (in the case of the satellites, information) over long distances in unpoliced areas (here, the upper atmosphere) are just as apparent now as they were to the historical trade in material goods. Similarly, satellite technology generates the need for zones of neutrality, though here we look at the allocation of orbital slots and issues of international regulation, rather than the neutral ground for trade provided by ancient ports of call.[2] What the new factors are, and how governments and businesses interact to shape the value of one route as opposed to another, are still open questions. Because these routes leave no marks and little in the way of associated activity, how these routes develop—and the impact of having one route rather than another—have not been examined.

Information is so valuable a commodity in the late twentieth century, and trade in information such a growing part of world balances and deficits, that it is productive to examine the metaphor of trade routes as a means of understanding current practices in law and regulation. It is for that reason that this chapter looks at the history of early eighteenth-century shipping routes as a source for common themes and major differences. This chapter, thus, explores the conceit that satellite patterns are trade routes that have their own agonizing histories and their own differentiated impacts. In the past, a trade route was an associated set of points which permitted ships to travel, receive coal for refueling, and to provide water, food and recreation for the sailors—in short, all stops necessary for goods to travel from Location A to Location B (and C and D), usually with the return of other goods (raw materials or manufactures). A good part of the history of colonialism can be read as the efforts of manufacturing and trading states to gain power or sovereignty over these points that were key to the maintenance of trading routes.

Along the coasts, these harbors were links in a complicated chain. Often, first a monopoly trading company and then a colonial power gained full dominion and sovereignty over the particular points in the trade routes (Auber, 1828; Horrabin, 1936; Juriaanse, 1943; Van Cleef, 1937). There were negotiations between the trader (or the government of the trader) and the local authority (king, tribe, city or otherwise). The reliable existence of these points was essential to investment and to the success of the trade. Sovereign entities often sought certain benefits for the concession, sometimes financial, sometimes otherwise (Kumar, 1996; Quiggin, 1949; Raychaudhuri, 1962). Points on ancient trade routes were valuable because raw materials could be added there as vessels moved from place to place. Since ancient times, trade routes favored ports that opened up to large consuming markets as well as ports where raw material could be taken on.

Today, satellites and their orbital slots constitute the points necessary for delivery of video (and other) signals over long distances. The trade route that information follows is superficially very different from its nautical predecessors. Because the process is electronic, painless, free of manual labor, and invisible, no novels—science fiction aside—will be written about information trade routes. No Herman Melville of global transmissions will arise. Lives are not risked. No coaling stations are required as intermediate stops between the original ports of debarkation and the ultimate ports of call. The economic need for two-way traffic is diminished because the costs of an empty ship returning are not present. With respect to the information colonies, the new order seems to deliver a manufactured product but appears not to obtain raw materials, a pattern strikingly different from the eighteenth-century model.

Yet the similarities between ancient trade routes and modern ones have the potential to instruct. The current powerful generation of communications satellites is located in a precise and limited geostationary orbit above the Equator, the only orbit that allows continuous contact between a satellite and a single ground station. Slots on this orbit are finite and, as a result, contested, bargained for and, to some extent, colonized (Finch, 1986). Particular orbital slots are often more important than others because of the particular terrestrial footprint a satellite can reach from those slots. A footprint that reaches a vast population or a wealthy population or a politically important one can be more valuable than one that does not. Governments seek to use such natural advantages as their terrestrial location to gain greater economic leverage, for example, more favorable orbital slots. Control of routes may be used to control the nature of the cargo— what information is carried (European programming, public service programming, anti-government programming) and what legal constraints are imposed (for example, indecency regulation or prohibitions on subversion or the advocacy of terror). Improvements in satellites add further complexities, just as changing shipping technologies did in seventeenth- and eighteenth-century trade routes.[3] There are moments, too, when existing patterns of trade routes are altered, sometimes permanently, by war, new technology or changing patterns of consumption. For the traditional trade routes, the opening of the Panama Canal or the Suez Canal reduced once important points on the trade route compass to impotency and brought new sites to prominence. Transitions from one direct broadcast satellite format to another or the introduction of communication satellite paths that do not rely on geostationary satellites may also change the relative value of orbital slots. Governments maintain the value of some orbits (their favored ports) rather than others by outlawing some receivers so as to preserve and enforce their determination as to preferred orbital slots and satellite systems (Price, 1994). They place pressure on channel service providers (the new networks) to use favored carriers, like Spain favoring Hispansat or Egypt Nilesat or Turkey Turksat. These deliberate governmental interventions increase the value of some trade routes and reduce others to nothingness. Low earth orbital satellites, much greater in number, with very different characteristics, may replace old technologies; and, combined with the Internet, may render existing attributes of value less reliable. Trade routes have always defined markets. They enrich the immediate environments of the ports of call by creating subsidiary needs for commercial support, such as the building or maintenance of ships or the provision of housing for those who came to ensure the security of the routes themselves. The route itself implied a particular form of trade, a scope of trade, a set of demands that were the very product of the route.[4] The opening of new routes in the sky for the distribution of images has radically altered the strategies of transnational corporations, just as the opening of new eighteenth-century routes altered the strategies of their equivalent business entities. These new routes in the sky also require new definitions of markets, as when states use the capacity of the new technology and the routes that are made available to reach out to their diaspora populations.

All of this suggests the need for a richer understanding of the geopolitical, economic, and technical factors that determine who controls which orbital slots, what satellites gain access to those slots and what program services are actually carried. Much of the literature of globalization deals only with the last point and its supposed cultural impact. But an understanding of the infrastructure—the way satellite routes come into being and are regulated—is necessary for an assessment of the consequences of information and entertainment flows. One way to begin this process is to examine some examples—small case studies—of the differentiation of satellite patterns. These examples help show how the struggles of users, governments and the international community mirror similar events in earlier efforts to control paths of commerce.

TONGA AND CONTROL OF ORBITAL SLOTS

A first example involves the Kingdom of Tonga, a bold pioneer in creating political control of orbital slots and turning that control to economic advantage (Ezor, 1993). In the late twentieth century, bureaucratic wiliness, not armed force, allowed Tonga to accomplish its objective of becoming a power in information routes. Assertions of the right to control these ephem-

eral harbors for the shipment of data must traverse the International Telecommunication Union (ITU) and its World Administrative Radio
Conferences (now known as WRCs). Modern bureaucracies, not distant
potentates, determine the existence of routes. It is neither papal decrees nor
regal ordinances, but bland officials in Geneva that organize lines on maps
of commercial consequence (Thompson, 1996). The dominant figures in
the battle for control over orbital slots wear suits, shirts and ties, not naval
uniforms. Trade routes emerge because of complex compromises and interrelationships among issues, not the sheer exercise of cannons or the
clever use of sophisticated maps.[5]

Tonga has been one of the most dramatic actors in the process of ac-
quiring orbital slots. Tonga was once representative of the point of view
that equatorial nations ought to have preferred access, almost by natural
law, to the geostationary orbit in outer space above. The equatorial states
asserted this right in the 1976 Bogotá Declaration (Gorove, 1991). The
view was argued in contrast to the strongly asserted position of the industrialized West that outer space was a kind of public domain not belonging
a priori to any state. The view of Tonga and others conflicted with international precepts that favored the highly developed nations by allocating
orbital slots to those countries first to have the financial and technological
resources to use the slots for satellites.[6]

In the 1980s, the ITU adopted a policy that, while rejecting the assertion
of the equatorial nations, did establish a process for claiming an orbital
slot which sought to leave some leeway for developing countries. Member
states could file their intention to use a slot. Then, if they in fact used it
within a reasonable period, they would actually have control of that slot.[7]
Tonga used this paper filing opportunity more than any other country. It
obtained claims on seven valuable slots even without drawing on its status
as an equatorial state. As with their counterparts, the terrestrial trade
routes, Tonga transferred use of its space to others, private telecommunications corporations, for economic benefits. Because neither the ITU nor
the "paper-satellite" countries had any means of policing the slot once a
corporation launched its satellite there, the orbital slot effectively became
a commodity controlled by the leasing corporate entity.

By 1997, the international community, at the ITU Radio Conference,
modified the procedures to lessen the likelihood of Tonga-like occupation
or warehousing of orbital slots. The 1997 plan shortened the length of time
a satellite application could remain on file from nine years (six plus an
automatic three-year extension) to seven years (five years plus a two-year
extension, conditional on an indication that a satellite was not launched
despite good faith efforts to do so). Still, an effort to impose financial prerequisites for the posting of allocation claims was beaten back. Language
endorsing "equitable access" was retained, recognizing some desire to ensure representation for developing countries. This compromise measure

gained support from Tonga and other equatorial countries. It was also favored by satellite businesses that preferred using these countries as ports of entry, rather than other, more truculent and difficult holders of orbital rights.

In March 1998, the national satellite company of Tonga, Tongasat, together with Russian-owned and registered Inspace Corp., announced a plan to launch an ambitious fleet of satellites to serve the Asian Pacific region, and perhaps beyond, using Tonga's seven ITU-registered slots. This "paper-plan" to use paper-satellites, if it were to occur, would have made Tonga a major telecommunications service provider, allowing the country to realize the profits of using its orbital slots, rather than only the income from selling the airspace (Keith-Reid, 1998). This plan has not been realized.

Think of this Tongan experience, repeated elsewhere, in trade route terms. A geographical location (be it an ocean port or an orbital slot) might have the potential to be of great value to traders. For it to become an active site within a trading pattern, however, requires more: a degree of investment, security, establishment of a physical port with attendant facilities. Tonga had gained the right to a slot, but only with further activity could that slot actually become part of a route that would bring financial and other benefits to Tonga. Sione Kite, then-managing director of Tongasat said, "We will prove the world wrong. They never expected us to have satellites up there in their wildest dreams."[8] Tonga's creative use of the definitions of "rights" to orbital slots is a gloss on the idea of the West's technological dominance in the demarcation of satellite use. We could compare revisionist historical accounts that criticize the predominant view of European dynamism in the demarcation of terrestrial trade routes from the seventeenth century onwards.[9] It is probable that some important traditional ports, part of the complex of seventeenth-century trade routes, gained their significance not through selection by the East India Company or its counterparts, or by location alone, but by the initiative and ingenuity of preexisting political forces.

Ironically, the United States, which had been one of the strongest critics of Tongasat on the international scene, indirectly acknowledged that speculation in orbital slots was acceptable. The United States did this in 1996 through the auctioning by the Federal Communications Commission of an orbital slot for direct broadcasting services (DBS), alleged at the time to be the last DBS slot capable of "seeing" all of the continental United States. MCI agreed in 1996 to pay $682 million for this slot—a staggering sum that reinforced the point that some points on trade routes are more valuable than others.

The MCI DBS auction purchase also illustrated another point about orbital slots: that numerous countries may have claims to similar slots, leading to potential conflicts as we move in communications to a world with new mapping and new forms of boundaries. After MCI agreed to pay the huge price for its DBS slot, other companies suddenly became interested in Canadian and Mexican slots that offer the potential for a footprint that covers most of the United States, therefore theoretically able to reach the most lucrative audience in the world. This aspiration for competing slots would have been based on the general U.S. position that the distinction between the "domestic" and "international" satellite systems was no longer a meaningful one. The U.S. effort has been to establish the principle, largely based on the WTO agreement on telecommunications, that satellite transmissions should not stop at national borders. MCI was not pleased to find out that others might receive—for free or at greatly reduced prices—orbital slots somewhat similar to the one that MCI bought with a promise from the United States that it was the "last" of its type. Of course, MCI's unhappiness in this regard may be an illustration of a point that applied to trade routes as well: Investing heavily in one trade route for profit is usually accompanied by efforts to ensure that competitors cannot establish a route in the immediate vicinity.

The story of Tonga is, of course, an anomaly. As with trade routes of the past, it was not the actual, physical, terrestrial route or the points of transportation that ultimately counted, but the economic and political forces that controlled trade along those routes. Even if orbital slots are widely distributed among states, the arrangements to control satellites themselves, and the ultimate predominance of the West in the satellite trade, makes the analogy to the past more striking (Curtin, 1984).

COMPETITION TO CONTROL THE SATELLITES

Let us, thus, turn from the orbital slots themselves to the satellites that fill them. If the slots are the trade route equivalent of ports of call, then the satellites can be likened to the great trading vessels, especially when the entire system of uploading and downloading of signals is taken into account. Here there are many dramatic stories. One of the most dramatic involves the effort of private corporations seeking to break government satellite monopolies, mirroring, perhaps, swashbuckling efforts to enter government-controlled trade in the eigthteenth century. Take, for example, the long struggle of Rene Anselmo, creator of the fiercely independent PanAmSat, a U.S. private satellite operator later associated with Hughes Electronics, against the intergovernmental body that has been Intelsat. Anselmo saw that Intelsat, concentrating on the satellite transmission of data and telephone messages, was ignoring a trade opportunity for the shipment and distribution of broadcast signals through satellites. Anselmo saw an unserved geographical market as well, using satellites to link the United States to Latin America and to link parts of Latin America to one another.[10]

Intelsat, like the trading companies of old, used government power, treaties, discriminatory pricing and other techniques in the late 1980s and early

1990s to maintain its monopoly and squelch PanAmSat and Anselmo.[11] PanAmSat used a clever capability of navigating various government bureaucracies and banking firms to gain a foothold. The existence of these carriers meant new markets. The boom in global broadcasting channels, such as CNN, meant a profitable cargo source for PanAmSat.

The rise of the deregulatory mentality endorsing the theme of competition and of multilateral trade agreements in which government restrictions would be reduced, magnified opportunities for PanAmSat to deliver its signals to earth stations in Europe and elsewhere. In a cocktail of his own metaphors, Anselmo wailed about the monopoly in 1990 when he sought greater freedom to carry data over his system as well as video channels: "We were sent into battle with this monstrous worldwide telephone cartel with both hands tied behind our back. . . . Intelsat's response to PanAmSat was to launch a global boycott of the company, lobby to prevent and stall the launch of our satellite, and start a war of predatory pricing to drive us out of the market. And that was only the tip of the iceberg of unfairness that they have thrown at us."[12] Once the monopoly was avoided, Anselmo's company succeeded wildly, challenging the rules of access and use of trade routes in the sky.

There are many other stories about the use of control over satellites to gain the profits of the trade, other chapters in the drama of establishing empires of the sky. In the 1990s, Luxembourg's Societe Europeene des Satellites (SES) came into existence with its Astra satellite series offering the most aggressive opening to a broadly European audience. This satellite company is responsible for more than 75 percent of Europe's direct-to-home audience. Again echoing the history of trading companies, a consortium of banks with substantial public investment owns it.[13] At the end of the decade, SES was in high-stakes, fierce competition for a single point on the geostationary orbit, the valuable 29 degrees east satellite position reaching Europe.[14] SES claimed the right to that airspace, based on varying interpretations of a 1997 World Administrative Radio Conference Agreement, but so had Deutsche Telekom. Both had already placed satellites in that airspace in dangerous proximity. Eutelsat planned to launch a third within that same 28–29 degree space by the year 2000, violating the norm that satellites are usually positioned at least three degrees apart.[15] With the ITU as decision-maker, SES obtained the slot.

A third element of the infrastructure involves the programming services that use the satellite, much like the shippers whose cargoes filled the vessels of seventeenth-century trade routes. Just as those trade routes reorganized markets for goods, satellite footprints reorganize markets for information. There are numerous examples of trade routes creating the possibility of trade and of physical distribution patterns inspiring new approaches to them. One recent example is Alfa TV.[16] Established by 25 countries in Central and Eastern Europe and the former Soviet Union, Alfa TV was proposed as a multilingual channel "to promote cooperation and reconcil-iation" in the region. With the support of the European Parliament and the European funding project called Eureka Audiovisuel, its task would be to use films and other cultural programs to reach an audience estimated at 400 million viewers, from Finland to Azerbaijan. Like other trans-European channels, such as the German-French Arte and the regional Euronews, Alfa-TV is presenting itself as an alternative to the oft-cited flood of American culture. It is the existence of new satellite routes that makes Alfa-TV and its cohorts possible, just as it was the existence of the great new foci of Hudson Bay and Goa that created new forms of cross-cultural imagining, respectively, between English, French and Native American fur traders or Portuguese, Asian and African in earlier times. Like these centers of trade, which were not exclusively dominated by any one cultural group, alter-natives such as Alfa-TV resist the imposition of one cultural model in the ever-expanding stream of information available by satellite (Curtin, 1984).

THE LAW OF SATELLITE TRADE ROUTES

One of the most intriguing questions is whether particular trade routes—historically or at present—are selected not just for their geographical span, but because of the legal environment that surrounds them: whether there is a relationship of pathway to law, and law to cargo. Points within dis-tribution patterns traditionally have barred certain cargo or put them in quarantine (one can think of animals or seeds or people). Such rules may have made some routes preferable to others. Now we can ask how gov-ernments that have control over an orbital slot regulate its use to affect the cargo in programming. In 1993, for example, the Secretary of State for what was then National Heritage (now Culture, Media and Sport) in the United Kingdom sought to block the marketing of subscriptions to allegedly pornographic broadcasts arriving in the country via direct broadcast sat-ellite (i.e., a signal that came straight from a satellite to a small receiver at a person's home or place of business). The particular route selected for the delivery of the service, called Erotica Rendez-Vous, involved the "uplink-ing" (the sending from the ground) of the signal from France to a tran-sponder within the Eutelsat satellite system for transmission into the United Kingdom.

The route selected meant that the legal structure of the European Union applied to this transmission, especially the 1989 Television Without Fron-tiers Directive. Under that regime, the law precludes officials in the recipient country, in this case the United Kingdom, from unilaterally prohibiting the programming, as could have been the case had the programming originated from outside the European Union. Because of the trade route selected by the programming source, the United Kingdom was obliged to mediate with the host authority, in this case France, to discuss its official finding that

British standards were violated. Under the European law applied to images distributed within the Union, if distribution of Erotica Rendez-Vous is lawful in the country of origin (or where the sender is established), then under the Directive, UK officials cannot act alone to block it. The European Directive gives member states the power to "suspend retransmission" of a service (originating from within the Union) only if it "manifestly, gravely and seriously" harms children by "impairing their moral development," as defined in Article 22 of the Directive. The United Kingdom and France may have sharply different views on what constitutes manifest and grave impairment of a child's moral development.[17]

It is still somewhat unclear what British officials can do, even with a domestic law that provides the secretary of state to "proscribe" a foreign satellite service deemed to be "unacceptable." Many are the voices that say that regulation of programming as cargo is not only indefensible, but also technologically impossible. Still, the British government can preclude cable television operators from carrying a violating signal that arrives via satellite; it can try to prevent the sale of decoders and it can make it a crime to market a proscribed signal or to advertise in connection with such a signal. What it cannot actually do is make the signal itself go away. In terms of trade routes, the significance of European law is that the transportation of signals from one country within the Union to another is a trade route with a law of content that differs from a trade route that originates outside the Union.

MED-TV

A quite different story about the cultural and political implications of the choice of trade route involves an extraordinary satellite service called MED-TV. MED-TV was established in London to distribute programming via satellite to the Kurdish population worldwide. MED-TV especially sought to reach Kurdish minorities in Turkey, Iran and Iraq. Its programming, produced in large part in Belgium, was a mix of news, entertainment and education, important to a historically diasporic community of 35 million engaged in, among other things, trying to rediscover and redefine Kurdish nationhood and reaffirm its language and culture. Naomi Sakr has called MED-TV a "kind of Kurdistan in space," as it provided a culturally unifying function despite the lack of a Kurdish homeland or single territorial base. Satellite broadcasting has proven a superior method of information exchange amongst Kurdish people because it neither relied on literacy (levels remain low, especially among women who remain in the home) nor involved complications of print media ranging from unstable mailing addresses to state censorship and circulation prohibitions. The service was also relatively inexpensive and was obtainable even in remote villages (Sakr, 1999).

Not all saw the implications of MED-TV in such a positive light. Turkey viewed MED-TV as virtually the media arm of the PKK, the separatist Kurdish force that has been engaged in armed conflict with Turkish government troops and has been deemed by Turkey to be a significant threat to the integrity and indivisibility of the country.[18]

For an entity like MED-TV, selection of a trade route for the distribution of its images was a complex matter. It sought a mode that would involve the least possible intervention, either directly by Turkey or by other governments at Turkey's behest. For example, its transmission was originally on the Hotbird satellite. But for viewers to turn their receiving dishes to Hotbird meant they were conspicuous in comparison to their neighbors, whose dishes were turned to a different, Eutelsat-originated satellite, which carried traditional Turkish entertainment channel services. The difference in the attitude of the dish could be perceived by the authorities. To protect its viewers, MED-TV had to shift, therefore, from Hotbird to Eutelsat.

Another element of political choice of route arose from the very transponders on the Eutelsat system that would be used by MED-TV. Access to Eutelsat's transponders, given the structure of the satellite service (it is owned by Eurovision, a cooperative effort of state entities), has political implications. These transponders are controlled by public agencies; the states that control those agencies have relations with Turkey. Stories were told of MED-TV securing time on a Slovakian-controlled time slot only to have the Turkish Foreign Minister obtain a cancellation through bilateral discussions. MED-TV was unceremoniously bounced from various transponders on Eutelsat and their contracts for access canceled. Put in trade route terms, because of the contraband nature/status of the cargo, the reliability of MED-TV's cargo arrangements was at risk.

One solace, an anchor, as it were, was MED-TV's license, or authorization to broadcast. Whatever their political goals, the choice of a relatively secure legal and political system that would govern the delivery of their information was one of MED-TV's most important goals and was a vital part of the strategy for obtaining transponder space to reach the relevant audience. The organization "established" itself in the United Kingdom, a technical term that meant that they were qualified, under British law, to receive a license from the UK's Independent Television Commission. This resulted in MED-TV's being subject to the ITC's content standards. However, receiving a British permit allowed MED-TV to claim that it met British broadcasting standards. This might, therefore, increase the chances that its programming would be subject only to legal, as opposed to extra-legal, constraints. At the danger of pushing the metaphor too far, the MED-TV decision could be perceived as a rough equivalent of flying the British flag on the main mast.

Turkish officials mounted an extensive campaign to pressure the British government to withdraw MED-TV's license and close the producer down.

They contended that MED-TV was a "political organization" and therefore, under UK legislation, precluded from obtaining a British license. In February 1998, the Independent Television Commission, charged with supervision of licensed entities in Britain, penalized MED-TV for three broadcasts, for a total fine of approximately $150,000. According to the Commission, despite formal warnings, MED-TV violated the impartiality requirements of ITC's programming code. In one breach, according to the ITC, a "40-minute long program consisted entirely of a political rally organized by the PKK." The violation was that "No context was supplied and there was no balancing material." In a second breach of impartiality requirements, MED-TV "seemingly endorsed" the on-camera condemnation of a United States list of terrorist organizations. A third transgression of the ITC's rules (involving neutrality of journalists) involved "personal comments" from a MED-TV journalist in the field, namely a description of the more pro-government Kurdish Democratic Party as "treacherous and murderous."[19] Finally, in 1999, the ITC withdrew the license, finding that the station had too often violated standards of objectivity and impartiality. Soon thereafter, MED-TV closed down.

The point here is not the validity of the ITC decisions, but the legal and political consequences for MED-TV of choosing (or being forced by circumstances to choose) a particular route for the origination and transportation of its satellite-borne information. MED-TV, in fact, could be the poster-child for the idea that there are vital implications, in terms of the capacity to achieve a safe passage between sender and receiver, of the choice of path for transmission. MED-TV's history has been one not only of British sanctions, but, within Turkey, specific army and police raids to destroy satellite receiving antennas that would be capable of retrieving the MED-TV signal. Those in charge of the Kurdish broadcasting entity were constantly searching for alternative means of assuring a route in which access to production facilities, uplinking, satellite access and downlinking into Turkey could be achieved as seamlessly as possible, free of government intervention.

Although MED-TV was on some levels a success, the hostilities toward it and the successful attempts to close it down, should prompt a reevaluation of some of the predictions for the potential of satellite communications. Channels like MED-TV are both "deterrestrialized," meaning that they address audiences in multiple geopolitical territories, and "deterritorialized," in that they may be based abroad, target primarily foreign audiences, and hire foreign nationals. The "deterritorialized" world can be seen as organized vertically into nation-states and horizontally into "overlapping, permeable multiple system[s] of interaction," along lines of shared interests, opinions, beliefs, tastes, ethnicities and religions. For some time, scholars have been weighing the implications of the supposedly disintegrating value of territory. In 1961 historian Arnold Toynbee posited that in the information age, diasporas could be "the wave of the future," supplanting the nation-state. Waves of information can serve to affirm nations that supersede existing states, or they can affirm the power of existing nation-states, reaffirming and relegitimizing their existence and their regulatory powers (Toynbee & Castells, cited in Verlhust, 1999).

States have passed stringent laws regarding access to satellite channels. These measures are imperfect at best: Cheaper and easier access to technology, from satellite dishes to wireless cable systems, enable the flouting of regulations such as the bans on satellite dishes in Saudi Arabia and Iran. Furthermore, sporadic enforcement of the ban in Saudi Arabia and declarations that the ban was unconstitutional in Iran have rendered these measures ineffectual. Even in Algeria, where a military coup in 1992 ended that country's political aperture, residents continued to turn to francophone news and analysis. Sharing satellite dishes and "improvised cabling" (read "stealing") further lower the cost of obtaining satellite transmissions. Governments can no more prevent the spread of this contraband than the Spanish viceregal government could entirely prevent the circulation of yellowing philosophical texts. Furthermore, technology allows its spread to happen at a much greater speed and reaches a much wider audience.

There is a much more powerful restraint on this spread of information than attempts to rid remote villages and urban shantytowns of their television access, namely control of the material being broadcast. Although access to satellite television can cost as little as U.S.$10 per month, the start-up costs for a channel runs into the millions. The Saudi Middle East Broadcasting Centre (MBC) was half-jokingly referred to as "My Broadcasting Company," as within several years the financial support of private investors apparently shifted to King Fahd and his associates. As we have seen before, even those private channels broadcasting from outside the region (based instead in England, France or Italy, to circumvent state restrictions on content) are subject to international pressure exerted by incensed governments and the preferences and judgments of private management and investors. Power relations within individual states and between them drive satellite transmission in the Arab world in a far greater way than had been optimistically predicted.[20]

ORBITAL SLOTS AS CULTURAL GATEWAYS

There are other examples, often trade related, in which countries have used slots from time to time to regulate access of information and entertainment to their populations, much as governments have often used ports of entry as a caliber of openness. Some countries, such as Malaysia, control trade routes by establishing a monopoly of information distribution in a favored orbital slot and restricting the use of the slot by limiting channel services to the control of those friendly to the government. Canada wishes to enforce its Canadian cultural content effort by prohibiting its citizens from gaining access to signals that travel through orbital slots not under Canadian control. It has, in the past, sought to criminalize the sale of receivers that allow the receipt of signals from satellites in orbital slots of American origin. Iraq has prohibited and confiscated satellite dishes capable of receiving signals from the West, particularly transmissions thought to be culturally subversive. There is some distant affinity to trade routes here, in the use of points of entry to control the kinds of products that would otherwise pass to affected populations, or in other words, the use of the power of the trade route for cultural screening. The BBC published excerpts of recorded prayer sermons at Teheran University on September 16, 1994, by an Imam for whom screening and banning was essential:

Satellite transmission, broadcasting the programs of foreign television networks, is not designed to increase the scientific knowledge of nations. Rather it has been developed to mislead the youth. . . . They [the West] do not transfer their knowledge . . . [or] their experience of modernizing technology. What they transfer is something which drags families into corruption.[21]

Such cultural screening is by no means unique to the Islamic world. Almost two centuries ago, in its efforts to retain its tenuous hold on its American colonies, Spain prohibited the transport, sale and distribution of subversive documentation inspired by Enlightenment philosophy. National and international regulation of trade routes is a complicated matter. The debates discussed in the ITU on actual control of orbital slots, the concept of "equitable access," and the debate between the developed and developing countries over *a priori* and *a posteriori* approaches to regulation, have not been the only ones to arise. Twenty years ago in the United Nations, countries were already debating whether an international regime could be established that controlled the content in the trade of images. A sweeping draft convention would have imposed a set of substantive standards on satellite-delivered information, excluding from television programs transmitted by satellites "any material publicizing ideas of war, militarism, nazism, national and racial hatred and enmity between peoples as well as material which is immoral or instigative in nature or is otherwise aimed at interfering the domestic affairs or foreign policy of other States."[22]

CONCLUSION

The complexity of corporate structures, the intricate relationships between business ventures and governments in the satellite field, and the difficulty of public accessibility of contracts for the transmission of program services, all turn the current, intricate patterns of transportation of satellite images around the world into a black box of unknown content. Scholarship, partly as a consequence, has looked at what seemed most apparent about this traffic for a very long time, namely that programming has its source in values and in production in the West, often the United States, and its impact elsewhere (Schiller, 1976; Tunstall, 1977). But as this picture changes, details will be far more important, including details about the ways trade routes in imagery and data are shaped and restricted. This will have to include closer examination of how governments use such powers as they still attempt to retain control of the ways information is received within their borders, and how they use their control over orbital slots.[23] Not for nothing has the rhetoric of the global entrepreneurs, like Rupert Murdoch, changed from the claim of borderless skies to a claim of deference to states.

Trade routes, of whatever vintage, have always been constituted of a series of physical points where ownership or control has been vital. More than that, however, these points, taken together, had geopolitical implications as they transformed into ports, concessions, warehouses, colonies, sources of raw material and markets for products. For the old trade routes, any government or power seeking to maintain the value of any particular point along the route was expected to struggle for that point's exclusivity, its competitive advantage, or its access to raw materials or markets. Trade routes in the sky, too, have their elements of exclusivity. Orbital slots have increased value if they or the satellites that occupy them do not increase in supply or if the demand for them keeps exploding in volume. For the satellite routes, as for their predecessors, technology increases supply while participants seek to retain control and quasi-monopolistic power.

In the broadcast era, when terrestrial transmitters were the exclusive technology, international concern had, historically, been to avoid the possible invasion of the domestic space of one country from its neighbor, especially for propaganda purposes. There were exceptions, such as the implicit acceptance of short-wave radio as a space for transnational services, symbolized by the use of spectrum by the BBC, the Voice of America and hundreds of other external services. But bilateral agreements—for example, between Mexico and the United States—were designed to insure minimal intrusion along the long borders. In the Cold War, the Eastern bloc's choice of SECAM for its color television technology was a technological break with the West's PAL. With the recent inception of the post-Soviet era, the use of international pathways for external services, like Radio Liberty, has been freshly debated. There are new disputes about Radio Marti, directed at Cuba, and Radio Free Asia, directed, among other places, at China and Vietnam, showing that traditional technologies continue to play an important role in the transportation of political imagery.

For the first 50 years of broadcasting, the entire motivation of a virtually united international community was to establish trade routes that assumed a national gatekeeper. With some important exceptions, "harm" was largely defined as the intentional spillover of spectrum use from one national zone into another. Terrestrially, the use of directional antennas, the reduction of power and the careful designation of spectrum were sufficient largely to accomplish the international consensus. As a 1930s international covenant put it:

The High Contracting Parties mutually undertake to prohibit and, if occasion arises, to stop without delay the broadcasting within their respective territories of any transmission which to the detriment of good international understanding is of such a character as to incite the population of any territory to acts incompatible with the internal order or the security of a territory of a High Contracting Party.[24]

Today, despite the fact that the technological capabilities of the satellite implicate issues of national identity, there is no international consensus on the rules that should guide the establishment of trade routes in the sky. The world is sharply divided into camps on how and whether to restrict routes by which that content gets delivered. Some consider that transportation in images should (indeed, must) be subject to national controls. Malaysia and India, in recent broadcast reform proposals, require that any information or imagery that is sent down from a satellite to people within its borders must first arise from within the territory, a so-called uplinking requirement. The tendency of some countries to require uplinking within their boundaries is an example of what Saskia Sassen has called reinstalling the local (Sassen, 1996, 1998). Despite the dizzying potential for free exchange of information available through satellites, some states are attempting to assert a sort of digital trade monopoly, exclusively controlling the exchange and distribution of information transmitted by satellite, or at the very least its points of entry and departure.[25]

On the other hand, multilateral trade negotiations which resulted in the World Trade Organization have dramatically asserted the idea of reducing barriers to free flow of services, including information and programs. The position has often been sounded that free trade in goods and economic growth is not possible without a free trade in information. As part of the ideology surrounding these multilateral negotiations, government restrictions on transmission of imagery and programming whether tied to national assertions or not, are condemned as violations of the human right to receive or impart information. The U.S. position, consistent with these views, is generally to assert that access to orbital slots, to licenses, and to markets should be as free as possible of public regulation. But, as we have seen, free trade does not necessarily mean random patterns of distributing information.

These new trade routes are not visible, linear, nor functionally evolved from prior methodologies. Invisible and "post-modern," the new routes will break some traditional categories, but reinforce others. They will crisscross regional lines, produce information spills such as pornography on the Internet, and allow diasporic groups to communicate among themselves. Seemingly indivisible by national boundaries, these routes prod existing sovereigns to search for ways in which these borders can be rehabilitated. They are almost solely about trade in information, though trade in information leads to changes in trade and development of physical products. Enveloped in technology, masked by complexity, it is apparent that the configuration of these satellite routes have an important relationship to democracy and culture and to the spaces for public debate. A focus on the details of these structures of distribution, the satellite routes of the distant firmament, is a necessary aspect of communications studies in the future.

NOTES

The author would like to acknowledge Henry Goldberg, Julian McGougan and Phillip Spector, who reviewed this chapter and made very useful comments. Kristina A. Boylan also assisted in historical research and revision.

1. Until the mid-nineteenth century, international, long-distance communication could be on the order of years. Steamships, canals and train reduced the lag to months. But it was not until the invention of the telegraph cable that a same-day exchange became possible (Curtin, 1984). Telephones, and following them, the Internet, have reduced the time lag to seconds.

2. The ancient definition of the port, *portus*, is "a place through which merchandise is carried." In this sense the routes and ports of the system of satellite communication can be compared to their terrestrial predecessors (Curtin, 1984).

3. The focus of this chapter is on geostationary satellites, which have been virtually the only kind of satellites operating commercially. Over the next few years, however, commercial operations by low earth orbit (LEO) satellites will commence. For these satellites, the concept of orbital slots is entirely irrelevant, but the concept of orbital planes may nonetheless make the trade route metaphor relevant. The orbital paths taken by LEO constellations are not randomly selected, but rather are intended to traverse the major population zones of the world. In addition, the satellite themselves typically are designed with steerable antennas, which enable them to focus on populated areas even as the satellites move in and out of direct viewable range.

4. The classic example is the "spice trade," the route from China and Southeast Asia through to Europe developed by Asian, Middle Eastern and Mediterranean traders. Only comparatively small quantities of pepper and spices, in comparison to other cargoes, were transported along this route, but their high ratio of value to weight not only made the trips worthwhile (even circumnavigation of Africa or across the Pacific), but determined the routes and stops at ports of call as well (Curtin, 1984).

5. The ITU (originally the International Telegraphic Union) was established in 1865. It has sought to encourage cooperation among its member countries to improve global telecommunications and offer technical assistance to developing countries. Its Radio Conferences, held every second year, allocate orbital space to member countries.

6. This could be seen as contradictory to the first world countries' rhetoric of free trade, which they then circumvent by enabling a preference for industrialized nations with satellite-building capacities. A historical parallel can be found in late eighteenth- and early nineteenth-century British and French criticism of Spain's monopoly on trade with its American colonies. After Latin American independence, Britain and France then vied for exclusive trade concessions with the new nations, in seeming disregard of their earlier arguments for the benefits of opening markets to diverse foreign trade (Miller, 1993).

7. The ITU structure that exists for registration of orbital slots developed out of a telecommunications environment in which each country, including the United States at the outset, was the single monopoly carrier for virtually all telecommunications traffic. Intelsat was created by this "club" of carriers as a cooperative intended to establish satellite links among the monopolies, much as the same club members had created undersea cable links among themselves. The theory was that each country, through (typically) its government-owned monopoly, would control the domestic orbital slots over its own region, while Intelsat would control the international slots. The ITU orbital slot registration process made more sense when a telecommunications monopoly model existed than when a more open, competitive approach evolved.

8. "Tongasat Set to Lead Asian Satellite Consortium," *Communications Today*, January 19, 1998.

9. For example, Europe did not create the aforementioned links on the "spice route" between Asia, Africa and Europe, ultimately used for European benefit. On the contrary, the Europeans were late entries into networks of trade which had existed for almost a thousand years previously and had been evolving since. Shifts in political alliances and transportation technology did alter the importance and predominance of some ports (for example, overland trading routes through Central Asia being supplanted by maritime trade from Asia to Europe and Africa), but overall it was not geographical innovation on the Europeans' part, but the harnessing of new technologies, the creation of new trade structures and an increasing reliance on military strength to defend those structures that gave the West its predominance in world trade (Curtin, 1984).

10. In the late 1970s and early 1980s, as the owner of the largest U.S. Spanish-language television network, Anselmo sought to import Spanish-language programming from Latin America. Because the transmission of this programming would be international, the FCC required Anselmo's network to use Intelsat for the transmissions, even though U.S. domestic satellites were technically capable of carrying the traffic and would have done it at rates that were 50 percent or less of Intelsat's. Although the U.S. government eventually allowed some transborder communications via U.S. domestic satellites, Anselmo became so enraged that he decided to compete directly with Intelsat in the provision of international satellite services.

11. "PanAmSat Lobbies FCC for Greater Freedom," *FinTech Telecom Markets*, July 26, 1990.

12. There is an important relationship—illustrative of the legal creation of sites—between Anselmo's PanAmSat and the legal adventurousness of Tongasat. When Anselmo and others filed at the FCC in the early to mid-1980s for what were then called "separate system" licenses (because they were "separate" from the Intelsat system), the issue of orbital slots serving international routes first arose. If

indeed it would be possible to compete directly with Intelsat, then orbital slots over the oceans—which theretofore had been of interest solely to Intelsat—were suddenly of great potential value. Tongasat, led at that time by an American entrepreneur, was one of the first to recognize this potential and to recognize that the ITU's procedures essentially allowed any nation, no matter how small, to file for large numbers of these valuable slots.

13. Following a flotation, SES has a large number of Luxembourg-based shareholders as well.

14. This slot was valuable even though Astra already had six satellites at 19 degrees east for two reasons: First, they needed to have three degrees of separation or they have to share frequencies, reducing their value; second, because most DBS dishes are in a fixed position, the introduction of competition in delivery to those dishes undermines monopoly rent.

15. "Eutelsat Promotes 290 East Slot," *Cable and Satellite Express*, March 26, 1998 (p. 9), available in LEXIS < World Library, ALLWLD File; "Hostilities Resumed in SES-Eutelsat Star Wars," *Cable and Satellite Europe*, April 1998.

16. "Alfa TV—A Multilingual Satellite TV for Europe and FSU," *BBC Summary of World Broadcasts*, January 16, 1998.

17. Regina v. Secretary of State for the National Heritage *ex parte Continental Television BV*, April 30, 1993: [1993] CMLR 387 (dismissing an appeal from a denial of injunction to prevent the United Kingdom from banning reception, viewing and advertising of the pornographic channel Red Hot Television, emanating from Denmark).

18. "Turkey Calls on USA to End MED-TV Broadcasts," *BBC Summary of World Broadcasts*, August 30, 1996; "MED-TV Off the Air after UK, Belgian Police Raids," *BBC Summary of World Broadcasts*, September 27, 1996; "Turkish Premier Discusses MED-TV with Tony Blair," *BBC Summary of World Broadcasts*, December 19, 1997; also see Hassanpour (1995).

19. This history is recounted in Price (1998).

20. Sakr (1999), passim.

21. "Emani-Kashani: West Interested in Transfer Not of Technology but of Corruption," *BBC Summary of World Broadcasts*, September 19, 1994; The Middle East; Iran; ME/2104/MED, available in LEXIS < News Library, BBCSWB File.

22. Draft convention on principles governing the use by states of artificial earth satellites for direct television broadcasting. U.N. Doc. A/8771 (1972), art IV.

23. For a discussion of human rights and the Indian Broadcasting Bill, see Templeton (1998).

24. International convention concerning the use of broadcasting in the cause of peace, September 23, 1936, Art. I, 186 L.N.T.S. 301.

25. The structure of Spain's restrictions on trade and exchange with its American colonies serves as a historical parallel (Zahedieh, 1986). Of course, as Zahedieh demonstrates, non-Spanish traders and others who wished to exploit the system soon found ways of circumventing crown regulations, for example, by striking deals with merchants in Seville or Cádiz to deliver non-Spanish manufactured goods to or raw materials from the colonies, all through the legally-defined "Spanish" ports.

REFERENCES

Auber, P. (1828). *Supplement to an analysis of the constitution of the East-India Company and of the laws passed by parliament for the government of their affairs, at home and abroad, East India Company.* Goldsmiths'-Kress Library of Economic Literature. London: Parbury, Allen, and Co.

Curtin, P. D. (1984). *Cross-cultural trade in world history.* Cambridge: Cambridge University Press.

Ezor, J. I. (1993). Costs overhead: Tonga's claiming of sixteen geostationary orbital sites and the implications for U.S. space policy. *Law and Policy in International Business,* 24(3), 927–942.

Finch, M. J. (1986). Limited space: Allocating the geostationary orbit. *Northwestern Journal of International Law & Business,* 7(4), 788–802.

Gorove, S. (1991). *Developments in space law: Issues and policies.* Dordrecht, the Netherlands: Kluwer Academic Publishers.

Hassanpour, A. (1995, November 7). *Med-TV, Britain, and the Turkish State: A stateless nation's quest for sovereignty in the sky.* Unpublished paper presented at the Freie Universitat Berlin.

Horrabin, J. F. (1936). *The opening-up of the world.* London: Methuen & Co.

Juriaanse, M. W. (1943). *Catalogue of the archives of the Dutch coastal government of coastal Ceylon, 1640–1796.* Colombo: Ceylon Government Press.

Keith-Reid, R. (1998, March 11). *Tonga pushes for Pacific-owned communications network.* Associated Press Newsfeed.

Kumar, A. (1996). *Java and modern Europe: Ambiguous encounters.* London: Curzon Press.

Miller, R. (1993). *Britain and Latin America in the nineteenth and twentieth centuries.* London: Longman.

Price, M. E. (1994). The market for loyalties: Electronic media and the global competition for allegiances. *Yale Law Journal,* 104(3), 667–706.

Price, M. E. (1998). What price fairness? *Media Studies Journal,* 82, 83.

Quiggin, A. H. (1949). *Trade routes, trade and currency in East Africa: The occasional papers of the Rhodes-Livingstone Museum.* Rhodes-Livingstone Museum, Livingstone, Zambia.

Raychaudhuri, T. (1962). *Jan Company in Coromandel, 1605–1690: A study in the interrelations of European commerce and traditional economies.* 's-Gravenhage, the Netherlands: M. Nijhoff.

Sakr, N. (1999). Frontiers of freedom: Diverse responses to satellite television in the Middle East and North Africa. *The Public/Javnost: Journal of the European Institute for Communication and Culture,* 6(1), 102–106.

Sassen, S. (1996). *Losing control? Sovereignty in an age of globalization.* New York: Columbia University Press.

Sassen, S. (1998). *Globalization and its discontents: Essays on the new mobility of people and money.* New York: New Press.

Schiller, H. I. (1976). *Communication and cultural domination.* White Plains, NY: International Arts and Sciences Press.

Templeton, M. A (1998). Human rights perspective in the broadcasting bill debate. In M. E. Price and S. Verhulst (Eds.), *Broadcasting reform in India: A case study in the uses of comparative media law.* New Delhi: Oxford University Press.

Thompson, J. C. (1996). Space for rent: The international telecommunications union, space law, and orbit/spectrum leasing. *Journal of Air Law and Communications,* 62(1), 279–288. Cites Stern, M. L. (1982), Communications satellites and the geostationary orbit: Reconciling equitable access with efficient use. *Law and Policy of International Business*, 14(3), 859–864.

Tunstall, J. (1977). *The media are American.* New York: Columbia University Press.

Van Cleef, E. (1937). *Trade centers and trade routes.* New York: D. Appleton-Century Company.

Verhulst, S. (1999). Diasporic and transnational communication: Technologies, policies and regulation. *The Public/Javnost: Journal of the European Institute for Communication and Culture*, 6(1), 29–36.

Volokh, E. (1995). Cheap speech and what it will do. *Yale Law Journal* 104(7), 1805.

Zahedieh, N. (1986). The merchants of Port Royal, Jamaica, and the Spanish contraband trade, 1655–1692. *William and Mary Quarterly*, 43(4), 573–593.

Chapter 10

Globalization Ltd.: Domestication at the Boundaries of Foreign Television News

Akiba A. Cohen

Globalization has become a buzzword. It has also come to mean different things to different scholars and practitioners in various fields, including international comunication (Boyd-Barrett, 1997), and there already exist many questions and myths about it (Ferguson, 1992). In an interview in *Newsweek*, Klaus Schwab, the Swiss professor of economics who founded the World Economic Forum more than 30 years ago, speaks of three basic components of globalization: capital, technology and knowledge ("Interview," 1999). In response to a question, Schwab stated, "Rolling back globalization reminds me of the workers in Manchester in the last century who tried to stop industrialization by smashing the machines." Thus, globalization is a fact of life and is here to stay.

But surely not everything is or can be global or globalized. It is not my purpose here to survey, analyze or critique the various meanings that have been attached to the concept of globalization, nor to participate in the burgeoning academic discussion as to whether or not globalization has indeed led to a world culture (Wallerstein, 1997) or to American or Western cultural imperialism (Braman, 1996). Instead, my objective is to focus on one domain of what may be considered, prima facie, as a "classic" example of globalization, but to suggest that in fact it is not so. I am referring to foreign news in general—and particularly to foreign news on television.

In this chapter I wish to put forth three related arguments: First, that while globalization may be an appropriate term to describe certain processes that take place around the world with regard to many goods and services, including many cultural products, television news should be considered exempt; second, that the main reason that television news in general, and foreign news in particular, do not fit the principles of globalization are the contents and cognitive attributes of television news and the way they interact with its production and delivery; and third, that one of the prime mechanisms by which some of these limitations of globalization are dealt with is by the process of domesticating the news.

PRODUCTS AND SERVICES CROSSING BOUNDARIES

My point of departure, which I believe is indisputable, is that there exist today multinational conglomerates which produce a variety of goods (e.g., automobiles and food) and services (e.g., banking and telecommunication), which are consumed daily around the world by millions of people of different religions, cultures and ethnic backgrounds. Moreover, the media in their various manifestations—films, CDs, books, certain newspapers, magazines and radio stations, and of course television—probably represent the most pervasive and powerful examples of global presence as well as real influence on norms, values and behavior.

Furthermore, I would suggest that the prerequisites for global use of many of these goods and services are quite minimal, thereby making them quite easily available and socially acceptable. Thus, for example, in order to drive an automobile, to prepare a ready-to-eat meal, withdraw cash from an ATM machine or use a cellular telephone, all one needs to do is to acquire some basic skills and follow a few simple operations. In most places, the way each of these goods and services is consumed is basically the same, although there are instances in which local rules and customs restrict the use of certain products, which may slightly modify their nature or use. For example, each country may have slightly different traffic rules, including speed limits, parking regulations and so forth, and outlets of certain worldwide food chains may not serve alcohol or pork or mix cheese and meat in certain countries due to religious customs, even if their standard menus include such ingredients. As for ATM machines, the limits on cash withdrawals may differ from one location to another while the use of cellular phones may be prohibited in certain areas in some countries and not in others. But by and large, with regard to most material goods and services that are distributed around the world, globalization indeed seems to work.

The situation regarding media products is quite different, however. Such products are created in certain cultural milieu, and in most cases, the language in which the product was created is of central importance. Thus a book written in Chinese is first and foremost intended for Chinese people, a film produced in Portuguese is mostly relevant for the Portuguese, and a television situation comedy produced in Burbank, California, is intended first of all for the English speaking population of America. Of course, this does not mean that such products cannot be exported from their country of origin and distributed in other countries and cultures. They are indeed, and they thus represent further evidence of globalization. But in these situations the products must be converted, modified and adapted for local consumers: readers, cinemagoers and television viewers.

As indicated, the key variable is language. In the process of transporting fictional contents in literature, film and television programs across national boundaries, little is necessary nor can actually be done with the product other than providing the text in the local language (Cohen & Roeh, 1992). If the language in the importing country is the same as in the country of origin (e.g., Hollywood films being exported to the United Kingdom or British films to the United States), nothing needs to be done with the product, and it is virtually always presented as it was originally created, even though some elements may be missed entirely or misinterpreted, such as British humor being unfamiliar to Americans. If the language is different, however, it must be rendered into the language of the importing country via total translation.

In the case of books, the text is merely translated, not that this is always an easy operation. In the case of audiovisual products, translating the dialogue into the vernacular is done either by dubbing, when the cost of this expensive process can be justified and absorbed (usually in large markets) or by subtitles (in smaller markets). In this translation process, too, certain elements and nuances in the text or the dialogue may be lost, such as when an appropriate term or phrase might not be available or when a metaphor may not be meaningful in the importing culture. Other minor alterations can also occur in the course of adapting a film or a television program, such as certain (usually brief) segments being deleted due to censorship in the importing country or changing or omitting the placement of commercial breaks initially planned for certain points in the scenario. But overall, it seems reasonable to argue that most fictional programming is presented very similarly to the way it was originally produced.

The literature of the past two decades or so is rife with theoretical discussions and empirical examples of differential "readings" of media products by audiences. The notion that different people interpret a poem or a novel in different ways is not new (Bakhtin, 1981; Eco, 1979). The adoption of this idea to television and the pursuant discussions about it in the context of "reception theory" have expanded it to fictional television contents (e.g., Liebes & Katz, 1986). The common thread in all these approaches is that consumers, both readers and viewers, digest, interpret and make sense of the contents according to their personal repertoires and cultural backgrounds.

LIMITS ON THE GLOBALIZATION OF TELEVISION NEWS

Some scholars, notably Jensen (1986), have put forth the argument that similar processes occur with regard to non-fictional contents, that is, news.

While I cannot but agree that news viewers also make inferences from what they see based on their accumulated knowledge, ideology, politics and comprehension of what is presented in the news items, I wish to draw what I believe is an important distinction between television fiction and television news in the context of globalization. This distinction is in fact the pivot of the thesis that I present in this chapter. Accordingly, as I have briefly illustrated above, when fictional television contents cross cultural or national boundaries, very little needs to be done with them in the host country other than to have them translated. On the other hand, for news items to be relevant and understood by viewers in countries other than where the events took place, they must be prepared and presented in an appropriate fashion with the audience of the non-origin country in mind.

News from abroad, or what is commonly referred to as "foreign" news, can cross (or enter) borders in three basic ways: (1) as so-called "global news" broadcasts such as CNN-International or BBC World Television; (2) as a newscast from another country (often, but not necessarily, a neighboring one), usually by means of cable or satellite); and (3) as part of the domestic station's newscast, the material being provided by its own correspondents who are based (or sent) abroad or with the aid of material supplied by various news gathering agencies (e.g., Reuters Television or Worldwide Television News), as well as regional news exchange services (e.g., Eurovision or Asiavision).

The first type, the so-called global news broadcast, is of potential relevance to the concept of globalization, due to some presumed effort being made by news editors and producers in Atlanta or London to be relevant to people around the world. The major problem with these broadcasts is that they are in English and that they therefore cater to English speakers; hence, only such people can attend to them in a meaningful way (assuming that the contents are not heavily American and British, which they often are). And while one can perhaps get a sense of being in a "global village" by watching identical contents at the same time together with several other million people who are doing the same thing around the globe, this is not the critical force behind this genre of news. Thus while its proponents may believe that this form of news is indeed what globalization is all about, it is at best a very modest mutation of the concept.

The second type of transmission—newscasts from other countries—are quite readily available, but are relatively uninteresting to most viewers. This is part of the repertoire of numerous cable systems that make it possible for viewers in one country to see programs, including news, from other countries. Examples can be American newscasts viewed (in English) by Canadians across the border, French news seen in Germany (or vice versa), Chinese news picked up in Hong Kong and even the British SKY News channel, which is available, via satellite, in many parts of the world. However, the contents of these newscasts are not selected, nor are they geared toward, non-local viewers, and nothing is done by the producers to make them especially relevant. In fact, in many such cases, the language is foreign and many of the events reported are unfamiliar and hence lack relevance and meaning. Thus this type of news does not purport to be, nor is it in fact part of, what would be considered as "true" globalization.

The third type of news broadcast is clearly the most important and most interesting. Here, "foreign" news is brought to the home audience in an attempt to make it relevant and meaningful. Local news producers use reports by their own correspondents or utilize raw footage that they receive from various sources to construct a story for their viewers, and local editors create both the text and the context for these stories, often by "domesticating" the news (Cohen, Levy, Roeh & Gurevitch, 1996). Accordingly, many of the same stories are frequently reported around the globe, very often using the same visual materials that were obtained from the same source (or sources), although the final product presented in each country is bound to differ in certain ways. Thus, this form of news is closer to the concept of "glocalization"—a term coined by Robertson (1994)—than to globalization. I shall return to domestication later in the chapter.

In short, these three types of "foreign" news point to some of the limitations of the concept of globalization, or put another way, globalization does not seem to be a highly pertinent concept apropos news. This is surely a seeming paradox. On the one hand, probably more money, time and effort have been invested in and achievements made in technological developments in the growing field of broadcasting and telecommunications than in most other fields. These developments have indeed made it possible for messages to be transmitted around the world, in real time, from even the most remote corners of the earth as well as outer space. Also, political and economic organizations have been established to manage and regulate these amazing feats with the goal of providing more and more people with knowledge and information. On the other hand, it is precisely the medium of television and the news messages that it delivers, which most people rely upon for their daily ration of information (e.g., Robinson & Levy, 1996), which is so difficult for viewers around the world to decipher and make sense of (Cohen, 1998; Gunter, 1987).

COGNITIVE DIFFICULTIES WITH TELEVISION NEWS

In fact, I wish to suggest that despite the relative popularity of television news compared with other media, it is the most difficult and complex format for presenting current affairs. Numerous studies have found that the information gain from television news is relatively small. It has also been demonstrated that while many people do not really understand the news, their exposure to it provides a false impression that television helps them understand (see, e.g., Adoni & Cohen, 1978). Indeed Katz (1977) had even gone so far as to characterize television news as a "bias against understanding."

More recent research in this area has tended to examine specific news-related and audience-related variables. However, these studies have not paid much attention to the overall changes in the nature of television news. In recent years, TV news has become less informative and more entertaining, a notion that has been aptly coined "infotainment." This is due, at least in part, to the rapidly growing number of news-producing stations, increased commercialization and competition, and the vigorous pursuit of ratings. This worldwide trend, especially in what were traditional public service stations, mostly in Europe, has prompted many services to produce faster-moving and seemingly more dramatic news in an MTV-clip-style, which might in fact further inhibit the audience's ability to follow what is going on and to make sense of the news. There seem to be many reasons for this.

Research on the content of the news indicates that despite some communality, there is much variability in what is presented each evening across the world (e.g., Malik & Anderson, 1992). News is about internal and international politics, crime and law and order, national defense, economics, business, labor relations, commerce, industry, agriculture, health, welfare, education, communication, housing, the environment, energy, science and technology, social relations, religion, culture and other topics. News is about people, objects, places, processes and combinations thereof. Some news is characterized as "hard" while some is "soft." Some issues in the news are simple and straightforward while many others involve complex, intense and insolvable social conflicts. In some news there is little or no emotion, while other items are heavily laden with graphic footage.

Some of the news is about events that took (or will take) place in relatively close proximity to the viewer (neighborhood, city or country) while other news deals with events that originate in other countries, often on the other side of the globe. While foreign news is typically less prominent in newscasts, it is gaining popularity in some places. This is due at least in part to the ever-increasing sophistication of media technologies as well as global geopolitical changes and the greater degree of interconnectedness among nations, such as the creation of the European Community; the dissolution of the Eastern European block and the expansion of NATO; worldwide financial crises; the intervention of the United Nations and NATO in the affairs of other nations; and the resolution of long-standing conflicts.

For viewers to make sense of the news, they must possess certain abilities and characteristics that they don't always have. Viewers enter news (and other) viewing situations with their own idiosyncratic and personal histories, repertoires, experiences and knowledge, which are the product of complex and cumulative cognitive and affective on-going socialization and acculturation processes.

It has been suggested that people develop mental schemas for many concepts and categories, including events, people, places and processes. These mental images contain cognitive and affective traces of phenomena that have been internalized following auditory and visual exposure to information (Taylor & Crocker, 1981). Accordingly, each new bit of information that reaches the individual, directly or via the media, is either integrated into an existing schema or leads to the creation of a new one, and the more elaborate one's cognitive structure, the easier and more successful it is to process, absorb and integrate new information and to make sense of it. Finally, the interaction of news content and viewer properties leads to certain modes of recall and comprehension of the news.

Certain formal features of news items and newscasts create further problems for viewers. Newscasts consist of quick successions of very brief and unrelated items with no time to pause between them, and with little or no context or background provided. Thus both proactive and retroactive interference occurs. In the former process, a particular item interferes with learning the next one, whereas in the latter an item interferes with learning the preceding one.

Given the audiovisual imperative of television news, editors and producers place emphasis on both channels and the interaction between them. At least five visual elements are of interest, which makes things difficult for viewers. First, the brevity of the news items including rapid editing with many cuts and very brief scenes. Second, editing of footage in non-chronological order, by using video fragments from several (often unrelated) sources, including file or archival material of previous events. Third, complex editing of interviews with the interviewer often unseen and unheard. Fourth, the use of graphic and emotional material such as war, terrorism, disasters and accidents in which the visual material, can "mask" the main information which is presented in the verbal text (e.g., where the event took place, how and why it happened, who and how many victims there were, etc.). Finally, computer graphics, which have become a prominent device in television news, including superimposed text on pictures and simultaneous presentation of two or more visual scenes.

Regarding the audio portion of the news, eight points should be mentioned. First, the speed at which newscasters read the news is usually much faster than most people can read. Second, there is the use of long, complex and sometimes incomplete and incoherent sentences. Third, there is the use of a high linguistic register that is often above the level of the typical audience member. Fourth, there is the use of references to many names of people, places, institutions, organizations, concepts, acronyms and metaphors, as well as to foreign language terms, which are unfamiliar and lack relevance and meaning. Fifth, just as there are very briefly edited visual components, so, too, there are very briefly edited verbal "soundbites," which are sometimes only one or two seconds long, with hardly any time to identify the speaker. Sixth, while a basic ingredient of news items is interviews, the viewer is often not privy to the questions put to the interviewee and doesn't know what was asked. Seventh, the audio portion of news items is sometimes not limited to the language of the anchor, reporter and the domestic people-in-the-news, but includes a voice-over translation of what the person said. And eighth, items also contain "natural sound" of voices and noises heard during the event (e.g., chanting of demonstrators, gunfire, sirens, etc.), all of which make it more difficult to decipher what is being said.

The final factor that makes the television news item such a difficult stimulus to process is the often lack of correspondence between the audio and video information (Graber, 1996). Sometimes there is perfect correspondence between the two types of information, sometimes there is absolutely no relationship between them, while most often there is only a moderate degree of correspondence.

As noted earlier, technology has made it possible to transmit and receive audio and video information from almost anywhere in real time. This, combined with possibly increasing interest in certain quarters in foreign news has been prompting news stations to expand their coverage of such events. This is the good news. The bad news, however, is that the reporting of foreign news is even more prone to the variety of problems explicated above. Thus, for example, foreign news would typically be concerned with more conflict, drama and tragedy, hence the greater likelihood of compelling visual material. At the same time, such foreign items tend to be shorter and contain more unfamiliar names, places, processes and institutions. Foreign events also contain segments in foreign languages thus requiring translation and the use of voice-over or printed captions. Add to this the fact that the audience in one country is inherently less familiar with the issues of other countries, and the processing of foreign news becomes all the more difficult.

THE DOMESTICATION OF FOREIGN NEWS

The question as to whether or not television news producers are aware of the problems that viewers have with the news has not been thoroughly investigated. However, given the way news is generally produced, the impression one gets is that producers are not terribly mindful of them or their audience. And yet, a growing phenomenon seems to be occurring, especially with regard to foreign news.

When an event takes place in another country, an attempt is often made to domesticate the story for the local audience. At the conceptual level, domestication is a process in which "journalists sometimes construct foreign news stories in ways which attempt to create links of meaning between the stories and the history, culture, politics, society, etc. of the viewers" (Cohen, Levy, Roeh & Gurevitch, 1996). Domestication can be done in a variety of ways: by drawing direct or indirect comparisons between the country where the event took place and the country of broadcast; by making analogies, using metaphors or providing some historical and/or cultural context to the country of broadcast; or by reporting on the possible impact of the event on the country of broadcast or on its citizens residing or visiting in the country where the event occurred.

The footage used in such items is provided by the station's correspondent or, more often, by one of the television agencies or regional news exchanges, by a broadcaster in the country of origin, or even by a non-journalistic source such as homemade video. However, decisions as to which visual segments and soundbites to use, how to edit and package them, what narration to provide in the language of the country of broadcast, and where to place the item in the line-up of the newscast, are all made by each broadcaster for its viewers. As a result, even more than one station within the same country, each having access to the same raw material, may present its respective audience with a different final product.

Identifying and analyzing instances of domestication can be done in quantitative research by using predetermined categories as well as by using less rigorous qualitative methods. In their quantitative analysis of a two-week sample in 1987 of newscasts in 11 European and Middle Eastern member countries of Eurovision's News Exchange Service, Cohen, Levy, Roeh and Gurevitch (1996) found relatively few instances of domestication. And yet, a qualitative analysis during that sample period provided some interesting examples of domestication regarding several news stories: the Soviet peace forum held in Moscow and hosted by Mikhail Gorbachev; strife in Beirut with clashes between the Shiite Amal militia and Palestinians residing in refugee camps; unrest in Seoul, South Korea, as student protestors clashed with police shortly before the Olympic Games; and national elections held in Italy and in Ireland (1996, pp. 92–102).

There are in the literature several other good examples of domestication, although not all of them are referred to as such. One example comes from the Middle East, during the days of the *Intifada* (the Palestinian uprising of the late 1980s and early 1990s). The American networks habitually presented reports on the clashes in the West Bank and Gaza. Bob Simon, the CBS correspondent in Israel, coined the phrase "The Wild West Bank of the Jordan," thereby creating a double metaphor of the Wild West, an old-time American cliché, and the West Bank of the Jordan, a modern geopolitical term, the combination of which might indicate to the not-too-sophisticated American viewer what the whole thing is about. When an incident took place in the village of *Nahalin*, not far from Bethlehem, in April 1989, Simon pointed to an Israeli helicopter hovering above the city and referred to the skyline as the place "where three wise men once saw a star in the East." Later the report showed Jewish settlers practicing target-shooting and Simon's voice-over talked about "the People of the Book . . . writing their own laws." By using these various techniques Simon attempted to bring this Mideast story back home to the typical Christian viewer in the American Midwest (Roeh & Cohen, 1992).

Another example comes from the intervention of U.S. troops in the Civil War in Somalia in the early 1990s. Besteman (1996) writes, "By the end of 1991, journalists, pundits, and politicians had settled upon an explanatory scheme for analyzing the situation in Somalia. The image of a country unable to rid itself of ancient rivalries became a journalistic mantra, invoked by reporters throughout the media" (p. 121). "We feel safe because, on the one hand, we could never imagine kinship-based genocidal warfare happening *here*; on other hand, Somalia provides us with a model for ethnic conflict among minorities, recent immigrants, and the underclass that denies the powerful dynamics of race and class" (p. 130).

Several examples of domestication of news concern the situation in the former Yugoslavia. In a poignant article, Meštrovic (1995) lashes out at the way the American media used metaphors, euphemisms and fiction to conceptualize the Balkan War. He gives, among others, the following examples: Bosnian Muslims being referred to as new Palestinians, the Bosnian Muslims as Native Americans on reservations or "safe havens," the Croats as Nazis, and the existence of "tribes" in Europe.

In another reference to the American networks, Sadkovitch (1996) discusses how they dealt with the horrors of the war in Bosnia in 1991–1992:

The revelations regarding death camps, massacres of civilians by Serbian forces, and the Serbian policy of ethnic cleansing forced the media to find new rationalizations for the inaction of Western governments. . . . By recasting the crisis in American terms, commentators and journalists could avoid grappling with complex Balkan politics and Serbian atrocities by arguing that moral outrage was helpless against the stubborn realities of ancient hatreds, an impotent UN, and an indifferent and neo-isolationist American public. (p. 133)

Another impressive study of television coverage of the war in Bosnia (Gow, Paterson & Preston, 1996) presents a detailed analysis of one week in 13 countries during May 1994. As could be expected, the various stations presented the events of the day each using a particular frame. Examples that the authors provide relate to two visits: that of the Russian patriarch, Aleksei II, to the former Yugoslav republics, and the pilgrimage to Mecca by Bosnian President Alija Izetbegovic. Several stations made use of one or both of the trips to present a historic-religious angle of the conflict, thereby domesticating the story for their respective viewers.

As this chapter was being written and revised, I noticed some additional examples of domestication. In April 1999, the world's attention was on Kosovo. Most television stations around the world had been reporting on this continuing harsh story and to a large extent the footage available to most of the stations was the same, having been provided by NATO Headquarters, Serbian Television and various television agencies whose reporters had been expelled from Kosovo itself. And yet, the unfolding story as it was being told around the world was not the same. First and foremost, although there was a major element of human suffering in the story, its framing no doubt depended upon the political stance of the countries of broadcast. The pictures of refugees streaming across the border from Kosovo to its neighboring countries created associations of the Holocaust and other human tragedies, while at the same time controversy had arisen in some quarters as to the extent of the suffering and the legitimization of comparing that crisis to the situation of World War II. It is ironic that in addition to images of trainloads of people being transported across the border—a clear visual association with the deportation of Jews during the Nazi era—Yugoslav television made several references to U.S. President Bill Clinton as a Nazi.

Finally, as this chapter was being revised, another example, in fact one of the best, surfaced. In August 1999 a devastating earthquake hit northwestern Turkey and tens of thousands of people were killed. The first day of the reporting in several countries that I was able to monitor dealt with and focused upon the tragedy in Turkey. Fortunately for Turkey and for the media organizations, the event occurred in an important geopolitical part of the world that is highly accessible to television coverage (some earthquakes and other natural disasters in more remote locations have received significantly less worldwide coverage). As the magnitude of the Turkish quake became apparent, stations around the world began to focus not only on the Turkish story, but also on their respective homefronts. Thus emphasis was placed in the reports filed from Turkey by correspondents "parachuted" to the scene on the condition of the nationals of various countries living in Turkey, on the efforts by various rescue teams sent to Turkey from many countries, and on the extent to which the various countries of broadcast were prepared for such an eventuality if an earthquake would take place in their territory. Thus the Turkish calamity became a series of stories focusing on domestic aspects of the countries of broadcast. By doing so the various television services (as well as other media) made the Turkish catastrophe more relevant to people around the world.

CONCLUSIONS

In this chapter I have argued that although technology as well as marketing strategies make it possible for television news to be broadcast across the globe, this fact alone should not automatically categorize such newscasts as part of the phenomenon of globalization. I have tried to suggest that while the broadcasting of many television genres seen around the world can be considered within the realm of globalization, news differs because, by its very nature, it must be made pertinent and immediately meaningful on a daily basis to its local audiences, and for this to occur, raw news materials need to be continuously adapted for the local political and cultural context.

The need for this adaptation is especially poignant because of the overall cognitive difficulties involved in processing television news in general and foreign news in particular. Thus the process of domestication serves as a counterpoint to that of globalization. "[It] may be thought of as a necessary corrective to discussions of media globalization. Assumptions and arguments concerning the globalization of television news are often so imbued with the spirit and the vision of the 'Global Village' that they typically ignore the counter pull generated everywhere by audiences situated within their own cultures" (Cohen, Levy, Roeh & Gurevitch, 1996, p. 152).

What is ironic is that while domestication of the news is important and often necessary in making news meaningful to viewers, the process itself often adds even more elements and more information, thereby creating potentially even greater complexity and overload, hence making domesticated foreign news items even more difficult for viewers to cope with than domestic stories.

Nobody can predict the future. But indications are that the coming years will see continued advancements in media technology—assuming that the sky is indeed the limit—as well as increasing interest of people in the affairs of others, given the great interdependency that we are witnessing in our day and age. These developments should, on the one hand, lead to increased interest among broadcasters to expand their services and to provide coverage of events from all corners of the earth to everyone. On the other hand, we are witnessing increasing economic pressures by news organizations to cut costs, which has led to recent curtailment of certain news services, the shutting down of news bureaus in various cities and countries, and greater reliance upon television news agencies to provide materials for broadcast. This seems to have upgraded the importance of regional news services, which is manifest by the tremendous volume of "traffic" in the numerous satellite feeds available each day.

What this might ultimately mean is that with the increased availability of news about other countries, cultures and societies, there will be a growing trend toward greater domestication of such news for the benefit of respective audiences around the world. Thus, not only the quantity of news supply will grow but so will the quality of its reception and internalization by international audiences. Perhaps this will even serve to promote more and better understanding and cooperation among nations and peoples of the world.

REFERENCES

Adoni, H., & Cohen, A. A. (1978). Television economic news and the social construction of economic reality. *Journal of Communication*, 28, 61–70.

Bakhtin, M. M. (1981). *The dialogic imagination*. Austin: University of Texas Press.

Besteman, C. (1996). Representing violence and "othering" Somalia. *Cultural Anthropology*, 11(1), 120–133.

Boyd-Barrett, O. (1997). International communication and globalization: Contradictions and directions. In A. Mohammadi (Ed.), *International communication and globalization* (pp. 11–26). London: Sage Publications.

Braman, S. (1996). Interpenetrated globalization: Scaling, power and the public sphere. In S. Braman & A. Sreberny-Mohammadi (Eds.), *Globalization, communication and transnational civil society* (pp. 21–36). Cresskill, NJ: Hampton Press.

Cohen, A. A. (1998). Between content and cognition: On the impossibility of television news. *Communications: The European Journal of Communication Research*, 23(4), 447–461.

Cohen, A. A., Levy, M. R., Roeh, I. & Gurevitch, M. (1996). *Global newsrooms, local audiences*. London: John Libbey.

Cohen, A. A., & Roeh, I. (1992). When fiction and news cross over the border: Notes on differential readings and effects. In F. Korzenny & S. Ting-Toomey (Eds.), *Mass media effects across cultures* (pp. 23–34). Newbury Park, CA: Sage Publications.

Eco, U. (1979). *The role of the reader: Explorations in the semiotics of texts*. Bloomington: Indiana University Press.

Ferguson, M. (1992). The mythology about globalization. *European Journal of Communication*, 7(1), 69–93.

Gow, J., Paterson, R. & Preston, A. (1996). *Bosnia by television*. London: British Film Institute.

Graber, D. (1996). Say it with pictures. *Annals of the American Academy of Political and Social Science*, 546, 85–96.

Gunter, B. (1987). *Poor reception: Misunderstanding and forgetting broadcast news*. Hillsdale, NJ: Lawrence Erlbaum Associates.

Interview: The realities of globalism. (1999, February 1). *Newsweek*, 74.

Jensen, K. B. (1986). *Making sense of the news*. Aarhus, Denmark: Aarhus University Press.

Katz, E. (1977). Das Verstehen von Nachrichten [Understanding news]. *Publizistik*, 22(4), 359–370.

Liebes, T., & Katz, E. (1986). Patterns of involvement in television fiction: A comparative analysis. *European Journal of Communication*, 1, 151–171.

Malik, R., & Anderson, K. (1992). The global news agenda survey. *Intermedia*, 20(1), 8–70.

Meštrovic, S. G. (1995). Postemotional politics in the Balkans. *Society*, 32(2), 69–77.

Robertson, R. (1994). Globalization or glocalization? *Journal of International Communication*, 1(1), 33–52.

Robinson, J. P., & Levy, M. R. (1996). News media use and the informed public: A 1990s update. *Journal of Communication*, 46(2), 129–135.

Roeh, I., & Cohen, A. A. (1992). One of the bloodiest days: A comparative analysis of open and closed news. *Journal of Communication*, 42(2), 42–55.

Sadkovitch, J. J. (1996). The response of the American media to Balkan neo-nationalisms. In S. G. Meštrovic (Ed.), *Genocide after emotion: The post-emotional Balkan* war (pp. 113–157). London: Routledge.

Taylor, S. E., & Crocker, J. (1981). Schematic basis of social information process-ing. In E. T. Higgins, C. P. Herman & M. P. Zanna (Eds.), *Social cognition: The Ontario symposium* (Vol. 1, pp. 89–134). Hillsdale, NJ: Lawrence Erlbaum Associates.

Wallerstein, I. (1997). The national and the universal: Can there be such a thing as world culture? In A. D. King (Ed.), *Culture, globalization and the world-system* (pp. 91–106). Minneapolis: University of Minnesota Press.

Chapter 11

(Re)asserting National Television and National Identity Against the Global, Regional and Local Levels of World Television

Joseph Straubhaar

Globalization of television is clearest at two levels. There is a strong globalization of media operations toward the advertising-based commercial market paradigm. That is accompanied by a systematic shift in the forms or genres of programs that are produced, so globalized content models or patterns tend to spread. They are, however, adapted to local cultures and circumstances, a process described by Robertson (1992) as glocalization. This process in turn is driven and bounded by audience desire for cultural proximity and relevance. Within these new structural boundaries, regional, national and local producers also receive new resources to work with, both material (finance and technology) and symbolic (ideas and models). This interplay between globalizing structures and regional, national and local producer's agency in content can be looked at in terms of structuration (Giddens, 1984).

Globalization theorists sometimes underestimate the continuing power of the nation state to structure the circumstances within which most media industries still operate, even though these national producers now have to compete with global, cultural-linguistic regional and local producers as well. This chapter offers some theoretical analysis of the relations between the global, regional and national levels of television production, flow and consumption.

FROM CULTURAL IMPERIALISM TO GLOBALIZATION

One of the enduring problems in international communication has been how to theorize and explain the international flow and impact of television across cultures. Critical scholars in the 1960s–1980s often analyzed problems of unequal television flows and structural inequalities of television production in the world in terms of media imperialism (Lee, 1980) and dependency (Fox, 1992), but more recently these approaches have fallen under critique as overly simplistic. In seeing the major industrialized countries as dominant and Third World countries as dependent, these theories have missed much of the complexity of change in industries, genres and audience reception in the Third World or periphery.

The current discussion tends to focus on the globalization of cultures within a world capitalist economy (Featherstone, 1990; Wallerstein, 1991). The globalization approach in general posits that the world is becoming a single world society, "more uniform and standardized, through a technological, commercial and cultural synchronization emanating from the West, and that globalization is tied up with modernity" (Pieterse, 1995, p. 45). There is a great deal of discussion about the globalization of television, particularly as it is being driven by the spread of satellite and cable television technologies around the world. There is a fear of a renewed cycle of one way television flows out from the United States, adding complete U.S. television channels, such as CNN, MTV, Nickelodeon and the Cartoon Network to the already large export of U.S. film, television programs and music.

The discussion on globalization focuses less on dominant and dependent nation-states, more on globalized cultural actors, corporations and governments, as well as globalized audiences. This view of globalization diminishes too much the continuing importance of national governments, national producers and national identity among communication audiences in selecting and interpreting cultural products and messages. In much of the world, such as Eastern Europe or the Middle East, we currently see a rise of ethnic nationalism that reflects a search for identity and seems to extend to cultural consumption. The globalization discussion also often overlooks the rise of a new level of television flow and impact, that within regions of the world. A number of national/local television networks, like Brazil, Egypt, Hong Kong, India and Mexico, export to surrounding regions, similar or proximate in culture and language. More rarely, some operations, like Star TV, produce for a supranational region, like Greater China, defined by culture and language.

MULTILEVEL APPROACH

This chapter will focus on television within a world system that includes several levels of operation, investment, production, flow and impact. There is a level that is truly global, one that is supranational regional or geolinguistic, one that is national, and others that are subnational or "regional" (within the nation) and even local. In fact, some of the most current theorization of globalization recognize that "what globalization means in structural terms, then, is the *increase in the available modes of organiza-tion*: transnational, international, macro-regional, national, micro-regional, municipal, local" (Pieterse, 1995, p. 50, emphasis in original). These levels correspond to levels of official government interactions, international or-ganizations and nongovernmental organizations, international media and other firms, and cultural flows and interactions as well. These levels are not necessarily in conflict. Pieterse (1995, p. 50) observes that "Globali-zation can mean the reinforcement of both supranational and sub-national regionalism." The main argument of this chapter is that the role of geocultural regions needs to be emphasized more, so that they can be fit into the more sophisticated interpretations of globalization that are emerg-ing, such as Pieterse's (1995). However, this chapter argues that it is clearer to think of television within a world system in which the term global is reserved for phenomena that are truly global, distinguishing those that are regional, national and local within the world system.

The global level of analysis is in fact increasingly crucial. There are sev-eral kinds of globalization relevant to television. Some of the new cable and satellite channels, such as CNN or the Cartoon Network, take the same content to worldwide audiences, although some "global" channels are cre-ating regionally or locally adapted versions. Some television programs, such as *Dallas* or *Baywatch*, still are syndicated to flow globally to be broadcast nationally or locally. Quite a few national and local productions derive from formats or genres that have spread globally beyond their places of origin. Even more basically, the models for broadcasting are being spread globally as private, commercial, entertainment-oriented stations and net-works continue to spread into more nations.

Ferguson's excellent discussion of the myths of globalization raises sev-eral key problems: the idea that the world is becoming one homogeneous culture, largely fed by the U.S. culture industries; that big cultural indus-tries, like those of the United States, have an automatic advantage due to economies of scale and the polish of their products; and that differences of time, space and geography are eroded by technology (1992). This chapter will critique the ideas of globalization such as the worldwide homogeni-zation of television, the erosion of national and cultural differences and domination of all by U.S. productions.

At the level of reception and audience impacts of television, some audi-ences do primarily watch globalized channels. We argue that those audi-ences are most often upper middle and upper class elites, since access to new channels is often limited by economic capital and interest in them limited by cultural capital. However, almost all audiences are touched by some aspect of globalization, at the level of program flow, genre, or broad-cast model.

We propose that, in terms of media and media flows, a phenomenon equally significant to globalization, per se, may well be "regionalization" of television into multicountry markets linked by geography, language and culture. These might more accurately be called the geocultural or cultural-linguistic (Wilkinson, 1995) markets, rather than regional markets, since not all these linked populations, markets and cultures are geographically contiguous.

For example, the United States is clearly still the main media exporter in the world. The United States dominates certain kinds of production, like feature films, which require huge investments, and certain kinds of television genres, like action-adventure, which also require big budgets and don't require a great deal of cultural capital or sophistication to understand. However, the "global" flow of television outward from the United States is probably strongest among the Anglophone nations of the world, such as the United Kingdom, Anglophone Canada, Australia and the English-speaking Caribbean, where U.S. television exports tend to be most popular and best understood (Straubhaar et al., 1992). These are also among the few countries which manage to export television, film or music back to the Anglophone U.S. market. Within this geocultural sphere, Canada and the English-speaking Caribbean are most closely tied to the United States by geographic proximity, notably being under the direct reach or footprint of U.S. television satellites, but also by migration, by language and, at least in the case of Canada, very strong cultural similarities or cultural prox-imities (Straubhaar, 1991).

There are a number of other geocultural markets emerging: Western Europe, where the European Community has been trying to create a region-wide cultural market; Latin America, linked also to other "Latin"-based language markets in Italy and France; a Francophone market linking France and its former colonies; an Arabic world market; a Chinese market; and a Hindi or South Asian market.

While globalization increasingly dominates current discussion of television flows and impacts, Tomlinson (1991) observes that most of the media imperialism and cultural imperialism discussion assumes that the primary actors are nations. Many of the studies done on media flows, media models, etc. are national case studies. Until the recent discussion of globalization, few studies focused on anything larger (or smaller) than the nation-state. Nearly all of the policy discussion about these issues has taken place within national governments, by academics speaking to national governments, or by national government representatives to institutions like UNESCO where much of the international debate has taken place (McPhail, 1989). Through frequency licensing, satellite orbit controls, market definition, financial incentives, cultural policy and advertising and other financial controls, national governments still define the primary market realities of television. Even "regional" actors like Star TV, even within relatively coherent cultural regions, like Greater China, still find their audiences defined and to some degree controlled by the national governments of China, Taiwan, Singapore, etc. (Chan, 1994).

However, the view of the nation as a cultural unit is changing. Very few nations are ethnically homogenous, Portugal, Greece, Iceland, Norway, Malta and perhaps, Germany and Japan. Most have fairly large minorities (Smith, 1981). If language is a primary characteristic of culture, then most nations are multilingual and not homogenous nation-states (Schlesinger, 1987). This opens up a large area of interest in media, including television in many areas, which address media audiences of smaller than national scope. Many local audiences would like to see programming in their own languages, addressing their own cultures. If this local audience shares a language, like the Chinese minority in Malaysia, with a larger geolinguistic group, then they might import programming in their language and culture, as did the Malaysian Chinese, first with VCRs, then DBS, particularly Star TV (Chan, 1994; McDaniel, 1994).

In many countries, broadcast television has been seen as too expensive to direct toward groups smaller than nations. Even countries like Brazil, a large middle income country with an extensive commercialized television system, have only recently begun to address television programs toward regional and local audiences.

STRUCTURING WORLD TELEVISION SYSTEMS

This chapter proposes an analytical structure for understanding global, regional, national and provincial systems, in this case, those of television. At all levels, it is useful to distinguish the structural from the cultural. Television, for example, has both structural and cultural components. The main structural elements, at least for television, are economic frameworks, technological bases and institutional forms of organization and operation. These structural elements form boundaries within which cultural agents like television producers operate. The structures of television frame or limit what is possible. For example, commercial television systems tend to produce few documentaries, educational programs or one-episode dramas. However, within those boundaries, the same structures do also provide resources to cultural forces and agents to create and consume television and other cultural products. As Giddens argues, institutional structures provide both rules/boundaries and resources to those who work within them (1984).

Structuration theory is Gidden's effort to reconcile the effects of structures and institutions upon society with the existence of agency exercised by individuals and groups, which often seem to go against the determining effects of the structures (Giddens, 1984). "Giddens proposes that we consider structure as a duality including constraining rules and enabling resources" (Mosco, 1996, p. 11). Working within constraining rules or boundaries imposed by structures and institutions, but with enabling resources and guiding patterns often provided by those same structures, individuals and groups produce cultural products like television, move them around the globe, and make meaning of them within other patterns provided by culture.

The chief structural factors are technological, economic and political/institutional. These forces do tend to both enable and constrain social and cultural actions, products and meanings. This gets us beyond the narrow issue of determinism. For example, technology tends to enable new developments, such as satellites' ability to let television broadcasts cross borders. It can also present constraints, but the result over time tends to be a layering, additive effect of new possibilities. New technologies, such as broadcast or satellite television, don't necessarily eliminate other options based on earlier technologies. For example, although VCRs and satellite/cable television bring in the possibility of many new U.S. movies and programs for Latin Americans, only relatively small proportions have access to these technologies and many of them don't necessarily use them to watch the "new" U.S. content. Several recent studies in Brazil, for example, show many, if not most, users of satellite dishes use them to get better reception of national channels, not to import channels from Galaxy (Hughes), Sky Latin America (Fox, Televisa and Globo) or other international channels (LaPastina, Straubhaar & Buarque de Almeida, 1999).

Technological forces sometimes seem the most revolutionary because they can sometimes enable very rapid changes. As a part of globalization, technologies such as ships, airplanes, telecommunications and broadcasting can facilitate the rapid spatial extension of empires and political, economic and military systems across nations and regions. The rapid recent expansion of satellite television broadcasting is to many people a somewhat terrifying example of this kind of technological potential. However, while technology can extend the reach of an idea or a system, its actual impact depends on economic, cultural and political factors, as well.

Economic conditions shape the actual development of technological possibilities. Economic factors both enable and limit cultural developments. Economic relations with other countries and economic growth can enable new possibilities, such as bringing television broadcasting into a country. However, economic patterns can limit possibilities. For example, advertising as an economic system for financing television broadcasts both enables and limits the possibilities of the medium. Advertising tends to enable by increasing the money available for production. It also tends to limit broadcast program genres to certain types, predominantly entertainment, which often puts other kinds of programming, like development education, high culture and extensive information programming, out of bounds. For another example, poor income distribution can limit the number of people who can actually afford DBS television or the Internet, hence restricting those technologies to national elites or upper middle classes.

At the political or institutional level, the dominant structure is still the nation-state, although globalization analysts like to point out its decline relative to other more global actors, like multinational corporations. Nation-states still structure most ground rules of media, such as national market structures, ownership rules, production incentives and subsidies, financial rules, frequency assignments, technical standards and content rules. Recently, some regional groups are beginning to exercise power, and in certain policy arenas, like economic restructuring, international organizations like the World Bank, the International Monetary Fund and the World Trade Organization can exercise considerable power as well.

At the cultural level, this chapter focuses on the formation of language and cultural communities and the creation and flow of media, particularly television, within and across those communities. The key elements in the formation of communities are their own historical dynamics, particularly the development of language and cultural themes, the creation and maintenance of group cultural identities as a locus of meaning, and cross-cultural interpersonal interactions such as travel and migration between communities. The media, the main focus of this chapter, build on, reinforce and, by dint of the agency of both media producers and consumers, sometimes contradict both this cultural context and the larger structural context of economics, technology and institutions. Structuration emphasizes that human agency and even aggregate social forces are sometimes hard to predict from structural or even cultural forces.

Culture is clearly not just a force acted upon by technologies like television, institutions like the nation-state and economic patterns like advertising. This chapter explores this cultural process as hybridization, the synthesis of local cultures with the imported elements of culture brought in by globalization, through specific processes like electronic media, migration, inflow of genres and models and entrepreneurial action of global or regional companies.

GLOBALIZING FORCES

In much recent work on globalization, there has been a tendency to try to more fully consider both temporal and spatial aspects of international change (Giddens, 1991), including culture and media (Friedman, 1994). Several theorists, including Giddens (1991), Friedman (1994) and Robertson (1995), have raised the need to consider modernity as a crucial aspect of globalization. Tomlinson (1991) relates the media imperialism and globalization theorizations of media flows. He observes that much of the discussion of media imperialism had to do with spatial relationships, particularly U.S. domination of other nations or cultural spaces, versus temporal relationships or change over time, in which modernization re-places tradition and may itself be replaced by post-modernity (Tomlinson 1991, p. 69). "One way to attempt to simplify the level of complexity which the intensification of global flows is introducing in the figuration of competing nation-states and blocs, is to regard globalization as an outcome of the universal logic of modernity" (Featherstone and Lash, 1995, p. 2).

Globalization can be seen as both spatial, the outward geographic spread of ideas and forms, particularly those related to capitalism, and temporal, changes over time within many locales. This chapter will examine the concept of cultural hybridization as a temporal or historical aspect of modernization of culture. Over time cultures adapt via hybridization to a series of spatial extensions of technological and economic change emanating out from centers of global activity to the peripheries of the global system. Currently, we can see satellite and computer technologies and modern capitalism as rapid, recent spatial extensions of new forces of modernity, to which regional, national and local cultures must adapt.

Hybridization, which is treated at length below, is also a structuring process. It is an historical, temporal, reflexive cultural structuring process. Over time, cultures interact, mediated by technology, migration and institutional and economic forms. Frequently, those cultures hybridize, with local elements and imported ones combining to create new forms of culture, like Latin Americans fusing local culture into the imported soap opera to create the *telenovela*. Sometimes, the result of interaction is less than hybridization, with local cultures only slightly adapting to foreign elements. Many times, the impact goes beyond hybridization, with local cultures and languages being essentially extinguished, so that "By the most reliable estimates, more than half of the world's 6,500 languages may be extinct by the end of this century" (Hotz, 2000).

In terms of structuration (Giddens, 1984), actors in a culture are reflexive in several ways that may produce hybridization. Some hybridization processes are very conscious, as when a television station deliberately copies a foreign genre, like a specific game show, from videotapes and mixes it together with local cultural specifics. Some are relatively conscious, as when someone chooses to watch an imported television channel in English in order to practice their language skills. Some processes are less conscious but still reflexive, as when people slowly adapt elements seen on national television into their daily, local lives.

GLOBAL SPREAD OF MARKET CAPITALISM

For many writers from the neo-Marxist and dependency traditions, globalization is essentially the worldwide spread, over both time and space, of a world capitalist market, or in Wallerstein's formulation, a world capitalist system (1979). Economically, globalization is seen as the spread of capitalism as a system, of consumerism and commercialism as social ethics (often referred to as McDonaldization or Coca-Colalization), and of the growing penetration and power of international corporations. Culturally, it is still seen by many as Westernization, a variation on or updating of the idea of cultural imperialism and synchronization (Tomlinson, 1991). While economics are a basic issue, various critics of globalization see overly simplistic assumptions being made about the causality of economics, particularly the global spread of capitalism, in globalization and fear a new wave of economic reductionism which might oversimplify cultural phenomena (Boyne, 1990; Ferguson, 1992).

For many writers on globalization of television, foreign models for television are one major form of media imperialism (Lee, 1980). This line of analysis tends to focus on the importation of system-level models, such as commercial versus public service broadcasting organizational forms. To use a concept found in structuration theory (Giddens, 1984), systemic changes like shifting toward a more commercial, advertising-driven basis of financing broadcasting redraw the boundaries of what is possible within that system.

Commercial broadcasting is proliferating across the globe. The increasingly global commercial system pattern for television is reinforced by several factors. Perhaps most powerfully, more and more countries are being drawn into a world capitalist or market economy (Herman & McChesney, 1997; Wallerstein, 1979). Within this global market economy, both national and global firms pressure broadcasters to allow—indeed, rely on—advertising (Fox, 1975; Herman & McChesney, 1997). Janus (1981) and Mattelart (1991) argue that multinational firms have pushed particularly hard to commercialize systems and introduce advertising, since they have become used to promoting goods with advertising in other markets. Viewing publics also tend to push for more programming choices, as with British television in the 1950s, which is often met by allowing in more commercial channels.

Commercial television systems, like commercial film studios before them, require that cultural products succeed in drawing a large, profitable audience. In television, like film before it, these demands for commercial success lead to the emergence and standardization of certain successful formulas (Schatz, 1981). If we consider both the production companies and the genre formulas as social structures, then Giddens (1984) would remind us that structures both bound and enable the agency of those who act within them. More specifically, commercial film studios and commercial television networks essentially require cultural producers to work within the boundaries of certain successful genres or formulas. However, within those structural boundaries, producers find not only constraints but also resources.

CULTURAL HYBRIDIZATION AND MODERNIZATION

Within certain increasingly global economic constraints and influenced by successful global patterns, regional and national cultures still tend to assert their own content very strongly over time. What emerges is often a strongly localized or hybridized adaptation of what is considered current or modern in global patterns. Robertson goes so far as to call the process of hybridizing the local and global together as "glocalization" (Robertson, 1995). This chapter argues that hybridization is essentially the dominant pattern of cultural interaction over time. It is the temporal reflection of the local, national and regional absorption and adaptation of global patterns of modernity in culture. As new patterns borne by technological and economic forces enter cultures, they interact with what is already there, producing a new pattern best characterized at this moment as hybrid (Bhabha, 1994; Garcia Canclini, 1997).

For example, there is much current discussion of an Asian approach to modernity. Iwabuchi, interviewing Taiwanese young people, finds that they are more likely to choose and identify with popular music and television from Japan than from China because the Japanese material is seen as being more modern while still recognizably familiar within an Asian context. He argues that Japanese popular culture successfully adapts or Asianizes U.S. popular culture genres into more localized or regionalized forms (Iwabuchi, 1997).

One useful theorization is to reconsider globalization as a set of regionally differentiated patterns of modernization. Japanese popular culture and its cultural industry represent a transformation from what was perceived in the 1970s, that "The media are American" (Tunstall, 1977), into globalized and regionalized patterns of modernity that build on, but also transform patterns of modernity that seemed so specifically "American" in the first wave of U.S. television program export dominance in the 1960s and 1970s. For example, Iwabuchi in the "Sweet Scent of Asian Modernity" describes the Japanese adaptation of cultural industry globalization as de-Westernized modernization (Iwabuchi, 1997). This is a hybrid localization or nationalization of a "global" pattern.

HYBRIDITY AND GLOBALIZATION

Cutting across levels such as global, regional, national and local is the notion of hybridization of cultures across levels. "Post-colonial theory, in so far as it addresses complex, multilayered identities, has proliferated in terms of having to do with cultural mixing: religious (syncretism); biological (hybridity); human-genetic (*mestizaje*); and linguistic (creolization) . . . while the themes are old—'syncretism,' 'hybridity,' *créolité*, and *mestizaje* had already been invoked decades ago by diverse Latin American modern-isms—the historical moment is new" (Shohat & Stam, 1994, p. 41). For instance, in the 1920s and 1930s, Brazilian intellectuals created a project of indigenizing modern art by absorbing international influences into a base of indigenous and African culture, which they called cultural cannibalism or cultural anthropophagy (*anthropofagia cultural*) (Karp, 1994).

Latin American cultures are essentially syncretic or hybrid by definition. They have been created by the fusion of ethnic, religious, cultural and even linguistic traditions from indigenous peoples, Europeans and Africans (García Canclini, 1995). In contemporary terms, post-colonial theory deals with the cultural contradictions generated by the global circulation of peoples and cultural goods in a mediated and interconnected world, resulting in a kind of commodified or mass-mediated syncretism (Shohat & Stam, 1994, pp. 41–42). Current hybridity results from both the physical movement and mixture of peoples and the media-based flow of cultural products and representation of cultures.

GLOBAL PROCESSES, NATIONAL AND LOCAL IDENTITIES

In television and in other cultural industries as well, people use globally distributed forms to create cultural products which define and redefine what the national and the local are. Robertson observes that "globalization has involved the reconstruction, in a sense the production, of 'home,' 'community' and 'locality' " (1995, p. 30). Cultural producers use forms and genres that have spread globally to express ideas of what home is like. There is a subtle interplay between the global and local in television form and content. Robertson (1992) calls this "glocalization." This chapter sees it as one aspect of the historical, temporal process of hybridization.

For example, the soap opera has distinct roots in both English and French serial novels, which were carried over time in magazines and newspapers. U.S. radio and later television took this idea and developed a particular form of soap opera, to entertain and draw loyal audiences over time, but explicitly also to sell soap. In fact, for quite a long time, the shows were produced for radio and television networks by advertising agencies on behalf of soap manufacturers. Soap companies and advertising agencies took this successful genre abroad, particularly to Latin America. Latin American radio and television producers adapted the genre to their cultures and needs, moving it into prime time, aiming it at both men and women, changing the form of story telling and using local motifs, characters, humor, and so on.

In a sense, then, a global form is being localized, both for purposes of global capitalist development and for expression of local identity. The soap opera genre is still used to sell soap and, even more basically, to show local people an ethic or goal of consumption. For example, in one Brazilian soap opera in the late 1970s, a high point in the plot came when a man asked his wife if she would like a refrigerator and she burst into tears of joy (Fernandes, 1982). This consumption ethic is itself localized, with a refrigerator being an almost supreme ambition for lower class Brazilians, compared to something like an automobile in more developed countries. The consumption ethic is also met by local conditions of audience reception. A series of about 30 in-depth interviews by the author with working class and poor television viewers in São Paulo in 1989–1990 showed that they were not generally frustrated by being exposed to advertising for consumer goods that they could not have, but had fairly specific, limited and realistic consumer ambitions. They varied considerably in terms of how important consumption of goods had become to them; they were not uniformly permeated by a consumer ethic, although some were. This is a process over time, however. Interviewing in 1995–1996 by Hamburger (in progress) in a São Paulo slum indicated that people were fairly rapidly being swept into a consumer society, both by media exposure and by personal, daily life exposure to consumption in city life around them.

While a local soap opera such as the Brazilian one with the man, his wife and the refrigerator is delivering an adapted underlying global message about joining the lower ranks of an emerging global consumer economy, it is primarily carrying messages about the local culture. In fact, in Brazil and India, among others, the soap opera became a prime vehicle for creating elements of a "national" culture and spreading them among localized and regionalized audiences that had not always shared a great deal of common culture between them despite being with common national boundaries (Fadul, 1993; Mitra, 1993). In Brazil, a study in various regions showed that television, in particular the local adaptation of the soap opera, the *telenovela*, has created a focus on common national holidays versus local ones and has liberalized views on race and women's roles (Kottak, 1990). In India, nationally broadcast soap operas about Hindu religious myths have created more standardized versions of those myths around the diverse parts of India (Mitra, 1993).

In this example, the local adaptation of an increasingly global form of television illustrates that "the concept of globalization has involved the simultaneity of what are conventionally called the global and the local . . ." (Robertson, 1995, p. 30). In particular, we see a diffusion of some basic global forms related to the expansion of the world economy, but those globalized forms co-exist with and even promote local adaptations with the expression of unique local content. Interviews by the author with advertising executives in Brazil in 1977–1980 indicated that multinational advertisers had begun to prefer putting their ads in local productions with localized cultural content because the audience clearly preferred them. While cultural forms, particularly those related to consumption within capitalist societies, diffuse globally, they tend to be adapted locally. In fact, global diffusion of certain elements of consumer culture may well be more effective when those consumer elements are cast in local terms and adapted to local economic realities.

There is also a process of active resistance to globalization in some places. The example of popular rejection of cultural Westernization, mobilized effectively by Islamic clerics, in Iran was one of the first clear signals that not all cultures were going to easily adapt Western cultural elements. Barber speaks of two opposing trends, a "McWorld" of global homogenization versus the "Jihad world" of localizing or particularizing "lebanonization" (1992).

U.S. CULTURAL EXPORT HEGEMONY

A number of studies have described the twentieth-century domination of world culture flows by the United States (Guback & Varis, 1986; Nordenstreng & Varis, 1974; Schiller, 1971). Starting with films, popular music and then television, the United States has been the major exporter to the global market, even though its relative dominance is, we shall argue, declining.

Another way to look at the U.S. position in global flows is an interesting pilot case in both globalization and hybridization of culture and cultural industries. While the United States partakes of an Anglo-European cultural base, much of what makes its audio-visual products so successful in global markets is their hybridization of those cultural roots with the other cultures represented in late-nineteenth- and twentieth-century immigration into the United States by Eastern European Jews, Arabs, Latin Americans and Asians. American media drew on these diverse cultures and, even more importantly, had to appeal to all of them to succeed in the American national cultural marketplace (Read, 1976). Read and others note that U.S. cultural products were then well situated to succeed as exports because they had already achieved a kind of universalization by the absorption of various elements and the need to appeal to very diverse audiences. Tomlinson notes that fear of Americanization assumes a homogeneity to American culture that it probably does not have (1991).

Hollywood used this initial cultural advantage relatively well. Producers there developed interesting genres of film, music and television. They began to draw in much of the world's talent, film directors, actors, writers and singers from Europe and even Latin America (Read, 1976). This again heightened a certain type of universalism based on hybridization of "American" and other cultural elements.

The United States also capitalized on an emerging English linguistic hegemony, drawing on the global penetration of English under the British Empire as well as the twentieth-century expansion of the United States itself. As Hoskins and Mirus (1988) and others have pointed out, the fact of production in English gave the United States an export advantage in the global market of the twentieth century. The United States also has the advantage of having several wealthy media markets—the United States itself, Canada, Great Britain and Australia, as part of a narrower English-speaking geolinguistic market, in which the United States is even more dominant than in other markets where language and culture present greater barriers to popular acceptance of American cultural products.

FROM EXPORTING TELEVISION PROGRAMS TO EXPORTING GENRES

A 1972 study for the U.N. Educational, Scientific and Cultural Organization found that over half of the countries studied imported over half of their television, mostly entertainment and mostly from the United States (Nordenstreng & Varis, 1974). There is now some debate and questioning about whether U.S. dominance is slipping in world television markets. American television exports are increasing fairly rapidly in their dollar values and exports represent a steadily increasing share of television producers' profits (Hoskins & Mirus, 1988; Wildman & Siwek, 1988). Many shows now make more overseas than in the United States and a number of American producers are beginning to shape their programs to anticipate and maximize overseas sales. However, American television programs are also facing increased competition at a variety of levels: regional, national and local. More countries are also competing to sell programs to others. Some like Brazil and Hong Kong compete worldwide (Marques de Melo 1988). American programs remain attractive to world audiences; this seems particularly true of better educated audiences, who are likely to be more cosmopolitan in their tastes and previous exposure (Straubhaar, 1991a). Still, it seems that people more frequently look for television programming that is closer to their own languages, cultures, histories and religious values—more culturally proximate or close to them (Straubhaar, 1991a).

What has happened to replace American programming in a number of countries is the local adaptation of the American commercial model and American television program formats (Oliveira, 1990). In the process of diffusion, the "American" model has been generalized and adapted in a global model for commercial media. This fits the model of Robertson (1995) and others that a number of current transformations may be described as glocalization, the oftentimes deliberate adaptation of a foreign or global model to fit national circumstances. Robertson observes that Japan is in some ways the prototype for this approach and that Japan in fact developed the term "glocalization," which Robertson has popularized within globalization theory.

REGIONAL MEDIA AND CULTURES

A major trend of the last twenty years has been the "regionalization" of television into multicountry markets linked by geography, language and culture. These might more accurately be called the geocultural or cultural linguistic markets, rather than regional markets, since not all these linked populations, markets and cultures are geographically contiguous (Wilkinson, 1995).

Efforts to define cultural markets, particularly for television, by geographic regions have met very mixed success. There is the hope that for some regions that old common cultural traditions will bind diverse nations into a common cultural region that would welcome common television programming. Huntington (1993) has hypothesized that there are a limited number of "civilizations" based on underlying religious, language and cultural divisions, which create what he calls civilizations. If his analysis extends to culture as represented on television, then we might expect to see the Chinese market broaden to a "Confucian"-cultural influence area market, the Arabic language market broaden to an Islamic market and a Slavic-Orthodox market emerging out of the former USSR and Eastern Europe (Huntington, 1993).

Government policy makers and some industry programmers have proceeded along lines similar to Huntington's analysis. For example, the European Economic Community (EEC) has made an assumption that "Beneath the surface diversity of languages, tastes and artistic styles, there is a likeness, a kinship, a European dimension or identity based on a common cultural heritage" (Commission of the European Communities, cited in Schlesinger, 1991, p. 139). Some of the initial DBS efforts to target all of Asia, like Star TV, seem to have similar assumptions about a common culture underlying the apparent diversity of Asian cultures.

Critics such as Schlesinger (1991) think that success for the EEC efforts is unlikely because what they are attempting to define as "European" is in fact an uneasy geographical alliance of several very distinct language and cultural groups, such as the English-speaking, the German-speaking and the French-speaking groups which comprise both countries and subpopulations within other countries.

Geocultural markets are unified by language (even though different accents and dialects may divide countries somewhat). However, they go beyond language to include history, religion, ethnicity (in some cases) and culture in several senses: shared identity, gestures and nonverbal communication; what is considered funny or serious or even sacred; clothing styles; living patterns; climate influences and other relationships with the environment. Geocultural markets are often centered in a geographic region, hence the tendency to call them regional markets, but they have also been spread globally by colonization, slavery and migration.

There are waves or creation of regional or geolinguistic cultures and effects on local cultural identity from early recorded history (and before). They reflect a long history of cultural development and hybridization within earlier empires before the current European-dominated world system. These empires had very strong impacts, often spreading religion and culture beyond the reach of any boundaries of conquest, as with the spread of Buddhism well beyond India into much of Asia, or with the spread of Chinese customs through much of Asia. In a discussion of cultural imperialism, several Asian graduate students once joked with the author that current Western influence on Asia was nothing compared to earlier Chinese cultural imperialism.

However, current geolinguistic cultures such as the Arab world or the widespread Chinese population have formed in part in interaction with and reaction to the Western culture spread by European colonization. The indigenous peoples of North America were displaced by a primarily European civilization, although Mexico produced a *mestizo* or mixed ethnicity and culture of indigenous and European roots, which has substantial impact on the United States. In much of Latin America, a similarly mixed or hybrid civilization arose from indigenous, European and African cultures and peoples (Garcia Canclini, 1990).

These cultural similarities and common histories come together to define cultural markets to which television responds. Populations defined by these kinds of characteristics tend to seek out cultural products, like television programs or music, which are most similar or proximate to them. Whereas some scholars used to fear that the intrinsic attraction of U.S. cultural products would result in "wall-to-wall Dallas" around the world (Collins, 1986), it seems more likely that most audiences are really looking for cultural proximity (Straubhaar, 1991a), to see people and styles they recognize, jokes that are funny without explanation, and so on. To use another framework, people acquire a cultural capital based on their experience, family background and education which enables them to understand things (Bourdieu, 1984). When confronted with unfamiliar cultural products, people are likely to apply a cultural discount to them (Hoskins & Mirus, 1988), to reject them in favor of things that are more familiar, more amusing and more easily understood.

REGIONAL TELEVISION MARKETS

Since the benchmark study of television flow by Nordenstreng and Varis in 1974, more nations at virtually all levels of wealth are doing more of their own television programming. Production technology costs are much lower, production groups of experienced technicians and artists have been trained by now in most places (Santoro, 1990), and a number of low-cost program forms or genres have been developed, such as talk, variety and live music, among others. Some countries which have slowed their film production down rapidly continue to produce quite a bit of television programming. As ratings in many countries reflect, audiences usually tend to prefer local programming when they can get it.

Major regional television markets are developing in Spanish, Arabic, Chinese, Hindi, English and French. These are often called regional because they are focused around a world region tied together by common language, culture, religion and a history of being colonized by the same country (usually Great Britain, France or Spain). Increasingly, though, these cultural markets extend beyond neighboring countries to follow populations that have migrated throughout a larger region or even the world. For instance, the Chinese audience is centered on China and nations near it (Hong Kong, Singapore and Taiwan) but extends slightly further away to Chinese populations mixed in with others (Singapore, Malaysia) and further to Chinese speakers around the world. Such world spanning populations are not so much "regional" as they are defined by language and culture. They are reached and united through a variety of new technologies: video, satellite television and cable television. For instance, Turkish television is following Turkish guest workers into a number of Western European countries by satellite—those people are a major and profitable target of Turkish satellite television channels. Similarly, Arabs in Europe are a major target for the MBC Arabic satellite channel.

NATIONAL FORCES

Concern with both globalization and cultural-linguistic regionalization should not obscure the fact, that, as this chapter will demonstrate, television remains a primarily national phenomenon. Most television is watched via national systems. States as diverse as China and Brazil work to protect the national market for national broadcast television. Many states in Asia (Chan, 1994; McDaniel, 1994) and the Middle East (Boyd, 1993) specifically restrict international DBS. Others, like Brazil, focus on providing incentives to national broadcasters to ensure their competitiveness (Straubhaar, 1991b).

Further, unlike the situation observed in the early 1970s by Nordenstreng and Varis (1974), much if not most of that television, particularly in the prime time hours when most people watch, is produced at the national level (see Table 11.1). However, much of this national programming is produced using regionalized or globalized genres or formats, an interesting contradiction which echoes Robertson's idea that we are increasingly using globalized forms to produce the local (Robertson, 1995).

There are a number of crucial structural conditions which make national

Table 11.1
Percentage of Nationally Produced Programming in Prime Time and Total Broadcast Day

	1962		1972		1982		1991	
	Prime	Total	Prime	Total	Prime	Total	Prime	Total
Asia								
Japan	81	92	95	90	96	95	92	94
South Korea	73	76	80	79	89	87	89	86
Hong Kong	23	26	64	62	92	79	95	83
India			98	80	89	88	97	78
Latin America								
Dominican Republic	38	45	33	55	21	32		44
Chile	63	65	54	52	58	48	58	64
Brazil	70	69	86	55	64	63	72	
Colombia	65	77	81	75	83	66		
Hispanic United States			3	66	14	43	0	43
Mexico	63	59	68	62	58	57	46	67
Anglo United States	99	98	98	98	98	93	98	99
Middle East								
Israel			63	69	72	71	67	57
Lebanon	66	60	46	38	37	34	34	24
Caribbean								
Trinidad	26	24	46	42	31	18		
Jamaica	17	30	30	29	37	20		
Barbados	16	16	13	51	10	16		

Note: This table is based on samples of one week of programming for each year, which was categorized by expert coders from each country by genres and country or region or origin.

media production more likely. These structural conditions enable national cultural producers to resist the contrasting advantages of global and regional producers. Some of these are inherent to the size and type of economy at question, which are structural conditions that limit or enable the state itself to act in regulating or structuring media industries. *Market size* is a crucial boundary or limit to whether national industry grows. Very few small countries produce a great deal of television, even in Europe. Conversely, almost all large developing countries eventually become significant producers of television because the size of the market supports greater production. *Wealth* of a market is also a crucial boundary. As noted for cultural-linguistic markets above, it can compensate for market size, per se, if the market, like Japan, Taiwan or Hong Kong, is wealthy enough.

Some structural conditions are the result of interaction between global economic forces and national governments. While the global market pushes for certain kinds of commercial or financial structures (Herman & McChesney, 1997), the nation-state can still make certain decisions about how media institutions or industries are to be structured.

National commercial structure bounds or limits what kind of media products will be produced. If commercial success in a market is imperative, the most commercially successful program models will be adopted, local or foreign.

The *national financial base* likewise places boundaries around what kind of programming will be produced. Reliance on advertising tends to constrain programming options to those which are commercially successful (i.e., those that draw the largest or most economically attractive audiences). Government finance tends to give greater control over programming to government institutions and ruling political parties. License fees, like in Britain or Japan, tend to insulate programming more against government and commercial pressures.

Competition among media in a national, regional or global market may sponsor creativity but also tends to disperse resources among a number of competitors. Growth in national or regional television industries, particularly in their infancy, is sometimes enhanced by limiting the number of competing stations or networks.

Government policies are crucial for shaping industries and enabling them to act independently of foreign pressure, but style of government involvement may limit industry growth. The state can be a media actor on its own. It can be a facilitating or obstructive regulator and can create favorable conditions, such as subsidies for construction, R&D or other needs.

Other cultural industries can support or limit television industries. Television draws heavily on the strength of related local cultural industries (film, music, theater, recordings). If those are underdeveloped, too, that places another boundary to television production.

Within the boundaries placed by these political economy structures, developments tend to be non-linear and hard to predict, but we do see patterns among the groups of actors involved. The key groups of people involved are those involved in the management and direction of television, the entrepreneurs; those involved in the actual program planning and production, the producers; and the receivers or audiences.

Producer behavior follows commercial imperatives but will tend to follow the demands of the domestic market or audience when resources allow. Entrepreneurial behavior likewise will tailor operations to the programming interests of domestic (or regional or global) audiences and to domestic and foreign business needs and markets, with considerable differentiation among larger markets/systems. National cultures vary in their appeal to domestic audiences, although this tends to be a crucial local advantage. National media's ability to compete with foreign imports varies depending on homogeneity and acceptance of local culture.

Over time, the patterns of action and behavior by these kinds of actors tend to stabilize and form culturally defined boundaries. Among industry professionals, those tend to take the form of "the way we do things here," and among audiences, they tend to take the form of preferences for certain kinds of programming. Theoretically, these are both forms of reflexive cultural structuring (Giddens, 1984) and hybridization (Garcia Canclini, 1995).

NATIONAL TELEVISION MARKETS AS "IMAGINED COMMUNITIES"

Nations are "imagined political communities," according to Anderson, who says, "It is imagined because members of even the smallest nation will never know most of their fellow-members, meet them, or even hear of them, yet in the minds of each lives the image of their communion" (1983, p. 15). Similarly, other levels of community can also be imagined: globe-spanning views of a rock music youth culture, geolinguistic identification with Chinese culture even if one lives in Montreal, civilizations, a la Huntington, in which one's identity as Christian or Muslim may be more important than being Guatemalan or Indonesian, membership in a tribe which lives in a remote place in the Amazon barely aware of the other levels, including the "nations" of Brazil or Venezuela whose borders they might routinely cross. Anderson agrees that all levels of community larger than the village of face-to-face contact are imagined (1983, p. 15) and Tomlinson observes that "all cultural identities—be they national, regional, local—are, in one way, of the same order. They are all representations of belonging. . . . Where people think beyond the immediate presence of others, which is today almost everywhere, they 'imagine a community' to which they belong" (1991, p. 81).

Tomlinson (1991, pp. 81–82) notes that for Anderson, imagining a national community comes only with modernity, with the technological and economic changes that lead traditional people to be contacted by outside forces. For Anderson, the essential modernizing medium has been the national newspaper. Schlesinger (1987) criticizes Anderson, in fact, for not seeing that broadcast media easily flow across borders, leading to less clearly national "imagined communities."

NATIONAL TELEVISION PRODUCTION

Television genres have developed remarkably over the last 20–30 years, however. For example, a number of people have remarked on the changes the soap opera/serial/*telenovela* has experienced over time and the variety of forms it has taken in various settings (Allen, 1995). More importantly, in some ways, is that a number of very low cost genres have evolved which can be produced almost anywhere with the simplest and cheapest of equipment: news, talk, variety, live music and games. More and more nations are producing an increasing proportion of their own programming using such genres. Table 11.1 shows that a significant number of countries are doing over half of their own programming, both in the total broadcast day and during prime time, where audience viewing is concentrated and the most popular programs are usually placed.

CONCLUSIONS

Current formulations of globalization show less economic reductionism, less tendency to assume a monolithic and homogenizing globalization, more awareness that there is an active interplay between global, national and local (Friedman, 1994; Robertson, 1995). Recent work more often recognizes the existence of separate layers of global, supranational/regional national, subnational/regional, and local (Featherstone & Lash, 1995; Pieterse, 1995). Robertson (1995) asserts, with some logic and evidence, that most of the cultures we now think of as national or local have been touched and often partially shaped over the centuries by contact with other cultures at "national," regional and global levels. He argues that there is a certain pattern now of what we expect national and local cultures to look like, which is an aspect of what he calls glocalization. We can extend that same analysis to geolinguistic or cultural-linguistic regions. Certainly in television production, there is good evidence that regional productions of major genres are influenced by global developments in those genres, such as the global evolution of the soap opera, in which global, regional and national experiences interplay.

One of the strengths of the new globalization theorization is that it is more historically nuanced than much of the cultural imperialism debate. As Tomlinson (1991) pointed out, the cultural imperialism debate was often primarily concerned with the current geographic or spatial spread of media exports, which sometimes had the effect of neglecting complex histories of development prior to the advent of the medium under discussion. Tomlinson and others (Featherstone & Lash, 1995; Pieterse, 1995; Robertson, 1995) observe that it is necessary to add a historical dimension, which has been manifested as an analysis of modernity as part of globalization and vice-versa. This chapter also places that historical dimension for cultures as a tendency to hybridity between global and other outside elements and the local or national. Theoretically, this makes it easier to see how countries may have very distinct developments of certain kinds of "modern" television genres, like the soap opera or the variety show. Even more basically, it helps us understand that a commercial network employing modern advertising and cultivating audiences as consumers may be operating within a distinct capitalist modernity of their own.

The media imperialism and cultural synchronization theories assumed an epochal change in the power of media to affect cultures. Earlier generations of anthropologists had seen change in cultures from contact with other cultures as constant and normal. Friedman (1994), for example, documents a long history of empires, migrations and other strong forms of contact leading to cultural change. Current globalization theorists seem to be reverting more to this mode of thinking, seeing mass media as one recent wave in a very long series of cultural interactions on a global or nearly global scale (Friedman, 1994; Robertson, 1995).

Overall, within an increasingly internationalized world of television, we find a fairly compelling argument for looking at global, regional and national levels fairly equally. Much of the development from the 1970s to the 1990s has been the development of more national production by almost all countries. However, in several regions, particularly Latin America and the Arab world, regional trade in television has grown rapidly as well. Now the new technologies of cable and satellite television present a new level of globalization, simultaneous global exposure to some channels delivered by satellite. These media also present an equal if not larger opportunity for a new level of regionalization, channels targeted at geolinguistic groups across national borders. Both these new global and new regional channels will have an impact on nation-states' sovereignty and control, but perhaps no more than earlier waves of cultural change that preceded most of the current nation-states and will be absorbed by local cultures in much the same way.

The analysis of globalization can be strengthened by theorizing it in terms of structuration (Giddens, 1984). Structuration helps clarify the role of various institutional and cultural structures in refashioning the boundaries of possibility for various cultural producers, in some cases expanding them, in others imposing severe limits. Some early, even premodern forces, such as colonization, migration and racial and cultural hybridization have created social structures that still define boundaries of cultural production. At the current global level, cultural production boundaries are being most powerfully changed by the expansion of capitalist market economy forms into almost all nations. This places limits on certain forms of culture while enabling social actors to create others. Institutional and cultural forms of modernity tend to accompany capitalist globalization, but have their own logic. (This century has seen influential forms of socialist modernization and public or governmental/institutional modernization, as well.) Migration, driven by political and economic forces, also is powerful in redrawing social and cultural boundaries.

Regional and national structures can and do sometimes counter certain forces of globalization. Linguistic and cultural borders dating to both ancient and recent empires define supra-national markets which are either an aspect of or a competitor of global actors and markets, depending on just how broadly one defines globalization. Perhaps most importantly, nation-states still have the power to define crucial structures for media production. States employ political power, define aspects of cultures, license broadcasters, create market incentives, limit imports through quotas and counteract global actors who wish to penetrate national cultural space.

REFERENCES

Allen, R. C. (Ed.) (1995). *To be continued . . . : Soap operas around the world.* New York: Routledge.

Anderson, B. (1983). *Imagined communities: Reflections on the origin and spread of nationalism.* New York: Verso.

Barber, R. R. (1992). Jihad vs. McWorld. *The Atlantic,* 269, 3.

Bhahba, H. (1994). *The location of culture.* New York: Routledge.

Bourdieu, P. (1984). *Distinction: A social critique of the judgement of taste.* Cambridge, MA: Harvard University Press.

Boyd, D. (1993). *Broadcasting in the Arab world: A survey of the electronic media in the Middle East* (2nd ed.). Ames: Iowa State University Press.

Boyne, R. (1990). Culture and the world system. *Theory, Culture and Society,* 7, 57–62.

Chan, J. M. (1994). National responses and accessibility to STAR TV in Asia. *Journal of Communication,* 44(3), 70–88.

Collins, R. (1986, May–August). Wall-to-wall Dallas? The US-UK trade in television. *Screen,* 66–77.

Commission of the European Communities. (1985). *The European community and culture.* Brussels: Commission of the European Communities.

Fadul, A. (1993). *Serial fiction in TV: The Latin American telenovelas.* São Paulo, Brazil: Esccola de Comunicações e Artes, University of São Paulo.

Featherstone, M. (Ed.) (1990). *Global culture: Nationalism, globalization and modernity.* Newbury Park, CA: Sage Publications.

Featherstone, M., & Lash, S. (1995). An introduction. In M. Featherstone, S. Lash

& R. Robertson (Eds.), *Global modernities* (pp. 1–24). Thousand Oaks, CA: Sage Publications.

Ferguson, M. (1992). The mythology about globalization. *European Journal of Communication*, 7, 69–93.

Fernandes, I. (1982). *Memoria da telenovela brasileira*. São Paulo, Brazil: Proposta Editorial.

Fox, E. (1975). Multinational television. *Journal of Communication*, 25(2), 122–127.

Fox, E. (1992). Cultural dependency thrice revisited. Paper presented at the International Association for Mass Communication Research, Guarujá, Brazil.

Friedman, J. (1994). *Cultural identity and global process*. Thousand Oaks, CA: Sage Publications.

Garcia Canclini, N. (1990). *Culturas hibridas: estrategias para entrar y salir de la modernidad*. Mexico, D.F., Grijalbo: Consejo Nacional para la Cultura y las Artes.

Garcia Canclini, N. (1995). *Hybrid cultures: Strategies for entering and leaving modernity*. Minneapolis: University of Minnesota Press.

Garcia Canclini, N. (1997). Hybrid cultures and communicative strategies. *Media Development*, 44(1), 22–29.

Giddens, A. (1984). *The constitution of society: Outline of a theory of structuration*. Berkeley: University of California Press.

Giddens, A. (1991). *Modernity and self-identity*. Oxford: Polity Press.

Guback, T., & Varis, T. (1986). *Transnational communication and cultural industries*. New York: UNESCO.

Herman, E. S., & McChesney. R. (1997). *The global media: The new missionaries of global capitalism*. Washington, DC: Cassell.

Hoskins, C., & Mirus, R. (1988). Reasons for the U.S. dominance of the international trade in television programs. *Media, Culture and Society*, 10, 499–515.

Hotz, R. L. (2000, January 13). The struggle to save dying languages. *Los Angeles Times*, A1, 14–15.

Huntington, S. (1993). The clash of civilizations. *Foreign Affairs*, 72(3), 22–29.

Iwabuchi, K. (1997). The sweet scent of Asian modernity: The Japanese presence in the Asian audiovisual market. Paper presented at the Fifth International Symposium on Film, Television and Video—Media Globalization the Asia-Pacific Region, Taipei.

Janus, N. (1981). Advertising and the mass media in the era of the global corporations. In E. McAnany, J. Schnitman & N. Janus (Eds.), *Communication and social structure: Critical studies in mass media research* (pp. 287–316). New York: Praeger.

Karp, J. (1994, January 27). Cast of thousands. *Far Eastern Economic Review*, 46–53.

Kottak, C. P. (1990). *Prime time society—An anthropological analysis of television and culture*. Belmont, CA: Wadsworth.

LaPastina, A., Straubhaar, J. & Buarque de Almeida, H. (1999). Producers, audiences and the limits of social marketing on television: The case of O Rei do Gado, a telenovela about land reform in Brazil. Paper presented at the International Communication Association, San Francisco.

Lee, C. (1980). *Media imperialism reconsidered.* Beverly Hills, CA: Sage Publications.

Marques de Melo, J. (1988). *As telenovelas da Globo: Produção e Exportação.* São Paulo, Brazil: Summus.

Mattelart, A. (1991). *Advertising international: The privatization of public space.* New York: Routledge.

McDaniel, D. O. (1994). *Broadcasting in the Malay world.* Norwood, NJ: Ablex.

McPhail, T. (1989). *Electronic colonialism.* Newbury Park, CA: Sage Publications.

Mitra, A. (1993). *Television and popular culture in India: A study of the Mahabharat.* New Delhi: Sage Publications.

Mosco, V. (1996). *The political economy of communication: Rethinking and renewal.* Thousand Oaks, CA: Sage Publications.

Nordenstreng, K., & Varis, T. (1974). *Television traffic—A one-way street.* Paris: UNESCO.

Oliveira, O. S. (1990). Brazilian soaps outshine Hollywood: Is cultural imperialism fading out? Paper presented at the International Communication Association, Dublin.

Pieterse, J. N. (1995). Globalization as hybridization. In M. Featherstone, S. Lash & R. Robertson (Eds.), *Global Modernities* (pp. 45–68). Thousand Oaks, CA: Sage Publications.

Read, W. H. (1976). *America's mass media merchants.* Baltimore, MD: Johns Hopkins University Press.

Robertson, R. (1992). Globality and modernity. *Theory, Culture and Society, 9*(2).

Robertson, R. (1995). Glocalization: Time-space and homogeneity-heterogeneity. In M. Featherstone, S. Lash & R. Robertson (Eds.), *Global Modernities* (pp. 25–44). Thousand Oaks, CA: Sage Publications.

Santoro, L. F. (1990). Interview with the author, Professor, University of São Paulo, and Co-Director, TV dos Trabalhadores.

Schatz, T. (1981). *Hollywood genres.* New York: Random House.

Schiller, H. I. (1971). *Mass communications and American empire.* Boston: Beacon Press.

Schlesinger, P. (1987). On national identity: Some conceptions and misconceptions criticized. *Social Science Information, 26*(2), 219–264.

Schlesinger, P. (1991). *Media, state and nation.* London: Sage Publications.

Shohat, E., & Stam, R. (1994). *Unthinking Eurocentrism: Multiculturalism and the media.* New York: Routledge.

Sinclair, J., Jacka, E. & Cunningham, S. (1996). *Peripheral vision: New patterns in global television.* New York: Oxford University Press.

Smith, A. D. (1981). *The ethnic revival in the modern world.* Cambridge: Cambridge University Press.

Straubhaar, J. D. (1991a). Beyond media imperialism: Asymmetrical interdependence and cultural proximity. *Critical Studies in Mass Communication, 8,* 1–11.

Straubhaar, J. D. (1991b). Class, genre and the regionalization of the television market in Latin America. *Journal of Communication, 41*(1), 53–69.

Straubhaar, J. D., Campbell, C., Youn, S. N., Champagnie, K., Ha, L., Shrikhande, S., Elasmar, M. & Castellon, L. (1992). The emergence of a Latin American market for television programs. Paper presented at the International Communication Association, Miami.

Tomlinson, J. (1991). *Cultural imperialism.* Baltimore, MD: Johns Hopkins University Press.

Tunstall, J. (1977). *The media are American.* New York: Columbia University Press.

Wallerstein, I. (1979). *The capitalist world economy.* Cambridge: Cambridge University Press.

Wallerstein, I. (1991). *Geopolitics and geoculture: Essays on the changing world system.* Cambridge: Cambridge University Press.

Wildman, S., & Siwek, S. (1988). *International trade in films and television programs.* Cambridge, MA: Ballinger.

Wilkinson, K. (1995). *Where culture, language and communication converge: The Latin-American cultural linguistic market.* Austin: University of Texas–Austin.

Chapter 12

Restrictions on Foreign Ownership and National Sovereignty: Whose Issue Is It?

Georgette Wang

National sovereignty, generally considered the key in keeping effective boundaries among nations, has in recent years encountered unprecedented challenges from global forces. With political, economic and scientific activities increasingly conducted at the international level, the decline of the nation-state and national sovereignty is believed to be inevitable. As McGrew (1992) argued, the process of globalization has compromised four critical aspects of the nation-state: its competence; its form; its autonomy; and, ultimately, its authority or legitimacy.

Media and telecommunications industries have become regional and global due to the rapid development of communication technologies. This has contributed to the rise of internationalism[1] and globalism and, presumably, the decline of sovereignty. Ownership of telecommunication networks, especially those for basic services (which are regarded as the backbone of a country's communication system), can trigger concerns among policymakers over national sovereignty for two reasons: the need to keep telecommunications services under sovereign control for security considerations, and the need to regulate the flow of information and provision of services within national borders. It is for these reasons that basic telecommunication services were exempted from major international trade negotiations in the past, and it is for the same reasons that the ownership issue is worthy of our attention after the agreement to open basic telecommunication services for competition was signed by the 72 member nations of the World Trade Organization (WTO) in 1998. Is foreign ownership of telecommunications basic services still a concern? If yes, which nations have chosen to adopt a more liberal policy stand, and for what reasons? Is sovereignty no longer a major concern to these nations? Why not?

To give the above issues a thorough examination, this chapter begins with a review of past debates over sovereignty and transnational communication, and the policies adopted by different groups of nations in this regard. This discussion is followed by an overview of WTO members' decisions on foreign ownership restrictions in basic telecommunication services vs. the extent of market liberalization after the 1998 agreement was signed. Next, the degree of economic and telecommunications sector development in different groups of nations is analyzed in an attempt to explain the pattern of decision-making on foreign ownership restrictions. Finally, the implications of such decision patterns for national sovereignty and the global community are discussed in the conclusion.

NATIONAL SOVEREIGNTY AND COMMUNICATION TECHNOLOGIES: A LONG STORY

If we define national sovereignty as the ability of governments to control things taking place within their borders (Braman, 1995), then communication technologies have had a long history of challenging this ability. When the issue of Direct Broadcast Satellite (DBS) was brought up at United Nations meetings in the 1970s, the question of whether free flow of information or national sovereignty should take priority triggered heated debates among delegates (Fisher, 1990). In 1982, a set of principles regulating satellite broadcast was finally passed in a UN plenary meeting (Powell, 1985). However, when commercial DBS services were launched in the 1990s, most governments were still left to solve their own problems with transnational television.

The same arguments were repeated when transborder data flow (TDF) became an issue. With no consensus reached on a regulatory principle, governments once again found themselves caught in a quagmire of political, economic and technological forces, searching for solutions. Given this background, it should come as little surprise that the Chinese and Singaporean governments took the matter in their own hands when Internet communication began to challenge national laws and regulations (Wang, 1999).

RESTRICTIONS ON FOREIGN OWNERSHIP OF BASIC SERVICES

To a given sovereign state, the role and function of telecommunications services are quite different from those of transnational media such as satellite broadcasting or Internet. They contribute to, rather than challenge, "a nation's ability to control things within its national borders"—that is, unless they fall into the hands of foreigners. These concerns over foreign ownership are clearly evidenced in the following quote from the Consultative Committee on the Implication of Telecommunications for Canadian Sovereignty (Globerman, 1995):

Telecommunications, taken in the broadest sense, will form the infrastructure of the new industrial society that is now coming into being around the world. Canadian sovereignty in the next generation will depend heavily on telecommunications. If we wish to control our economy then we will require a sophisticated telecommunications sector developed and owned in Canada to meet specific Canadian requirements. To maintain our Canadian identity and independence we must ensure an adequate measure of control over data banks, transborder data flow and the content of information services available in Canada. Telecommunications, as the foundation of the future society, cannot always be left to the rigors of the market.

This statement points to two central concerns of governments in regard to foreign ownership in the telecommunications sector: (1) the control—including ownership, development and application—of telecommunications networks, which is seen as the key to national development and also a manifestation of sovereignty; and (2) the need to regulate content flow and service provision, another form of control which is often undermined by transnational media, which easily bypass national borders and hence all forms of government rules in reaching audiences and users.

Since the early 1980s the world market has seen extensive deregulation and liberalization in the telecommunications sector. By eliminating restrictions on foreign competition in domestic markets, liberalization pushes national industries to go overseas for continual growth and greater profit.

While deregulation is lauded as the key to globalizing the world telecommunications market, a number of nations have chosen to maintain some form of restrictions on foreign ownership in basic services. The restrictions on foreign ownership include stipulations that specify the kind of businesses that foreign companies may buy into, the extent to which they may do so and the conditions for such permission (e.g., reciprocity in policy treatment). They may not be effective in barring businesses that are capable of conducting transactions off-shore (e.g., electronic commerce) but they can bar or substantially limit competition from transnational corporations. Seen as an act defying the globalization trend and an indicator of protectionism, restrictions upon foreign ownership have been a major target for international negotiations, but these negotiations have not covered restrictions of ownership on basic telecommunications services.

For reasons of national security, social welfare or simply market value, basic services was the last area in telecommunications that was opened to foreign competition in many countries. In the past, national governments have been exempted from granting domestic treatment to foreign-owned carriers in basic telecommunications services in trade agreements such as the North American Free Trade Agreement and the General Agreement on Tariffs and Trade.

Today foreign competition has become increasingly difficult to avoid, including competition in basic telecommunications services. Under the terms of the World Trade Organization (WTO) Agreement on Basic Telecommunications Services and its associated Reference Paper, which took effect in 1998, 72 WTO member governments agreed to open their domestic markets in basic services to foreign competitors (Taylor & Jussawalla, 1998). The trade agreement, which covers all public and private telecommunication services that involve the end-to-end transmission of customer-supplied information and services provided through resale, requires that telecommunications operators based in other WTO member countries be permitted to compete in the national market on a most-favored-nation (MFN) basis.

To ensure open competition, this agreement provides a dispute settlement mechanism that enables any WTO member to challenge the laws, policies and regulations of other member countries, and to allege non-compliance with the Agreement in order to reduce barriers to competition.

One important consideration in demolishing domestic market entry barriers to foreign competitors in telecommunications is reciprocity—the opportunity to compete on the overseas market. Although the motivation of seeking overseas markets is typically driven by the need for economic expansion, free trade in telecommunications is also regarded as an important step toward a global information society. Pekka Tarjanne, Secretary General of the International Telecommunication Union (ITU) once said, "We will never have a global information society until we have a global information economy, and we will never have a global information economy without free trade in telecommunications and information services" ("Windows," 1997, p. 8; Wright, 1998, p. 267).

But even with basic telecommunications services opened to foreign competition, as all of the 72 WTO member nations have pledged to do, many have chosen to maintain restrictions on foreign ownership in this area.[2] A survey of the regulation of 69 WTO member nations which concluded the initial trade agreement in telecommunications in 1997 showed that over one-third of the total (25 of them, or 36 percent) have retained specific clauses on the restrictions of foreign ownership in their telecommunications law or regulations (See Table 12.1).

The 47 nations in the "no restriction" category include most of the members of the European Community and a few of the least developed nations. Included in the "yes" list were major economies in the developing world (e.g., Brazil, South Africa, Malaysia and Singapore) and also many top economic powers that are generally staunch supporters of free trade ideals (e.g., the United States, Japan and France).

Most of the restrictions have to do with the maintenance of a "golden

Table 12.1
Restrictions on Foreign Ownership and Range of Services Opened*

With Foreign Ownership Restrictions	Per Capita Income	Telephone Main Lines Per Capita	Without Foreign Ownership Restrictions**	Per Capita Income	Telephone Main Lines Per Capita
All					
Canada	19,290	0.621	Argentina	8,570	0.190
Colombia	2,280	0.140	Australia	20,540	0.492
France	26,050	0.570	Austria	27,980	0.496
Japan	37,850	0.479	Belgium	26,420	0.477
Korea	10,550	0.444	Chile	5,020	0.175
Mexico	3,680	0.097	Denmark	32,500	0.668
New Zealand	16,480	0.460	Finland	24,080	0.572
Portugal	10,450	0.400	Germany	28,260	0.551
United States	28,740	0.643	Greece	12,010	0.494
			Hong Kong	25,280	0.521
			Ireland	18,280	0.375
			Italy	20,120	0.451
			Luxembourg	—	—
			Netherlands	25,820	0.554
			Norway	36,090	0.684
			Spain	14,510	0.406
			Sweden	26,220	0.668
			Switzerland	44,320	0.670
Average	17,263	0.428	Average	23,295	0.497

Table 12.1 (continued)

With Foreign Ownership Restrictions	Per Capita Income	Telephone Main Lines Per Capita
Limited		
Belize	4,720	0.010
Brazil	4,430	0.310
Hungary	1,110	0.025
Indonesia	1,220	0.028
Philippines	3,590	0.193
Poland	32,940	0.562
Singapore	3,700	0.278
Slovak Republic	3,400	0.122
South Africa		
Average	6,889	0.191

Without Foreign Ownership Restrictions**	Per Capita Income	Telephone Main Lines Per Capita
Bolivia	950	0.067
Bulgaria	1,140	0.335
Czech Republic	5,200	0.328
Dominica	—	—
Dominican Republic	1,670	0.089
Ecuador	1,590	0.075
El Salvador	1,810	0.054
Grenada	—	—
Guatemala	1,500	0.039
Jamaica	1,560	0.118
Peru	2,460	0.066
Romania	1,420	0.164
Trinidad & Tobago	4,230	0.248
Turkey	3,130	0.246
Venezuela	3,450	0.122
Average	2,316	0.150

Very Restricted				Bangladesh	270	0.003
Antigua & Barbuda	—	—		Brunei	—	—
Ghana	370	0.004		Cote d'Ivoire	690	0.009
India	390	0.002		Mauritius	3,800	0.223
Israel	15,810	0.443		Pakistan	490	0.019
Malaysia	4,680	0.201		Papua New Guinea	940	0.009
Morocco	1,250	0.048		Senegal	550	0.013
Tunisia	2,090	—		Sri Lanka	800	0.019
				Thailand	2,800	0.079
Average	3,998	0.150		Average	1,293	0.047

—: Data missing from *World Development Report* (1999) or ITU database.

*Included in this list are the 69 WTO member nations which agreed to open basic telecommunications services in 1997; three more were added to the list when the agreement was signed in 1998.

**"Without foreign ownership restrictions" here means the absence of a special clause directed at restricting ownership of telecommunication services by foreign individuals or companies.

Sources: Analyses (http://www.analysys.co.uk/products/wto/background.htm), *World Development Report* (1999), International Telecommunication Union database on common carriers.

share," a stipulation that ensures that the dominant telecommunications operator must not come under the control of a single—especially foreign—operator. In most cases the ceiling of foreign equity is set around 40 to 50 percent (e.g., in Brazil, Korea, Mexico, Morocco, the Philippines, Poland, Singapore, Sri Lanka and Tunisia). Others, including Australia, France and Portugal have lower maximums (10 to 25 percent), but only for a few selected items such as radio-based services.

While one may take the absence of restrictions on foreign ownership as an indicator of the degree of market openness, it is interesting to note that the two do not seem to be necessarily related. In nine of the 25 nations with restrictions on foreign ownership of basic services, the market was open to competition in all telecommunication services, including basic services in local, national and international voice and data communications, and mobile services such as radio navigation, paging, personal communication and mobile satellite services. Japan, for example, removed the long-standing foreign equity limitations on Type I carriers and radio-based services in 1996, but has left a ceiling of 20 percent for foreign equity in its two major telecommunications service providers, KDD and NTT.

In nine other nations that impose no limits on foreign ownership in basic services, "very restricted"[3] competition is found in the telecommunications market. In Pakistan, for example, while no restrictions are imposed on foreign ownership, the existing monopoly over voice telephony, telegraph services and leased circuit services is not scheduled to phase out until 2004, with no commitment on commercial presence.

To sketch a profile for different nation groups, per capita income has been used as an indicator of the extent of economic development, and the penetration of telephone main lines has been used as an indicator of the scale of telecommunications services. The averages of the two indicators as shown in Table 12.1, demonstrate an interesting pattern. Irrespective of the presence of restrictions on foreign ownership, those nations with a more liberalized telecommunications market have higher average per capita income and telephone penetration. Of nations with a similar degree of market liberalization, those that impose restrictions on foreign ownership tend to be higher in both average per capita income and telephone penetration than those that do not impose such restrictions (with the exception of the fully deregulated group).

It is also interesting to note that the nations which have retained some form of restrictions against foreign ownership in their otherwise totally liberalized markets are home to seven of the ten public telecommunications operators with the highest revenues in 1997, and eight of the top ten cellular mobile operators among OECD (Organization for Economic Cooperation and Development) nations (OECD, 1999). On the other hand, over half of the nations that impose no restrictions on foreign ownership are developing countries where one telephone main line could be shared among over 30 people and telecommunications industries barely exist. If the lifting of foreign ownership restrictions can be seen as an indicator of loosening controls over "activities within its national borders" and a more liberal attitude toward national sovereignty, the implications of the above analysis would be contrary to what we have seen in previous debates on national sovereignty.

Tarjanne (1995) once raised the question of whether global communication technologies are crossing the "limits of national sovereignty." While no one has offered to answer the question, it is not difficult to sense national differences regarding where this "limit" lies.

Indeed it is no secret that the developed and the developing worlds hold distinctly different attitudes concerning transnational media, and have come in direct confrontation in more than one international meeting and conference in the past. In drafting the agreement on the "Peaceful Use of Outer Space"—an agreement on the uses of DBS, for example—national sovereignty was one of the points repeatedly brought up by delegates from developing nations (Pool, 1979). Concerns of developing nations over the influences of uncurbed transnational flow of information and television programs were illustrated in the Argentine draft of the DBS convention. In contrast to the U.S. draft, which advocated expansion of free and open exchange, the Argentine draft sought to subject DBS broadcast to "national sovereignty, the fundamental rights of states, the family and the individual" (Fisher, 1990, p. 121).

A similar version of the DBS debate was seen again over the issue of transborder data flow (TDF) when delegates from developing nations insisted that information be treated as a public good. The basis of their argument was the UN Resolution of Permanent Sovereignty over Natural Resources, which stated that sovereignty over natural resources was a "permanent and fundamental right of nations" (Adams, 1983, p. 410).

The stand that developed and developing nations adopted in the UN debate on DBS and TDF is typical of the policy attitude governments take regarding other issues of a similar nature. Those that are more competitive on the global market and have products to sell tend to advocate the elimination of all forms of barriers to trade and information flow, while those that are not as competitive tend to opt for protectionist measures, and national sovereignty becomes a justifiable last refuge.

In actual practice, however, government restrictions on foreign ownership of basic telecommunications do not fit the pattern described above. Several nations that have led the push for liberalization of the telecommunications market, and which are home to the most powerful transnational telecommunications corporations in the world, are found to have retained certain forms of restrictions on foreign ownership, while others have kept no specific clauses. Similarly, the developing world is also split on the issue of whether to keep restrictions.

While restrictions on foreign ownership may be seen as a strategy to protect national industries and enhance their competitiveness in world trading activities, the absence of such clauses does not necessarily mean the absence of restrictions altogether; they may be embedded elsewhere in the telecommunications law. For example, the United Kingdom keeps no restrictions on foreign ownership of basic telecommunication industries, but the British government reserves the right to block acquisition of more than 15 percent of the two largest companies by either national or foreign companies. In Spain, preliminary administrative authorization would be required if any individual or corporation, national or foreign, were planning to obtain control of over 10 percent of Telefonica equity.

Aside from general ownership regulations, licensing conditions may also create barriers to foreign investment. As indicated by Fredebeul-Krein and Freytag (1998), by requiring applicants to meet various criteria for the granting of a license, it is entirely possible for a government to impose obstacles against market entry by foreign parties.

Such sophistication in regulatory design, however, entails a heavy information and technical cost which is hardly affordable to regulators in developing nations, especially those in the lower-income group. In these nations, therefore, an absence of specific clauses on restrictions of foreign ownership in telecommunications laws and regulations is more likely to mean a thorough absence of restrictions. In Third World nations, where basic services are placed in the hand of state monopolies, the concern about losing control over telecommunications services may not be as serious, because the decision to accept or reject foreign investment rests with the government. The situation, however, is different in low-income developing nations, where basic telecommunications services are privatized or deregulated, as most Third World WTO member nations have pledged to do early in the next decade (Pogorel, 1997). In these cases, the absence of restrictions on foreign ownership calls for an explanation. Is exploitation by transnationals and national sovereignty no longer a concern? Is foreign ownership a feasible solution when national industries are struggling to survive?

Before a conclusion can be arrived at, it is perhaps necessary to look further into the differences among developing nations in the competitiveness of their telecommunications industries.

FOREIGN INVESTMENT: A WELCOME OPTION

As noted by Taylor and Jussawalla (1998), the 72 WTO member nations that signed the agreement account for nearly 93 percent of the total domestic and international revenue of U.S.$600 billion generated in this sector annually. Some authors, however, were also quick to point out that the agreement only covered 19 percent of the world population (Allen, 1998).

Table 12.2
Average Telephone Penetration in Four World Bank Income Groups

Income Groups	Average Per Capita Income/Group	Telephone Main Lines Per Capita/Group
U.S.$350 or below	245	0.006
350–1,230	703	0.056
1,230–4,520	2,607	0.150
4,520–25,700	12,738	0.355
25,700 or above	31,099	0.577

Sources: World Development Report (1999) and International Telecommunication Union data on common carriers.

This figure reminds us that of the 26 low-income nations listed in the 1999 edition of the World Bank's *World Development Report,* only one—Bangladesh—participated in the WTO agreement on basic services. While the gap between the developed and the developing nations may be alarming, equally alarming are the gaps within the developing world.

As shown in Table 12.2, average telephone penetration in low-income nations (per capita income below U.S.$350) is 6 per 1,000 people, which is close to one-tenth of the average of the upper-lower income group (per capita income from U.S.$350 to U.S.$1,230), and one-twentieth of that of the lower-middle income group (U.S.$1,230–U.S.$4,520). The gap is much larger than that between the high-income (above U.S.$25,700) and upper-middle income groups (from U.S.$4,520 to U.S.$25,700), or even that between the high-income and the lower-middle income groups (U.S.$1,230–U.S.$4,520). This difference in the size of the gap, and the differences in needs, are easily overlooked when "developing nations" are treated as a single category.

The key to narrowing these gaps is economic growth. According to a study by Hudson (1995), there was significant growth in the telecommunications sector in the low- and middle-income countries from 1980 to 1990. In the low-income economies, telephone density increased by an average of 19.7 percent when their economies grew by merely 4.2 percent. This growth, however, paled when compared with the growth in the middle-income nations: 23.9 percent growth in GDP and a 77.9 percent increase in telephone lines. For the low-income nations, also discouraging is the fact that the change is extremely modest given the basis of growth. Until the late 1990s, there was an average of one telephone line for more than 100 people, and the situation is unlikely to undergo drastic changes as long as a large majority of the population is scattered in rural areas

(Gifford & Cosper, 1998). While globalization is believed to be the trend of development, few African countries have undersea cable access to the rest of the world; for domestic and international services they had no choice but to rely on Intelsat (Gifford & Cosper, 1998).

Listed among the roadblocks for telecommunications growth in African nations are government control, red tape, corruption and language barriers, not to mention famine, civil war and political strife (Gifford & Cosper, 1998). Without an effective telecommunications infrastructure, African economies will likely remain stagnant, and how African operators are to accomplish the task of modernizing the system remains an open question. Despite optimism for future changes, the telecommunications market in African nations has enough difficulties in attracting foreign investment as it is. Putting restrictions on it would only compound the problem.

To the extent that Africa represents the plight of the world's low-income nations, it is not difficult to understand why restrictions on foreign ownership, or any form of protectionist measures, have not been as much concern to them. While middle-income developing nations were criticized for their intention to protect domestic companies which were incapable of competing with foreign entrants (Taylor & Jussawalla, 1998), the low-income nations had few industries to protect. Similarly while middle-income nations were concerned about the erosion of national and cultural sovereignty as transnational communications services continued to expand, many low-income nations remained "un-invaded." According to Gifford and Cosper (1998), Africa is a land that satellite broadcasters "aren't flocking to," although market demand may be slowly growing. To the poorest of nations, capital investment, domestic or foreign, is so much in demand that taking precautions to guard against harmful side effects does not seem to be high on the priority list.

Senegal is one good example of what foreign ownership means to telecommunications services in a developing nation. With telephone penetration of 13 per 1,000 people and per capita income of U.S.$550 (see Table 12.1), Senegal is among the poorer nations in the developing world. Sonatel, the Senegal telecommunications monopoly, was deregulated in 1996 under the new telecommunications law. A year later, the government approved the sale of a 33.33 percent stake in Sonatel to France Cable Radio, a subsidiary of France Telecom.

With the new regulatory regime, Sonatel retains the monopoly to operate public telephone services and telephone services between fixed points, but once privatized, these rights were ceded to its strategic partner, France Telecom, as a seven-year concession. In exchange, France Telecom has offered to invest in infrastructure and rural telephones, targeted at telephone services in 2,000 villages by 2005, as compared to 400 in 1997. Today Sonatel provides the country's cellular services and also Africa's first fully digitized telephone network.

According to an ITU report, Senegal already was one of the best performing sub-Saharan countries in telecommunications before France Telecom came into the picture. But without the capital, know-how and professional workforce of France Telecom, it would likely take Sonatel much longer to build a modern telecommunication system. What Senegal has lost in this arrangement is its independence in building and maintaining a telecommunications infrastructure, for its system now relies on France Telecom to function effectively. How to ensure that this trade-off is exercised in the interest of the nation in the long run is something that individual governments must, although often fail to, consider.

Obviously Senegal is not the only developing nation that sees the benefit of bringing foreign investment. Bulgaria, one of the socialist Eastern European nations, is another one that has committed to free and competitive communications market with no restrictions on foreign ownership in basic services. With a system that is plagued by poor staff policy, incompetent management and corruption, there is not yet a clear indication as how foreign capital may effectively be put to work and national interest protected.

THE CONCERN FOR NATIONAL SOVEREIGNTY: WHO CAN AFFORD IT?

The sovereignty argument, therefore, seems to have become a relevant issue with regard to global competition in telecommunications services, something to seriously consider in policy formulation only when nations have reached a certain level of growth.

Without further examination of telecommunications laws and regulations in the low-income nations, it would be premature to conclude that in the "no restriction" nations foreign ownership is indeed free from any form of restrictions. However, if the need for economic development has anything to do with a government's stand on sovereignty and how it is reflected in communications policies and regulations, this would not be the first time for such a connection to be found. In China and Singapore, for example, regulations on Internet communications are strict, yet not rigorously enforced for fear that so doing may have an adverse impact on economic growth (Wang, 1999).

If sovereignty is the right of a nation while economic growth holds the key to its survival, what we have observed is that nations tend to let down their guard on their rights when survival is at stake. Although the result of lifted market restrictions—a free market—is the same, it is erroneous to assume that the cause, the effects and the side effects are the same across nations.

In 1997, the year when the WTO Agreement on Basic Services was signed, Tarjanne noted the passing of "the old regime of international telecommunications based on national sovereignty and correspondent relations" ("Windows," 1997, p. 8; Wright, 1998, p. 267). However, he also noted that this is not the end of national sovereignty. Although the marketplace ideology has produced spectacular results in many countries, it has also raised new issues that require regulatory solutions at both the national and the international levels.

The question here is not what will replace national sovereignty in this age of global communication and information, or to what extent national sovereignty has been undermined, as some had feared (Braman, 1995; Pogorel, 1997), but rather, how it has been defined and redefined, used and shaped by national governments through the formulation of national policies and negotiation of trade agreements. As some critical theorists suggested, it is through the "practice of power relations and norm development" that sovereignty is structured and contested.

If such is the case, what we have learned from the restriction of foreign ownership is that, as the range, scale and complexity of international telecommunications services increase, the level of sophistication in regulatory design also increases. What regulators face is no longer just the challenge of new communication services brought within the scope of existing laws and regulations. In order to design licensing conditions so as to afford the greatest possible protection for the interests of the host country while enabling foreign investors maximize their profits, one would need extensive legal, technical, as well as market, information which is frequently unavailable in developing nations, especially in low-income nations. Key international telecommunications organizations are becoming increasingly commercialized (Taylor, 1998) while subsidies to developing nations produced by the accounting rate system are likely to be removed (Taylor & Jussawalla, 1998). As such, no solution is in sight for the problems faced by regulators in Third World nations.

As Tarjanne has suggested, we are not likely to go beyond the limits of national sovereignty in the near future. However, it is also important to note that the question of how to best structure sovereignty through policy has not only become a matter of needs, but also a matter of abilities, which may have become increasingly expensive to acquire.

NOTES

This study was sponsored by the Ecole Nationale Superieure des Telecommunications (ENST), France. The author would also like to thank Clare Liu for her assistance in data collection and analyses.

1. A term used by Pekka Tarjanne, Secretary General of the International Telecommunication Union, in a speech on the governance of international telecommunications.

2. Altogether 72 nations signed, but information is not available for the last three that decided to join.

3. The 69 nations were categorized according to the degree of market liberalization in the telecommunications sector. The "very restricted" markets are characterized by long-standing state monopolies in basic services.

REFERENCES

Adams, J. M. (1983). Canada's future TDF policy: Reconciling free flow with national sovereignty. *Transnational Data and Communication Report,* 6, 405–411.

Allen, D. (1998, July). The WTO telecommunications agreement. Paper presented at the International Telecommunications Society Conference, Stockholm, Sweden.

Braman, S. (1995). Horizons of the state: Information policy and power. *Journal of Communication,* 45(4), 4–24.

Fisher, D. (1990). *Prior consent to international direct satellite broadcasting.* Dordrecht: Martinus Nijhoff.

Fredebeul-Krein, M., & Freytag, A. (1998, July). The case for a more binding WTO agreement on regulatory principles in telecommunication markets. Paper presented at the International Telecommunications Society Conference, Stockholm, Sweden.

Gifford, J. M., & Cosper, A. C. (1998, April). Out of Africa. *Satellite Communication,* 34–38.

Globerman, S. (1995). Foreign ownership in telecommunications. *Telecommunications Policy,* 19(1), 21–28.

Hudson, H. (1995). Access to telecommunications in the developing world: Ten years after the Maitland Report. In G. W. Brock (Ed.), *Toward a competitive telecommunication industry: Selected papers from the 1994 Telecommunications Policy Research Conference* (pp. 235–248). Mahwah, NJ: Lawrence Erlbaum Associates.

McGrew, T. (1992). *Modernity and its futures.* Cambridge: Polity Press.

Organization for Economic Cooperation and Development (OECD). (1999). *Communications outlook 1999.* Paris: OECD.

Pogorel, G. (1997). Signification et implications de l'accord OMC sur l'acces aux services de telecommunications de base (MABTS). Unpublished paper, Ecole Nationale Superieure des Telecommunications.

Pool, I. S. (1979). DBS national culture integrity. In C. Nordenstreng & H. Schiller (Eds.), *National sovereignty and international communication* (pp. 120–153). Norwood, NJ: Ablex.

Powell, J. T. (1985). *International broadcasting by satellite.* Westport, CT: Quorum Books.

Tarjanne, P. (1995, September). The limits of national sovereignty: Issues for the governance of international telecommunications. A lecture to the Law School, University of California, Berkeley.

Taylor, L. A. (1998, February). The World Radio Communication Conference clears a path for broadband systems using non-geostationary orbits. *Satellite Communication,* 29–32.

Taylor, R., & Jussawalla, M. (1998, July). The WTO Basic Telecommunications Agreement: Evolving multilateral regulatory paradigms and the developing world. Paper presented at the International Telecommunications Society Conference, Stockholm, Sweden.

Wang, G. (1999). Regulating network communication in Asia: A different balancing act? *Telecommunications Policy*, 23, 277–287.

Windows of the World. (1997, March). *ITU News*, 8.

World Bank. (1999). *World Development Report*. New York: Oxford University Press.

Wright, D. (1998). The European Commission and the satellite industry combine forces to open markets. *Telecommunications Policy*, 22(4/5), 267–272.

Part IV

Crossing Boundaries

Chapter 13

Disneyfying and Globalizing the Chinese Legend Mulan: A Study of Transculturation

Joseph M. Chan

INTRODUCTION

Hua Mulan, a girl warrior who is believed to have disguised herself as a man and fought a war on behalf of her father, is a household name to the Chinese. She is at the heart of a legend that people learn in childhood and adolescence in mainland China, Hong Kong and Taiwan. The legend is passed from generation to generation through storytelling, poems, songs, comic books, short stories, textbooks, dramas, movies and television.[1] In 1998, the legend took on a new life when it became the theme of the Disney animated feature *Mulan*. Premiering in Singapore, *Mulan* was shown around the world, grossing about U.S.$300 million and making the list of Disney's most profitable movies.

This was the first time that Disney had ever drawn on an Asian story for making an animated feature. While Walt Disney used to draw his inspirations from British sources, most other features are retreads of familiar Western children's classics (Sinyard, 1988). Indeed, the story of Mulan was unknown in the West and in non-Chinese Asian countries. But the Disney touch has made it a global legend. *Mulan* is thus an ideal case for studying how a Chinese legend is Westernized and globalized by a multinational studio. At a more abstract level, this is a study of transculturation, the process by which one culture is transformed by another in their mutual encounters.

Methodologically, I rely on published interviews and documents for the analysis of the cultural dynamics involved in Disneyfying the Chinese legend. I also text-analyzed *Mulan* to identify the storyline, the major themes, the characters and the artistic style. The textual analysis enables me to relate the text to the observations made by *Mulan*'s producers and myself. To heighten my sensitivity and understanding of what Disney has done to the Chinese legend, I reviewed other versions of the Mulan story published as drama series, plays, novels and poems (e.g., Anonymous, 1997; Huang & Li, 1992; Tan, 1996). A constant reference is a short poem called the Ballad of Mulan that is widely regarded as the foundation of the story. While the Chinese version of the poem is readily available in any secondary school textbook in Chinese societies, Disney publishes an English translation in its official Web site.

In the sections to follow, I shall first explicate the notion of transculturation in connection with related concepts such as globalization, localization, hybridization and acculturation. Then I shall give a brief account of the animated movie *Mulan*. This is followed by a concrete analysis of transculturation as reflected in the Disneyfication and globalization of the legend. Finally, I shall revisit the concept of transculturation and its association with cultural authenticity, and the formation of global culture.

CULTURAL GLOBALIZATION AND TRANSCULTURATION

The discourse on the world's cultural order until the 1980s was heavily influenced by the notions of media imperialism and cultural imperialism (e.g., Boyd-Barrett, 1977; Lee, 1980). With Hollywood as the world's center of production, American media were viewed as a threat to indigenous culture in developing countries. The general fear was that the world media would be homogenized. The idea of sovereignty and associated concepts such as the nation-state, information sovereignty and cultural integrity were highly relevant in the discussion on the impact of Western media and culture.

The idea of imperialism began to lose its relevancy after the mid-1980s, when some developing countries such as the four small dragons of Asia achieved impressive economic development. Its irrelevancy deepened as radicalism lost its steam in the West. Even China, the world's stronghold of socialism, began to distance itself from ideological orthodoxy and adopted open and reformist policies, moving itself closer to the capitalist world. The theories of imperialism and socialism suffered from further loss of credibility when Eastern Europe collapsed in the late 1980s and early 1990s. The world seemed to have converged toward capitalism and a market economy.

In the midst of all these happenings, the world's economy has become more integrated than ever. The world seems to have converged toward capitalism and democracy. Meanwhile, the advent of information technologies such as computers, cable television, satellite television, the Internet and mobile telephony have effectively shrunk the world. The interrelationships between countries are increasingly characterized as interdependent, with the world viewed as a whole. It is against this backdrop that the idea of globalization began to gain popularity in news magazines and academic publications. As an extension of modernity, globalization is the process by which the world's economy, polity and culture are becoming a connected and interactive whole (Featherstone, 1990; Giddens, 1991). What happens in one place will have repercussions elsewhere. The unit of analysis in the discourse on globality is not the nation-state, but the world itself.

The idea of globalization is easily extended to the cultural realm to refer to the formation of a global culture. To some, this global culture is dominated by the West, and the associated threat is cultural homogenization. Cultural globalization is, in effect, Westernization. To others, the asymmetrical relationship is not tilted all to one side. The nation-state still has its autonomy and local culture may resist (Schlesinger, 1993; Sreberny, Winseck, McKenna & Boyd-Barrett, 1997). Indeed, while globalization is an important trend, it has to be understood in conjunction with localization: The global and local are relative to one another and both belong to the same dialectical process. This relativity and dialectical relationship are well captured by the notion of "glocalization," which Robertson (1995) uses to express the global production of the local and the localization of the global.

Cultural globalization is often argued by referring to the domination of Hollywood in the media world. Studies seldom show the actual process by which cultural globalization is done. One of the foci of this chapter is on how a local culture of a developing country is globalized, which is a subject that has received even less empirical attention. This rarity is related to the fact that the West, the seat of the world's globalizing force, seldom borrows from the cultures of the developing world. It is also a result of the general incapability of developing countries to globalize their cultures. But to Hollywood, what is local is American and what is American is global. In other words, the local and the global are unified in being American. This unification is based on the self-sufficiency of its domestic market and the keen American sense of cultural superiority.

On a more general level, cultural globalization and glocalization represent forms of transculturation which, as mentioned earlier, refers to the process by which a culture is transformed by another before or during synthesis. To make the concept more specific, I shall confine the use of the term transculturation to the transformation that takes place during cultural production and exclude the changes that the audience may introduce during reception. Of course, the changes during production and reception are closely interrelated. To say the least, the anticipated responses from the audience form an imagined feedback loop that informs the process of transculturation and cultural production.

The notion of transculturation is analogous to the concepts of cultural adaptation, acculturation and assimilation in cross-cultural communication. These ideas are often used to analyze how human groups, especially immigrants or ethnic minorities, respond to a dominant culture (e.g., Hood & Koberg, 1994; Tamura, 1994). For instance, a standard textbook on cross-cultural communication refers to acculturation or cultural adaptation as "an immigrant's learning and adopting the norms and values of the new host culture" (Jandt, 1998, p. 315). Acculturation and its related concepts are applied mostly to values, attitudes and behavior as expressed in interpersonal communication and at the level of individuals and groups. In contrast, the term transculturation is intended to refer mainly to, but is not limited to, mediated cultural forms, often at the level of organizations which are responsible for the formal production of culture. The transculturator can belong to either a dominant or a subordinate culture.

Transculturation is a form of cultural borrowing in which one culture reconfigures another for its own purpose. This is an extension of the observation that cultural borrowing, as a rule, serves self-aggrandizement despite the fact that the best intentions may be involved (Burton-Carvajal, 1994). For media organizations in a capitalist environment, making a profit is the ultimate driving force. Like globalization, which implies hybridization (Pieterse, 1995), the result of transculturation is also a synthesis of elements taken from two or more cultures. It is a form of boundary-crossing between the global and the local and between the foreign and the indigenous. The relative weights of the ingredients may vary in different cultural hybrids, but there is a tendency for the cultural producers to strike a balance between the foreign and the indigenous so as not to alienate their target audience. The basic premise here is that local cultural products owe their competitive edge over foreign ones to their cultural proximity, the audience's familiarity with the language and the cultural context they carry (Straubhaar, 1991).

This is a study of the processes by which a Chinese legend is transculturated by an American studio. It can be viewed as a study of the dialogue between cultures, only in this case the transculturator belongs to a dominating transnational force. Consequently, the transculturation is intricately linked to cultural globalization. I hope that this study will contribute to our understanding of the processes of cultural hybridization and globalization in the realm of popular culture.

THE STORY

The legend of Mulan[2] can be traced in folktales and poetry as far back as the fourth century (Li, 1992). Mulan is believed to have lived during the Han Dynasty (205 B.C.–A.D. 220). But there is no official record of Mulan's achievements in the history books of those times (Kurtti, 1998). Indeed, there is no conclusive evidence that Mulan was a real person at all. Nevertheless, many villages and counties in China claim even today that Mulan is their native daughter.[3]

The animated feature *Mulan* begins with the invasion of China by the Huns. Led by Chief Shan-Yu, the Huns breach the Great Wall and march on to capture China's Imperial City. The Chinese emperor immediately orders each family to send a male member to join the army in defense against the enemy.

Mulan is a free-spirited girl who does not readily conform to the traditional norms that are imposed on her. However, in an attempt to please her parents, she attends a match-making exercise. The exercise comes to an abrupt end when Mulan's good luck cricket, Cri-Kee, gets loose and sets off a series of mishaps. Angered, the matchmaker sends Mulan home in disgrace. The dejected Mulan is later consoled by her understanding father, who tells her that some of the most beautiful blossoms are late bloomers. Meanwhile, her father receives the Emperor's summon to serve in the army.

Noting that her father, a disabled veteran, is too weak for battle, Mulan shears her hair, dons her father's armor and sets out under the cover of darkness to join the army. Mulan's unconventional act has awakened her ancestral spirits, who, in an emergency meeting at the family temple, decide to send a powerful dragon to bring her home safely. Mushu, a self-centered and mischievous tiny dragon who has lost favor with the ancestral spirits, sees this crisis as his golden opportunity to regain his status as a family guardian. Mushu secretly takes the place of the powerful dragon and brings Cri-Kee along to join Mulan.

At the army camp, Mulan tries hard to play macho with her fellow soldiers. The wisecracks and antics of Mushu bring her both fun and trouble. At first, Mulan has great difficulty in measuring up to the requirements of military training. But Mulan refuses to give up. Her perseverance and cleverness finally earn her the respect of her peers and the commanding officer, Captain Shang.

Ready for battle, the troops move on and encounter the Huns army on a snowy mountain pass. Outnumbered and chased by the enemy, Mulan smartly creates an avalanche that sweeps away most of the Hun soldiers. Mulan is injured in the process, and her secret is revealed when the doctor attends to her wounds. Captain Shang is forced to discharge her from the army.

On her own, Mulan discovers that Chief Shan-Yu and his major warriors have survived and are heading for the Chinese Imperial City. Shan-Yu takes the Emperor hostage. Mulan devises various ways and risks her life to save the emperor. In the end, with the help of her fellow soldiers and Mushu, she wipes out the Huns and saves China. With the Emperor's blessing, Mulan returns home in great honor. Captain Shang visits her and stays for dinner, and perhaps forever.

DISNEYFICATION

The major agent of transculturation in popular culture is the media organization, the character of which has immense influence on both the production process and the end product. Starting out as a marginal operation
in 1922, Disney grew over the years to become first a successful niche
company and finally a multinational corporation whose business focuses
on movies, theme parks, other entertainment operations and real estate
(Gomery, 1994). Disney has become a "technical system" that involves not
only "the hardware, devices, machines, and processes," but also "the transportation, communication, and information networks that interconnect
them" and "the array of employees and regulations that make them run."
(Smoodin, 1994, p. 3) In this section, I shall draw on the case of *Mulan* to
examine some of Disney's organizational processes that help Americanize
and globalize a Chinese legend.

Location of Animation in Disney

The animated feature film, a movie form invented by Walt Disney, plays
a special role in the history of the studio. It has been an important source
of Disney's income ever since it struck gold with the release of the first
animated feature *Snow White and the Seven Dwarfs* in 1937 (Eisner and
Schwartz, 1998). After the death of Walt Disney in 1966, Disney's animation department went through a period of uncertainty. Under the leadership of Michael Eisner since 1984, Disney has been revived (Gomery,
1994). One of his strategies was to re-energize the production of animated
features, a strategy that has been rewarded with the box-office success of
The Little Mermaid, *Beauty and the Beast* and others.

The library of animated features that Disney has accumulated since the
firm's inception constitutes a valuable asset because they can be re-released
once every few years to a new generation. Re-released Disney films have
made as much, if not more, money on their second release than they did
on the first (Capodagli & Jackson, 1999). Since 1992, six of the eight top-
selling videos in the United States were Disney videos, with *Snow White
and the Seven Dwarfs* and *The Lion King* tied for the first position. The
animated features also owe their importance to the significant revenue that
tie-ins such as dolls, toys, books, music CDs, clothes, souvenirs and games
can bring. Without the cartoon characters that are made popular by the
animated features, many programs in Disney theme parks would lose their
appeal.

Mulan is Disney's thirty-sixth animated feature. It marks the first time
that Disney made use of an Asian story that was obscure to the rest of the
world. Disney's business requires a steady stream of new ideas and constant
reinvention of production. *Mulan* represents Disney's willingness to go any-

where in its effort to expand its cultural repertoire. According to *Mulan*'s co-director, Tony Bancroft, Disney has to find "new and interesting characters" from different "locales" and "cultures" so that they "don't all end up similar."[4] He thinks that it just "does not work to go to the same provincial town in Europe and see some classic tale being spun." The adaptation of foreign stories serves at least two organizational functions: It adds variety to Disney's productions, giving it a more global image; and it reduces the risk of production because these stories have stood the test of time in their home cultures.

The discovery and the final adoption of the Mulan legend bear testimony to Disney's organizational imperative. Initially, the animation team in Florida was assigned the job of producing a short called "China Doll," which was intended just for video.[5] The plot had a British Prince Charming taking the heroine away from all her problems. The huge box-office success of *The Lion King* in 1993 prompted Disney to scour the studio for more animation feature projects. As "China Doll" failed as a candidate, Disney turned to Robert San Souci, a children's book author and a frequent Disney consultant, who suggested that a Chinese poem called "The Ballad of Mulan" might make a good movie.[6] Meanwhile, another Disney feature, *Beauty and the Beast* (1991), grossed big box-office receipts, thus making Disney willing to take a risk that is greater than normal, the risk of producing a "Chinese" feature. This episode shows that serendipity sometimes interacts with organizational imperatives in fostering transculturation in a media organization.

The Disney Formula and Cultural Experimentation

To achieve efficiency, Disney has developed a formulaic approach to the production of content. A review of *Mulan* and other Disney animated features identifies these basic elements in its formula: good prevailing over evil, emotional, catchy songs, cute animal sidekicks for comic relief, young romance, funny in-jokes, an assorted supporting cast with a grumpy-to-dopey personality range and character voices performed by film stars.[7] Many of these elements have proven to be effective, as attested to by the wide popularity of Disney features around the world. That explains why the formula is used over and over again.

Although the Florida animation team that was responsible for the production of *Mulan* had never produced a feature before, the Disney formulaic routines were equally applicable. The inclusion of Cric-Kee and Mushu in the movie is a good illustration of the influence of the Disney formula. The original legend did not carry any hint of a family guardian dragon or other sidekicks. But a cricket and a dragon were added to make the movie more interesting. Being the sources of comic relief, the cricket and the dragon are intended to draw laughter from the audience. Their roles are analogous to those of the famed Jiminy of *Pinocchio* and the genie in *Aladdin*. At one point, the Disney production team toyed with the idea of making *Mulan* free of the sidekicks. But that version was overruled by Roy Disney, head of the animation department, who is reported to have said: "Why make an animated movie without the fantasy characters? Give us that cricket. Kids really enjoy it."[8] "[Mulan] is a nice story, but where are the great Chinese dragons and folklore and mythical creatures? When you think of China, one of the first things you think about are those hazy mountains and dragons everywhere." So the cricket and the tiny dragon were finally included to prove the rule.

However, Disney is not rigid with its formula. It allows experimentation to cope with novelties and to encourage re-invention. As mentioned earlier, the *Mulan* production team did try to do away with sidekicks although it yielded to the established formula in the end. An important deviation of *Mulan* from the traditional formula is the insignificant location of romance in the movie. The instinctive response of the producers was to treat the Mulan story with Disney's favorite formula for girl movies: beautiful rebel seeks love. But when compared with the original, the character they were trying to assemble was "too angry, too flirtatious and much too Western," weakening what Mulan was really all about.[9] After two years of working on it, Disney told the production team to rewrite. They finally produced a feature with only little reference to romance. Instead, it is a feature about the triumph of a young woman discovering herself. This shows that a media organization such as Disney does not just work by established routines, but also allows room for trial-and-error testing in its search for the most desired results.

Americanization and Universalization

Given the equal importance of the domestic market and the global market to Disney, there is a tendency for Disney to give a foreign culture an American and universal spin. Americanization and universalization are done along with essentialization. The producers have to identify what are to them the key elements of the original culture and subject them to transformation that will help meet the needs of the transculturator. For Disney, its challenge is to sell its animated feature to the Americans and people in other parts of the world. This entails the processes of Americanization and universalization, which are most clearly reflected in the retreads it gives to the themes of the *Mulan* story.

Filial Piety vs. Reciprocal Love

The original story, as interpreted by most Chinese, is about filial piety, which is traditionally ranked as the most important virtue. The Chinese have a special term for filial piety, *xiaodao*, which, according to Confucius, carries these meanings: (1) supporting and caring for one's parents; (2) reverence and obedience; (3) continuing the ancestral line; (4) glorifying the family name; and (5) mourning and ancestral remembrance (Yu, 1984). In Chinese culture, *xiaodao* is the supreme ethical principle that begins with serving one's parents, extends to the duties toward one's sovereign, and ends in the establishment of one's personal character (Lin, 1992). Mulan is believed by many Chinese to have joined the army on behalf of her father out of *xiaodao*. That explains why Mulan was included in China's list of "Twenty-four True Daughters" and why she was bestowed the title of "General of Filial Piety" in temples and by emperors over the years (Ning, 1995).

In the Chinese legend, Mulan was first of all a dutiful and filial daughter. But in the movie *Mulan*, the notion of filial piety was diluted and given a secondary role. Obedience was not stressed at all. Unlike the Chinese version of the story, the Disney Mulan does not even seek the consent of her father before joining the army. She just leaves a letter and sneaks off in the middle of the night. However, it would be an exaggeration to claim that Disney has totally abandoned the idea of filial piety. What remains in *Mulan* is the idea of honoring one's family, which is a concept that can be more readily understood by people of other cultures.

To the Disney producers, Mulan represents a foreign ideal that cannot be taken for granted. As Mulan's character designer Dean DeBlois explains, "I think [the pivotal relationship of the movie] evolved out of the notion that we were dealing with a 'foreign' ideal, doing something purely out of honor, a duty that you're born to uphold and therefore do without question. Honor is a pretty universal concept, but to label it as honor and not give a specific example of why a person would want to live up to that— we found ourselves tripping over it" (Kurtti, 1998, p. 116). Instead, DeBlois says that they had to make *Mulan* so "universal" and "emotional" that it would lock the audience into the characters and get their empathy.

Why does Mulan leave home for the army? That is the key relationship for the movie. The Disney producers think that acting out of obligation is not convincing to the audience who are foreign to the ideal of *xiaodao* (Kurtti, 1998). After much thought, they finally decided that Mulan does it out of her love for her father. What is stressed here is a close and intimate father-daughter relationship. Love, as portrayed in *Mulan*, is reciprocal, and not obligatory as implied in *xiaodao*. The scene most reminiscent of this father-daughter love is when Mulan's understanding father tells her that she may be a late bloomer in a heart-to-heart chat in the garden. In the eyes of the modern audience, such love helps justify Mulan's decision to take her father's place in the army.

The Feminist and Individualistic Touch

The theme of *Mulan* was further Americanized or Westernized when Disney gave it a feminist and individualistic touch. While individualism has long been part of the West's cultural fabric, feminism has begun to take hold. In the United States, for instance, it has become politically incorrect to make public references biased against the female. More women have come to be recognized as individuals equal to men. A strong theme that underlines Mulan's behavior is her pursuit of identify. In the theme song by Mulan, she admits that she will never pass for a good bride or a good daughter, and emphatically asks who she really is inside. After Mulan is forsaken by her colleagues upon discovery of her sex, she confesses that she might have gone through all the ordeal not because of her father, but because of her desire to achieve something on her own. This stress on individuality, particularly for a female, is at odds with China's feudalistic past.[10] To Disney Feature Animation President Peter Schneider, the search for who we are, the search for self, is an ever-ongoing process and universal theme (Kurtti, 1998, p. 11). He thinks that "*Mulan* is a very intimate, personal story about a loyal and brave girl who's going to find *herself*" (Kurtti, 1998, p. 189). That is supposed to be the "timeless relevance" of the *Mulan* tale (Kurtti, 1998, p. 11). Barry Cook, the co-director, shares this observation, saying: "[Mulan]'s not only endearing, she's resourceful and heroic and she doesn't need a man. I think *she celebrates the importance of an individual* [italics added]. She shows what a difference one person can make."[11]

But Disney stopped short of making *Mulan* a manifesto of women's liberation. It takes a middle-of-the-road approach. It refrains from going to the extremes of feminism. It understands that most audiences are in the middle and extremism may alienate the mainstream.

Decontextualization and Recontextualization

To be persuasive, all stories have to be contextualized. The more contextualized a story is, the more believable it will be. In Americanzing a story, it has to be essentialized, stripping away its context and identifying its core elements. Then the story is reconfigured and recontextualized. To Disney, whether the context in the Americanized story really matches that in the original story is of secondary importance. As Mulan is a Chinese story and Disney wants it to retain the Chinese flavor, it is first of all decontextualized and then recontextualized against the cultural backdrop of China. This is achieved by situating the new story amidst cultural icons such as the Great Wall, willow trees, pavilions, Buddha caves and Tiananmen Square.

Another method of recontextualization is to retell the story by an internal logic that sounds convincing to the potential audience. From the perspective of the Disney production team, what is crucial in developing an animated story is to identify the characters and the key relationships. Once these are set, the characters will interact in ways as if they are living out a life of their own. The feisty and fire-breathing Mushu, for instance, is assigned the task of making fun. It does so at various occasions. Mulan, an independent and thoughtful girl, will show her character as the situation warrants. Originally, the production team had a lot more of the villain, a lot more of Mushu and a lot more romance. But as all of those things "didn't stack up to what was happening in the movie," they became "untrue to themselves" and the Disney team took them out,[12] attesting to the operation of the internal logic.

Transfiguration

Transfiguration, or the change in cultural forms, affects the ways the original story is transculturated. Given that Mulan is a legend rather than a historical document, there is more room for Disney to exercise its imagination. To *Mulan*'s co-director, Barry Cook, that knowledge was "liberating" because they could let their "imaginations" kick in (Kurtti, 1998, p. 25). The lack of details in the original legend also makes it easier for Disneyfication. What people know about Mulan is mostly from a short poem that carries only a sketchy story. This leads another of *Mulan*'s co-directors, Tony Bancroft, to say that the lack of details "gives [them] a chance to elaborate on [Mulan's] character and the characters around her."[13]

The cultural form of the end product also affects the scope of adaptation. Animated features are freed from the basic cinematic expectation that they convey an "impression of reality" (Burton-Carvajal, 1994, p. 139). Instead, cartoons are supposed to convey "impressions of irrationality, of intangible and imaginable worlds in chaotic, disruptive, subversive collision." It is therefore more acceptable for Disney to introduce cute animal sidekicks and fun-packed action.

This illustrates that the genre and the type of media involved have important implications for transculturation. An elaborate story carried by a novel, for instance, is expected to exert greater influence on the adapted version. Meanwhile, a television series can afford being more faithful to the original novel because it is longer in duration. But if the resulting format is a one-and-a-half-hour movie, there is a greater chance for the original story to be essentialized and transformed. What is ultimately retained, discarded and reinvented during transculturation appears to depend on the interactions between the genre, media type and the intentions of the producers.

Assertions of the Original and Cross-Cultural Referencing Mechanisms

Although the Mulan story has been transformed in some significant ways, some core elements of the original legend remain. There are limits to Disneyfication. The *Mulan* story is about a Chinese girl warrior who is willing to sacrifice herself for her father. As mentioned earlier, the Disney production team did at first try hard to turn it into a romance, with a beautiful rebel seeking love. But the resulting story lost the strong image of an independent and capable girl conveyed by the original story. The deficiency finally led the producers to opt for a story that was closer to the original, although much effort had been spent on developing the romance version. This shows that the original culture always serves as a basis for comparison, affecting the extent to which it is changed during transculturation.

The commitment not to misrepresent a given culture on the part of a media organization also has an effect on the scope of cultural transformation. Such a commitment is a function of its cultural sensitivity which, in turn, is linked to the social structure. Disney animation has angered several ethnic groups in the recent past: Arab-Americans for the lyrics of an *Aladin* song, Native Americans who felt *Pocahontas* was unnecessarily sexualized and blacks who took issue with the interracial makeup of voice talent in *The Lion King*.[14] Now Asian Americans are becoming a more visible and outspoken minority in the United States. It is not in the interests of Disney to extend the stereotypes of Asian Chinese such as Charlie Chan and Fu Manchu that once dominated the screen.

Disney has built-in mechanisms for cross-cultural referencing. The hiring of Asians and Asian Americans helped give a Chinese touch to *Mulan*. For instance, Chen-Yi Chang, an artist originally from Taiwan, was hired to oversee and design the characters of *Mulan*. He was a key force in conceptualizing the "look" of the key characters, including their costumes (Kurtti, 1998). Under his influence, for instance, the Disney artists applied the Chinese ideal of beauty, an egg-shaped face and cherry blossom lips, to Mulan.[15] Likewise, Chinese-American scriptwriter Rita Hsiao helped shape the story and dialogue. With the assistance of Chinese musicians, Eastern music played on temple flutes, guzheng (a Chinese zither) and the two-string erhu, feature prominently in songs, while the musical score is a conscious mingling of East and West.[16]

Another mechanism for cross-cultural referencing is field trips to familiarize high-ranking production team members with the Chinese context. Invented in the late 1980s, field trips have become part of Disney's filmmaking process (Kurtti, 1998). The idea is to get a first-hand feel of the actual location of their screen stories. The influence of the field trip shows in the movie, as evidenced by the presence of Chinese scenes such as pavilions, tomb slabs, vertical flags and Buddha caves. The influence also shows in the heavy use of spareness and simplicity, a visual style often found in Chinese art. Organizationally, the field trip is instrumental in enhancing the team's respect for cultural authenticity, unifying the team by sharing an experience and a common frame of reference, fostering a team spirit and strengthening their vision of the story.

Although Disney had a determined respect for the original tale, *Mulan*'s co-director Tony Bancroft admitted that there were limitations: "We knew we had to respect the material. This is a beloved story to the Chinese people. We also knew that we weren't going to make a Chinese picture. We couldn't. We're not Chinese. We have a different sensibility, a different storytelling style" (Kurtti, 1998, p. 24). This disclaimer represents the ultimate orientation of Disney products. That explains why *Mulan* includes scenes such as Mushu reading a modern newspaper, Mulan eating sausage and fried egg for breakfast, the ancestral spirits rocking to Western music and Eddie Murphy voice-acting for Mushu in a street-smart lingo. The Disney producers are uncomfortable in following the principle of authenticity to its logical conclusion. What they fear is that if *Mulan* were to seem too exotic, too foreign, audiences might not warm up to it. The basic principle involved is to include enough foreign elements to convey a unique experience, but not so much as to send people away.

GLOBALIZATION

Since the early 1930s, Disney has been part of transnational capitalism (Smoodin, 1994). As of today, the foreign market is of growing importance to Disney and, for that matter, to other American studios as well. As indicated in Table 13.1, while 59.2 percent of *Mulan*'s gross receipts (U.S.$2.971 billion) are derived from the overseas market, many other blockbusters such as *Armageddon, Saving Private Ryan* and *Godzilla* also rely on the foreign market for more than half of their revenues.

Globalization is the natural extension of Disneyfication. *Mulan* is globalized when it is successfully marketed through Disney's worldwide distribution network. Without the global network, *Mulan* would be confined to the United States. Japanese animated features are sometimes comparable to Disney productions in quality, but they fail to match their importance in the global scene. This has to do with the relatively limited reach of the Japanese products. In addition to the exhibition chains, Disney also has a global network for the distribution of merchandises, books, toys, clothes, television and videos. All these outlets and activities intermesh to form a sophisticated infrastructure that takes a long time to build. Over the years, Disney has successfully gained people's trust in its animated features and other products. The establishment of a world brand is thus crucial for cultural globalization.

Table 13.1
Top 20 Films in the United States, 1998 (ranked by domestic box office in U.S. millions of dollars)

Rank	Movie Title	U.S. Domestic	Foreign
1	*Armageddon*	201.6	306.4
2	*Saving Private Ryan*	191.0	242.3
3	*There's Something About Mary*	175.8	171.1
4	*The Waterboy*	154.8	4.3
5	*A Bug's Life*	151.7	41.0
6	*Dr. Dolittle*	144.2	141.5
7	*Deep Impact*	140.5	208.3
8	*Rush Hour*	140.4	36.0
9	*Godzilla*	136.0	239.7
10	*Lethal Weapon 4*	129.7	141.7
11	*The Truman Show*	125.6	122.8
12	***Mulan***	120.6	176.5
13	*Patch Adams*	108.6	n.a.
14	*Enemy of the State*	106.0	65.7
15	*You've Got Mail*	104.1	13.2
16	*The Mask of Zorro*	93.8	135.9
17	*The Rugrats Movie*	93.6	n.a.
18	*Antz*	90.3	76.3
19	*The Prince of Egypt*	87.3	93.9
20	*The X-Files*	83.9	103.1

n.a. = figures were not available at the time this table was compiled.

Source: Adapted from Box Office Report, *Entertainment Weekly*, February 5, 1999, p. 34.

Disney has the know-how for both domestic and international marketing, without which globalization is all but empty talk. In releasing *Mulan* in the United States, Disney's marketing department searched its soul as *Hercules* and *The Hunchback of Notre Dame* failed to measure up to expected returns.[17] For fear that it might have overhyped its animated features and made the public cynical, it used a relatively restrained approach. Subsequently, the "noise level" associated with *Mulan* was reduced, doing away with hype such as a Central Park premiere. But when it comes to selling kids on *Mulan*, Disney was not taking any chances. The TV ads aimed at children were divided up by gender and stereotype rules. Shows with a big audience of boys got ads featuring action, war and thundering

Huns; shows for girls got more of the emotional and father-daughter scenes.

Disney is experienced in localizing its marketing strategies to make its globalizing effort more effective. This includes the use of famous local actors in dubbing and promoting the movies when marketing its movies overseas. For instance, with the Cantonese version of *Mulan*, Jackie Chan, the world-famous kung fu actor, was hired to represent Captain Shang. The Cantonese dubbing is often emotionally charged. Hong Kong Cantonese slang was used in dialogue and songs. Similar techniques were also applied to the Mandarin and other versions.

Quality is of special importance to a cultural product that aims at global distribution because of the intensity of international competition. Disney is in an advantageous position in this regard. First, it has access to the best talent in the United States and the world. Nearly 700 Disney artists, animators and technicians contributed to the final production of *Mulan*. Second, it was produced with the state-of-the-art animation facilities. For the making of *Mulan*, several innovations in Computer Generated Imagery (CGI) were created after one-and-a-half-years of experimentation at the Orlando Studio.[18] They enabled the production of a breathtaking sequence in which 2,000 Huns on horseback spill through a mountain pass in full attack mode. Third, Disney can afford investments that can hardly be matched by its competitors in other parts of the world. It spent U.S.$100 million and took five years to make *Mulan*. Not all Disney productions are well received. But given Disney's capital, expertise and equipment, they stand a better chance. Without the tremendous resources that have been put into *Mulan*, it would have been less likely that it would become globalized.

Part of Disney's scheme of globalization is the international division of labor. Like other cartoon giants such as Hanna-Barbera, Marvel and Warner Brothers, Disney sent its scripts, storyboards and voice tracks to Asian artists to draw, shoot and assemble, mainly by hand.[19] Most "offshore factories" of the American animation industry are located in Japan, southern China and the Philippines, where labor is cheaper and more reliable (Lent, 1998). As pre-production work is done mainly in the United States, it is doubtful whether this global division of labor has made the final products any more Asian.

WHOSE STORY? DOES IT MATTER?

In this section I would like to relate to several important theoretical issues in the discussion on cultural boundaries and globalization in view of the findings. One major concern relates to the idea of cultural integrity. I shall demonstrate how transculturation and cultural hybridization have blurred the boundaries between indigenous and foreign cultures, rendering the concept of cultural integrity problematic. Another concern relates to the controversy over the impacts of Western media products. I shall briefly discuss how reception may vary with the orientation of the nation-state and the social locations of the audience. In addition, I shall assess whether Disney, as exemplified by *Mulan*, is part of cultural imperialism. Finally, I shall sum up our understanding of the process of transculturation and relate it to the search for cultural boundaries.

Cultural Authenticity, Hybridization and Global Culture

A common reaction of Chinese audiences to *Mulan* is that it is not authentic. That is why many reviews of *Mulan* in Chinese societies paid much attention to the ethnic mistakes Disney had made. There is no question that the Chinese legend has been Americanized and Disneyfied. But the question of authenticity is complicated by the fact that Mulan has also many Chinese versions, ranging from being a historical person involving supernatural beings (Anonymous, 1997) to a female's search for equality and liberation (Zuo, 1935). The reinvention of Mulan in Chinese societies continues up to the present time. Mulan is extolled as a figure of patriotism and nationalism by schoolteachers in mainland China. Hong Kong and Taiwan have produced different television drama series on Mulan. As we shall see later, the Taiwanese version has even been influenced by Disney's *Mulan*.

That the Chinese do not agree among themselves as to what really constitutes the Mulan legend speaks to the increasing difficulty in differentiating the authentic from the hybridized, and the indigenous from the foreign in cultural formation. While the core story of the legend persists in all these versions one way or the other, their authors are recreating the story in accordance with their personal and organizational agenda and the cultural context of their times. This is perhaps a long-standing practice of human beings, as Disney asserts: "Storytellers for all time have taken core story material and adapted and changed it for their audience, their era, and their point of view" (Kurtti, 1998, p. 23). But in a time of transnational capitalism, this is done more than ever consciously and calculatively.

The diversity of Chinese versions of the Mulan story suggests that transculturation can take place across time within the same culture. The culture of any country is always in a state of flux. The meaning of a given culture is subject to reinterpretation over time. Like the Disneyfication of Mulan, the reinvention of the Mulan story on Hong Kong and Taiwanese television represents cultural transformations that respond to market consideration, the inner logic of audio-visual drama and modern times. It is almost impossible for any commercial audio-visual drama not to be given a modern interpretation. The huge revenues that *Mulan* earns around the world speak to its popularity among people in various cultures. To most audiences, be they Chinese or otherwise, *Mulan* is first of all a story: What matters is not its authenticity, but enjoyability. The more enjoyable a cultural product is, the more the audience can tolerate its foreignness.

Mulan is not genuinely Chinese, nor is it all American. It has become a transcultural text: a combination of old and new, traditional and modern, East and West, collectivism and individualism, female submissiveness and women's liberation, filial piety and reciprocal love between father and daughter. This represents an important way by which the world's cultures are being hybridized to form what can be called a global culture. Not only is it a hybrid in content, but also in visual style. On the one hand, the Disney team draws from traditional Disney productions and the films of David Lean for the expansive scale and sense of composition. On the other hand, it is inspired by both Chinese and Japanese arts traditions, including the choreography of Japan's Akira Kurosawa and the use of negative space characteristic of Chinese paintings.[20]

The worldwide success of *Mulan* has added a Disneyfied version of a Chinese legend to the world's popular culture. It has drastically changed the parameters for the discourse and narration of the original legend. From now on, it will be difficult for a re-inventor of Mulan not to have a dialogue with the Disney version. Indeed, the Taiwanese television drama series on Mulan has shown evidence of *Mulan*'s influence. The series introduce some playful supernatural characters such as the kitchen god and other gods to the story. They remind one of the roles played by Mushu and the ancestral spirits in *Mulan*. Again, like *Mulan*, the heroine is portrayed as a girl who ventures on a trip to realize her potential as an individual. However, Disney's *Mulan* has not ruled out the other reinventions. The Taiwanese television series, for instance, differs from *Mulan* in that romance is given a prominent place, with the kitchen god and two supervising officers competing for the girl warrior. It even played on the power struggles in the imperial court and the animosity between Mulan and her mother-in-law.

Anyway, that *Mulan* has become a source of inspiration for Chinese productions on the same subject speaks to the blurring of boundary between global and local culture. What is initially a local and indigenous story is Americanized and globalized. The globalized version, in turn, is localized and reinvented for the home market.

Empowerment or Cultural Domination

There is fear among some governments at the receiving end of Disney productions. To the mainland Chinese government, for instance, the success of Disney films implies the erosion of their control over Chinese cultural icons. In a letter to a Shanghai animation studio in 1996, Chinese President Jiang Zemin expressed the hope that children in China would soon have their own cartoon heroes.[21] Plans were subsequently made to pursue Chinese rivals for U.S. favorites such as Mickey Mouse and Donald Duck.

In the last analysis, nation-states have the ultimate control over accessibility to foreign culture. Although *Mulan* is popular around the world, there is no guarantee that it is welcome in its "homeland." Chinese officials, who let in only 10 foreign movies a year to protect their own industry, declined to import *Mulan* at first because of Disney's release of the pro-Tibet movie *Kundun*.[22] They changed their mind after Disney launched an aggressive damage-control effort that culminated with meetings in Beijing with senior Chinese leaders. To many people's surprise, *Mulan* flopped in the Chinese box office. It was estimated that *Mulan* would gross about U.S.$1.3 million in all Chinese cities, fulfilling only one-sixth of the anticipated income. The failure is attributed to poor timing, the prevalence of pirated videos and the Western outlook of the movie.

The meanings of a transculturated product are realized only when it is consumed. Such meanings are always localized and individualized. One well-known example is the diverging readings that audience may have of the American television series *Dynasty* (Liebes & Katz, 1990). A brief review of some of the movie reviews in Chinese societies and the United States shows that the rule of polysemy should apply to the reception of *Mulan*. As demonstrated by Lull (1991), even the Chinese audience interprets state-controlled television in diverging ways, ranging from preferred reading to oppositional reading. Researchers should therefore factor in greater activeness on the part of the audience in the discourse on the impact of transcultural text.

To many adults in mainland China, nationalistic and ideological boundaries are still clear, the "foreign look" of *Mulan* often results in some kind of negative evaluation. For instance, a movie reviewer at the *Beijing Youth Daily* said he was "disappointed" by *Mulan*, which portrayed Mulan as an independent, rebellious and yet successful female, an image that is unfaithful to the original story.[23] Worst of all, he found that Mulan did not succeed on her own, but only with the help of a funny guardian dragon Mushu. He regretted that a Chinese heroine had become just another name in Disney's list of movie titles. But the general public, especially the young and children, appear to be less critical, as attested by another report in the *Beijing Youth Daily*: "The cinemas showing *Mulan* during the weekend were filled with happiness. Throughout the show, the cinema was filled with the laughter of both primary and secondary school students. They were attracted by the beautiful pictures, as well as the lively and humorous plots."[24]

To many American reviewers, *Mulan* represents female empowerment. Unlike other female characters in Disney's animated films, Mulan wins her place by using her brains and relying on her courage and instinct, even when all the odds seem to be against her.[25] *Mulan* poses another role model besides the all "white-skinned girls of European ancestry" represented by Snow White, Cinderella and Sleeping Beauty, whose "salvation as woman comes from being chosen by equally white, handsome princes who live in European castles in the sky."[26] Many ethnic Chinese in the United States also appear to be happy with the ways *Mulan* recasts the stereotypes of Chinese women from being submissive to independent, cheerful and clever. All these observations lead one to ask: Whose story is *Mulan*? Does it matter if it is a liberating story?[27]

This assessment of *Mulan* tends to disagree with the strong traditions in the critical school and cultural studies which view Disney and its products as part of the Yankee cultural chauvinism, if not cultural imperialism (see for instance, Smoodin, 1994). By these traditions, Donald Duck was criti-cized for the "imperialist ideology" it carries (Dorfman & Mattelart, 1975). Disney's animated feature *The Three Caballeros* was treated as instance of "one Hollywood dream factory constructing its Other(s)" for self-aggrandizement (Burton-Carvajal, 1994). The *Cinderella* cartoon movie of 1949 was criticized for segregating the sexes (Kelley, 1994). The moral and political order as created by Disney is biased in favor of white capitalist society (Rojek, 1993). Disney is seen as a major economic and cultural force that has the power to shape the needs and desires of children (Giroux, 1999). *Mulan* appears to have reflected Disney's growing consciousness of changing culture in the United States and other parts of the world. It has become more sensitive to the contribution of foreign culture in its business of cultural globalization. In this particular case, the movie product is almost universally approved because of its female empowerment. One does not have to deny the dominating role of Disney in the world of comics and its ultimate concern for profit before one can endorse the emancipatory nature of *Mulan*. This case study of *Mulan* should have shed light on the process of transculturation regardless of the ideological stance one may take. It shows that products of a Hollywood studio can be liberating.

TRANSCULUTRATION AND THE SEARCH FOR CULTURAL BOUNDARY

To recap, transculturation refers to the ways by which a culture is trans-formed by another before it is absorbed. In search of a desired result, it is a continually evolving process involving both organizational routines and experimentation. As demonstrated by *Mulan*, transculturation in the area of popular culture is subject to the imperatives of a media organization. It will scour the foreign cultural gene pool for inspiration and raw materials in order to diversify its products and cultural repertoire. The foreign culture will be treated by routines and formulae that have been established for the efficient processing of cultural materials. However, these routines and formulae are flexible enough to cope with novelty and to allow trial-and-error experimentation.

To make transculturation manageable and to appeal to an expanded target audience, the imported culture is often decontextualized, essentialized, universalized and reconfigured before recontextualization, which is often achieved through the use of cultural icons and a convincing storyline. In the case of *Mulan*, while it is recontextualized against the general cultural backdrop of China, the Chinese legend is made a personal discovery story rather than a story about the obligatory behavior of a filial daughter. Although this is a study of how a dominating culture assimilates the local legend of another culture, the processes mentioned above, on the whole, should apply when the transculturator belongs to a subordinate culture— only in this case the original will be essentialized and *domesticated*, rather than universalized, to meet with the specific needs of the home audience.[28]

Transculturation may also involve the transfiguration of cultural forms, which affects the extent to which the original culture is changed. *Mulan* shows that the less historical and less detailed is the original story, the greater is the room for creativity. The animated feature is a cultural form that favors reinvention and the exercise of imagination. The transculturator's commitment to authenticity also has a bearing on cultural transformation. The inclusion of cross-cultural referencing mechanisms such as field trips and the hiring of cross-cultural experts will help retain the core and flavor of the original culture.

The product of transculturation is not just a physical mix of two different cultures. It is always a hybrid formed as the result of a chemical reaction between the two, with the whole being greater than the sum of the parts. During the transculturation process, the producers are trying to define and redefine the cultural boundaries. In the end, they settle on a new boundary that seems to be acceptable to their target audience and to themselves. Once produced and consumed, the hybridized product will form an integral part of the transculturator's culture, thereby increasing its foreign content. What is foreign becomes indigenous. By the same token, the hybridized product demonstrates to the original culture how a given cultural artifact can be alternatively interpreted. What is domestic has become foreign. This will in turn help redefine the boundary of the original culture.

Cultural boundaries are socially constructed and are always in a state of flux, especially in this age of global communication when all cultures are interconnected (Chan, 2000). It is through the hybridization of the foreign and domestic cultures that cultural development is achieved. The cultural boundaries are blurring: what is considered to be foreign at a time will be rendered indigenous if it has been successfully synthesized; the resultant culture, undeniably national, will then serve as a new basis for further hybridization. While the domestic culture of a nation may change as a result of transculturation and hyrbridization, its cultural genetic base will remain relatively stable. So are people's cultural identities that are tied more to their blood, soil and religion. Cultural boundaries are not to disappear overnight. Human beings have a constant need for them. Cultural boundaries will continually be defined and redefined.

Peter Berger (1997) observes that there are four faces of global culture, including the internationalization of the Western intelligentsia's values, the international business culture, popular culture and the spread of Evangelical Protestantism. This is a study of transculturation and globalization in the realm of popular culture. It should be rewarding for one to compare the processes of transculturation and cultural globalization across the above realms. The comparison can be extended to different cultural forms and different media. Finally, how these processes relate to various indigenous cultures should also make an interesting research agenda.

NOTES

1. A notable movie version is a 1969 musical, *Lady General Hua Mu Lan,* produced by the Shaw Brothers of Hong Kong.
2. See *Mulan,* Movieweb [On-line], available: www.movieweb.com/movie/mulan.
3. The Chinese official news agency Xinhua reported that experts in Henan province reached the conclusion that Mulan was a native of Dazhou Village, Yucheng County, Henan. There people could still find her tomb and memorial temple. See "Origin of Chinese Heroine Mulan Confirmed" (1999).
4. Strauss (1998).
5. Pearlman (1998).
6. Brown (1998).
7. For a brief observation, see Sinyard (1988).
8. Pearlman (1998).
9. Ibid.
10. The values that prevailed in Mulan's time are captured in one of the movie's songs, "Honor to Us All."
11. Strauss (1998).
12. Ibid.
13. Ibid.
14. Ibid.
15. Amy (1999).
16. Seno (1998).
17. Brown (1998).
18. Amy (1999).
19. "That's not all, folks" (1995).
20. Linehan (1998).
21. "Mickey Mao" (1996).
22. McDonald (1999).
23. Guan (1999).
24. Zhou (1999).

25. Ryerson (1999).

26. Huson (1999). For a relatively detailed analysis of women characters in Disney's animated features, see Solomon (1998).

27. This evaluation of *Mulan* should not be extended to other Disney features whose ideologies and values are problematic for many researchers. See Bell et al., 1995.

28. This is analogous to the domestication of news, which, according to Akiba Cohen and his colleagues (1996), is a process by which journalists construct foreign news stories in ways that attempt to create links of meaning between the stories and the history, culture, politics and society of the home viewers.

REFERENCES

Amy, S. (1999, February 14). Mulan's big bag of tricks. *New Straits Times* (Malaysia). [On-line]. Available: http://web.lexis-nexis.com/universe/do...&_md 5=5404fa99d4d53913350913b9ddfdb0bd.

Anonymous. (1997). The biography of a loyal, filial, brave, enthusiastic, and unusual girl. In Z. Hou & Li Q. Li (Eds.), *The rare ancient versions of Chinese novels* (Book 9, pp. 249–477). Shenyang, China: Spring Wing Press (in Chinese).

Bell, E., Haas, L. & Sells, L. (Eds.) (1995). *From mouse to mermaid: The politics of film, gender, and culture.* Bloomington: Indiana University Press.

Berger, P. (1997). Four faces of global culture. *The National Interest, 49,* 23–29.

Boyd-Barrett, O. (1977). Media imperialism: Towards an international framework for the analysis of media systems. In J. Curran, M. Gurevitch & J. Woolacott (Eds.), *Mass communication and society* (pp. 116–135). London: Edward Arnold.

Brown, C. (1998, June 8). Woman warrior. *Newsweek* (U.S. edition), 64.

Burton-Carvajal, J. (1994). Surprise package: Looking southward with Disney. In E. Smoodin (Ed.), *Disney discourse* (pp. 131–147). New York: Routledge.

Capodagli, B., & Jackson, L. (1999). *The Disney way.* New York: McGraw-Hill.

Chan, J. (2000). No culture is an island: An analysis of media protectionism and media openness. In G. Wang, J. Servaes & A. Goonasekera (Eds.), *The new communication landscape* (pp. 251–264). London: Routledge.

Cohen, A., Levy, M., Gurevitch, M., & Roeh, I. (1996). *Global newsrooms, local audiences: A study of the Eurovision news exchange.* London: J. Libbey.

Dorfman, A., & Matellart, A. (1975). *How to read Donald Duck: Imperialist ideology in the Disney comic.* New York: International General.

Eisner, M., & Schwartz, T. (1998). *Work in progress.* New York: Random House.

Featherstone, M. (1990). Global culture: An introduction. In M. Featherstone (Ed.), *Global culture: Nationalism, globalization and modernity.* (pp. 1–14). London: Sage Publications.

Giddens, A. (1991). *The consequences of modernity.* Stanford, CA: Stanford University Press.

Giroux, H. (1999). *The mouse that roared: Disney and the end of innocence.* Landham, MD: Rowman & Littlefield.

Gomery, D. (1994). Disney's business history: A reinterpretation. In E. Smoodin (Ed.), *Disney discourse* (pp. 71–86). New York: Routledge.

Guan, Y. (1999, April 26). "Mulan" and the difficulty to differentiate the female from the male. *Beijing Youth Daily*, 7.

Hood, J., & Koberg, C. (1994). Patterns of differential assimilation and accuulturation for women in business organizations. *Human Relations*, 47(2), 159–167.

Huang, S., & Li, S. (Eds.) (1992). *On Hua Mulan*. Beijing: Chinese Broadcasting and TV Press (in Chinese).

Huson, R. (1999, February 16). Filial piety or independence? *St. Louis Post-Dispatch*, B7.

Jandt, F. (1998). *Intercultural communication: An introduction*. Thousand Oaks, CA: Sage Publications.

Kelly, K. (1994). A modern Cinderella. *Journal of American Culture*, 17(1), 87–92.

Kurtti, J. (1998). *The art of Mulan*. New York: Hyperion.

Lee, C. C. (1980). *Media imperialism reconsidered*. Beverly Hills, CA: Sage Publications.

Lent, J. (1998). The animation industry and its offshore factories. In G. Sussman & J. Lent (Eds.), *Global productions: Labor in the making of the "information society"* (pp. 239–254). Cresskill, NJ: Hampton Press.

Li, S. (1992). On Mulan. In S. Huang & S. Li (Eds.), *On Hua Mulan* (pp. 1–16). Beijing: Chinese Broadcasting and TV Press (in Chinese).

Liebes, T., & Katz, E. (1990). *The export of meaning: Cross-cultural readings of Dallas*. New York: Oxford University Press.

Lin, A. (1992). *A study on the concept of filial piety in Confucianism*. Taipei: Wenjing Press (in Chinese).

Linehan, H. (1998, October 18). No time to sing. *The Irish Times*, weekend section, 73.

Lull, J. (1991). *China turned on: Television, reform, and resistance*. London: Routledge.

McDonald, J. (1999, February 23). Disney's *Mulan* debuts in China after long political delay. Associated Press. Dateline: Shanghai, China. Section: International News.

Mickey Mao: China hopes to promote its own cartoon heroes to co-exist with Disney characters. (1996, August 3). *The Economist*, 32.

Ning, S. F. (1995). *On the Chinese culture of Xiao*. Beijing: Minorities University Press (in Chinese).

Origin of Chinese heroine Mulan confirmed. (1999, February 18). Xinhua News Agency. Dateline: Zhengzhou. Item No.: 0218086.

Pearlman, C. (1998, June 4). Mulan earns her stripes: *Mulan* banks on a brave new girl. *Chicago Sun-Times*, SHO3.

Pieterse, J. (1995). Globalization as hybridization. In M. Featherstone, S. Lash & R. Robertson (Eds.), *Global modernities* (pp. 46–68). Thousand Oaks, CA: Sage Publications.

Robertson, R. (1995). Glocalization: Time-space and homogeneity-heterogeneity. In M. Featherstone, S. Lash & R. Robertson (Eds.), *Global modernities* (pp. 25–44). Thousand Oaks, CA: Sage Publications.

Rojek, C. (1993). Disney culture. *Leisure Studies*, 12(2), 121–135.

Ryerson, N. (1999, April 5). Mr. Showbiz movie guide: *Mulan*. [On-line]. Available: http://mrshowbiz.go.com/reviews/moviereviews/movies/Mulan_1998. html, 1.

Schlesinger, P. (1993). Wishful thinking: Cultural politics, media, and collective identities in Europe. *Journal of Communication*, 43(2), 6–17.

Seno, A. (1998, June 5). Woman warrior. *Asiaweek*, 58.

Sinyard, N. (1988). *The best of Disney*. New York: Portland House.

Smoodin, E. (1994). Introduction: How to read Walt Disney. In E. Smoodin (Ed.), *Disney discourse* (pp. 1–20). New York: Routledge.

Solomon, C. (1998, June 26). Animated heroines finally get in step with the times. *Los Angeles Times*, Calendar, F18.

Sreberny, A., Winseck, D., McKenna, J. & Boyd-Barrett, O. (1997). Editor's introduction—Media in global context. In A. Sreberny-Mohammadi, D. Winseck, J. McKenna & O. Boyd-Barrett (Eds.), *Media in global context: A reader* (pp. iv–xxviii). London: Arnold Press.

Straubhaar, J. (1991). Beyond media imperialism: Asymmetrical interdependence and cultural proximity. *Critical Studies in Mass Communication*, 8(1), 39–59.

Strauss, B. (1998, June 14). Disney tries its hand at Chinese storytelling. *Boston Globe*, N8.

Tamura, E. (1994). *Americanization, acculturation, and ethnic identity: The Nisei generation in Hawaii*. Urbana: University of Illinois Press.

Tan, W. (1996). *The unusual story of Hua Mulan*. Taipei: Hanxiang Press (in Chinese).

That's not all, folks: Asia gets serious about drawing cartoons. (1995, June 22). *Far Eastern Economic Review*, 86.

Yu, C. P. (1984). Confucian and Biblical concepts of filial piety. Unpublished doctoral dissertation, School of Theology, Boston University.

Zhou, Y. (1999, April 20). Mulan brought happiness to cinemas. *Beijing Youth Daily*, 7.

Zuo, G. (1935). *Mulan joins the army*. Shanghai: Qizhi Bookstore Press (in Chinese).

Chapter 14

Mapping Transborder Imaginations

Eric Ma

Information technologies shrink the world. Boundaries collapse. Money, images, powers, ideas and theories travel around the world, in the split second of a mouse click. Tourists, migrants and entrepreneurs are crossing national boundaries at astonishing rates (e.g., Canclini, 1995; Castells, 1996; Friedman, 1994; Urry, 2000). As Appadurai (1996) argues, shifts and changes characterize the mediascape and ethnoscape of the contemporary world. The ways we theorize about transborder flow in the compressed time and space of the now globalized world would be very different from the ways we did just half a decade ago. Ten years back, we theorized about globalization as a transforming and homogenizing dynamic which would force us to revise theses in cultural imperialism, international communication and diffusionist modernization. Now many of us have experienced the various impacts of global dynamics. Yet the world is far from being one, and boundaries old and new are still around us. Globalization and cultural homogenization, as theoretical imaginations, have not been fully actualized, and perhaps they might never be.

In this chapter, I use the terms "border" and "boundary" to refer respectively to the geographical division between communities and the imaginary line between cultures. Borders are terrestrialized, while boundaries are regulated, but not fixed by borders. Boundaries are rendered highly mobile by media technologies and transborder exchanges. They can be dislocated by transborder media and embodied by travelers and migrants.[1] The thesis of globalization as cultural homogenization is in fact about the dissolution and redrawing of boundaries by transborder flow of cultural imaginations. Here, cultural imagination is used as a general term referring to a fuzzy collectivity of ideas, values, sentiments and imageries within an imagined boundary. It can be about a place, a culture, a social group, a nation, or a collective identity. Imaginations are not pure fantasies without empirical ground. Like Anderson's (1983) term "imagined community," cultural imagination about a place or a community is inferred from partial and fragmented experiences and generalized to the collectivity within the boundary of the imagined whole.

The main task of this chapter is to map the logic of transborder cultural imaginations. By understanding how cultural imaginations extend and reassert their boundaries across physical borders, theorists can pin down general claims of globalization in specific and analytic terms. Thus this is a reconsideration of globalization in terms of transborder cultural imagination. How do cultural boundaries reconfigure themselves in the process of globalization? How do dissolving yet always reasserting boundaries regulate the mediascapes and ethnoscapes across physical borders? What are the features and effects of transborder cultural imaginations? To tackle these questions, I will ground my analysis in empirical cases of border crossing migrants and imageries. I will generalize from the cultural imaginations and social practices of migrants who have crossed the physical border and cultural boundary from post-socialist China into the cultural spaces of Hong Kong in different periods of time. I have interviewed more than 50 families and asked about what they thought of Hong Kong before and after their migration.[2] Various media texts are also examined to trace the trajectories of imageries distributed, reproduced and appropriated across the Sino-Hong Kong border.

THE MATERIALITY OF CONSUMERIST MODERNITY[3]

This chapter is about the configurations of cultural imagination across borders. As the arguments proceed, I will talk more about the mutation and implosion of shifting cultural boundaries. However, this is not another work that recycles theses of postmodern mixing and blending of imageries and lifestyles. I want to argue, in this beginning section, that cultural imaginations across borders are rooted in the differentials of materiality between border sharing communities. By stressing the materiality of cultural imagination, I am not sliding to the opposite theoretical end of crude materialism. After years of debate between, and theoretical advances made by, theorists of political economy and cultural studies (Hesmondhalgh, 2000), it would be naïve to argue for a thesis which says that the "cultural" is determined by the "material" in a simple and linear chain reaction. Instead, I am proposing that transborder cultural imaginations, no matter how fluid and hybridized these travelling imageries may appear, are shaped and modulated by the materiality of the life worlds in concrete historical contexts.

This chapter is about the specific case of the Sino-Hong Kong border. From the interview data, it is quite obvious that the cultural imaginations about Hong Kong before and after the actual crossing of border are rooted most prominently in the materiality of consumer culture in Hong Kong. The border crossing experiences of the informants were characterized by vivid memories of material consumption. This was especially true among those who came to Hong Kong in the 1970s, when Hong Kong and China had a huge gap in material affluence. To my informants, the first taste of ice-cold Coca-Cola, a mouthful of a fresh California orange, the colors of trendy clothing and the comfort of wearing sports shoes, all left lasting impressions of the first encounter with Hong Kong culture. These sensory contacts of modernity can be quite overwhelming. Informants told me about the bright light of Hong Kong at night, which was in big contrast with rural China, where evenings were covered in darkness. On the way to Hong Kong, by legal or illegal means, immigrants could see the "heavenly" lights of Hong Kong in the distance. One informant recalled vividly that what amazed her most was that she did not need to shine her shoes in Hong Kong. "Hong Kong is clean and neat; the restaurants, and especially McDonald's, are nice and colorful." Back home in mainland China, her daily rituals were cleaning her shoes and preparing meals. Some informants recalled the astonishment when they first stood at the platform of subway stations. They experienced a sense of powerful control of huge mechanical operations, of speed and accuracy, of comfort and efficiency. All these imaginations of modernity were enveloped in the bodily senses of sight, sound and touch.

The superiority of Hong Kong's material culture over China's was instantly mapped psychologically into these encounters. The perceptions of Hong Kong's "superior" modernity and China's "deficient" modernity caught the imaginations of the immigrants. In fact, the material superiority of Hong Kong culture was in many cases recognized before the actual crossing of the China/Hong Kong border. Informants said they first encountered Hong Kong culture when relatives brought fashionable clothing and TV sets to the mainland. These conspicuous acts of giving were highly charged rituals serving multiple social and cultural functions. Informants remembered how homecoming rituals became public displays of wealth when relatives walked pass the village with conspicuous goods, attracting curious village kids running after them. They talked about how a newly acquired TV set was installed outdoors instead of indoors:

> In those days (the 1970s) nobody in my village would have a TV set. Having a TV set was definitely an indication of having a Hong Kong relative.

> I was very proud of our TV set. We put it in front of the main door. After dinner, people would bring a little chair and gather in front of our house waiting for the shows.

This served as a display of social superiority and was a remapping of social position within the rural communities. Those who had relatives in Hong Kong were seen as superior because of status markers brought to them from Hong Kong. Material goods served as iconic signifiers of what Hong Kong was like. They served as symbols of modernity and affluence. Meaning transfer is done powerfully by this material mediation (Miller, 1995, 1998). McCraken (1988) coins the term "diderot effect," which refers to the destabilization of lifestyle options by new acquisitions. New consumer goods can destabilize an individual's habitat by introducing alien items that are inconsistent with the existing lifestyle pattern. They out-shine existing furniture and clothing. This destabilization can be restored by either upgrading the old or hiding the new. When my informants were in China, the consumer goods from Hong Kong were transposed from an alien system of material culture across the border. Upgrading has not been feasible until quite recently, when the gap between Hong Kong and China started narrowing. Thus for them meanings were displaced into the future dream that could only be realized across the border. The newly acquired consumer goods served as material anchors of displaced meanings and as the first taste of a future dream. Gift-giving from the modern to the less modern is in fact implanting a "diderot effect" in the recipient family, which is then motivated to realize their dream by migration to the promised land. Migrants tend selectively to over-rate those aspects of modernity in which their home culture is deficient. The cultural imagination about Hong Kong and about modernity at large is rooted in these material differentials, which are one of the major driving forces behind global migration to sites of high-modernity.

ENTERING THE IDEOLOGICAL FIELD OF SOCIAL MOBILITY

As indicated in the previous discussion, transborder cultural imaginations are rooted in the material encounters before and after actual migration. However, border and boundary crossing are not just about "fluid" cultural experiences of lifestyle and material consumption. These cross-cultural experiences are also embedded in an ideological thrust of modernity of which capitalism is a major component. Material culture fuels the desire for better living and upward mobility. The cultural imagination of migrants is propelled by the perceived deficiencies of the developing modernity of the home culture and the material superiority of high modernity of the aspired culture. This desire for mobility, when boiled down to its ideological core, is constituted by discourses of liberalism such as consumption, individualism, freedom, competition and success.

To the mainland immigrants, after decades of collectivism, capitalism has become the "ideological other." It serves as the meta-narrative structuring the cultural imagination of an ideal new life in Hong Kong. Hong Kong's brand of capitalism is in fact embodied in the vivid experiences of material cultures discussed in the previous section. Informants talked spontaneously about their dreams of making big money or fulfilling their personal aspirations when they came to Hong Kong. The now classic mobility myth of capitalism—that one will succeed if s/he tries hard enough—works powerfully among migrants. This myth of ultimate success both works as justification for the difficulties encountered in migration and as the motivation to overcome discrimination against them in the host society.

Here, the "soft" label of cultural imagination exhibits the structuring force of ideological constitution. The aspiration for a modern lifestyle is shaped by the ideology of upward mobility, leaving an ideological imprint on the life stories of migrants. I will illustrate this process of cultural/ideological/personal articulation by tracing the reading of an award winning TV commercial produced in the mid-1990s. The commercial retells Hong Kong history through the story of a fisherman who struggled and overcame numerous hardships and finally made a decent living in Hong Kong. I have discussed the case extensively elsewhere (Ma, 2001b). Here I want to use it to highlight the discursive and reproductive power of cultural imagination. When I talked with my informants about this TV commercial, most of them expressed strong identification with the story and agreed strongly with the last line of the voice-over: "Whether you make a living in Hong Kong all depends on yourself." They said that the story of individual survival was their own attitude of life in Hong Kong. A few informants said in a matter-of-fact manner, "It is the history of Hong Kong."

Those informants who were born in Hong Kong or had come to Hong Kong more than 30 years ago were by and large subscribed to the ideology expressed in the commercial. However, more interesting and revealing were the accounts of those who migrated to Hong Kong just recently and did not have direct experience with the history described in the commercial. They arrived after those historical events, not before. Yet they could, with ease, recontextualize their own personal stories and intertwine them with the story of the nostalgic text. A "Miss Chau," a social worker who came to Hong Kong in the early 1980s, went into details of her teenage years in Hong Kong, telling me how she managed her father's noodle stall.

> Yes, in Hong Kong, you can only count on yourself. I stood all day in the street selling noodles. At that time I was only 15. I had to carry large packs of noodles up and down a 5-storey building. . . . We had to overcome lots of hardship in order to achieve the prosperity we now enjoy. My story is different from the commercial, but the feeling is the same.

The commercial relates the story of a particular group of fishermen in particular historical situations. Yet it demonstrates extraordinary power among new immigrants who do not share the same history. The nostalgic text is operating at the ideological level for mainland immigrants. These informants arrived in Hong Kong only after the 1970s; they had different life histories. But they were eager to cross the identity boundary and be assimilated into the collective life world of Hong Kong. Their easy identification with the fisherman reflected their desire to subscribe to Hong Kong's way of life; they were embracing Hong Kong capitalistic ideology rather than the historical specificity of the fisherman commercial. This shows an ideological compatibility rather than a nostalgic sharing of collective history.

The informants had learned and been practicing the ideology of the fisherman commercial when they arrived in Hong Kong. Ideology is constituted by and rereinforces social practices. When asked what they thought of Hong Kong before they came, they said that Hong Kong was a place where they could earn a living. No matter how vague a picture they had of Hong Kong, they had a clear idea that Hong Kong was a place full of opportunities. When they arrived in Hong Kong, they had to work very hard to earn a living. Material affluence did not come easily. Since they were somewhat marginalized by established Hong Kongers, most of them had very few friends. They worked on their own. In Hong Kong, they believed there was a way to move upward. They aspired to do so even if it meant a very dehumanizing way of life. In fact, upward mobility is not merely a myth in Hong Kong. All of my informants, although some are still confined to a low social class, manage to get some form of material rewards from their hard work. "Mrs. Mok" arrived in the late 1990s. She was a medical doctor in Beijing but was not licensed as a doctor in Hong Kong. She managed to save enough money to open a private home for the aged by herself. Her daughter was a university graduate who came to Hong Kong just two years ago. She could not find a job in Hong Kong because her academic qualification was not recognized. But she was still a true believer of the fisherman commercial. "I'll work two times harder. Like my mother, I believe I can finally succeed in Hong Kong." Their border crossing experiences illustrate that Hong Kong's capitalistic system is not perpetuated by "soft" cultural imagination, but is also sustained by "hard" disciplinary ideology and social practices. Culture, ideology and practice are mutually constitutive within the life world of a capitalistic society. Transborder cultural imaginations about modernity are densely rooted in the ideological network of capitalism. Cultural imaginations are "materialistic" as well as "ideological."

THE HYPER-REALITY OF CULTURAL REPRODUCTION

In 1998, I crossed the Sino-Hong Kong border on a field trip to visit a newly developed private housing estate in China. I shall call this estate "Five Star Villa." It is located in a coastal area about two hours' boat ride from Hong Kong. Typical of many other luxurious mainland property items, Five Star Villa targets both Hong Kong and mainland residents as potential homebuyers. These apartments and houses are much cheaper than those in Hong Kong but are considered quite expensive by mainland standards. Some Hong Kong people who cannot afford to buy a home in Hong Kong may buy one on the mainland. Other Hong Kong buyers may want to acquire mainland properties for future retirement. In recent years, marketing tours have been organized by developers to take Hong Kong buyers to these Hong Kong style villas on weekend trips, such as the one I joined on a Sunday in 1998.

My impression of this first visit was that Five Star Villa seemed to be a simulacrum which was reproduced as an imaginative reality, or realistic imagination, with houses, roads and gardens resembling those in Hong Kong. It was an imagination of Hong Kong recast into real properties. The names of small shops, buildings and roads within the area seemed to have been taken from a glossary of very stereotypical colonial Hong Kong names—Victoria Café, Nathan Road, OK Convenience Store, New Sino-Hong Kong Décor, Western Piano and New Styles Saloon. The streets and gardens in Five Star Villa differed from Hong Kong street scenes in that they were bigger and more decorative. The villa looked more like Hong Kong than the real Hong Kong, I would say. The interior decorations of display apartments exhibited excessive, hybridized and imagined Hong Kong styles blending with Western, classic and modern designs. There were red wines, elaborate dining sets, oil paintings, heavy curtains, "classic" Western furniture and Hong Kong show biz magazines peppered throughout these apartments. A golf cart was conspicuously parked in front of the door of the most expensive house for sale. The common swimming pool looked like those inside resort hotels, with non-stop Western "elevator music" and a team of waiters serving no one. The clubhouse was almost empty. There were only two very sexy ladies sipping cocktails by the swimming pool. During my visit, there were groups of locals peeping through the fence to check out the luxurious swimming pool and other exotic elements in the complex.

Potential buyers and owners of these properties take pleasure in being seen by the locals as rich and modernized men and women from Hong Kong.[4] There is also the pleasure of vicariously crossing the boundary of economic classes. In China, buyers from Hong Kong can afford to buy spacious homes, which are quite difficult to afford in Hong Kong.[5] A 1,000-square-foot apartment in Hong Kong, before the Asian economic crises in 1997, might have cost about H.K.$10 million (U.S.$1.3 million), but one could get a similar flat in mainland China for less than H.K.$500,000 (U.S.$64,700). Up-scale buyers in Hong Kong may find the decor of Five Star Villa vulgar and flamboyant. But grassroots or lower middle-class buyers may find it very gratifying to acquire such an extravagantly up-scale home at a bargain price. In fact, newly acquired mainland flats are used mainly as investments or weekend and vacation retreats only. Thus, their purchase is not really for the utility value but partly for future retirement needs and partly for the pleasure of having a high-class home. The imagination of an ideal and modern home in Hong Kong is reproduced as a hyper-reality, which is economically more viable, culturally more imaginative and geographically dislocated and transbordered from the modernized but expensive Hong Kong city space to the less modern but more affordable property market in China.

Five Star Villa looks like Hong Kong, in a hyper sense, because all those explicit references about Hong Kong have been placed in the foreground. Most Hong Kong owners live and work in Hong Kong and pay only infrequent visits to these mainland homes. The shops and apartments are mostly left vacant. During my visit, the empty streets and gardens somewhat resembled outdoor movie sets or studio constructions. Here, cultural imaginations about Hong Kong are reproduced as "imaginative reality" for the consumption of both Hong Kong buyers and local onlookers. The reproduction of this simulacrum is just one dramatic illustration of how cultural imagination is transformed into a hyper-reality across the border. Other examples include Hong Kong–style restaurants, fashions, magazines, private schools, and so on, which are constructed by inflating and reproducing stereotypical imagination about Hong Kong. Cultural imaginations are transformed into marketable commodities.

MEDIA TECHNOLOGIES, DETERRESTRIALIZATION AND RETERRESTRIALIZATION

Hyper-real transborder cultural imaginations are often mediated by information technologies. Hong Kong film and television productions have long been popular entertainment programs among Mainland audiences. They are carried by television stations or produced and circulated in videotape format (VHS) and more recently as video compact discs (VCDs), pirated or otherwise. Indeed, these extensive exchanges across borders are, as prescribed by postmodernist theorists, blurring and hybridizing boundaries between cultures. However, on closer examination, this blurring and hybridizing is not without patterns. The case of Five Star Villa is a dramatic example of "simulative inflation and reproduction" of cultural imagination. Decontextualized from local culture, popular imaginations tend to be inflated across the border. Some of my informants told me that, before they migrated to Hong Kong, their relatives warned them about the possibility of being shot or hurt by gangsters and gunmen in Hong Kong streets. The most obvious explanation is that many popular Hong Kong movies feature gangsters and triads in violent gunfights. To mainland audiences, these de-contextualized filmic representations become part of the general cultural imagination about Hong Kong. Understandably, mainlanders who reside in places geographically more distanced from Hong Kong tend to have much more inflated cultural imaginations.

Besides, inflated transborder imaginations are usually reconfigured in processes of deterrestrialization and reterrestrialization.[6] When cultural imaginations are deterrestrialized from the constraints of the local life world, they are freed from the restrictive local networks, rendering simulative inflation possible. Yet inflated imaginations can be reterrestrialized, or in other words, domesticated, by adding in the specificities, preferences and needs from the reception end. One very illustrative case is documented by one of my students who came to Hong Kong from the mainland.[7] *A Chinese Odyssey (Part I & II)*, a Hong Kong movie produced in 1995, has been very popular among university students in Beijing. The movie is a well-known Chinese legend remade into a delicate love story, featuring the famous Hong Kong actor Chiau Sing Chi as a romantic lover and a legendary hero. Quite popular at the time of its release, the movie has now more or less been forgotten by many Hong Kong viewers. Yet Beijing university students have been screening the VCD version of the movie in lecture halls and dormitory rooms for years since its release. The movie has been renamed *Big West Side Story* in China. As students are talking with each other and writing about it in e-mails and bulletin boards, more and more students are joining in the "Big Story Craze" and becoming, as they call themselves, "Big Fans." The reading and rereading of the film have been sustained year after year by interpersonal connections, low-tech VCDs and hi-tech Internet bulletin boards. In-coming students have been advised to study the film as an initiation to campus life and as a guidebook for intimate relations.

On further analysis, this micro case is constituted by macro cultural dynamics. As China is moving away from collectivism to "market socialism," individual fulfillment has been reprioritized as a culturally correct and politically legitimate pursuit. The issues of intimate relations, privacy, leisure and consumption have suddenly become big hits in China. In 1998, a best-seller entitled *Absolute Privacy* initiated the publication of a dozen more bestsellers on privacy, romantic love and marital and extramarital affairs (Ralph, 2000). The "Big Story Craze" can be seen as part of the unfolding concerns about individual rights and bodily pleasures. This micro cultural expression of the macro social shift is mediated by a Hong Kong movie, which has been translocated from the highly commercialized mediascape of Hong Kong to the highly localized networks of Beijing universities. The deterrestrialized movie has been reterrestrialized by rich and multiple layers of mediated and personal communications; a Hong Kong actor has been transformed into a guru who teaches young Beijing urbanites how to seek free and autonomous relations. The fact that this is mediated by a Hong Kong movie heightens the sense of being modern and liberal when they participate in the reterrestrialization process. The intensive reading of the film, the rich interchange between filmic representations and social practices, the active reworking of textual meaning in concrete settings and the thick mediation of chatrooms—especially ICQ, which is very popular among Chinese university students—and bulletin boards, all exceed the level of engagement of the movie with the primary audience group in Hong Kong.

COLLAPSED TEMPORALITIES

Another feature of transborder cultural flow is the collapse of temporalities. I will illustrate this feature by the "star text" of Chow Yun-fat. Chow is a Hong Kong movie star who has made a name in Hollywood. I use the term "star text" to refer to the integral and intertextual articulation of the star in movies, gossip columns, biographies and publicity materials (Dyer, 1979). As Tam (2000) argues, the star text of Chow in Hong Kong has a particular history. It has been fleshed out in two decades of television and movies, most recently in Hollywood films. Now the Hollywood Chinese Hong Kong star text of Chow has been circulated across the border into mainland China. It has become decontextualized from its historical root in Hong Kong's popular culture. In China, VCDs of Chow's previous movies and TV dramas have been redistributed in video shops and rerun on television. Thus some mainland audiences think that Chow is now making TV serial dramas and Hollywood movies at the same time. Historicity has been collapsed and imploded to form a new star text, which hybridizes different representations and temporalities. In Hong Kong, the representations of Chow have shifted over the years and intermingled with sociopsychological needs of Hong Kong society at large. In the 1970s, when Hong Kong was a rising Asian economy fueled by the optimism of upward mobility, Chow was famous for his office boy-cum-manager type of roles. From the 1980s to the early 1990s, when Hong Kong was experiencing its collective pride of prosperity and collective anxiety of sovereignty change, Chow became a multifaceted hero who was in some movies comedic and in others charismatic. He was a romantic hero who was faithful to his buddies, lover and family in times of extreme crises. More recently, Chow has become a Hong Kong man who is able to make a name in Hollywood (Lo, 2001; Tam, 2000). When this transnational star text is now repackaged and dislocated to the mainland audiences, the different temporalities and historicities have been collapsed to form a transborder and multilayered star text, utilizing

Chow as a grassroots worker, a romantic hero, a killer, a lover and a Chinese Hollywood star all at the same time. Chow has become a "generalized" China man who exhibits Orientalistic and diasporic characteristics. For cultural imaginations with specific historical formation, its historicity will be collapsed, imploded and generalized once it is deterrestrialized.

CONFLICTIVE MULTIPLICITY

In the first two sections of this chapter, I have talked about the material and ideological aspects of transborder cultural imaginations. Then I have proceeded to map the hyper-realistic, reproductive and mutational features of cultural imaginations when they are dislocated across borders. Recently, cultural flows across the Sino-Hong Kong border have become much more complicated. The dynamics of globalization have triggered these new complications. However, as I argued earlier, the fluidity and complicity of transborder cultural imaginations have strong structural and material roots. Since the 1990s, material cultures from all over the world have been flooding into the Chinese market, and the exchanges between Hong Kong and China have been more frequent (Kwok & So, 1995; Ong, 1999; Smart, 1998). In this period of dialectic interaction, transborder cultural imaginations have become unstable and even demonstrate some postmodern features. The crash of modernities with different levels of intensity produces fragments of postmodernity in quite a unique way. Let me elaborate with a specific case.

"Ah-Chor," a beautiful woman in her mid-20s, came to Hong Kong from Wen Zhou in 1996 to marry a Hong Kong man. Since the early 1990s, Wen Zhou has been saturated with modern commodities and has been called the little Hong Kong in China.[8] Hong Kong television programs, popular songs and entertainment magazines are well received in the community. Ah Chor recalled: "The girls and housewives in Wen Zhou all dress up like the movie stars in Hong Kong. Girls dare not go out without wearing makeup. They think that all Hong Kongers live like those in the magazines." However, when Ah Chor first came to Hong Kong, she was surprised by the way Hong Kong people dressed. "Lots of girls didn't wear makeup. And they were wearing ugly gray and black." Ah Chor quickly "dressed down" like her Hong Kong friends. When she went back home to China a year later, she had a very different opinion about the dress code of her former neighbors. "They are too sexy, too fuzzy, they seem to be living in an artificial world." What is interesting was the way Chor was judged by her Chinese friends. Ah Chor wore a plain T-shirt and jeans, and her friends asked, "Why are your dressing like a beggar? Look how ugly you are." Her neighbor, a medical doctor, secretly asked Chor's sister whether Chor had married a bad husband in Hong Kong.

Hong Kong consumerist modernity, the image, the imagined and the imaginary[9] are dislocated to this community by the Hong Kong media. The imagination becomes an organized field of social practice. A dislocated mediascape dissolved into life. The symbolic is realized as a "little Hong Kong," while the real Hong Kong becomes plain and ugly. As Bauman (1992, 1997) phrases it, reality has been made ugly by the beauty of the vision. This brief moment of simulation points to the discursive reproduction of consumerist modernity with a postmodern bend. When modernization and marketization become official, when consumer products become available in China, the discursive power of Hong Kong culture is released in various parts of China, reproducing social practices based on imaginations of Western modernity relayed through Hong Kong.

In the 1980s and early 1990s, China was modeling Hong Kong, but it has recently developed its own cultural edges and economic power to complicate Sino-Hong Kong exchanges. As China catches up with the race of modernization, the cultural boundary between Hong Kong and China becomes fuzzy and unstable. The sovereignty transfer in 1997 further softened the cultural boundary of the two places. Now the Sino-Hong Kong territorial border has become more administrative than political. Hong Kong culture has been resinicized (Ma, 1999); on the other hand, Hong Kong's brand of modernity is exported, reproduced and localized in other parts of China. More and more Hong Kong entrepreneurs and opportunists are exploiting the possibilities offered by the developing Chinese market (Ong, 1999). Hong Kong consumers are flooding into Shenzhen and other coastal cities to consume China's bargain-priced consumerist modernity during the weekends and holidays. But here postmodern theories are not in full purchase. Postmodern features like symbolic simulation, hybridization and blurring of boundaries are phenomena that can be framed within the juncture of dislocated "modernities." They arise in between the overlaps of high modernity at the satellite site of Hong Kong and the developing modernity in post-socialist China. The discursive fragments refracted from the crashes between two or multiple modernities exhibit postmodern features, but they are all within the fold of a compressed and asymmetrical process of modernization (Lash, 1999; Wittrock, 2000).

In this chapter, I have moved away from the general theoretical claims of cultural homogenization and hybridization. I have tried to describe the patterns and configurations of cultural imaginations in more precise and analytic terms. The cases discussed in this chapter have illustrated how transborder flows of cultural imagination are rooted in materiality and ideologies. Transborder cultural imagination can be deterrestrialized, inflated, collapsed and reterrestrialized into the internal social network and circuits of meaning construction. These are especially true in times when information technologies are speeding up the circulation of cultural imaginations. And finally, hybridization and multiplicity can be situated in the contemporary historical juncture where different modernities are pressing on to each other as mutual points of reference and overlapping exchanges. Mapping these configurations of transborder imaginations can be considered as one of the many beginning steps to develop theories of globalization in more sophisticated and substantial terms.

NOTES

This chapter is derived from a paper entitled "Consuming Modernity," presented at the conference "In Search of Boundaries: Communication, Nation-States and Cultural Identities," The Chinese University of Hong Kong, Hong Kong, 1999. The conference paper has been rewritten into two papers. One is the present chapter and the other is entitled "Consuming Satellite Modernities," forthcoming in *Cultural Studies*. While this chapter focuses on the configurations of transborder imaginations, the *Cultural Studies* paper will examine the role of satellite cities in the global network of transborder exchanges.

1. For recent theorization of border and boundary, see Michaelsen and Johnson (1997) and Welchman (1996). For a poetic treatment, see Chambers (1994).

2. This chapter is part of a project entitled "Advertising the Hong Kong Identity." The project is funded by the Hong Kong Research Grant Committee. The initial questions of the research were: How do different waves of immigrants learn to be Hong Kongers when they came to Hong Kong? What is the role of television commercials in "teaching" new immigrants the Hong Kong way of life? From this point of departure, I started to interview immigrants and their families. Apart from talking about their "boundary crossing experiences" and their "consumption histories," we shared with them a set of selected TV commercials of the past 20 years. These commercials were stored in a notebook computer, so we could screen and talk about them when we touched on relevant subjects.

3. Part of the material in this section is taken from Ma (2001a).

4. For a discussion on the psychological process of identity formation in modernity, see Giddens (1991).

5. See Cheng (2000) for a study of Hong Kong property market.

6. For theory on the media and modernity and the effect of deterrestrialization, see Thompson (1995).

7. She provided me with some of the letters and essays written by Beijing students about a Hong Kong movie *A Chinese Odyssey*.

8. For an account of the fashion in post-Mao China, see Li (1998).

9. In this context, Benedict's imagined community (1983) can be extended to include dislocated imagination of a far away "satellite community" of modernity.

REFERENCES

Anderson, B. (1983). *Imagined communities: Reflections on the origin and spread of nationalism*. London: Verso.

Appadurai, A. (1996). *Modernity at large: Cultural dimensions of globalization*. Minneapolis: University of Minnesota Press.

Bauman, Z. (1992). *Intimations of postmodernity*. London: Routledge.

Bauman, Z. (1997). *Postmodernity and its discontents.* New York: New York University Press.

Benedict, A. (1983). *Imagined communities: Reflection on the origin and spread of nationalism.* London: Verso.

Canclini, G. (1995). *Hybrid cultures.* Minneapolis: University of Minnesota Press.

Castells, M. (1996). *The rise of the network society.* Cambridge: Blackwell.

Chambers, I. (1994). *Migrancy, culture, identity.* London: Routledge.

Cheng, H. L. (2000). Buying a home, buying a dream: Meaning systems of home in contemporary Hong Kong. Unpublished M.Phil thesis, Communication Division, The Chinese University of Hong Kong.

Dyer, R. (1979). *Stars.* London: BFI Publishing.

Friedman, J. (1994). *Cultural identity & global process.* London: Sage Publications.

Giddens, A. (1991). *Modernity and self-identity: Self and society in the late modern age.* Cambridge: Polity Press.

Hesmondhalgh, D. (2000). Cultural studies and political economy as positive achievements. Paper presented at the Crossroads in Cultural Studies Conference, June 21–25, Birmingham, United Kingdom.

Kwok, R., & So, A. (Eds.) (1995). *The Hong Kong–Guangdong link: Partnership in flux.* Hong Kong: Hong Kong University Press.

Lash, S. (1999). *Another modernity: A different rationality.* Oxford: Blackwell.

Li, X. (1998). Fashioning the body in the post-Mao China. In A. Brydon & S. Niessen (Eds.), *Consuming fashion* (pp. 71–89). New York: Berg.

Lo, K. C. (2001). Double negations: Hong Kong cultural identity in transnational cinematic representations. *Cultural Studies,* 15(3/4), 200, 275–295.

Ma, E. (1999). *Culture, politics and television in Hong Kong.* London: Routledge.

Ma, E. (2001a). Consuming satellite modernities. *Cultural Studies,* 15(3/4), 444–463.

Ma, E. (2001b). Re-advertising Hong Kong: Nostalgic industry and popular history. *Positions: East Asia Cultures Critique,* 9(1), 131–159.

McCraken, G. (1988). *Culture and consumption: New approaches to the symbolic character of consumer goods and activities.* Bloomington: Indiana University Press.

Michaelsen, S., & Johnson, D. (Eds.) (1997). *Border theory: The limits of cultural politics.* Minneapolis: University of Minnesota Press.

Miller, D. (1995). Consumption as the vanguard of history: A polemic by way of an introduction. In D. Miller (Ed.), *Acknowledging consumption* (pp. 1–57). London: Routledge.

Miller, D. (Ed.) (1998). *Material cultures: Why some things matter.* Chicago: University of Chicago Press.

Ong, A. (1999). *Flexible citizenship: The cultural logics of transnationality.* Durham, NC: Duke University Press.

Smart, J. (1998). Transnationalism and modernity in the South China region: Reflections on future research agendas in anthropology. In S. Cheung (Ed.), *On the South China track* (pp. 56–70). Hong Kong: Hong Kong Institute of Asia-Pacific Studies.

Ralph, R. (2000). The privacy rage: Discourse of intimacy and suffering in 1990s China. Paper presented at the Crossroad Cultural Studies Conference, June 21–25, Birmingham, United Kingdom.

Tam, V. (2000). Star text: Transnational meanings of Chow Yun-fat. Paper presented at Transnational Chinese Film and TV conference, April 19–21, Department of Cinema and Television, Baptist University, Hong Kong.

Thompson, J. (1995). *The media and modernity*. Cambridge: Polity Press.

Urry, J. (2000). Mobile sociology. *The British Journal of Sociology*, 51, 185–203.

Welchman, J. (Ed.) (1996). *Rethinking borders*. Minneapolis: University of Minnesota Press.

Wittrock, B. (2000). Modernity: One, none, or many? *Daedalus*, 129, 1–29.

Chapter 15

Sweet Comrades: Historical Identities and Popular Culture

Michael Curtin

In the months leading up to Hong Kong's return to Chinese rule in 1997, it was often remarked in the global press that this was the first time that a colony failed to make the transition from servitude to independence. The observation of course betrays a Eurocentric presumption that colonialism somehow prepares a society for a leap onto the global stage as a fully sovereign nation-state. But perhaps more importantly, it presumes—despite much recent scholarship to the contrary—that postcolonial identities are somehow stable and coherent, that Kenyans, Indians and Malaysians emerged from the colonial era as fully formed publics that were distinctive from their neighbors. Thus in 1997 it was often remarked that Hong Kongers were so different from their mainland counterparts that it would be hard to imagine the territory being folded back into China and subjugated to the alien authority of the national Beijing government. It was presumed by some commentators that the colonial experience had produced a society with a distinctive collective identity that was perhaps more Western than Eastern. Nevertheless, most everyone—Hong Kongers included—acknowledged that the majority of the territory's inhabitants are ethnically Chinese and therefore presumably share important cultural and historical capital with their counterparts across the border. In other words, Hong Kong seemed to be both "authentically" Chinese and yet decidedly different. It therefore presented political, economic and social paradoxes, both for the Chinese government and for international institutions. Interestingly, these problems were in large part symbolic and most centrally connected to questions of identity. As the territory moved inexorably toward postcolonial status, how might one think of Hong Kongers in relation to national and transnational systems? How might Hong Kongers themselves reflect on issues of identity? What are the relationships between being a Hong Konger and being Chinese? How might the processes of boundary construction and maintenance be affected by the transfer of sovereignty?

Such questions will continue to preoccupy many institutions in the newly constituted Special Administrative Region (SAR) of Hong Kong. The courts are now deliberating over thousands of claims filed by mainlanders seeking "right of abode" in the territory; businesses are puzzling over new patterns of ownership that show the increasing influence of mainland investors in the Hong Kong economy; and educators are hard at work striking a balance among Cantonese, English and Mandarin as potential languages of instruction. The territory's enormously prolific media institutions are also confronting new questions as they adjust to the transition. The film industry has been hit particularly hard, because in addition to the uncertainties engendered by the transfer of sovereignty, its access to overseas markets in East and Southeast Asia has been undermined by changes in local media regulations, new exhibition technologies, media piracy and Hollywood competition (Curtin, 1999; Leung & Chan, 1997). The industry faces significant economic and political problems that can only be resolved by attempting to recover some of its lost audiences and by actively searching for new audiences beyond the borders of the SAR. Of all the potential new markets it might pursue, the mainland offers both the greatest promise and the greatest peril. To single-mindedly pursue mainland viewers by skewing creative content to meet their tastes could mean risking the loss of audiences in Hong Kong and in existing export markets. Yet to ignore mainland audiences is a difficult proposition for an industry teetering on the brink of financial ruin.[1] In response to these complex conditions, media practitioners seem to be employing several different strategies. Some prefer to redouble their efforts in service of traditional Hong Kong cinema audiences; some are aggressively hailing mainland audiences with products that are fashioned as distinctively "Chinese"; and some are focusing their attention on cosmopolitan audiences with products that might be seen as transgressing or transcending conventional boundaries.[2]

This chapter provides a cultural, historical and critical perspective on the vicissitudes of identity politics in Hong Kong cinema. The first part of the chapter briefly reflects on scholarly work regarding identity and popular culture in Hong Kong, and the second part then analyzes a commercially successful and critically acclaimed Hong Kong feature film that premiered on the eve of the handover, in the fall of 1996. *Tim Mat Mat* ("Sweet One"), which was released to English-speaking audiences under the title, *Comrades, Almost a Love Story*, seemed to strike a responsive chord with audiences and critics precisely because it focuses on issues of identity and diaspora. The film explores the unstable nature of contemporary social and political boundaries within the framework of a commercial, romantic melodrama. As an historical artifact, it conveys the complex identity issues at

Li Chiao (Maggie Cheung) and Li Xiao-jun (Leon Lai) experience the challenges and reversals of diasporic Chinese in *Comrades, Almost a Love Story*.

stake in Hong Kong during the second half of the twentieth century and resolves these issues not by valorizing a distinctive Hong Kong identity nor by promoting a national Chinese identity, but by collapsing the boundaries of identity and advancing a cosmopolitan consciousness that is grounded in the lived experiences of the Chinese diaspora.

In an industry that is currently experiencing the worst downturn in 25 years, the film seems to propose that one way to restore the popularity and profitability of Hong Kong film is to actively transgress and transcend the boundaries of identity that have influenced Hong Kong film throughout its history. *Tim Mat Mat* seeks to accommodate changing political, social and economic forces without being pulled into a nationalist worldview and without taking up a defensive form of localism. The film presents a kind of cosmopolitanism that is historically aware but which avoids reductive categories of identification. It navigates boundaries rather than maintains them. It undermines conventional categories of identity rather than observes them. A careful reading of the film is not intended to suggest that all films follow this pattern or that audience responses are uniform. One can find powerful separatist and localist tendencies at work in many parts of Hong Kong society and throughout East Asia as well. Yet, as we will see, cosmopolitan cultural products like *Tim Mat Mat* mark a significant new development in the culture industries of the territory and the film is therefore worth discussing in some detail. In order to understand how it departs from prior narrative patterns, one first needs to talk briefly about identity politics in southern China and some of the ways that Hong Kong popular culture has managed them in the past.

THE POLITICS OF CHINESENESS

People living in the southern part of China have been reflecting on their "Chineseness" for at least one thousand years. Debates over Chinese identity have in part revolved around questions of allegiance to the imperial government and in part around issues of cultural identification—shared artistic, mythological and linguistic traditions. But perhaps most centrally, debates about Chinese identity often refer to ethnicity. According to current government statistics, 93 percent of the inhabitants of China are Han Chinese (Ramsey, 1987). Such pretensions to ethnic homogeneity seem daunting in a country of more than 1 billion people, for it suggests an unproblematic and primordial connection that legitimizes a vast and sprawling apparatus of state power by effacing important social, cultural and historical differences. Consequently, the return of China's sovereignty over the territory was seen by the Beijing leadership as an uncontested fact of history and ethnicity, since most Hong Kong families migrated from the mainland and therefore should be counted as Han Chinese. From the government's perspective, fraternity is presumed, since Hong Kongers share the same mythical origins as their mainland counterparts.

Yet beneath this veneer of cultural and political unity, one finds a much more contested set of identities stretching back many centuries, especially in southern China. The issues are complicated, and for many years, orthodox histories of China tended to marginalize the development of the south, which tended to obscure the fact that Chineseness has been a subject of ongoing social and cultural contest throughout the imperial and national eras of China's history. For example, one recent revisionist account suggests that during the Song dynasty (960–1279) southerners were clearly distinct from populations to the north by virtue of ethnicity, language and cultural practice. Yet those differences were sometimes effaced by local elites in the south who sought to consolidate their power by claiming a Han Chinese cultural identity, which might thereby align them more closely with northerners who dominated the authoritarian imperial state. These elites actively rewrote their identities in a number of ways. "From the Song dynasty onward," contends Helen Siu (1993, p. 23), "the population in Guangdong who claimed to have a common cultural ancestry with those in the North created myths and regional historiographies, compiled genealogies, and built ornate ancestral halls with literati pretensions." They sought to "rediscover" their connections to a lost Han identity and, not coincidentally, to consolidate their ties to each other and to the imperial court. Many of the major lineages in the Pearl River Delta claim their ancestors migrated south from the central plains during a period when nomads threatened the Han settlements. "Lineage membership was at once proof of cultural identity and a shrewd strategy for strength in numbers, for social mobility and political legitimacy," according to Siu (p. 23; see also Sage, 1992).

Unable or unwilling to contest the power of the imperial regime, southern elites focused much of their energy on land reclamation projects in the Pearl Delta, yielding rich, fertile farmland. As they grew to become wealthy landlords, they turned their attention to the development of elaborate cottage manufacturing operations that, by the nineteenth century, sold goods in markets throughout the world. This emerging merchant class furthermore exported labor and invested in overseas business operations throughout East and Southeast Asia (Ang, 1994; Seagrave, 1995). According to Siu, "different dynasties centered in Beijing tolerated the region's unorthodox diversity and benefited from the wealth it generated" (p. 26).

Meanwhile, in Hong Kong, a multiracial merchant society, emerged during the 19th century due to growing commercial ties among England, India and the Pearl River Delta.[3] Identity issues in the colony were no doubt complex, but perhaps just as importantly, recent historical accounts suggest that Hong Kong was not an isolated island of aberrant diversity perched on the edge of a homogeneous, Chinese nation. Rather, Chinese identities in Hong Kong were perhaps no more complicated than Chinese identities in much of the Pearl Delta. Indeed, Chun takes the argument to its logical extension by suggesting that, "Prior to the Nationalist Revolution of 1911, there was no cognate notion in Chinese of society or nation as a polity whose boundary was synonymous with that of an ethnic group" (Chun, 1996b, p. 113). Sun Yat-sen, the revolutionary hero and founding leader of the Republic, sensed the problems of forging a national identity when he observed that the Chinese polity was no more unified than "a dish of loose sand" (Chun, 1996b, p. 114).

With the fall of the Qing Dynasty and the emergence of a modern form of Chinese nationalism, the situation apparently remained quite complicated. Since the modern nation-state is premised on the notion of popular sovereignty, the Communist and Nationalist governments took on the role of promoting collective identity through the active production and promotion of particular cultural forms. Each state sought to delimit not only what it meant to be a citizen, but what it meant to be Chinese. As Chun puts it, "the public space of culture is then an abstract space, not just an empty, homogeneous space etched in the minds of the equal, autonomous individuals that constitute Anderson's 'imagined communities' but also a space framed by the possibilities of identity" (Chun 1996a, p. 52). Those possibilities were powerfully shaped and contested by political and bureaucratic factions. Consequently, Chun suggests that notions of Chinese ethnicity are less a matter of primordial connection than of political intention. Ethnicities, like identities, are socially constructed under specific historical circumstances and they almost invariably are the product of intense social struggle.

During the post-dynastic era, the two most powerful poles of official Chinese identity were advanced by the Communist and Nationalist regimes. Although the Revolution physically separated the two camps across the Taiwan straits, they nevertheless continued to struggle over the terrain of culture and identity. The Kuomintang (KMT) in Taiwan promoted itself as the guardian of "traditional Chinese culture" and instituted a series of initiatives aimed at sustaining the fiction that the island regime was the last bastion of authentic Chinese culture and therefore the legitimate heir to succeed the Communist regime in Beijing. Meanwhile, the mainland government used similar tools of language, ethnicity and history to promote a vision of the People's Republic of China as the most advanced state of development in Chinese society—a society that adopted a Stalinist policy of multiculturalism that positioned the Han majority at the center of a host of ethnicities (Chun, 1996a).

HONG KONG IDENTITY AND POPULAR CULTURE

Hong Kong culture industries emerged at the nexus of these conflicting claims regarding ethnicity, culture and identity. Attempting to navigate this complex terrain, they fashioned products that changed dramatically over time, just as the circumstances of their audiences would change. For example, the Hong Kong film industry first began to take off with the introduction of talking pictures, as Cantonese-speaking audiences in the south responded enthusiastically to films produced in Guangzhou and Hong Kong during the 1930s (Fonoroff, 1988; Law, 1995; Teo, 1997). So popular was Cantonese cinema that Hong Kong would quickly grow to be one of the most significant film production centers in China.[4] Drawing upon the patronage of the Pearl Delta elite and the Chinese merchant class in the colony, and benefiting from educational and intellectual contacts with distant parts of the world, Hong Kong became a cosmopolitan center that nevertheless based the appeal of its films on a distinctive variety of Chinese culture and identity. Moreover, it did so outside of the realm of state control. In the socially bifurcated context of Hong Kong, the British colonial administration showed little interest in forging allegiances with the local Chinese populace and even less interest in popular film. Thus the industry flourished with little state interference regarding matters of content or style. By steering a non-political course at the level of manifest content, studios were able to produce films that were not only widely popular with Hong Kong audiences but also with mainland audiences in the Pearl River Delta and with southerners who had migrated abroad (Choi, 1990; Leung & Chan, 1997).

Whether motivated by aspiration, deprivation, or persecution, millions of southern Chinese dispersed throughout Southeast Asia and other parts of the world during the nineteenth and twentieth centuries established Chinese communities in such cities as Bangkok, Jakarta and London (Ang, 1994; Seagrave, 1995).[5] Hector Rodriguez (1997) contends that the turmoil of modernization and diaspora helped to make cinema an especially important form of popular culture in these overseas communities. For during the early years of the Hong Kong movie industry, many films specifically drew upon or reflected upon traditional cultural forms, especially Cantonese opera and legend. They served as a site where one might indulge in nostalgic longing for a lost past and as a place where one might reflect on the role of tradition in a rapidly changing social environment.[6] One of the most popular recurring characters in Cantonese cinema was Wong Fei-hong, a practitioner of Chinese medicine, a dutiful father, an upright leader of his community, and a martial arts expert who employed his skills only as a last resort and always in the defense of the oppressed. Not only did the character help audiences reflect upon tensions between tradition and modernity, but Wong also defended the integrity of southern Chinese culture in the face of challenges posed by northerners and foreigners.[7]

It is important to stress that this early era refers to *Cantonese* cinema rather than Hong Kong cinema. That is, Hong Kong was the location where filmmakers produced movies for a widely dispersed Cantonese population. The cultural and linguistic affinities that these audiences shared harkened back to the dynastic era and set Cantonese cinema apart from the official cultural policies of the Communist and Nationalist regimes, as well as the British colonial government. The success of this cinema was predicated upon identities that distinguished themselves as regional rather than national. Cantonese cinema was condoned but never embraced by any of the governments that exercised power over its audiences. It was, in that sense, a marginal—and one might even say, an oppositional—cinema, serving audiences in Hong Kong, Taiwan and southern China, as well as diasporic audiences in cities such as Bangkok, London and Jakarta. In most instances, these were audiences who saw themselves at the margins of political power.

Despite the vibrant success of studios during the 1930s and 1950s, box office returns began to decrease in the mid to late 1960s, and Cantonese film production ground to a virtual halt in the early 1970s. The reasons for the decline of Cantonese cinema are many and complex, among them the exhaustion of traditional genres and the competition from better financed Hollywood and Mandarin-language films (Choi, 1990; Fu, 1997; Teo, 1997). But perhaps just as important was the shift in population. As Lee (1991) notes, the influx of mainland Chinese moving to Hong Kong began to subside in the 1960s and many of those who migrated to the colony during the 1940s and 1950s had settled down and had begun to raise families. Local demographics began to skew younger and the colony began to experience the emergence of a locally based youth culture. This younger generation was raised on both Western and Chinese popular culture. Furthermore, as Lee contends, the culture industries began to respond to these audiences by appropriating Western media forms and inflecting them with both Chinese qualities and local qualities. This trend accelerates with the introduction of television in 1967. J. M. Chan (1992) points out that broadcast television came to Hong Kong at the very moment when the colony's demographics shifted significantly. For the first time since the 1940s, a majority of the population was actually born in Hong Kong, and the preponderance of locals would only increase over the succeeding decades. With the pace of migration slowed down by official government policy, Cold War tensions and the erection of a barbed-wire frontier, media for the very first time turned their primary attention to Hong Kong itself, producing extremely popular variety shows, local dramas and television news. Chan suggests that this shift in population and this transformation in the culture industries moved the local population to a new level of social awareness. Six years after its introduction, television receivers could be found in more than 80 percent of all homes. With only two Cantonese-language channels, one of which overwhelmingly dominated the ratings, Hong Kong television during the 1970s was a truly broad-based collective viewing experience. Shedding a "refugee mentality," local television became the primary site were local journalists and artists intensively reflected upon the meaning of life in Hong Kong (Chan & Choi, 1989; Kung & Zhang, 1984; Lo & Ng, 1996).

Most powerfully, Eric K. W. Ma (1999) explains how television dramas delineated the distinctive qualities of what it meant to be a Hong Konger, as opposed to Chinese, Cantonese, or a British colonial subject. Interestingly, the most important faultline of this identity formation became the distinction between Hong Konger and mainlander, more or less collapsing the categories of Cantonese and Chinese, and marking them as a collective "Other." Focusing on a television series that premiered in 1979 and that proved to be the most popular melodrama of the era, Ma shows how *The Good, the Bad, and the Ugly* established categories of opposition that suggested that mainlanders were naive, crude, provincial and potentially lawless. Hong Kongers were by comparison portrayed as educated, hard-working and cosmopolitan. This set of distinctions was conveyed through a personal family history in which an established Hong Kong family is thrown into turmoil by the arrival of a long lost son from the mainland. As the story unfolds over the course of 80 episodes, the Chian Wai character (familiarly know as Ah Chian) comes to stand for the contaminating influence that threatens community and civility within the territory. Writes Ma:

The differentiating process not only stigmatized the newcomers, but was also essential to the "discovery" of the collective identity of the established populace. Stigmatizing outsiders seems to go hand in hand with the identity formation process. The established group came to be called Hongkongers, leaving their Chinese identity in the shadows, while the newcomers were given a collective name "Ah Chian", a label carrying a derogatory sting. In Hong Kong "Ah Chian" has been the most popular name for newcomers from mainland China for more than a decade. (p. 62)

What is perhaps most interesting about this television series—other than the fact that it coined a popular sobriquet for mainlanders—is that it marked a significant shift of identifications. Not only were Hong Kongers shedding the refugee mentality but they were also distinguishing themselves from Cantonese regional culture. Whereas 40 years before, people and ideas used to flow across the colonial border regularly, thereby blurring Cantonese Hong Kong into Cantonese China, now there emerged distinctions that were marked by wealth, attire, behavior and culture. Not surprisingly, they were also marked by language. Hong Kong Cantonese developed a sound and velocity that was different from mainland Cantonese. It also developed a rich and rapidly changing local idiom that incorporated distinctive cosmopolitan influences, casually borrowing words and concepts from English, Mandarin and other languages.

Word play became one of the hallmarks of Hong Kong television, especially comedy, and it is the career of one extremely popular television comedian that helped to mark the revival of the film industry. After establishing himself in television, Michael Hui moved over to the film medium in the mid-1970s and began directing and starring in a series of films that proved popular not only in Hong Kong, but in overseas markets as well. His global appeal is no doubt attributable to his brilliant physical comedy and a series of impeccably-timed gags. As film critic Law Kar remarked, "Michael Hui is to comedy what Bruce Lee is to the martial arts: they both reign supreme" (Law, 1984, p. 65). Yet Hui was also renowned for playing an important role in reviving Cantonese-language cinema and most especially for showcasing the Hong Kong variety of Cantonese, helping to make it a new standard for the industry (Teo, 1997). Just as importantly, Hui's brand of humor marks another significant break from the legacy of regional Cantonese cinema as he inverts the Wong Fei-hong character for comedic effect. In many of his early films, such as *Boon Gan Baat Leung* (literally, "Half Pound, Eight Ounces," English title *The Private Eyes*, 1976) and *Moh Dang Bo Biu* (literally "Modern Bodyguards," English title *Security Unlimited*, 1981), Hui plays a mean-spirited boss who serves himself rather than his employees or his community. While navigating the tensions of modern life in Hong Kong, Hui's character abandons Confucian morals in pursuit of fame, fortune, sex and modern conveniences. Hui strips the character of all traces of traditional dignity in favor of a single-minded pursuit of worldly pleasures. Inevitably, the character's aspirations are dashed within the course of the narrative, which allows Hui to close the film with a comic moment of humility, which points to the character's potential for rehabilitation and renewal. Yet this potential is not posed as a restoration of balance between East and West or tradition and modernity, but rather as the emergence of a modern sense of reflexivity. Hui's character will be rehabilitated not by reconnecting to the Chinese past nor by embracing Western modernity but by traversing the pitfalls posed both by tradition *and* modernity. He is an indigenous Hong Konger—a comedic representation of an identity commonly advanced in popular culture during the 1970s.

Jenny Kwok Wah Lau argues that this ambivalence marks another break with Cantonese cinema of the 1950s and 1960s. "In the previous era, theater audiences, many members of whom were refugees from China, were generally China-centered. That is, they identified themselves more with the (romanticized) China than with Hong Kong and were quite willing to position Hong Kong as the "Other." Some of the older films, while exposing problems such as greed and exploitation as Hong Kong's capitalist faults, also implied that social virtues were to be found in China" (Lau, 1998, p. 29). Lau suggests that the popularity of Hui's films marked a shift in public attitudes, since his characters do not find solace in the sacred virtues of traditional China. Rather a majority of the audience now saw the territory as home and expressed enthusiasm about popular culture that explored the rewarding but often troublesome aspects of Hong Kong life.

Others followed Hui in the successful transition from television careers to film careers. Like their work in television, these filmmakers addressed themselves primarily to Hong Kong audiences rather than Cantonese or Chinese audiences. This isn't to suggest that all Chinese content or references were emptied out of the films but rather to point toward the establishment of a film style that was grounded in a locality that was intersected by regional, national and global forces. The emergence of a young, locally born audience as well as the arrival of a "new wave" generation of filmmakers meant that Chineseness and Cantoneseness were no longer privileged points of reference. And perhaps somewhat unexpectedly, instead of becoming a more insular and localized cinema, Hong Kong films proved to be fascinating to audiences in overseas Chinese communities, which had also experienced a slowing of new migration and the emergence of hybrid identities. These audiences, like their counterparts in Hong Kong, were younger and had grown up in diasporic communities, confronting new and complex identity issues that could no longer be salved by traditional Chinese melodramas or opera films. Fueled by success, Hong Kong cinema developed a distinctive style and content. Picking up on trends that began in the 1960s, film locations became more modern and more opulent, narrative more playful and irreverent, and visual style more fluid and more cinematic. Emerging from the plural influences at work in the territory, Hong Kong cinema proved popular at home, overseas, and, during the 1980s, on the mainland where audiences were undergoing the shift from Mao's Cultural Revolution to Deng's Four Modernizations (H. M. Chan, 1997; Gold, 1993).

During the 1980s and into the early 1990s, the Hong Kong film industry became incredibly prolific, producing movies in a wide variety of genres, some aimed at very local audiences and others targeted for regional or global release. But what it failed to produce during that period were films that cast mainlanders in sympathetic lead roles. Some films that were set outside of Hong Kong featured sympathetically portrayed Chinese roles, but mainland characters within the local context were invariably presented as villains, layabouts or comic foils. Thus the distinctions at work in early Hong Kong television carried over to cinema, even despite the fact that the fortunes of the colony changed dramatically in 1984 with the drafting of an agreement between leaders in Beijing and London to restore Chinese sovereignty over the territory. Even during the run-up to 1997, filmmakers did not see their audiences as ready for dramas that would sympathetically portray mainland characters in leading roles. This is not to say that during the 13 years leading up to the handover, Hong Kong films failed to seek any sort of accommodation with the inevitable transition. In fact, exploring Chinese cultural and historical legacies was a major function of cinema during this period, as if discovering a shared heritage might help to make a shared political system more tolerable (Sek, 1997). Some critics even refer to a process of "resinicization" and have shown how specific media institutions in the territory explicitly pursued a production policy that would promote Hong Kong's reintegration with China (Chan & Lee, 1991; Curtin, 1998; Ma, 1999). Despite such trends, however, the figure of the mainlander was still held at arm's length within the context of film narrative. Even movies like *Biu Je, Nei Ho Ye!* (literally, "Cousin, You're Great Stuff!" English title, *Her Fatal Ways* parts I to IV, 1990 to 1994), which arguably featured a fond and amusing portrayal of the lead mainland character, nevertheless sustained an emotional distance by making her the comic foil of each episode. Truly sympathetic mainlanders did not appear in lead dramatic roles.

It is therefore significant that *Tim Mat Mat*, released on the eve of the handover, featured two mainlanders as lead characters in a melodrama about their migration to Hong Kong. Interestingly, the director of the film, Peter H. S. Chan, had no particular nostalgia for China and little direct experience of the mainland, other than two very short business trips. He furthermore sees Hong Kong's immigrant culture as that of his parents' generation, one for which he has a playful curiosity, but no deep attachment.[8] In his early 30s on the eve of the handover, Chan is part of a Hong

Kong generation that finds itself uneasy with representations of nationalism and even representations of cultural China. He describes himself as having more in common with people his age from New York, London and Bangkok than with mainland Chinese. Indeed, Chan suggests that the film is as much about the migration from rural to urban life (a universal theme) as it is about issues of Chinese identity. And yet he wanted to make a film that explored the connections between Hong Kong and the mainland, and just as importantly, he wanted to make a film that might be marketable in China, which is perhaps one of the most important future markets for Hong Kong filmmakers (P.H.S. Chan, 1997; *Report*, 1997). Thus the impending handover marked a complicated moment for Chan. Coming off the success of an enormously popular comedy, *He's a Woman, She's a Man*, and pressed to do a sequel by his distributor, Golden Harvest, Chan agreed to do so as long as Golden Harvest would finance another, more personal film project of dubious commercial value (Chan, 1997). The results proved otherwise. *Tim Mat Mat* was a significant box office success in Hong Kong and internationally, doing especially well in overseas Chinese communities in Southeast Asia and the West. Applauded by critics and members of the film community, *Tim Mat Mat* virtually swept the Hong Kong Film Awards in the spring of 1997, winning an unprecedented number of awards in nine major categories, including Best Film, Best Director, Best Actress and Best Supporting Actor. It also won top recognition for screenplay, cinematography, art direction and film score (Chung, 1997). Box office and critical response seemed to suggest that the film was emblematic of public sentiment at the time of the handover, especially since it dwelled on relationships between Hong Kongers and mainlanders.

Tim Mat Mat provides a narrative interrogation of the boundaries of identity, but in doing so, the film confronts enormously complicated issues, given the history of political and cultural relationships between the two groups. For example, how might one evoke a sense of connection between Hong Kongers and mainland Chinese without conjuring up the ghost of nationalism? Without suggesting a relationship of dominance or privilege? Without lapsing into a dangerous nostalgia? Significantly, Chan produces an innovative tale of migration within the framework of a stylistically hyperconventional romance. Featuring three of Hong Kong's most popular entertainment stars, the film comforts audiences at the same time that it significantly disrupts conventional boundaries of ethnicity and difference. The complexity of the film emerges from the ways in which it weaves a tale out of the popular history and mythology of Hong Kong identity. As such, it is open to a variety of interpretations and no doubt that was part of its appeal to audiences. What follows, however, is one potential reading of the film that suggests the ways in which the director tries to appeal to mainland audiences as well as established audiences in Hong Kong and overseas. In so doing, the narrative plays out the problems migration and identity in ways that depart from earlier practices that prevailed in Hong Kong cinema.

SWEET COMRADES

The story begins on March 1, 1986, as a train from the Chinese border pulls into the Kowloon station in downtown Hong Kong. Li Xiao-jun (played by the Cantopop singer, Leon Lai), asleep on the train, is rousted by a comrade and wearily gathers up his bundles and heads for his Aunt Rosie's house, which turns out to be a brothel. He is gruffly turned away by two young women who can't make sense of his Mandarin speech or his "mainlander" attire. Like hundreds of thousands before him, he is stigmatized as the crude outsider but is ultimately rescued by his elderly Aunt, who sets him up with a job in "the transportation business," riding a bicycle about the streets of Tsimsatsui, a district of Kowloon, delivering chickens from a butcher shop to restaurants. Making H.K.\$2,000 a month (U.S.\$260), he reflects upon the fact that he now earns more than the mayor of his hometown, Tiensin. He dreams of bringing his girlfriend to Hong Kong and writes letters to her describing his often difficult adjustment to the city. But mixed with his reservations is a wide-eyed sense of wonder that is perhaps best conveyed by his momentous decision to visit a place where "Wusih people have never been."

Cued up in a long line at McDonald's, Li Xiao-jun can barely contain his excitement as he reaches the counter where he once again painfully runs up against his linguistic and cultural difference. Unable to speak Cantonese or English, and awkwardly out of place, he becomes the mark for Li Chiao (played by Maggie Cheung, one of Hong Kong's leading dramatic actresses), a counter clerk at McDonald's who moonlights as a recruiter for an English language school, receiving commissions for each student that she enrolls. She convinces him to join a class where the instructor (played by renowned cinematographer Christopher Doyle) provides rather unorthodox English lessons that draw upon bawdy sequences from old Hollywood westerns as models of informal dialogue. Nevertheless, the school becomes Li Xiao-jun's entry into Hong Kong society and Li Chiao becomes his reluctant mentor.

Li Chiao's reluctance stems not only from Li Xiao-jun's geeky behavior but also from Li Chiao's singleminded fixation on building her bank account. She works three jobs, wears a pager and visits her ATM machine regularly for the pure pleasure of checking the balance in her savings account. Shot from the perspective of the machine, these visits convey an almost erotic relationship that seems to displace all other forms of interpersonal connection. Indeed, as we watch Chiao insert her card, we notice Xiao-jun hovering behind her, peeking over her shoulder. At turns, Chiao

Li Xiao-jun peers over Li Chiao's shoulder as she looks at an ATM screen, admiring the growing balance in her savings account.

seems either completely oblivious as to his presence, or she seems irritated by his intrusion upon this moment of private pleasure.

Ackbar Abbas (1997) suggests that such imagery conveys a kind of reverse hallucination in Hong Kong culture and society. Given that Hong Kong developed as a colonial society whereby political expression was significantly circumscribed and given that the same condition will persist under Chinese rule, Abbas observes that many Hong Kongers have channeled their enthusiasms toward economic activities and consumerism, leading to a worldview that is often distorted by reverse hallucination. Writes Abbas, "If hallucination means seeing ghosts and apparitions, that is, something that is not there, reverse hallucination means *not* seeing what *is* there" (p. 6). Such distortions seem to be at work in *Tim Mat Mat*, since Li Chiao shows more interest in Li Xiao-jun as an exploitable business partner than as a lover, a friend, a comrade, or even a fellow citizen. She fails to see the friendship that is there because she is focused on a dream of material well being. She suffers from the kind of emotional inertia that often characterizes immigrants who are so bent on success and assimilation that they have little time to reflect on what either of those things might mean.

As time passes, however, Chiao and Xiao-jun grow to become close friends. Exhausted by their labor and by their efforts to assimilate, they form a personal bond that grows more intense as they begin to confront a series of reversals of fortune. On Chinese New Year's Eve of 1987, the two set up an outdoor market stall to sell audio tapes by Teresa Teng, a Tai-wanese vocalist who, during her early career, spent time in Japan where she perfected a singing style based on traditional Chinese ballad and con-temporary pop music. Her career then took off after she signed with a Hong Kong music company that promoted her work to Chinese audiences around the world. Not only did Teng become a favorite of Hong Kongers and diasporic Chinese, but, with the loosening of social constraints in post-Mao China, she also became a favorite of mainland audiences who were wrestling with the transition from the Cultural Revolution to the Four Modernizations. Although frowned upon by government authorities, the Taiwanese singer's recordings were widely copied and distributed through-out the mainland, leading to a popular maxim that even if big Deng (Xiao-ping) rules China by day, little Teng rules by night.[9] Indeed, she became the first truly global Chinese star of the post-Mao era.

Yet the irony is that Teng's music became a boundary marker in the eyes of some Hong Kongers. When she first emerged as a singing star, Teng and other Mandarin-language (Mandopop) singers were very popular in the colony, especially on television variety shows, such as *Enjoy Yourself To-night*. But the tastes of Hong Kong audiences shifted dramatically during the cultural awakening of the 1970s and, as the territory developed its own Cantopop artists, Teng's music began to seem out of place, not only lin-guistically but stylistically. Its lilting tones and leisurely tempo, as well as its connection to traditional Chinese ballad made it seem less cosmopolitan than the upbeat rhythms and contemporary lyrics of singers like Sam Hui, Alan Tam, Anita Mui and Sally Yeh. Some disdained Teng's music as suit-ing the tastes of Mainlanders and Taiwanese, while failing to connect with the changing lifestyles of "authentic" Hong Kongers. Denizens of the city, especially the younger generations who had been born there, were actively trying to distinguish themselves from other Chinese in matters of language and taste. Teng's music served as one such marker of distinction. For oth-ers, however, Teng's music continued to represent a sense of connection to a larger Chinese cultural context.

As they set up their market stall in 1987, Xiao-jun warns Chiao that they should not be too optimistic about their business venture, as his aunt had told him only mainlanders enjoy Teresa Teng's music. Li Chiao retorts that the newspapers say 20 percent of the Hong Kong population is main-lander. "They are all over. They are just not recognizable, unlike you," she says in pointed reference to his immigrant mannerisms. Indeed, the pros-pects for success are even greater, she confides, since, "Between you and me, 50 percent is mainlander. Comrade Li Xiao-jun, we're gonna make a lot of money." Yet despite the fact that immigration statistics are in their favor, their commercial venture proves disastrous. Throughout the night, the two entrepreneurs fruitlessly attempt to hawk the cassettes, shouting out the virtues of Teng's music to a passing crowd that seems completely indifferent.

Later, as they console each other, Li Chiao recalls that last year in Guangzhou her cousin sold 4,000 cassettes with little effort at all. Li Xiao-jun replies that Hong Kong people are different. His aunt cautioned him that even passionate Teresa fans wouldn't buy cassettes in front of the busy crowds on New Year's Eve because then everyone would think they were mainlanders. Given their desire to be recognized as locals, potential customers would not want to risk a public declaration of musical taste that might betray their social origins.[10]

Indeed, it turns out that Li Chiao's business judgment betrays her origins as well. The comparison she makes between 1986 and 1987 reveals for the first time that she was in Guangzhou only last year to witness her cousin's success selling Teng cassettes. Recognizing that Guangzhou is 100 miles inland from Hong Kong, Xiao-jun surmises that, like him, Chiao is also a recent immigrant from China. "I knew it!" he exalts. "We're comrades!"

"No way!" she replies with a wounded look of embarrassment and then defiance. "We [Guangzhou Chinese] speak Cantonese. We get Hong Kong TV. We are so much closer to Hong Kong."

Sensing the fragility of Chiao's claim to a Hong Kong identity, a claim that would be significantly compromised by lumping her into a category that would include an awkward northerner like himself, Xiao-jun attempts to console her. "You're right," he says tenderly. "Your look, your gesture, your face, your hair are so Hong Kong."

This dialogue sequence marks a significant turn in the narrative, for the two characters now begin to move beyond public posturing. The acquisitive inertia that had dominated Chiao's worldview begins to slacken and the reverse hallucination that had kept them from seeing what is there begins to dissipate. They lay aside reductive categories of identity and, from this point onward, they are no longer comrades nor are they immigrants who position each other within the hierarchies of assimilation. Xiao-jun is no longer a Mandarin-speaking northerner and Li Chiao is no longer a Cantonese-speaking southerner. They become lovers who care less about the politics of identity or geography than they do about the quotidian struggles that make their experiences emblematic of the lives of millions of other migrants who came before them.

Darrell Davis (1998) contends that the two characters are living a mythology of immigration: "It's a script profoundly recognizable by any Irish, Italian, or Jewish—or Vietnamese refugee. It is composed of universal emotions that accompany odyssey and migration: yearning for a better life (or escape from a bad one), anticipation, arrival, hardship, vulnerability, ghettohood, assimilation, disappointment, discrimination, surprise, and (maybe) fulfillment" (p. 59). Yet unlike most other movie scripts, *Comrades* does not advance a conventional tale of ethnic struggle, family solidarity, or mainstream assimilation. It is not a story of "us against them." The characters are not defiantly proud mainlanders who seek to perpetuate their way of life, nor are they enthusiastic immigrants who develop a passionate attachment to Hong Kong. Assimilation is for them a matter of convenience, a necessary prerequisite to success. Moreover, assimilation and success in Hong Kong are presented as peculiarly indeterminate, unstable and fleeting. Consequently, the characters are pressed to develop a cosmopolitan consciousness in response to their encounter with diaspora and their relationship becomes emblematic of a move beyond conventional identities, politics and family attachments.

As the couple grows closer, their connection to relatives at home seems more remote. Instead, it is their enthusiasm, their good fortune and their romantic relationship that sustain them until, tragically, the Hong Kong economy experiences a dramatic downturn in 1987 that virtually wipes out Li Chiao's savings. She is forced to go to work at a massage parlor where she apparently abstains from providing supplementary services to a few wealthy patrons and therefore must compensate by providing basic services to a large clientele. Exhausted from work—her hands aching from the arduous and relentless labor—she finds consolation in the kindness of her companion. But one night while they are out for a walk, they stop in a jewelry store where Xiao-jun buys a bracelet for his girlfriend at home and an identical one for Chiao. She is stunned when she reflects on the meaning of the gesture.

As they leave the shop and walk slowly along the crowded street, her epiphany unfolds as she realizes that her relationship with Xiao-jun is more a convenience than a commitment. A handheld camera frames the couple tightly as crowds swirl about them. In a single, unedited shot that lasts more than three minutes, the camera records their dialogue while they walk along the street, their faces periodically illuminated by the lights of shop windows and neon signs. The effect is more documentary than melodramatic, as the two comrades move through pools of light and shadow. "I don't know where I'm going and I don't know what I'm doing," says Li Chiao. "A few days ago I called mom and told her I was going to hit the jackpot in the stock market, but now I'm penniless and deep in debt. What have I done? I don't know what will happen tomorrow. I'm scared. What would you think if your girlfriend slept with someone?"

If the first part of the film was governed by the affective inertia of material aspiration and the second part was structured by the affective inertia of romantic love, then this is the moment when the narrative momentum is abruptly interrupted and Li Chiao begins to see her situation in a new light. "Comrade Xiao-jun," she concludes, "I am not what brought you to Hong Kong and you are not what brought me to Hong Kong." With the exhaustion of her fortune, her body and now her love affair, Chiao panics at her loss of orientation. The garish blend of street lights and the hustling crowds now suggest a frightening reversal. The brassy universe of neon promotions that once seemed to promise opportunity and choice, now seem to harshly contrast with her desperate, lonely circumstances. She tells Xiao-jun it is time to acknowledge their differences. Whereupon she dashes away, leaving him standing alone and bewildered at the intersection of a busy street. The extended shot that framed the dialogue sequence is then edited to a slow-motion point-of-view shot, as the audience, like Xiao-jun, watches Chiao disappear into the bustle of the evening crowd. This abrupt shift from a *cinema verité* documentary style to melodramatic slow motion seems necessary in order to contemplate the meaning and fragility of relationships in a city such as Hong Kong. By step-printing the filmed recording of Chiao's flight, the moment is extended. Her disappearance into the crowd—which in on a Hong Kong street can happen in the blink of an eye—is preserved in the memory of a brooding Xiao-jun, who chooses not to pursue her but instead to follow his original dream to save enough money to bring his fiancée to Hong Kong.

After they part, Chiao becomes romantically involved with one of her massage clients, Pao (played by Eric Tsang Chi-wai), a gangster who is ruthless in his professional life, but exceptionally kind and tender with her. Subsequently, Chiao's fortunes begin to change and she becomes a successful businesswoman in the fashion and real estate industries. In the meantime, Li Xiao-jun finally brings his fiancée to Hong Kong and arranges a wedding ceremony. Both lead characters have seemingly realized their dreams, and Chiao attends Xiao-jun's wedding accompanied by her new partner, Pao. But even across the boundaries of their respective relationships, Chiao and Xiao-jun recognize the powerful and unresolved nature of their attraction. They secretly renew their affair and resolve to tell their spouses about their need to be together. But fate intervenes when the police close in on Pao, and Chiao decides that she must support her partner in his time of need. She joins him as he flees Hong Kong and goes into hiding. Xiao-jun of course is heartbroken, but decides nevertheless that he must divulge his true feelings to his wife. The original dream that brought him to Hong Kong no longer governs his emotions and behaviors. The couple divorces and he migrates to New York City, where he takes a job in the "transportation business" delivering meals for a restaurant run by a friend of his from Hong Kong.

At this point the narrative develops along parallel tracks, for it turns out that Li Chiao and Pao also end up in New York, planning to finally settle down, start a family and buy a house. But fate once again intervenes, as Pao is killed by a street gang and Chiao finds herself alone. She renews her struggle for material success and security. Working long hours, she strives to establish herself in her new home, ultimately securing a green card that gives her legitimate immigrant status in the United States. Yet her success only resurrects her need to connect with her past. She buys a plane ticket

Li Chiao and Li Xiao-jun, finally reunited in front of an electronics store in New York City.

to return home to China and, as she leaves the travel agency, she hears the news on television that Teresa Teng died tragically of an asthma attack at the age of 42. The date is May 8, 1995, 9 years after Chiao first crossed the border, leaving China behind. The disheartening news of Teng's death conjures up affective ties to her past. In a state of distraction, Chiao wanders through the streets of Manhattan as the news reports play on the soundtrack accompanied by the Teresa Teng song "The Moon Speaks for My Heart."

Although director Peter Chan contends that the figure of Teresa Teng is little more than a plot device that ties the two lead characters together (P.H.S. Chan, 1997), this closing sequence goes to some lengths to elevate Teng's significance above the level of romantic narrative. The news reports detail the singer's career and her tragic demise at her home in Thailand, where she lived in retirement. We are told that her initial popularity in Taiwan spread to audiences around the world and finally, in the mid-1970s, to mainland China. "In big cities or small villages, people could hear her songs anytime, anywhere," according to the newscaster. "Her songs won the hearts of Chinese all over the world. People said, anywhere there are Chinese, you can hear Teresa's songs." Indeed, just as her music seemed to bring Chinese people together, this final song unexpectedly reunites the two main characters of the film as they mournfully gaze at a television news report in the shop window of an electronics store.

Teng's music is also featured prominently in other parts of the film, including the title, *Tim Mat Mat* (*Tian Mi Mi* in Mandarin), which is drawn from one of Teng's most popular songs. In a review of the film, Davis (1998) contends that the lyrics to the song have little meaning, but "because of its simple melody and its plaintive, throaty rendition by Teng, [the song] carries a painful, inarticulate sweetness" that appeals to audiences around the world. "Those who recognize her voice are the new China," says Davis, "united not by ideology but by sentiment. Coming from Taiwan, itself an orphan island, Teng was a wanderer all over Asia, winning over Japanese, Hong Kong, Southeast Asian and especially mainland Chinese audiences. This sentimental Chinese identity is or depends on a condition of exile bound by fellow feeling, nostalgia, and homesickness. . . . Teng's music addresses them in their separation, and touches all but the youngest" (p. 60). Nevertheless, this community is not one that can be exploited by political regimes that pretend to represent all Chinese people. Indeed, many of Teng's most avid fans fled just such regimes. Davis suggests instead that "Teng's appeal hints at a decentralization of China, loosening it from a specific physical homeland" (p. 60) and, one might argue, loosening Chinese ethnicity from the grip of Nationalist or Communist regimes. For the very antipathies that have animated political and social differences among Chinese throughout this century are now in a state of dramatic flux. The transnational popularity of *Tian Mi Mi*—both the song and the film—encourage us to reflect on this moment of transition.

CONCLUSION

Perhaps the lyrics to "Tian Mi Mi" are practically meaningless or only based on sentiment, and perhaps the same could be said of Peter Chan's hyperconventional romantic melodrama, but one might nevertheless contend that such commercial artifacts evoke powerful affective responses outside the official arenas of Chinese national identity. The manifest content of these artifacts is apparently apolitical, but the increasing transnational flow of such imagery seems to anticipate major social, economic and political shifts. Teng's far-flung success was unanticipated, but more recently, one can see a younger generation of pop music stars whose careers are increasingly predicated on these new patterns of circulation. For example, even at the height of recent tensions between the mainland and Taiwan governments, Beijing's Faye Wong was enjoying top status on the music charts in Taiwan at the very moment when Taiwan's Zhang Hui-mei was performing for sell-out crowds in Beijing. Political conflict regarding issues of national sovereignty seemed to have little impact on audience responses or media industry practices. Moreover, the broad reach of singers like Wong and Zhang has been noted by Cantopop singing stars who are now releasing Mandarin-language albums in addition to their Cantonese CDs.

Music company executives are making very calculated attempts to bring into being a Chinese media market that pulls together mainland, Taiwanese and overseas Chinese audiences. Obviously, the styles and themes of the music are quite diverse, but the key to these singers' success seems to be a mixing of global, national, regional and local influences. In a prior era, Teresa Teng's distinctive contribution was to combine Western, Japanese and Chinese formulas to produce a musical style that embraced rather than subverted conventional forms. In a sense, her music could be considered a hyperconventional hybrid style that became the vehicle for expressing shared sentiments of longing, loss and migration.

A similar thing might be said about Peter Chan's film, which taps the conventions of Hollywood romance and documentary realism while adding the irreverent stylistic flourishes of Hong Kong cinema in order to tell a story with broad sentimental appeal.

Yet Peter Chan reaches even farther than that. The conventional stylistic qualities of the film allow him to focus his attention on themes of longing and displacement that move beyond reductive categories of Hong Konger/ mainlander, East/West, as well as the myriad status distinctions that exist within and between Chinese communities. The film is not about the struggle for survival among a particular family or clan. Nor is it an emblematic struggle of Chinese people against the West. It is, instead, a broadly accessible allegory about the ongoing endeavor to negotiate complex and phantasmagoric forces in a rapidly changing world. Buffeted by transnational migration, black markets, marginal labor economies, property speculation and global capital flows, these characters hold fiercely to their personal ambitions as their only points of orientation. Although the film bows to the conventions of melodrama by allowing fate to take its course in reuniting the couple, the narrative nevertheless resists the temptation to resolve the plot complications within the context of a national or local identity.

Instead, *Tim Mat Mat* closes with long, lingering point-of-view shots as the two characters gaze at each other in front of an electronics shop window in New York City. At this final moment of epiphany, Chiao and Xiao-jun seem to realize that their dreams were not what they originally believed them to be. Their aspirations for success in Hong Kong and their nostalgic longing for home imposed boundaries that made it difficult for them to appreciate their interpersonal proximity. Yet over the course of the film, boundaries disappear, as do binarisms. The mainlander becomes a Hong Konger and then something else that is not attached to a particular place, but to a certain attitude about the world and about relationships. This suggests something different from a localized or resinicized perspective. Fulfillment in this context is not conditioned by geography, status or politics. Fulfillment is perhaps the ability to penetrate those reverse hallucinations that had originally driven Chiao and Xiao-jun apart. It is only when the two characters shed their attachment to Chinese and Hong Kong identities, as well as the dreams that go with them, that they are able to discover the interpersonal rewards of an everyday world that is constantly shifting under their feet.

If we recall the rough historical periodization that was advanced earlier, we might generalize by saying that early Cantonese cinema was motivated by the need to sustain regional cultural affinities among a diasporic population and that Hong Kong cinema of the 1970s and 1980s was animated by a need to establish a hybrid local identity. This was followed by a period in which many filmmakers searched for some reconciliation with the culture and politics of China in anticipation of 1997. More recently, however, directors like Peter Chan seem to be working through the problematic of shifting boundaries and identities from a different perspective. Policing or refashioning the distinctions between Hong Konger and mainlander seems less urgent to Chan. He has no nostalgia for China and expresses no particular attachment to a Hong Kong identity (P.H.S. Chan, 1997). Indeed, he is a filmmaker who is in the process of globalizing his career by working both in Hong Kong and Hollywood, where he produces films that might be best described as pitched at a young, urban demographic that is alert to local cultural trends and fashions but is also transnational in outlook.[11]

Ackbar Abbas has written about Hong Kong directors who, like Chan, seem to be reaching beyond "the available binarisms [that] tend to confuse more than they clarify questions of identity. To take one example," observes Abbas,

Hong Kong culture cannot simply mean focusing on Hong Kong as a subject, laudable as that may be, in an attempt to fathom the mysteries of its identity. What is both culturally and politically more important is the development of a new Hong Kong subjectivity, that is, a subjectivity constructed not narcissistically but in the very process of negotiating the mutations and permutations of colonialism, nationalism, and capitalism . . . It is, I am trying to suggest, a subjectivity that is coaxed into being by the disappearance of old cultural bearings and orientations, which is to say that it is a subjectivity that develops precisely out of a space of disappearance. (Abbas, 1997, p. 11)

Using the concept of disappearance, Abbas analyzes the work of directors such as Wong Kar-wai and Stanley Kwan, whose films problematize the visual image and destabilize conventional narrative patterns in search of a new subjectivity. What is interesting about Chan's film is that he explores a similar terrain not through formal innovation, but through a hyperconventional portrayal of the dilemmas of postcolonial subjectivity. Although he is clearly a more commercially motivated film maker than Wong or Kwan, Chan nevertheless aspires to escape conventional identity categories; an aspiration that apparently is shared by some Chinese audiences, as well as audiences in Korea and Japan, where the film has enjoyed notable success. If there is a sentiment that links these audiences, it grows out of a shared experience of extremely rapid change that cannot be explained by the integrative narratives of Chinese civilization and ethnicity nor can it be explained by local narratives of uniqueness. If Chan's film comes up short, it is because the conventions of the romantic melodrama can only allow him to gesture at the history of the momentous decade in which the film is set. The narrative suggests that identities are historically contingent and unstable, but it makes only a limited effort to explore the social forces that produce, sustain and transform categories like Chinese, Hong Konger, comrade and migrant. The characters struggle to survive in an environment shaped by a globalizing economy, a postcolonial transition and a national policy of modernization. Yet the film makes only oblique reference to how such forces set boundaries on personal mobility and imagination.

Currently, the Hong Kong film industry is experiencing a severe downturn that is attributable to a variety of forces, among them piracy, changing modes of distribution, oligopolistic practices and competition from Hollywood. Of course, this is not the first time that it has hit a serious slump, and many believe that the industry will eventually turn the corner and be restored to its prior well-being. But what will be the factors that bring it back to life? Some say the industry is waiting for Chinese officials to eliminate restrictions on the distribution of Hong Kong films to the mainland, opening new and potentially lucrative markets. Others say that piracy and distribution problems throughout Asia must be resolved before any improvements can be made. Perhaps just as importantly, however, Chan's film seems to suggest that revival may be dependent on new narrative strategies for addressing a widespread Chinese audience. On the one hand, this can be accomplished by resinicizing film narratives so that they dwell upon historical and cultural legacies shared by audiences throughout East Asia. Film and television costume dramas like *Once Upon a Time in China* and *Justice Bao* seem to pursue this strategy quite successfully. On the other hand, the industry also seems to be experimenting with contemporary narratives that acknowledge shared cultural and historical experiences but which nevertheless avoid reductive categories of identity. Such films tap shared sentiments and explore shared dilemmas without promoting a particular brand of identity politics or nationalism. They depend not on traditional ethnicities or identities but instead search for new affinities and new possibilities.

One can certainly detect this trend in the films of directors like Wong Kar-wai and Stanley Kwan, but this tendency can also be discerned in Jackie Chan's ongoing attempts to fashion films with transnational appeal that nevertheless spring from the martial arts tradition of Chinese cinema (Fore, 2001). Similarly, one can detect it in the many recent attempts to attract the attention of an increasingly interconnected East Asian youth culture whose affinity depends not on a shared national identity but upon a shared experience with cultural products that circulate among young people in cities like Tokyo, Hong Kong, Shanghai and Seoul. Several recent films have specifically targeted this audience. For example, *Storm Riders*, one of the most commercially successful films of recent years, brought Hollywood high-tech special effects to bear on a science fiction narrative derived from Japanese manga and headlined by some of Hong Kong's most popular young film stars. Likewise, *Tempting Heart* shrewdly constructs a coming-of-age narrative from the perspective of young people experiencing first love while enduring the social pressures of growing up in Hong Kong and Japan. The success of such films points toward new possibilities that refashion audience boundaries and affinities in response to changing social, economic and political conditions. Such a response sheds prior notions of local identity while refusing nevertheless to participate in dominant national narratives of Chineseness. Should such strategies succeed, and should they become more widely emulated by filmmakers in the territory, they could mark the advent of a new period of Hong Kong cinema.

NOTES

1. See, for example, the extensive discussion of this dilemma among industry personnel at the 1997 Hong Kong film festival (*Report*, 1997).

2. The argument that follows is not intended to privilege one strategy over another or to suggest that only three patterns of response exist. Nor is it intended to diminish the significance of films that follow a more "localist" or nationalist pattern of response. See for example, Lai (1997) and Sek (1997).

3. Although multiracial, Hong Kong was neither integrated nor multicultural. It was instead a highly segregated colonialist regime.

4. Part of this can also be attributed to the fact that both the Nationalist and Communist factions were suspicious of the divisive potential of dialect cinema. The Nationalists even adopted a policy that officially embraced Mandarin-language film production to the exclusion of "dialect" films. Although never enforced, the policy encouraged many studios to relocate from Guangzhou to the British colony of Hong Kong, where they could ply their trade under the benign neglect of colonial authorities (Fonoroff, 1988; Teo, 1997).

5. These were not the first waves of immigration. Overseas Chinese settlements can be traced back several hundred years earlier, for example, the Peranankan Chinese in Indonesia. Nevertheless, overseas immigration increased dramatically in the nineteenth century.

6. Also note that Hong Kong became a center for multi-language film production—not only Cantonese but Fukienese, Hokkien and later Mandarin. Each was intended to serve particular diasporic cultural communities, such as, for example, Hokkien audiences in Singapore and Taiwan.

7. Indeed, the character is so resilient and important to Cantonese cinema that he would later be resurrected to great effect by such diverse contemporary filmmakers as Tsui Hark, Jackie Chan and Corey Yuen.

8. For example, see his earlier film, *San Naan Hing Naan Dai* (literally "Once

Upon a Mid-Autumn Festival," English title, *He Ain't Heavy, He's My Father*, 1993).

9. In Chinese characters, both Deng Xiao-ping and Teresa Teng have the same family name, adding an elegant sense of irony to this comparison.

10. As Linda Lai points out, Chan's interpretation of Teng's popularity is a narrative device and should not be mistaken for historical fact. Teng was and still remains popular with many Hong Kongers. Indeed, even today if one visits a major music store in Hong Kong, such as HMV, one will find that Teresa Teng's music is still popular, given the fact that the amount of shelf space devoted to her CDs is far larger than many other contemporary Hong Kong singers. Nevertheless, Chan's point remains that matters of taste often play a powerful role in establishing and sustaining group affinities and social boundaries. And of course these boundaries change. So although Teng's music was very popular in Hong Kong during the 1970s, it was most enthusiastically embraced by mainland audiences during the 1980s.

11. Other members of the Hong Kong film community are following a similar career trajectory, including John Woo, Stanley Tong, Jackie Chan and Chow Yun-fat. Chan is making this career move while fully aware that Hong Kong artists constitute little more than the "flavor of the month" in Hollywood, a place that is renowned for voraciously appropriating talent from around the world. Thus, Chan says he hopes to stay active in both places given the uncertainties of such trends within the entertainment industries (P.H.S. Chan, 1997).

REFERENCES

Abbas, A. (1997). *Hong Kong: Culture and the politics of disappearance*. Hong Kong: Hong Kong University Press.

Ang, I. (1994). On not speaking Chinese: Postmodern ethnicity and the politics of diaspora. *New Formations*, 24, 1–18.

Chan, H. M. (1997). The labyrinth of hybridization: The cultural internationalization of Hong Kong. In G. A. Postiglione & J.T.H. Tang (Eds.), *Hong Kong's reunion with China: The global dimensions* (pp. 169–199). Armonk, NY: M. E. Sharpe.

Chan, J. M. (1992). Mass media and socio-political formation in Hong Kong, 1949–1992. *Asian Journal of Communication*, 2(3), 106–129.

Chan, J. M., & Lee, C. C. (1991). *Mass media and political transition*. New York: Guilford Press.

Chan, K. C., & Choi, P. K. (1989). Communications and the media. In T. L. Tsim & B.H.K. Luk, *The other Hong Kong report* (pp. 293–316). Hong Kong: The Chinese University of Hong Kong Press.

Chan, P.H.S. (1997). *Personal interview*, April 11.

Choi, P. K. (1990). From dependence to self-sufficiency: Rise of the indigenous culture of Hong Kong, 1945–1989. *Asian Culture*, 14, 161–176.

Chun, A. (1996a). Discourses of identity in the changing spaces of public culture in Taiwan, Hong Kong and Singapore. *Theory, Culture & Society*, 13(1), 51–75.

Chun, A. (1996b). Fuck Chineseness: On the ambiguities of ethnicity as culture as identity. *Boundary* 23(2), 111–138.

Chung, W. (1997, April 14). "Comrades" among friends at awards. *South China Morning Post*, 1.

Curtin, M. (1998). Images of trust, economies of suspicion: Hong Kong media after 1997. *Historical Journal of Film, Radio and Television*, 18(2), 281–294.

Curtin, M. (1999). Industry on fire: The cultural economy of Hong Kong media. *Postscript*, 15(4), 20–43.

Davis, D. W. (1998). Comrades: People on the make. In *Cinedossier: The 34th Golden Horse Award-Winning Films* (pp. 56–61). Taipei: 1998 Taipei Golden Horse Film Festival.

Fonoroff, P. (1988). A brief history of Hong Kong cinema. *Renditions*, 29/30, 293–308.

Fore, S. (2001). Life imitates entertainment: Home and dislocation in the films of Jackie Chan. In E.C.M. Yau (Ed.), *At full speed: Hong Kong cinema in a borderless world* (pp. 115–142). Minneapolis: University of Minnesota Press.

Fu, P. S. (1997). The turbulent Sixties: Modernity, youth culture, and Cantonese film in Hong Kong. In Law Kar (Ed.), *Fifty years of electric shadows: Hong Kong cinema in retrospective* (pp. 34–46). Hong Kong: Hong Kong Urban Council.

Gold, T. B. (1993). Go with your feelings: Hong Kong and Taiwan popular culture in greater China. *The China Quarterly*, 136, 907–925.

Kung, J., & Zhang, Y. (1984). Hong Kong cinema and television in the 1970s: A perspective. In C. T. Li (Ed.), *A study of Hong Kong cinema in the Seventies* (pp. 14–22). Hong Kong: Hong Kong Urban Council.

Lai, L.C.H. (1997). Nostalgia and nonsense: Two instances of commemorative practices in Hong Kong cinema in the early 1990s. In Law Kar (Ed.), *Fifty years of electric shadows: Hong Kong cinema in retrospective* (pp. 90–99). Hong Kong: Hong Kong Urban Council.

Lau, J.K.W. (1998). Besides fists and blood: Hong Kong comedy and its master of the Eighties. *Cinema Journal*, 37(2), 18–34.

Law Kar. (1984). Michael Hui: A decade of sword grinding. In C. T. Li (Ed.), *A study of Hong Kong cinema in the Seventies* (pp. 65–70). Hong Kong: Hong Kong Urban Council.

Law Kar. (Ed.) (1995). *Early images of Hong Kong and China*. Hong Kong: Hong Kong Urban Council.

Lee, P.S.N. (1991). The absorption and indigenization of foreign media cultures: A study on a cultural meeting point of the East and West: Hong Kong. *Asian Journal of Communication*, 1(2), 52–72.

Leung, G., & Chan, J. (1997). The Hong Kong cinema and its overseas market: A historical review, 1950–1995. In Law Kar (Ed.), *Fifty years of electric shadows: Hong Kong cinema in retrospective* (pp. 136–151). Hong Kong: Hong Kong Urban Council.

Lo, T., & Ng, C. B. (1996). The evolution of prime-time scheduling in Hong Kong. In D. French & M. Richards (Eds.), *Contemporary television: Eastern perspectives* (pp. 200–220). New Delhi: Sage.

Ma, E.K.W. (1999). *Culture, politics, and television in Hong Kong*. London: Routledge.

Ramsey, S. R. (1987). *The languages of China*. Princeton, NJ: Princeton University Press.

Report of Conference on Hong Kong Cinema. (1997). Hong Kong: Hong Kong Urban Council.

Rodriguez, H. (1997). Hong Kong popular culture as an interpretive arena: The Huang Feihong film series. *Screen*, 38(1), 1–24.

Sage, S. (1992). *Ancient Sichuan and the unification of China*. Albany: State University of New York Press.

Seagrave, S. (1995). *Lords of the rim*. London: Bantam Press.

Sek, K. (1997). Hong Kong cinema from June 4 to 1997. In Law Kar (Ed.), *Fifty years of electric shadows: Hong Kong cinema in retrospective* (pp. 114–125). Hong Kong: Hong Kong Urban Council.

Siu, H. F. (1993). Cultural identity and the politics of difference in south China. *Daedalus*, 122(2), 19–42.

Teo, S. (1997). *Hong Kong cinema: The extra dimension*. London: BFI Publishing.

Tu, W. M. (Ed.) (1994). *The living tree: The changing meaning of being Chinese today*. Stanford, CA: Stanford University Press.

Part V

Getting Personal

Chapter 16

Globalization and Me: Thinking at the Boundary

Annabelle Sreberny

INTRODUCTION

I have received great pleasure in the reaction that is evoked when telling people the title of this chapter: Almost without fail, people have laughed. And that's also made me stop and wonder: Is this just an impossible joke, a mad attempt to juggle the impossible—the huge earth-encompassing notion of globalization and the tiny little dot that is me? I remain intrigued by the encounter between the terms for a number of reasons.

1. It cuts through many other intermediate levels of possible connectivity/ identification such as the "national" or the "local," even the "group/community," which are continually evoked in discussions about globalization. Frequently, it appears as if the visual imaginary of such "levels" is of ever larger concentric circles emanating out from a "me" in the middle. But this is a simplistic and static image since we increasingly can, and do, interact with different peoples-at-a-distance in a variety of ways, through travel, person-to-person communication, mediated communication, in ways that cut across distance. I want to ask directly how am "I" affected by globalization, and conversely what does my life have to do with globalization? I want to see if it is possible to explore unmediated the relation between these two concepts, or levels of analysis, and what is gained by doing so.

2. The literature on globalization is an abstract, masculist and public discourse, and thus we are invited to think of the processes of globalization in the same way. A more immediate, personal, experiential, supposedly feminized voice might try to anchor abstract processes in particular lives, exploring both at the same time. Thus perhaps we can cut across, or through, the absurd space and bipolar division of the macro-analytic and

294   *Getting Personal*

the micro-experiential. Perhaps ironically, in the slow recognition of the growth of choice and personal identity construction (albeit if only for some) in the new networked society, the almost taboo construct of the "individual" is making a surprise return, not simply as consumer or audience member, but as an active creator of his/her own life. It is a moment when different forms of narrativity—the masculist conceit of holding the entire world in a single sentence versus the feminist conceit that each individual life needs telling—need to be brought together. Theories of globalization have to "come down to earth" and become better grounded in the variegated experience of ordinary lives.

3. *Contra* Giddens (1990) who argues that "there are no others" in the sense that the peoples of the world are now reasonably transparent to each other, I want to play with another resonance in the phrase, that is, "we" are all the others' others, and explore how we process and live that. I wish to argue that since identity-construction is always a social process, the encounters with more "others" that globalization can bring about can challenge old identity structures and provoke new ones over and over again. I want to show how globalization is an old and on-going set of processes, not necessarily very contemporary nor indeed encountered only once. By focusing on comparatively recent narratives of "private lives" I also want to promote a reflexive sociology that recognizes transnational processes, that shows how the construction of identity is an on-going process, how static group categories and conceptions of ethnicity and diaspora are constantly being challenged, and how the "I" of lived experience encounters many different "thems" in the course of a life. Beck describes reflexive modernization as a process that deepens and broadens insecurities (1997, p. 38) so that "in regard to life situation, life conduct and social structure, there is a conflict of large-group categories and theories versus theories of individualization and (intensifying) social inequality" (1997, p. 38). The focus here is on the blurring of various boundary categories and the on-going reconstruction of identities, group and individual, as new global forms of structuration, global figurations, invite and produce new forms of global awareness and connectivity, Elias's (1987) abstract stretching of connectedness. Indeed, I have argued that they already do. Thus not only through some abstract logic, but also through the increasing interactions of our lives, the play between the "global and me" will become stronger.

Among the boundaries that increasingly interest me, in relationship to my academic work, are the boundaries between the intellectual and the emotional, the objectivity and the subjectivity of viewpoints. Academic writing is hubristic, ego-ruled, with little fear of autership, yet as soon as we start to write, the "I" disappears. Standpoint theory is a useful and welcome development, the importance of clarifying from where one stands to see. But much of the time, it is insufficiently personal, based on a claim to categoric belonging rather than a textured subjectivity. I want to press for a radical subjectivity that not only tries to account for why I, the articulating academic, find a certain issue of value to explore but more importantly, how my subjectivity resonates with and through the subject matter as I analyze it. The theoretical purchase of this position is of course not new. It speaks to historical debates lodged at the heart of social theory (see Pels, 2000) as well as on-going controversy as to its value. It echoes more contemporary voices within feminism that support, even desire, such acts of "getting personal," as Nancy Miller describes them (1991). It resonates with the radical voices within psychotherapy that highlight the potential significance of therapeutic counter-transference as a method of radical subjectivity to further political debate (Samuel, 1993); and with the arguments within contemporary anthropology about the processes of "writing culture" and the broad debate about reflexivity as a key element of late modernity (Beck, Giddens & Lasch, 1994). Where one used to think through transnational processes, reflexivity too often deteriorates either to a kind of anecdotal, even armchair, tourism, or to an overly politicized and binary post-colonial analysis of "here" and "there," "them" and "us." I want to try to argue that "them" and "us" continually shifts, even within the course of one human lifetime, let alone the course of anything remotely stable or coherent enough to be called a community. The boundary is always unstable, always being rewritten.

THE ISSUE OF THE BOUNDARY

The very notion of "boundary" is wonderfully provocative, playing on the edge of so many of our most profound ways of being in and thinking about the world. At the end of his essay "The Instincts and Their Vicissitudes," Freud (1915/1991) talks about "the three great polarities that dominate mental life." These are activity/passivity, which he calls the biological polarity; ego/external world, which he calls the real; and that of pleasure/unpleasure, the economic polarity. The boundary of the inside-outside is thus one of the most basic, ordinary and fundamental differentiations we make; it is ontologically primary in our self-development. And it is deeply problematic. Where is the line to be drawn? Even our supposedly self-evidently bounded physical self depends continuously on taking in air to the lungs, food into the belly (Klein, 1987). Our most intimate moments are about violations of, intrusions into, the body. Birth is a cascade out of another's body. The baby sucking hungrily on the mother's breast is at its most joyous as well as most dependent. Much sexuality and most reproduction usually still depend on the transfer of bodily fluids, of penetration. The outside needs to be taken in, trusted. Our physical boundaries, particularly those of women, are continually violated, penetrated, renegotiated.

And our psychological self is itself a social product, the outcome of these early interactions with intimate others, imbued with oedipal taboos, a superego based on the superego of our parents, and on-going socialization through schooling, community/peers and the media. The very process of achieving a bounded self, a rounded ego, is through the internalization of good objects and good others. Others are already encoded in us: this family, not that; this language, not that; this group affiliation, not that. Social categories are always already a part of us, and while they bind us to some, they also set us apart from others. The process of individuation is also a profoundly social one.

Such ambiguity around identity-formation echoes Norbert Elias, who long critiqued the notion of *homo clausus*, the notion of an isolated individual, a "we-less ego" looking out from a sealed mind trying to gain knowledge of an external world of objects. Instead Elias proffered the notion of *homine aperti*, open people, bound together in various ways and degrees. Everyone is somehow interwoven into a network of people, and the experience of this is thought about and referred to by means of pronouns and related concepts (Mennell, 1992). Elias (quoted in Mennell, 1992, p. 265) says:

One's sense of personal identity is closely connected with the "we" and "they" relationships of one's group, and with one's position within those units of which one speaks as "we" and "they". Yet the pronouns do not always refer to the same people. The figurations to which they currently refer can change in the course of a lifetime, just as any person does himself. This is true not only of all people considered separately, but also of all groups and even of all societies. Their members universally say "we" of themselves and "they" of other people, but they may say "we" and "they" of different people as time goes by.

Thus, not only is our psyche configured by and with others, but our self is lived out relationally, and not only do the patterns of relations between people change (the figurations, as Elias describes them), but also the structures of people change, not least in the nature of the boundaries of their "I," "we" and "they" (Mennell, 1992, p. 265). So, the boundary is a challenge. To reach it, even to surpass the limit, is to gain the most runs in cricket. The boundary can be constructed positively, it does good things. It contains, holds in, supports. Where there is a boundary, there might also be a center, a place of belonging.

But the boundary also limits, divides, cut us off from others. In holding in, it might constrain. It can also hold out, at bay, those who are not wanted, who are not like us. Boundaries usually need policing, surveillance and censors. They are points of contention, of exercises of power. Thus, if we go "in search of boundaries," whether conceptual, physical or legal, it is in most cases to discover that they demand to be challenged, transgressed and reconstituted, over and over and over again.

The emerging paradigm of globalization is challenging boundary-definitions, especially of a society-bound sociology and the nation-statecentric conceptual models of international communication (Sreberny, 1999). Among the two most powerful challenges to the long-accepted territorial boundedness of national, indeed our social, identities come from the transborder processes of the media and of migration (Appadurai, 1996); we might also add markets.

Again, Elias offers useful concepts with which to think through these emerging global processes. He offers an account which links micro-level and macro-level theorizing about identification processes, based on detailed empirical evidence. One of Elias's arguments is that the long-term trend in the development of human society has been toward larger and larger networks of interdependent people organized in more and more interlocking layers (Mennell, 1992, p. 178), the essence of the civilizing process. Is this not, in essence, what the emergence of crossborder networks of affiliation, the development of transnational communities, constitute? I think it's worth noting the plurality, the multiplicity of possible connections for individuals and groups that contemporary migration, travel, information technologies and political movements summon up. While the notion of a singular "global consciousness" makes sense at the level of emerging awareness, its enactment seems to take multiple forms. Globalization does not mean a singular universalism, one all inclusive formation, but rather the emergence of many transnational, interwoven and overlapping, economic, social and political formations.

Of course this has profound effects on who we think we are. Group commonality, "culture" in the anthropological sense, or more precisely, "habitus," is based on the modes of conduct, taste and feeling which predominate among members of particular groups. Identity is then the conscious awareness by members of a group and implies some degree of reflection, articulation, emotional connection, the sharing of commonalities and differing from others, which results in a particular "we-I balance," as Elias describes it (1991). This might change over time as long-term increases in the scale and complexity of social interdependence produces more and more complex layers of "we-image" in people's habitus and sense of identity. However, and at the same time, not only has the individual mode of self-experience altered in the process of social development, but the preoccupation with the experience of the single isolated adult individual has itself emerged out of the European civilizing process from the Renaissance on. The most important thing is that "habitus and identification, being related to group membership, are always—and in the modern world where people belong to groups within groups within groups—multilayered" (Mennell, 1992, p. 177).

I want to pay attention to the attenuation of one kind of linkage, between the nation and the state. I then want to look at the dynamics of another kind of emergent linkage, between global processes and the individual.

THE COHERENCE OF UNITS OF ANALYSIS:
DISAGGREGATING THE HYPHENATED NATION-STATE

The central unit of analysis of much of social theory, and certainly of most work in international communication, the hyphenated nation-state, can no longer (if it ever could) be taken so simply for granted. It is evident that the nation and the state have for a long time been each other's project (Appadurai, 1990); nations only gain recognition on the international stage when their political coherence is recognized in (preferably UN-ratified) statehood. States remain thin political structures without a national consciousness, a collective identity to which to bind adherence.

Habermas (1998) reminds us that we have to acknowledge that the nation-state has definitively superceded older political formations, but is itself under pressure from the complex of global processes, which now pose problems (the environment, nuclear weapons, biotechnologies, genetic modification, etc.) that can no longer be solved within the existing framework of nation-states. Developing out of two separate processes—the formations of states and a growth in self-awareness of nations—the nation-state solved two main problems. One was its internal and external sovereignty over territory (spatial power), and the other was over its members, citizens (social power). Peoples become nations through the concrete form of a particular form of life, becoming a political community shaped by common descent, common language, culture and history. Yet historically the nation was a contrasting concept to *civitas*, implying shared descent and geographic and cultural integration, but not (yet) political integration. Slowly, ruling estates challenged the power of the court, and the nation of the nobility gave way to the nation of the people, the imagined community propagated in national histories, which "made possible a relation of solidarity between persons who had previously been strangers to one another" (Habermas, 1998, p. 402).

Yet, what Habermas underlines is that "to the extent that this idea took root, however, it became apparent the political concept had inherited the power to generate stereotypes from the older, prepolitical concept of the nation as an index of descent and origin. The positive self-understanding of one's own nation now became an efficient mechanism for repudiating everything regarded as foreign; for devaluing other nations, and for excluding national, ethnic and religious minorities" (p. 402). But national self-consciousness also provided the cultural background against which "subjects" could become politically active citizens. "Thus the achievement of the nation-state consisted in solving two problems at once: it made possible a new mode of legitimation based on a new, more abstract form of social integration [which of course echoes Elias]. But it also led to a double coding of citizenship: legal status in terms of civil rights also implies membership in a culturally-defined community. The nation-state has thus played a key role in containing political subjectivity as well as defining cultural identity." This kind of imagery resonates somewhat with recent experience in Hong Kong in terms of the handover of collective "belonging" from Britain to China, from "inside" one old empire to a role within a new political and geographic context. Yet, throughout it all, Hong Kong itself as an entity remains deeply imbricated and a significant player in a multitude of global financial, commercial and cultural dynamics.

Thus what Cheah (1998, p. 22) has described as "the loosening of the hyphen between nation and state in globalization" may be broadly understood as a weakening of the relationship between "political" issues and identity/cultural issues and the containment of the Other. Even more importantly, I think, each half of the concept can be said to be challenged and is suffering a boundary collapse. The boundary problems of nation-states can be addressed by two spatial metaphors: the problem of the "inside/outside" divide, as Rob Walker (1993) has described it, but also "globalization from above" and "globalization from below" as Richard Falk (1994) has described the processes. Thus the territorial spatiality of these constructs is under challenge as well as their adequacy as units of analysis.

In regard to states, three major implications of globalization processes and theories can be noted. The first is clearly the emergence of other levels of political actors "above" the single state, emergent supra-state structures. Sometimes these are geographical contiguous regions, as with the EU, but there are many organizations of multiple states centered around common military, economic and increasingly cultural interests and goals: UNESCO, NATO, OAU and G8. More academics are realizing the potential significance of the "cultural discount" and acknowledging the emergence of regional linguistic-cultural zones of media production (Sinclair, Jacka & Cunningham, 1995; Straubhaar, 1997).

The second is the emergence of new forms of global solidarity politics from "below" the state: popular, grassroots forms of political groupings and imagination that are building new forms of global solidarities, a global civil society. This includes the network of networks that comprises the global movements of feminism (Sreberny-Mohammadi, 1998); the human rights movement, perhaps most obviously embodied in Amnesty International, or the environmental movement, exemplified by Greenpeace and Friends of the Earth. NetAid harnessed contemporary pop music, locales such as Wembley Stadium and the Internet, to create a new global consciousness of development issues, and the demonstrations around the WTO meeting in Seattle vividly showed the value of the Net to coordinate political activities. States can no longer contain political activity, as it spills out above and beyond the territorial boundary. But neither can they end political activity by simply expelling it. Exile politics thrives with the Internet, as well as with fax, broadcasting and print technologies. Indeed, perhaps nothing has so vividly exemplified deep interconnectivity than the speed with which the Lovebug virus spread in the spring of 2000, mocking the global networked society and revealing its vulnerability.

The third involves the increasing recognition of internal inequality around different forms of power, political and economic, and different and hierarchically structured areas of influence, the public and private spheres, of patriarchal states. Gender issues often lurk behind male defense of the national culture, which becomes part of the project of defending the sexual purity of women. Both must be protected from the incursions of foreigners; the penetration of one affects the other.

In regard to nations, the other side of the hyphen, the problematics are different ones, and I'll highlight three.

The first is the argument that the nation is always a structure-in-dominance, with other potential, lurking "nations" within the boundary. The "nation" represents the successful, dominant ethnie and, as Chakrabarty has nicely expressed it, "the argument about hybridity is most effective when purity has become the ideology of the oppressor" (Chakrabarty, 1998, p. 470). Thus, instead of continuing to ask, "How do we protect national identity?" it would be more useful and creative to ask, "How do we construct a political and cultural environment in which the multiple identities of our subjects can find expression?"

The second is connected: Far too much theorizing in international communication has operated with the assumption of the singularity and authenticity of the idea of national culture. In very simple terms, we have seen nothing wrong in talking about the effects of "American" culture on "India" (even about the effects of the "West" on the "East"). Yet all the work of post-colonial and subaltern studies must surely sensitize us to the argument that colonial culture is not simply packed-up with the colonizers' suitcases nor can it be simply cleaned out if you polish hard enough. But then neither is the culture of the colonies kept so easily at arm's length; not only does the empire write and video back, it moves in next door. The resonances with the Hong Kong experience are self-evident, most obviously in the legacy of English-language fluency.

Post-colonial theory invites us to think about the perverse cultural legacies of colonialism not just as a burden or as necessarily undermining something indigenous and of greater value, but as rich additions, shifts of global cultural capital, which will give the South huge cultural dynamism and flexibility in the future, in a way to which much of the North has little claim. For example, an international student from the Cameroons who speaks fluent English and French as well as African languages and local dialects, has a different purchase on the global cultural ecumene than the monolingual English undergraduate whose only travel abroad is to the rave enclaves of Ibiza or Corfu. Where and with whom does the cultural competence, flexibility and indeed, understanding of the future lie?

The third is the changing nature of affiliation that challenges the terri-torially bounded identities offered by the hyphenated nation-state so that we need to "think ourselves beyond the nation" (Appadurai, 1993; Sha-piro, 1994; but also see Hollinger, 1995) to the challenges of post-nationalism. The massive migrations that this century has witnessed have produced "diasporas," transnational communities, networks of affiliation (fueled by mixes of financial, economic, political, cultural, familial and emotional linkages) that run across many national boundaries, alternate forms of globalization to the circuits of established wealth and power. What is important about such terms is that they function not simply as conceptual categories—although they do do that—but that they describe already-existing social formations in which people invest considerable af-fection and with which strong identifications are made. Diasporic communities exist across national boundaries, but also within a number of national boundaries, altering the spaces in which they function—perhaps a new dynamism of entrepreneurship, new cuisine, new black markets. Thus, the state no longer contains our political and cultural identifications, and the nation has become just one possible site of affiliation.

ARE WE ALL DIASPORIC NOW?

But the new categories run the risk of too rapid hypostatizations, as the old "ethnics" have been suddenly reconstituted as "diasporas." I have ar-gued that work on ethnic communities often presumed a looking inward to assimilate in the new host environment; work on exile presumed a look-ing backward in nostalgia to old home; while the emerging diasporic con-sciousness looks around in a globally scoping gaze (Sreberny, 2000). Even while a certain particularistic identity is being maintained, in this case Ir-anianess, this is happening within a novel trans-national figuration that alters not only the nature of Iranianess (residents in Britain talk of speaking Pinglish; perhaps residents in France speak Frarsi?), but also the places where it is enacted (Green Lanes in North London is a microcosm of Med-iterranean culture and politics with Iranians, Kurds, Turks, Turkish Cyp-riots, Greek Cypriots cheek by jowl in comparative commercial harmony). Only comparative analysis of diasporas settling in more than one location could fully tease out what the migrant community brings with it, and how it is reconfigured within the existing political and cultural economy of the new host location.

It is clear that diasporic groups such as Iranians, with 2 million people dispersed since the Revolution, do often produce new media which bind many local nodes togther in an globally dispersed network, real and virtual transnational communities. But it is also clear that there is considerable internal differentiation among Iranians even in relation to this diasporic consciousness. Within the Iranian communities in London it is middle-aged

Table 16.1
The Recent History of a Surname

pre-1945:	Srebrny (numerous)		
1945:	Srebrny (2)		
1948:	Srebrny (3)		
1951:	Srebrny (1)	Sreberny (3)	
1956:		Sreberny (4)	
1962:		Sreberny (3)	
1976:		Sreberny (2)	Sreberny-Mohammadi (1)
1978:		Sreberny (2)	Sreberny-Mohammadi (2)
1981:		Sreberny (2)	Sreberny-Mohammadi (3)
1985:	Srebrny (1)	Sreberny (1)	Sreberny-Mohammadi (3)
2000:	Srebrny (1)	Sreberny (2)	Sreberny-Mohammadi (2)

males who are the political nostalgics, still deeply cathected to the Islamic Republic and actively devouring diasporic news media and political publications for information and analysis; women are the pragmatic day-to-day realists, watching their children grow up not so foreign (Sreberny, 2000). Everyone does not inhabit a diasporic consciousness in the same way, and there are different constructions and experiences of "being Iranian" whether one is looking back toward the Islamic Republic, in toward the new host environment, or around to the internal religio-cultural, political and economic diversity among Iranians-out-of-Iran. The notion of "we" alters, depending on the definition of the "they."

But even this is insufficient. We remain stuck in comparative statics, appearing only to acknowledge differentiation around gender, generation and some other categories. Yet the processes of indentification and affiliation with others, of moving toward and moving out of groups and relationships are dynamic, fluid. And the best way I can think to demonstrate some of this fluidity is to finally come to "us" and "me," families of birth and construction, and to focus on one highly symbolic and public aspect of ourselves, our surname. Allow me some brief story telling which includes at least two diasporic movements (see also Table 16.1).

WHAT'S IN A NAME?

My father, David Chaim Srebrny, was a major in the British Army, having introduced himself in Palestine, where he was an illegal alien, having arrived on an illegal ship from Italy in 1939. He got to Italy from Czechoslovakia, and before that from Poland, making each move as the changing social conditions disallowed him to study medicine since he was a Jew. His professional status brings acceptance into the army, and potential Britishness.

Of his family, only one sister survived. There are two Srebrnys in the world, until she marries.

After being demobbed, he met and married my mother. She is a *Kindertransportee* from Germany, sent away as a teenager by her mother in May 1939; my grandmother herself managing to get out in July. My parents settle down in North London where he ran a general practice. Their erstwhile national affiliations have been annihilated in violence; while born a Pole and a German, each was effectively stateless. They apply for citizenship. As part of that astonishingly named process of "naturalization," my father decided to "Anglicize" his name. He joked about becoming Sirberny, so able to make my mother Lady Berny. But he didn't risk that, and in 1950 they became Sreberny, simply adding a second "e" between the uncompromising string of consonants that had previously been his name. It didn't help enormously, because it's the odd pairing of "s" and "r" at the beginning of the name that is so ineffably foreign to English. You just have to hiss and then roll it out, tongue on the roof of the mouth.

Through my adolescence and on, I was called Shreberny, Streberny, Strawberry and Shrewsbury—endless permutations of orthography, but rarely the correct one—and have always known when my name was about to be called from any class register or any social queue by the deep intake of breath needed to try to spit the name out. Since my father's death in 1962, my mother, brother and I have been the only Srebernys in the world.

On completion of a university degree, I go to the United States, attracted by the rise of the women's movement, the anti-war movement, the radicalism in its air. While a waitressing graduate student, I meet an Iranian taxi-driving graduate student. After marrying Ali, I gradually took on the professional name of Sreberny-Mohammadi. If, as in other realms, size matters, this was one of the longest. It signified a meeting of West and East, of Judaism and Islam, of Britain and Iran. Perhaps it helped legitimize my writing about the Middle East. It became the symbol of my hybridity, although not Ali's, who remained steadfastly only Mohammadi. It was bestowed upon our two daughters. I and our daughters are the only three people named Sreberny-Mohammadi in the world.

My brother gets angry. He begins to think that Sreberny is inauthentic, a giving-way to social pressure, an act of an insecure migrant. He wishes to restore the earlier version. He calls himself Srebrny. Now there's one Sreberny; one Srebrny and three Sreberny-Mohammadis. (There are lots and lots of Mohammadis, in Isfahan and beyond).

My husband and I separate. I sever our names. I return to Sreberny. Dehyphenate. In 2000 there are two people called Sreberny, one Srebrny and two Sreberny-Mohammadi.

The above is not just a holocaust story, although it is also that. It also includes stories of the choices of the second generation, potentially called "sleeping with the enemies," and the identities of the third. Nor yet is it post-colonial, if only for the simple reason that Iran was never directly colonized. It embodies diasporic movement with no hope—or desire—for return (to either Germany or Poland for my parents) although my brother, the second generation, now lives in Berlin. It also includes a highly nostalgic diasporic dispersion, as Iranians out of the Islamic Republic, and the yearning of a middle-aged man for return. It includes love, marriage and children: a Pole marrying a German; a Jew marrying a Muslim; a mother sending her daughter away to survive; it includes physical and cultural exits and entrances, bilinguality, *multiculti*. It is a story of the continual undermining of groupishness: loss of Polish and German identities; marginalization from one's "own" community, including the religious; living abroad. And it produces cosmopolitan children with dual-nationality, bilingual and bireligious heritages for whom the world is a number of clubs to which they can stake claims. Earlier choices are revoked, reworked, our orientations shifting back and forth.

While I want to claim the specificity and particular detail of "my/our" story, I also want to argue that this kind of story, this kind of cross-cultural, cross-national complexity is not strange at all in the twenty-first century, but doesn't fit well into the monofactoral, monoethnic, frames by which "difference" is usually constructed. These many different points of arrival, many different relationships, a considerable amount of physical and social movement across borders is the stuff of contemporary globalized existence.

CONCLUSION

So why the hubris of such self-declaration? Certainly I would like to claim that these intimate stories of my family of birth and my family of choice have attuned me to the liveliness, and complications, of boundaries; the problematics of identity and belonging. My hope would be that, through a radical subjectivity that takes seriously and reflexively one's own identity-affiliations, their bases, their shifting valences, their mutative centrality in one's own life, one might gain a certain humility in the study of "others" and certainly in an encounter with the Other's claims.

I want to identify a triple dynamic at work. On the one hand, a slowly emerging global awareness, manifest in many ways, which supports the Eliasian notion of the civilizing process being about increasingly large/long—and abstract—chains of identification.

The logic of Elias's argument is that social development has tended toward larger, more interdependent and more abstract social units, latterly nation-states but with the spread of global figurations have come new transnational networks and lines of affiliation and an emergent global consciousness. The loosening of ties to the nation and the political containment of activity within states does not, of course, mean their withering. It means, however, that they become simply one site of our multiple allegiances, one node of our political solidarities, another layer in our multiple identities.

At the same time, other/older kinds of identifications are also maintained. Diasporic communities and ethnic groups through particularist media and cultural expression, promote a strengthening of parochial identities—although this awareness is often understood to cross territorial boundaries and to have severed the connection to land that such identities once may have had. Home is increasingly where you live, not the "homeland" for which one may perhaps nostalgically yearn but which becomes a figment of fantasy.

But I think a third step is also necessary. The argument that forms of "groupishness" are changing has implications for the individual self that is subject to a greater variety of claims for attachment than ever before. "We" have been told over and over again that the post-modern subject is fragmented, no longer unitary, multiple. But now we can perhaps interpret that in a slightly different way: It is not because of our collective dissolution into existential fragments, but because of the increasingly multiple social claims for allegiance made upon the individual by a myriad of groups and collectivities which offer some sort of partial belonging in return. It is not that "we" have lost social affiliation. Rather, "we" (or many of "us") have gained a great many: to different locales of residence (countries, cities, places); different national and local cultures, systems of ideas, interest groups. The ties may be weaker (although Granovetter [1972] has pointed to the strength of weak ties), but they are multiple. We experience divided loyalties, conflicts of interest, and in that process of understanding and empathizing with both sides, may work to solve conflicts rather than exacerbate them.

Thus, perhaps ironically, a process of individuation, or reflexive modernity, is not to be conceived as the free-floating cosmopolitan who has transcended all social ties but to the "universal" but rather as a more (not less) radical cosmopolitanism, experienced through ties to more and more differentiated peoples and interests, and understanding that as the contemporary social logic. To think of ourselves, each self, as a container of difference, not the site of sameness, might be a huge leap of imagination, but one that seems worthwhile. There's a lot more to be explored in the encounter between globalization and me, and you.

REFERENCES

Appadurai, A. (1990). Disjuncture and difference in the global cultural economy. *Public Culture*, 2(2), 1–24.
Appadurai, A. (1993). Patriotism and its futures. *Public Culture*, 5, 411–429.

Appadurai, A. (1996). *Modernity at large: Cultural dimensions of globalization.* Minneapolis: University of Minnesota Press.

Beck, U. (1997). *The reinvention of politics: Rethinking modernity in the global social order.* Cambridge, MA: Polity Press.

Beck, U., Giddens, A. & Lasch, S. (1994). *Reflexive modernization: Politics, tradition and aesthetics in the modern social order.* Cambridge, MA: Polity Press.

Chakrabarty, D. (1998). Reconstructing liberalism? Notes toward a conversation between area studies and diasporic studies. *Public Culture,* 10(3), 457–482.

Cheah, P. (1998). Introduction Part II: The cosmopolitical today. In P. Cheah & B. Robbins (Eds.), *Cosmopolitics: Thinking and feeling beyond the nation* (pp. 20–44). Minneapolis: University of Minnesota Press.

Elias, N. (1987). *Involvement and detachment.* Oxford: Basil Blackwell.

Elias, N. (1991). *The society of individuals.* Oxford: Basil Blackwell.

Falk, R. (1994). The making of global citizenship. In B. van Steenbergen (Ed.), *The condition of citizenship* (pp. 127–140). London: Sage Publications.

Freud, S. (1991). The instincts and their vicissitudes (originally published in 1915). In A. Dickson (Ed.), *On metapsychology: The theory of psychoanalysis* (pp. 105–138). Penguin Freud Library, Vol. 11. Harmondsworth: Penguin.

Giddens, A. (1990). *The construction of modernity.* Palo Alto, CA: Stanford University Press.

Granovetter, M. (1972). The strength of weak ties. *American Journal of Sociology,* 78(6), 1360–1380

Habermas, J. (1998). The European nation-state: On the past and future of sovereignty and citizenship. *Public Culture,* 2, 397–416.

Hollinger, D. (1995). *Postethnic America: Beyond multiculturalism.* New York: Basic Books.

Klein, J. (1987). *Our need for others and its roots in infancy.* London: Routledge.

Mennell, S. (1992). *Norbert Elias: An introduction.* Dublin: University College Dublin Press.

Miller, N. K. (1991). *Getting personal: Feminist occasions and other autobiographical acts.* New York: Routledge.

Pels, D. (2000). Reflexivity—one step up. *Theory, Culture and Society,* 17(3), 1–25.

Samuel, A. (1993). *The political psyche.* London: Routledge.

Shapiro, M. (1994). Moral geographies and the ethics of post-sovereignty. *Public Culture,* 6, 479–502.

Sinclair, J., Jacka, E. & Cunningham, S. (Eds.) (1995). *New patterns in global television: Peripheral vision.* New York: Oxford University Press.

Sreberny, A. (1999). Globalization and the nation. In *World social science report.* Paris: UNESCO.

Sreberny, A. (2000). Media and diasporic consciousness: An exploration among Iranians in London. In S. Cottle (Ed.), *Ethnic minorities and the media* (pp. 179–196). London: Open University Press.

Sreberny-Mohammadi, A. (1997). The many cultural faces of imperialism. In P. Golding & P. Harris (Eds.), *Beyond cultural imperialism: Globalization, communication the new international order* (pp. 49–68). London: Sage. Publications.

Sreberny-Mohammadi, A. (1998). Feminist internationalism: Imagining and building global civil society. In D. Thussu (Ed.), *Electronic empires: Global media and local resistance* (pp. 208–222). London: Arnold.

Straubhaar, J. (1997). Distinguishing the global, regional and national levels of world television. In A. Sreberny-Mohammadi, D. Winseck, J. McKenna & O. Boyd-Barrett (Eds.), *Media in global context: A reader*. London: Arnold.

Walker, R.B.J. (1993). *Inside/outside: International relations as political theory*. Cambridge: Cambridge University Press.

Index

About the Contributors

JOSEPH M. CHAN is professor and former director of the School of Journalism and Communication at The Chinese University of Hong Kong. His research interests include international communication political communication and information technology. He served as a Harvard-Yenching Scholar and as president of the Chinese Communication Association.

AKIBA A. COHEN is professor and chair of the Department of Communication at Tel Aviv University. He is a former president and an elected fellow of the International Communication Association. His main interest is the comparative analysis of television news.

MICHAEL CURTIN is an associate professor of communication and culture at Indiana University. He is the author of *Redeeming the Wasteland: Television Documentary and War Politics* (1995) and co-editor of *Making and Selling Culture* (1996) and *The Revolution Wasn't Televised: Sixties Television and Social Conflict* (1997). He is currently working on a book about the film and television industries in East Asia.

TODD GITLIN is professor of culture, journalism and sociology at New York University. He is the author of *The Whole World Is Watching*, *Inside Prime Time*, *The Sixties*, *The Twilight of Common Dreams*, *Sacrifice* and the forthcoming *The Infinite Glimmer of Images: On Saturation, Speed, Politics and Other Modern Disappointments*.

ALICE Y. L. LEE is an assistant professor in the Department of Journalism at Hong Kong Baptist University. Her major research interests include media education, new communication technologies and the sociology of education.

PAUL S. N. LEE is professor and director of the School of Journalism and Communication at The Chinese University of Hong Kong. His research interests include international communication, telecommunications policy, development communication and media criticism. He is the author of *International Communication* (in Chinese), editor of *Telecommunications and Development in China* and co-editor of *TV Without Borders: Asia Speaks Out* (with Anura Goonasekera).

MARK R. LEVY is professor and chairperson of the Department of Telecommunication at Michigan State University. A former editor of the *Journal of Communication*, Dr. Levy's current research focuses on the social and societal impact of new communication technologies.

ERIC MA is an assistant professor in the School of Journalism and Communication at The Chinese University of Hong Kong. He is the author of several books in Chinese on the popular culture of Hong Kong and a book in English entitled *Culture, Politics and Television in Hong Kong*. His publications appear in *Gazette, International Journal of Cultural Studies* and *Social Text*.

BRIAN L. MASSEY is a visiting member of the communication-processes faculty at the University of Connecticut, and formerly was an assistant professor of communication studies at Nanyang Technological University, Singapore. He is a former print journalist and U.S. Peace Corps volunteer.

BRYCE T. McINTYRE is an associate professor in the School of Journalism and Communication at The Chinese University of Hong Kong. His research interests include Internet regulation and applications in Southeast Asia. A former print journalist, he has published several journalism textbooks.

TOBY MILLER is professor of cultural studies and cultural policy at New York University. He is the author of *The Well-Tempered Self, Contemporary Australian Television, The Avengers, Technologies of Truth* and *Popular Culture & Everyday Life*. He also edited the following books: *SportCult, Film and Theory* and *A Companion to Film Theory*. He edits the journals *Social Text* and *Television & New Media*.

MONROE E. PRICE is professor of law at the Benjamin N. Cardozo School of Law, Yeshiva University, and co-director of the Programme in

Comparative Media Law and Policy at the University of Oxford. He is the author of *Television, Public Sphere and National Identity*.

CLEMENT Y. K. SO is an associate professor in the School of Journalism and Communication at The Chinese University of Hong Kong. His research interests include the development of communication as an academic field, citation analysis, new communication technologies, the sociology of news and the Hong Kong press.

ANNABELLE SREBERNY is a professor at the Centre for Mass Communication Research at the University of Leicester. Her books include *Small Media, Big Revolution; Gender, Politics and Communication* and *Globalization, Communication and Transnational Civil Society*. She is particularly interested in transnational communities and diasporic media, and radical subjectivity as a method of cultural analysis.

JOSEPH STRAUBHAAR is the Amon G. Carter Professor of Communication at the University of Texas Radio-TV-Film Department. He previously taught at Brigham Young University and Michigan State University. He has published extensively on international media studies.

GERALD SUSSMAN is a professor of urban studies and communications at Portland State University. He is the author of *Communication, Technology, and Politics in the Information Age* (1997) and co-editor of *Global Productions: Labor in the Making of the "Information Society"* (1998) and *Transnational Communications: Wiring the Third World* (1991).

GEORGETTE WANG is professor and dean of the College of Social Sciences at National Chung Cheng University, Taiwan. Her field of research is communication technologies and culture, in which she has widely published.

FRANK WEBSTER is professor of sociology in the Department of Cultural Studies and Sociology, University of Birmingham, United Kingdom. He is author of several books, including *Theories of the Information Society* and *Times of the Technoculture: From the Information Society to the Virtual Life*.